JFK

JOHN F. KENNEDY

JOHN F. KENNEDY

BY JUDIE MILLS

FRANKLIN WATTS
NEW YORK | LONDON | TORONTO
SYDNEY | 1988

Library of Congress Cataloging in Publication Data

Mills, Judie.
John F. Kennedy / by Judie Mills.
p.   cm.
Bibliography: p.
Includes index.
Summary: The life and political career of the thirty-fifth
president with biographical information about the members
of his family.
ISBN 0-531-10520-2
1. Kennedy, John F. (John Fitzgerald), 1917-1963—Juvenile
literature.   2. Presidents—United States—Biography—
Juvenile literature.   3. Kennedy family—Juvenile literature.
[1. Kennedy, John F. (John Fitzgerald), 1917-1963.   2. Presidents.
3. Kennedy family.]   I. Title.
E842.Z9M55   1988
973.922'092'4—dc19
[B]
[92]   87-29470   CIP   AC

For my family

Thanks to all *my editors:*
Margaret Ribaroff, T. Maker,
Frank Sloan, and especially
Marjory Kline.

It's impossible to express
my gratitude to Mike Mills
and Mary Ellen Casey,
except to say . . . this is
their book too.

CONTENTS

PART II
JACK

PART III
JFK

**JOHN F.
KENNEDY**

PROLOGUE

I, John F. Kennedy

He stood bareheaded in the bitter cold, his breath frosting the air. Only days before, the Forest Service had sprayed green dye on the lawns of Washington, hoping to give the capital a touch of spring. But a blizzard left the city covered with eight inches of snow, and Army flamethrowers had to be used to melt the ice on the streets and sidewalks. At dawn the snow stopped, and by noon the sky was blue and cloudless.

do solemnly swear

Twenty thousand people, wrapped in blankets and scarves, ringed the eastern front of the Capitol building. A million more lined the streets, eager to catch a glimpse of his limousine as it made its way toward the inauguration site. Across the country, eighty million people sat expectantly before their television sets to witness the swearing-in of the youngest man ever elected to the presidency.

that I will faithfully execute

The brilliant Washington sunlight seemed to reflect the mood of America itself. For months, Kennedy had urged, "Let's get this country moving again!" Today, January 20, 1961, the United States would take up the challenge he had made so often during the presidential campaign.

the Office of President of the United States

That his vision of the country's destiny was unspecified seemed less important than what America would be leaving behind. An economic depression had no sooner ended than a world war began. The United States had won that conflict, only to plunge into a cold war in which it appeared communism would prevail. Now, after a decade and a half of Russian triumphs, Americans were ready to follow their charismatic new president into the future.

and will, to the best of my ability

The years ahead would not be without difficulty. The day before, Kennedy had been briefed on the problems which would be his to solve: Cuba, Southeast Asia, the economy, civil rights. Then, just before one o'clock, in the less than a minute it took to recite the oath of office, he assumed those burdens as president of the most powerful nation on earth. It was a position he had never expected to hold, for Kennedy had entered politics as a reluctant substitute for his older brother.

preserve, protect and defend

His parents were sitting in the front row during the ceremony, Joe Kennedy wearing the same coat he had worn twenty years before as ambassador to Great Britain. For a moment, Rose and Joe thought of the young man they too had once expected to be standing there. Then they squeezed each other's hands. No words were necessary between them on this triumphant day, the day their second son became the thirty-fifth president of the United States.

the Constitution of the United States

As Kennedy completed the presidential oath, he took his hand from the family Bible, in which the joys and sorrows of generations had been recorded. At that same moment, thousands of miles away, bonfires were being lit at the spot from which Patrick Kennedy had set sail for America. Today was more than a beginning. It was also an end, the end of a journey which had begun more than a century before on a small island on the other side of the Atlantic.

so help me God.

PART ONE

THE KENNEDYS

1

NO IRISH
NEED APPLY

In the middle of the nineteenth century, thousands of Irish poured out of their country, fleeing the starvation and disease of the Potato Famine.

The island had first been invaded by Britain in 1169. Over the next five hundred years, the Irish rebelled again and again, but eventually England's domination was complete. Having conquered Ireland, the British carved up its countryside into large estates, as rewards for those who had crushed the rebellion. Few of the landlords stayed behind to look after their new properties. Instead, the estates were divided into tiny lots and rented back to the Irish, who were somehow expected to turn England's conquest into a profitable venture.

The only way farmers could earn money to pay the rent was to export almost everything they raised. Cattle, pigs, chickens, eggs, oats—all were sold to the British. The Irish kept only one source of food for themselves: the inexpensive and easily-cultivated potato. The farmer fortunate enough to have an acre and a half of land could raise enough potatoes to feed himself, his family, and his livestock for a year. Most of those who scratched out a living from the soil existed miserably in windowless mud huts, animals and people sharing the single room. They were the lucky ones.

Although every possible patch was in use, there wasn't enough land to go around—so that in a population of more than nine million, almost one-third was always on the verge of starvation. By the 1840s, conditions in Ireland were said to be the most deplorable in Europe. But the Protestant landlords cared little how the "inferior" Catholic Irish lived, as long as their properties continued to yield both food and rent. Among Britain's officials, the sole concern was that Ireland might rise again in rebellion, and a member of the House of Commons summed up his government's attitude by saying the Irish must be ruled "not by love but by fear." Neglected and exploited, Ireland teetered on the edge of disaster.

In 1845 the disaster struck. Blight hit the potato crop, and that food, for which there was no substitute, began to rot in the ground. The Irish had only two choices: leaving themselves nothing to eat, they could go on exporting their animals and grains to earn money for the rent; or they could keep what they raised and be evicted from their farms. Most thought the blight would pass—but if they gave up their land, all hope was lost. Under armed English guard, wagon-loads of produce continued to be sent from Ireland, while starving people watched along the roadside.

In desperation the Irish dug up the rotten potatoes, eating them raw since they were too weak to dig for peat, their source of fuel. Fires that had burned in the hearths of the mud huts for more than a century began to go out. Unable to even boil water, much of the weakened population fell ill with typhus or cholera.

England officially continued to look the other way, and by the end of the decade more than a million people had died of hunger and disease. Those who still lived saw only one option: emigration.

Families sold their clothes, their bedding, their kettles, their tools, anything that would bring in money to send at least one child to the place where everyone was thought to be prosperous: "the States." British shipping lines were happy to cooperate. No one wanted the Irish in England, and fares to North America were kept as low as possible, with the result that conditions on the ships were unfit for livestock. But to stay was to die, and by 1848 the Irish were leaving by the hundreds of thousands. One of them was Patrick Kennedy.

The trip across the Atlantic took over six weeks, with the passengers locked below deck for most of the journey. The Irish were crammed into a space in which a grown man could not stand, given rotting food and contaminated water, denied sanitation facilities. Although many were ill with typhus or cholera, no medical care was provided.

Patrick's chances for survival were not good: one out of three perished in the "coffin ships."

More than half of those who lived through the crossing landed in New York. But because the fare to Boston was less expensive, many chose it as their destination—among them Patrick Kennedy and Bridget Murphy. Despite the unromantic circumstances, the two had met and fallen in love on board ship, and were married soon after their arrival. To the Kennedys, as it had to other immigrants, Boston proved to be a shock.

There, in the Cradle of Liberty, in a city which had itself suffered British rule, a city in which the very concept of America had begun, Catholic immigrants discovered that all men were not, after all, created equal. The descendants of *Mayflower* passengers wanted nothing to do with those who had made the trip in steerage. Boston's power and wealth would remain where they had always been: with the Protestants on Beacon Hill. The only Irish admitted to that exclusive neighborhood went as unskilled laborers or as servants; for more responsible or better-paying positions, ads were careful to specify "No Irish Need Apply."

Patrick was fortunate to find a job making whiskey barrels—steady employment, since the immigrants often turned to alcohol to forget their surroundings. The slums were appalling. An average family lived in a single small room. In one tiny damp cellar with a ceiling only five feet high, eighteen people made their home. Another cramped basement housed thirty-nine. Unable to afford rent for both a shop and a place to live, many immigrants sold food in these same filthy cellars, spreading diseases from the makeshift grocery stores.

Deprived of proper nourishment, sanitation, or medicine, Irish children, it was said, were "born to die," and over 60 percent of the first Irish-Americans did not live to the age of five. Yet the Kennedys were determined to raise a family. First came two daughters, then a son, then a third daughter. The little boy died of cholera, but in January 1858, another son was born: Patrick Joseph, whom they called P.J. Defying the statistics of the slums, all four children survived. Their father, however, would not live to see the little boy reach his first birthday. Patrick died on November 22, the victim of another cholera epidemic.

Although his adopted country had rewarded him only with poverty, Patrick Kennedy left a rich legacy. He gave America its most remarkable political family.

In 1858 Kennedy triumphs were still far in the future. At the time of Patrick's death, the prospects of his children looked bleak. Life in the slums had been difficult enough, even with Patrick's meager support. Without that income, his daughters and son seemed doomed to the destitute existence of most Irish families. But Bridget Kennedy was a fighter. She took a job in a small shop which sold toiletries and household articles—and, after years of saving, bought the store and put her children to work behind the counter.

As a boy P.J. helped out in the shop; in his teens, he dropped out of school to take a full-time job on the waterfront. With an Irish background and limited education, there was little hope that P.J. could avoid the drudgery and alcoholism which were the fate of so many of his contemporaries. But P.J. had two unusual resources: his family and his determination.

At first P.J. contributed his salary to help Bridget make the shop a success. But once it became financially secure, he began putting aside part of his earnings for a business of his own. Since the door to enterprise was shut tight against Irish ambition, his freedom from an immigrant existence would have to be achieved within the very community from which he longed to escape. At age twenty-two, P.J. found his way out: he bought a saloon.

Irish immigrants sought relief from their misery in two ways—gossip and drinking. A neighborhood saloon was conducive to both, and young Kennedy's was one of the most successful. P.J. was an unusual Irishman; he preferred lemonade to whiskey, and would rather listen than talk. A sober, silent bartender was in a position to learn a great deal about his customers, and before long P.J. had heard the secrets and ambitions of almost everyone in the area. His patrons soon realized that if a man needed a free drink, a small loan, or a sympathetic ear, P.J. Kennedy could be counted on. Admiration of the young man resulted in a business so prosperous that he was able to expand: first into partnership in two other saloons, then into a liquor importation firm.

Next came the opportunity for a second career. By 1885, when Boston elected its first Irish mayor, immigrant descendants outnumbered the Protestant Yankees. Through the political process, the city's immigrants now had the power to control their own fate, and Irish names became commonplace on the ballot. The Democrats, party of the Boston poor, saw in P.J. a natural candidate for office, and their choice of the twenty-seven-year-old Kennedy to run for the Massachusetts House of Representatives resulted in a landslide victory.

One year later P.J. continued his progression upward by marrying Mary Hickey, daughter of a prosperous businessman. The Hickey family had already achieved great success by Boston Irish standards, and some in that community thought this time young Kennedy had aimed a little too high. But P.J. saw no reason to doubt his ability as a breadwinner, and as time passed it was obvious that Mary Hickey had done very well for herself. Her husband's climb out of the shanty neighborhoods of his youth continued upward, rung by rung, through election to the state Senate, to partnership in a bank, to a position of genuine power behind the scenes in Boston. Along the way, he and Mary raised a family: two daughters and a son. The boy's name was Joseph P. Kennedy.

Thirty years after his grandfather's death, Joe was born into a world Patrick could never have imagined. Compared to many other immigrants, his family was well-to-do—the sort of Irish, it was said, who could afford to have fruit in the house even when nobody was sick. But there was still a long way to go. No matter what advantages the Kennedys could offer Joe and his sisters, their name was Irish and their fortune had begun in a saloon. The last rung on the ladder that P.J. had climbed out of Shantytown ended far short of Beacon Hill. Joe Kennedy would spend his life trying to scale slippery new heights of respectability, and eventually, acceptance of that Irish name would reach far beyond Boston.

Although there were few ways to escape the prejudice with which even the most eminent Irish-Catholic families were regarded, a good education was at least a step in the right direction. The Kennedys decided their son should attend Boston Latin, an elite Protestant prep school which included five signers of the Declaration of Independence among its alumni. Scholastic competition at the school was intense, and Joe did poorly in every subject except mathematics. Yet in spite of his grades and his background, young Kennedy's charm and athletic ability eventually won over most of the other students. By his senior year, Joe was president of the class and star of the Boston Latin baseball team. His .667 batting average, the best in the city, earned Joe the Mayor's Cup, which was presented by another Irishman, Mayor John F. Fitzgerald.

On that happy occasion, P.J. and the mayor consented to pose together, smiling at the camera. It was a rare moment in an uneasy relationship; for all their mutual interests in Boston politics, there was no affection between the two. P.J. considered the flamboyant

Fitzgerald a brash and publicity-hungry little man who shamelessly paraded his Irish background. At a moment's notice, the mayor would launch into a lengthy speech filled with blarney, or—worse yet, as far as P.J. was concerned—burst into song in his quavering tenor. Fitzgerald's sweet voice had even earned him the nickname "Honey Fitz," which repelled P.J. all the more. But the final insult to P.J.'s straitlaced sensibilities was that Honey Fitz was rumored to have a wandering eye for the ladies, while his stoic wife stayed home and quietly raised their six children.

The mayor was no less distasteful to P.J. than P.J.'s son was to the mayor. Fitzgerald, once a member of the U.S. House of Representatives, had now achieved the office to which every Boston Irish politician aspired. Naturally, Honey Fitz regarded his family as superior to the Kennedys. And he was horrified that his beautiful daughter Rose had fallen in love with young Joe.

P.J., however, wasn't interested in Fitzgerald's opinion. Joe's future would not be determined by City Hall, or by the other authority that held sway over Boston's Irish—the Church. Although the local Catholic hierarchy thought all their young men should attend parochial schools, the Kennedys knew the direction their son must take if he was to escape the stigma of his heritage. And if Boston Latin had been far up the slope of P.J.'s ambitions for Joe, Harvard was the summit.

Joe found acceptance at college much more difficult than at prep school. Snobbish Protestant classmates looked with disdain at one whose grandparents had come to America by boat, and whose schooling was paid for with money made selling whiskey. But Joe stuck it out, developing at Harvard traits he would display throughout his life. He despised those classmates who sneered at all things Irish, yet he sought out that same elite group, quick to accuse them of prejudice if he sensed a snub. Since his religion and ancestry denied him membership in the best clubs, he ridiculed their importance while yearning to be admitted.

During summer breaks Joe made his first foray into business. He bought a sight-seeing bus for a few hundred dollars, and after two seasons, ended up with a profit of five thousand dollars. But in school, the academic approach to finance bored him, and he dropped out of a banking course. An undistinguished student, Joe could not repeat even the one glory of his days at Boston Latin. His prep school batting skills had deserted him, and he warmed the bench of the university baseball team. Joe finally won his letter during the Yale game in his senior year, when the team captain requested that young Kennedy be put in the lineup—because a friend of P.J.'s had made it clear that the captain's own postgraduation business plans would depend on Joe being in the game.

After three generations in America, a family principle had been laid down: Kennedys would get what they wanted, even if it meant cutting a few corners in the process. And the Yankee establishment could either accept it—or go to blazes.

In 1912, armed with ambition, confidence, and a Harvard degree, Joe Kennedy entered the business world. Unlike Joe, most of his classmates would enjoy an inevitable progression toward the boardroom, the path smoothed by Protestantism, tradition, and family connections. Joe believed that banking—*money*—was the only way to achieve true power and prestige. Yet his experiences at Harvard had proven that the effortless course of others would be denied to him. He was Irish and Catholic; no generations of Kennedys had preceded him in the exclusive fraternity of Boston finance.

But the Irish had political control that could be used, not to beat hopelessly against the front door of the establishment, but to gain entry through the side. So Joe Kennedy, calling on the influence of his father and others, had himself appointed as a bank examiner at an annual salary of fifteen hundred dollars. For eighteen months he traveled the state, inspecting statements and ledgers, learning how the banking business really worked, soon convinced it was a world he would be able to conquer.

Then Columbia Trust, a small neighborhood bank of which his father was a founder, was threatened by a takeover from the largest bank in Boston. For once even P.J. seemed helpless, and turned to his son for assistance. Joe charged into battle. With no assets except his own confidence, he borrowed heavily, bought stock, lined up proxies, and won enough support to avert the takeover. The Columbia's grateful directors promptly elected Joe, who had just turned twenty-five, president of the bank. Fascinated by the David-and-Goliath struggle, the press claimed that Joe was the youngest bank president in the city, the country, or perhaps even the world. The success and publicity made Joe more self-confident than ever. When an admiring interviewer asked him what he hoped to achieve in life, he replied, "I want to be a millionaire by the age of thirty-five."

Joe's performance had awed not only newspaper reporters and the officers at Columbia Trust, but Honey Fitz himself—who now regarded the young man as a suitable son-in-law. This was another Kennedy triumph, because bright and beautiful Rose Fitzgerald was unquestionably the prize catch in the shallow sea of Boston Irish society.

At fifteen, when she became the youngest graduate in the history of her high school, Rose was also voted the prettiest senior in the city. Because her shy mother shunned the spotlight, Rose had been, since early girlhood, her father's official hostess. She attended many of the inevitable political functions which required the mayor's presence, as well as the numerous other social occasions which Honey Fitz simply wanted to attend—averaging, a contemporary account said, "two dinners and three dances a night, to say nothing of six speeches."

The mayor traveled just as energetically outside the city, and his lovely daughter, whom he called "my rambling Rose," often went with him: throughout the United States, to Central America, to Europe. A reporter noted Rose was "brimming with animation and charm and girlish spirits. . . . Undoubtedly her father's influence upon her life has broadened her outlook, so that she lives much more vividly than most girls of her age." Poised, cultured, and gracious, Rose was the perfect complement to the boisterous Honey Fitz, never giving any sign if his exaggerated Irishness embarrassed her. She was also a skilled pianist, accompanying her father again and again as he broke into a chorus of "Sweet Adeline"—a sentimental ballad the mayor had first used as a campaign song and which he now regarded as the municipal hymn of Boston. He sang it so often that in some countries he visited, people thought it was the national anthem of the United States.

Only three things had ever clouded the adoring relationship between Honey Fitz and Rose: her attraction to Joe Kennedy, her choice of a college, and the scandals which would eventually finish her father's career in public office. Rose had been admitted to Wellesley, then the leading women's school in the country. But by September 1907, a few days before she was to enroll, her father was under political fire. A list of municipal employees showed that one out of every forty-two people in Boston was drawing a salary from the city. The mayor had even created positions such as "City Dermatologist" and "Rubber Boot Repairman" for his cronies, and the *Boston Journal* began running a series of articles devoted to the "amazing exposure of payroll graft."

The mounting criticisms convinced Honey Fitz that his daughter should attend a Catholic school to make a better impression on the Irish voters, and Rose dutifully entered the Academy of the Sacred Heart in Boston. In spite of her obedience and self-discipline, the decision was a bitter one. With all the tragedies Rose would eventually endure, she told a writer seventy-three years later, "My biggest regret is not having gone to Wellesley." It proved to be a needless sacrifice. Disclosures of graft continued, and in December 1907 the mayor lost his bid for another term in office. To spare his favorite daughter the embarrassment of the political scandal, and to avoid losing her to Joe Kennedy, Honey Fitz a few months later sent Rose to the Academy of the Sacred Heart in Holland. There she developed the self-control and religious devotion which would characterize her life. But a lasting commitment to Catholicism had not lessened her attraction to Joe, and the couple kept up a secret correspondence between the convent and Boston.

When she came back to America the following year, Rose enrolled at the Academy of the Sacred Heart in New York, from which she graduated in June 1910. By then Honey Fitz had weathered the storm and rewon the mayoralty, so Rose finally went home to Boston. In the fall of 1911, as Joe started his senior year at Harvard, she began two year's study at the New England Conservatory of Music. November 1913 saw the announcement of Fitzgerald's candidacy for reelection, but one last scandal marked the end of his days in City Hall. The mayor, it was widely rumored, was having an affair with a young woman named Toodles Ryan. Pleading ill health, Honey Fitz withdrew from the race, and in February 1914 relinquished his beloved office forever.

The only Fitzgerald victory that year belonged to his daughter. In October 1914, Rose Fitzgerald and Joseph P. Kennedy were married—an occasion that marked not only the alliance of two remarkable people, but the beginning of an American political dynasty.

Rose and Joe began their life together in a small frame house in suburban Brookline. Here, in the last modest home in which they would ever live, the Kennedys spent four years filled with personal and professional satisfactions.

The year 1915 marked the arrival of their first child, Joseph P. Kennedy, Jr. Eight more children would follow, but none, to Joe, would ever rival the significance of his eldest son. The little boy was far more than a namesake. Indeed, to his father, Joe Jr. symbolized the ultimate investment in the future. It was too much to hope that in his own generation an Irish-American could achieve the greatness to which Joe Kennedy aspired; but through Joe Jr., his father vowed, the family would reach its destiny. Honey Fitz agreed, telling reporters his grandson would go to Harvard, serve as mayor of Boston, governor of Massachusetts, and finally as "President of the United States."

On May 29, 1917, a second son was born, a son for whom Joe would have considerably scaled-down ambitions. The baby was named John Fitzgerald after his grandfather; his parents called him Jack. By the time of Jack's birth, his father was general manager of the Bethlehem Steel shipyards. Two years later, the thirty-one-year-old Kennedy had become a manager in the Boston branch of a brokerage house where, he knew, the real money was to be made. Joe thought it was time to get started on compiling his fortune; after all, he would be thirty-five in just four more years.

During those years, three daughters—Rosemary, Kathleen, and Eunice—were born. The Kennedys moved to a much larger house a few blocks away, hired a housekeeper and a nursemaid, bought a car. And Joe, who had never doubted he would, achieved his goal of becoming a millionaire.

The fortune came from many sources. It was widely believed that the Kennedys, who had always been in the business of supplying liquor, went right on doing so during Prohibition. It was perhaps that income which gave Joe a stake to invest in the stock market, where he made enormous profits using inside tips learned at the brokerage firm, a practice that was not illegal in the 1920s. But working for someone else was not Joe Kennedy's style, and he was soon successful enough to open his own business as a "private banker." His interests sprawled in several profitable directions: real estate, banking, more extensive investments in the stock market. Motion pictures were becoming popular, and Joe, as usual, was quick to recognize a sure thing. Calling the movie industry "a gold mine," he bought into a chain of New England movie theaters; then he went into distribution, where there were even greater profits.

Now in a position to emulate other wealthy Boston families, the Kennedys took a beach home in Cohasset, just south of the city on Massachusetts Bay. It proved to be an unpleasant summer. The women snubbed Rose, daughter of that disgusting little man who had been mayor; their husbands blackballed Joe, son of an Irish barkeep, from membership in the local country club. To Joe, it was the bitter lesson of Harvard all over again. "I was born here. My wife was born here. My kids were born here," Joe said. "What the hell do I have to do to be American?" But obviously acceptance of *Irish*-Americans would not be found in Cohasset—or in Boston.

If they weren't going to be allowed into Yankee society, the Kennedy family would become its own exclusive circle. Thereafter, all their summers were spent at then less fashionable Hyannis Port—only a few miles farther out, on Cape Cod, but a world away from the Protestant establishment. And in 1926, the Kennedys, who now included another daughter, Patricia, and a third son, Robert, moved to a place in which they could truly "be American": New York. There, in a city where people of every heritage spent their days in the pursuit of money, Joe Kennedy could compete with the best of them. Wealth had not kept the Kennedys from feeling they were trespassers in their own hometown, but away from Boston no dream was impossible. As Rose and the children boarded a private railroad car to set off for their new home, a friend asked Joe what he wanted out of life. "Everything," he replied.

2

THE ARCHITECT
OF OUR LIVES

The Kennedys rented a house in Riverdale, an exclusive section of the Bronx. It was an ideal location for the growing family, with excellent schools nearby for the five oldest children. Although at that time wooded and rural, Riverdale was only a few miles from Manhattan, so that Joe could commute to look after his financial interests in the city. But as soon as the family was settled in its new home and he was established in Wall Street, Joe was off to another city which beckoned with opportunity: Hollywood.

For the next thirty-two months, Kennedy was back and forth from one coast to the other. New York was the financial center of the country, and where his wife and children lived; California was the capital of the movie industry. It was also the home of Hollywood's reigning queen, Gloria Swanson. Kennedy loaned the actress money to form her own production company, but the relationship extended far beyond a mutual interest in films, and their affair soon became an open secret on both coasts. Honey Fitz's wife had spent years ignoring rumors of his philandering, and Rose, following the example set by her mother, chose not to acknowledge Joe's romance with one of the most famous women in the world. There were more important things to think about than Gloria Swanson. Rose had given birth to another daughter, Jean, and she now had eight children to raise.

Rose Kennedy was as skilled an executive in the home as her husband was in business. She oversaw a large staff of nurses, governesses, maids, cooks, housekeepers, and gardeners—and supervised her troop of children no less closely than she did her domestic help.

Rose was a compulsive note-writer. During the day, any small scrap would do: a cash register slip, a piece of wrapping paper. She also kept a note pad at her bedside, so that even during the night no thought would go unrecorded. There were notes all over the house, admonishing her children to turn out the lights, and on their pillows, prompting them to wash their faces before going to sleep. Most of all Rose wrote reminders to herself, pinning them to her clothes so she could keep track of her daily chores, tearing each off after the task had been taken care of.

But Rose's paper work extended far beyond her notes. She kept an index file, with a card for each child, on which she listed a variety of statistics: date and place of birth, of baptism, of First Communion, of Confirmation; weight (recorded weekly); shoe size; names of doctors; vaccinations; illnesses; visits to the dentist; results of physical examinations.

Jack's card was especially full, since he, more than any of the other children, was prone to childhood illnesses: scarlet fever, whooping cough, measles, chicken pox, bronchitis, appendicitis, asthma, as well as chronic back pain, a delicate stomach, and frequent headaches. Perhaps because he was so often sick or convalescing, Jack became an avid reader. An early favorite, which Rose thought very silly, was called *Billy Whiskers*: the adventures of a goat. Later he became fascinated with tales of King Arthur.

Rose wanted everyone else in her family to enjoy reading. But she had very definite ideas about what was appropriate, and with the exception of *Billy Whiskers*—which she said was allowed in the house only because his grandmother Fitzgerald had given it to Jack—books were chosen from library lists Rose made up for each child. As they became older, the *New York Times* was added to their required reading, and at mealtimes they were usually questioned about some item which had appeared in the paper. In the Kennedy household, meals were not a time for small talk; in addition to current events, appropriate dinner conversation was history or religion. The subject was often chosen to coincide with the time of year, and few topics escaped the scrutiny of Jack's inquisitiveness and humor. One Easter, when the little boy thought Rose had chattered on long enough about Christ being taken by donkey to Jerusalem for the Crucifixion, Jack asked, "Mother, we know what happened to Jesus, but what happened to the donkey?"

Because of her own devout beliefs, Rose insisted that religion be an important part of each child's life. Grace was recited before every meal, prayers were offered every night before bed, the saying of the rosary was a family event. Regular attendance at mass was mandatory, and religious holidays were strictly observed. But even as a youngster, Jack's irreverent attitude toward Catholicism worried his mother. At church on the Good Friday when he was six years old, Rose told all the children to wish for a happy death. Jack said he was instead going to wish for two dogs.

He was also a trial in other ways. Rose had clocks put in every room so that no child ever had an excuse not to show up on time for lunch or dinner. Anyone who arrived after the meal had begun had to start with the course then being served. Four-year-old Bobby took his mother's rule so seriously that on one occasion, afraid of being late for the first course, he ran through a plate-glass door and was severely cut. But Jack, whose chronic tardiness was a life-long characteristic, often got to the table just in time for dessert— although later he usually managed to cajole a full meal from the cook. Sometimes, in his eagerness to get to the kitchen, he would forget another family rule: no child was to leave the table before Rose. Then it would become a race between the mother and her absentminded son, with the rest of the family trying to stall Jack to make sure Rose got to the door first.

The sight of their mother scurrying from the dining room, or walking around like a human bulletin board in a dress covered with bits of paper, might have made Rose seem a comic figure. Her children, however, knew better than to laugh, since Rose kept a ruler in her desk and never hesitated to use it to spank a child who had misbehaved.

Rose instigated many systems to maintain order in her sprawling household. She sent the children off in different-colored bathing suits and caps to help her keep track of them while they were swimming, but dressed them in similar street clothes so one would not be jealous of another. This backfired in the case of Joe Jr. and Jack, because the younger boy would often help himself to an outfit of his brother's. Joe Jr. had a bad temper and the two had to be pulled apart more than once. The skinny and sickly Jack always lost.

Although Rose deplored the fistfights, competition between the children was not only encouraged, but demanded. Competing was a Kennedy compulsion, and winning was the only acceptable outcome. All the children were expected to be the best at whatever they attempted. If they were hurt, they were not to cry. When they lost, they were to try harder and do better the next time. Rivalry between family members was inevitable, and most obviously so between the two oldest brothers, who were constantly trying to outdo each other. In spite of Jack's persistence, Joe Jr. usually came out on top. One memorable incident involved a bicycle race in which the two boys went around the block in opposite directions. As they approached head on, neither would give way. Joe Jr. didn't get a scratch; Jack had to have twenty-eight stitches.

Despite a never-ending series of cuts, bruises, and broken bones, Rose felt athletic activity was just as important as intellectual pursuits. A physical education teacher was employed to lead the group in calisthenics every morning at seven o'clock. The children took lessons in golf, skiing, and tennis. In 1927, Joe Jr. and Jack were given the first of what would eventually be several Kennedy sailboats, and began competing in sailing races, which they understood they were always to win. Contests were a part of life, and the yard was an almost constant scene of a game of baseball or touch football.

Life in the Kennedy household was a careful balance of sports and scholarship. Rose never missed an opportunity to be instructive, and even walks through the neighborhood were used as a way to expand a child's vocabulary. "Look at that fence and give me three adjectives to describe it," she would say. Some parlor games also served a purpose. There were "Twenty Questions" and charades, at which Jack particularly excelled, but Rose's favorite was one in which she would toss out an arithmetic problem: "Five times three, add one, divide by four, multiply by eight, subtract two, divide by three, divide by two. What's the answer?"

While math was an important and appropriate subject, money was not. The children were told their father was well-to-do, that money brought civic and social responsibility, that it was not to be foolishly or ostentatiously spent; then the topic was dropped. The only time it was ever discussed was on "Pay Day." Starting at age five the children were given allowances of a dime a week, with raises on each birthday. All of them agreed the allowances were much too small, and when he reached the age of ten, Jack decided to do something about it:

A Plea for a raise
By Jack Kennedy
Dedicated to my
Mr. J.P. Kennedy
Chapter I

My recent allowance is 40¢. This I used for areoplanes and other playthings of childhood but now I am a scout and I put away my childish things. Before I would spend 20¢ of my ¢.40 allowance and In five minutes I would have empty pockets and nothing to gain and 20¢ to lose. When I am a scout I have to buy canteens, haversacks, blankets searchlidgs poncho things that will last for years and I can always use it while I cant use a cholcolote marshmellow sunday with vanilla ice cream and so I put in my plea for a raise of thirty cents for me to buy scout things and pay my own way more around.

Finis

The increase was granted, and the saga ended with Chapter I. It was one of the few times that Jack ever appeared to be aware of his finances.

Jack was not the only young Kennedy who was oblivious to financial responsibility, and there was some doubt in their father's mind that even his enormous income could keep up with the family's ability to go through money. Their only concept of finances, Joe thought, was that money was what he earned, and what Rose and the children spent—sometimes to an alarming extent. "I don't know what's going to happen to this family when I die," he said one night at dinner. "No one appears to have the slightest concern for how much they spend." Warming to his subject, he turned his attention to one of the girls. "And you, young lady, you are the worst." He went on in such a tirade that the object of his wrath burst into tears. "Well, kid, don't worry," Jack consoled his sister. "The only solution is to have Dad work harder."

Even Joe Kennedy had to laugh, and the tense moment passed. Still, the remark reflected Jack's casual attitude toward money. Throughout his life, he never carried cash, and continually had to borrow from whatever parent, brother, sister, or friend was handy.

Money, companionship, support: the Kennedys always relied on each other. They grew up a close-knit little band, encouraged by their parents to be at the same time one another's greatest rivals and best friends. Joe and Rose had succeeded in creating their own society, one in which their rejection by the Boston elite could never be repeated. But the reason for that snub was not forgotten. For all their insistence that the children be aware of United States history, Rose and Joe saw to it that Irish history was never discussed. Their plans for the future depended on the Kennedys being *American.*

Nineteen twenty-nine was an eventful year for the United States, and for the Kennedys. P.J. died in May, and Joe, a continent away in Hollywood, couldn't get back in time for the funeral. Shortly after his father's death came the abrupt end of his relationship with Gloria Swanson. "I questioned his judgment," the movie star later said. "He did not like to be questioned." Guilt over missing P.J.'s funeral and the trauma of his breakup with Swanson persuaded Joe to finally get out of motion pictures. Five million dollars richer, Kennedy returned permanently to the East. Home was now a mansion in Bronxville, a small, secluded village just north of New York City.

In October 1929, the bottom fell out of the stock market, and as the nation plunged into a terrifying economic depression, Joe soared above it. Having received accurate stock tips from the young man who shined his shoes, he decided he wanted no part of a market that could be so easily predicted. While others had been going mad buying stock, Kennedy had been selling. Then, when those who had bought imprudently were forced to get rid of their stock at a great loss, Joe had plenty of capital with which to pick up bargains. Wealthy people all over the country had been wiped out, but Joe was richer than ever.

The financial woes of others were of little concern to Joe. But ruthlessness and occasional cruelty were characteristics of only the professional man. As a father, Joe was loving, fiercely loyal, and generous. The country's economic chaos made him worry about the future of his family, and Joe decided to establish a million-dollar trust fund for each of the children. A friend, publisher William Randolph Hearst, didn't think much of the idea. "If you make them independent, they won't need you. They'll leave you," Hearst warned. "If that's the only way to hold them, I've been a lousy father," Joe replied, and went right ahead with his plan to give each of the nine children a guaranteed income from the interest on their trust funds.

In 1932, the size of his family, which Kennedy considered his true fortune, had increased with the birth of a son, Edward. But the romance between Joe and Rose had obviously cooled. For thirteen years, there had been a new baby almost every eighteen months. Four years had elapsed since Jean's birth, and Teddy would be their last child. Although Rose appeared to take her husband's return as calmly as she had borne his absence, she began to spend less time at home.

In the six years after Joe relocated in the East, his wife made seventeen trips abroad, no doubt motivated by Joe's continuing affairs with women. Neighbors commented that as Rose's limousine went down the road, Joe's limousine would be coming up, bringing him a visit from still another mistress. But Joe, too, was often away. When business interests took his father all over the country and to Europe, Joe Jr. stepped into the role of surrogate parent during summers at Hyannis Port. The young boy took his responsibilities toward his siblings very seriously, and despite Jack's occasional reluctance to accept his brother's position as head of the family, Joe Jr.'s word was regarded as final. During the winters, however, the children, like their parents, had also begun to scatter. Bronxville was less a home than a point of departure for their boarding schools.

Still, neither distance nor time could weaken the bond between the Kennedys. Even if their physical relationship had ended, Rose and Joe were forever united in their devotion to the children. And the rivalries among brothers and sisters, a competition for the approval of two extraordinary parents, affected not at all their love and loyalty for each other. Whatever happened, there would always be the family.

Despite his prolonged absences, authority in the Kennedy household, for so many years the sole province of his wife, had now passed to Joe. As the children grew older, his would be the predominant role, "the architect," Rose said, "of our lives." She relinquished her solitary position without regret, quietly accepting her husband's judgment in all matters except that of where the children would be educated. Rose thought they should go to Catholic schools. Joe disagreed—at least in the case of their eldest son. P.J. had insisted that Joe attend Boston Latin, as a first step in overcoming the stigma of an Irish name. Now Joe Jr., the heir apparent to all his father's dreams, was enrolled at Choate, an exclusive Protestant prep school in Wallingford, Connecticut.

As the second son, Jack was somehow a little less important in the Kennedy scheme of things, so Rose was allowed to have her way. He had not done well at private schools in Brookline and

Riverdale, and his mother decided Jack's performance would improve in a Catholic boarding school. She selected Canterbury in New Milford, Connecticut, the only parochial school he would ever attend.

But Jack's eighth-grade year there was undistinguished. He admitted to at first being "pretty homesick, but it's O.K. now." His spelling tended to be creative. He knew Rose would like to hear that he went to church every day, and wrote her that "I will be quite pius I guess when I get home." Although he had learned to play "baggamon," classroom work was a bore. "If you study too much," Jack explained to his mother, "you're liable to go crazy." This attitude was reflected in his grades, which, except in English, continued to be mediocre. The school told Rose and Joe their son should be doing better.

In a letter to his parents that fall, the young man showed just how successful had been the family rule that money was not an appropriate topic for conversation. One year after the stock market crash, the most devastating economic event in his country's history, Jack wrote asking for a newspaper subscription, saying he "did not know about the market slump until a long time after. . . . " Having exhausted his attention span for financial matters, Jack's letter returned to the only subject he really cared about: sports. He signed off with a request that his parents send him some golf balls.

Jack desperately wanted to be a good athlete like his older brother, but he lacked Joe Jr.'s natural skills. He tried out for football, a sport he loved passionately, but could not make the first team—although a classmate, Sargent Shriver, commented on how "spunky" Jack was, in spite of being thin. His size and health were an ongoing concern. His back continued to bother him; he was unable to gain weight; he was always tired. In the spring, Jack was hospitalized with appendicitis and had to leave Canterbury for the rest of the second semester.

When the time came for Jack to return to school, Joe put his foot down and decided his second son might do better by following the splendid example of Joe Jr. In the fall of 1931, Jack was enrolled at Choate. It was taken for granted, however, that Jack could not match the achievements of his older brother, and Rose wrote the Choate headmaster to tactfully caution that Jack was "quite different from Joe Jr." Ironically, a few years later the perplexed headmaster, who had obviously not taken Rose's warning to heart, would write the Kennedys to wonder how two brothers could be so unalike.

Joe Jr. was a conformist in a traditional school that rewarded conformity. Faculty and students alike were charmed by the young man's amiable disposition, his attractive appearance, his good grades, his athletic ability. And Jack, at Choate as in the Kennedy household, was simply the younger brother who didn't quite measure up. Although he was more quick-witted than Joe Jr. and could have outdone his brother scholastically, Jack refused to do classroom work that he found dull and tedious. Instead, he attempted to emulate the older boy's athletic success, but he could not compete with his brother's natural talent and good health.

Joe Jr. gave Jack no encouragement in his struggle to make the football team, or in little else. In spite of the gregariousness and generosity young Joe showed his friends, an acquaintance said he was "sarcastic and overbearing and disapproving and challenging" toward Jack. When the boys played football, Joe Jr. would lob the ball to others, and then throw it as hard as possible at Jack, teasing unmercifully if his younger brother couldn't catch it. He was determined to let Jack be no more of a challenge on campus than at home, where Joe Jr. always dominated.

Once, just before the two were going to Hyannis Port for Thanksgiving, Jack delighted in being able to write his parents that Joe Jr. was ill and wouldn't be able to eat the holiday dinner. "Manly youth," the young man added sarcastically. That his flawless brother could actually get sick seemed to Jack a sort of triumph, a rare victory in their rivalry that he was eager to report. Joe Jr. knew better the sort of news his parents wanted to hear. His letters always included a dutiful list of his latest achievements and, for Rose's benefit, an account of his religious activities. Jack's perfunctory notes were less satisfying: "Received the prayer book and would you please send me a muff because it is cold." The brief letters also caused his parents to despair of Jack's ever learning to spell. He mentioned he had attended "football pracite," and requested Rose send him a "choclate pie with whipt cream."

Other letters from Choate came frequently to the Kennedy household—reports from the headmaster on Joe Jr.'s scholastic excellence, his endeavors in sports, his popularity; on Jack's poor grades, his illnesses, his ability to get into mischief. "Jack studies at the last minute, keeps appointments late, has little sense of material values, and can seldom locate his possessions," said one report. The barrage of criticism did nothing but rob Jack of his already fragile self-confidence. There was no doubt about it. To his parents, his teachers, and to himself, Jack Kennedy was simply outclassed by his older brother.

The differences between the two boys became even more obvious in the spring of 1933, when Joe Jr. was given an award as the senior who best combined scholarship and sportsmanship. Jack had accomplished absolutely nothing in two years of prep school, while his brother was leaving Choate in a final burst of glory, ready to take on the next challenge—this time in England.

Joe Jr. had been admitted to Harvard, but his father decided that the young man should first go abroad to study for a year with Harold Laski at the London School of Economics. It was a decision which astonished even Rose. Laski was a socialist, and Joe Kennedy, a capitalist to his very soul, disagreed with everything Laski had ever written or taught. Still, the Depression had upset economic order throughout the world. Communism, socialism, and capitalism would all struggle for dominance in the years ahead, and Joe felt it was necessary for Joe Jr. to understand the economic theories which would challenge the American system of free enterprise. After all, young Joe was not only destined to be a wealthy heir to his father's fortune; like Honey Fitz, Joe Kennedy had long ago decided his eldest son was also going to be president of the United States.

With Joe Jr. in England, Jack was at last on his own, free from the constant unflattering comparisons with his brother. As far as the school and his parents were concerned, it didn't seem to help. Without his older brother to bully and boss him, Jack became even more of a problem. He continued to pour his limited energies into making mischief instead of good grades. Rose declared he was a nuisance, wasting his own time and that of his teachers. She was particularly annoyed that a crate of oranges she had sent Jack from Florida had all been tossed out his window at passersby below.

There were many times in his years at Choate when Jack was simply too sick to get into trouble. During the summer of 1933, he had his tonsils and adenoids removed, an event that Rose dutifully noted on Jack's index card on which she had kept track of all his physical problems for sixteen years. But when as a junior Jack became severely ill, the fact was not mentioned in the card file. Although he would be sick over and over again for the next decade and a half, Jack's pattern of poor health as a young adult would prove to be a less easy diagnosis than a bout of measles or chicken pox. Whatever the cause, he was all but incapacitated for much of one semester his junior year. His studies were even more neglected, his attempts at athletics came to a halt, and his pranks were temporarily curtailed. But only temporarily.

By the fall of 1934, when Jack began his senior year at Choate, his father had become an important man in government. Although Joe had emerged from the stock market crash richer than ever, the Depression frightened him. The country's banking system had completely broken down. Life savings of millions of people had been wiped out, and one-fourth of the labor force were unemployed. The president of the United States, Herbert Hoover, seemed helpless. "Economic depression," he said, "cannot be cured by legislative action or executive pronouncement." But the man who had run against Hoover in 1932 believed otherwise. Franklin D. Roosevelt was determined to cure the nation's financial problems by the very congressional and presidential acts that Hoover had rejected. Joe Kennedy agreed with him. Joe knew no nation could long survive the fiscal chaos that was blighting America. And if the economy totally collapsed, even the vast Kennedy fortune would collapse with it.

Motivated more by pragmatism than by patriotism, Joe had gone into action. Giving his not inconsiderable support to Roosevelt, he contributed heavily to the Democratic party and worked to line up other influential backers. When FDR was elected, Joe confidently waited for appointment to an important government position; secretary of the Treasury, he thought, would be just about right.

As one by one the major posts—including secretary of the Treasury—were filled, Kennedy had yet to be summoned to Washington. This was not the way Joe had been reared. In the world of Boston politics, those who backed a candidate were rewarded for their support. Roosevelt, however, had a different philosophy: one did not bestow a powerful position on an ambitious ally. Instead, he offered Kennedy the ambassadorship to Ireland.

Joe was outraged. To be approached about a job with little prestige was bad enough. But that the position would emphasize a heritage Kennedy had spent his lifetime trying to escape was the last straw. Stung and embittered, Joe turned once more to the pursuit which had never disappointed him—making money.

Then the new president began to have second thoughts. It was one thing to have Joe Kennedy as an important ally; it was quite another to have him as a disenchanted adversary. Kennedy was a very wealthy man with many influential friends. As little as Roosevelt wanted to put Joe in a position of power, to ignore him altogether could prove politically dangerous. Some appropriate post must be found to give Kennedy what he regarded as his long-overdue reward.

A Senate committee had recently ended an investigation of the stock market, and politicians and public alike were appalled at its findings. The dramatic tales of millionaires throwing themselves off tall buildings at the time of the crash did not reflect what was now taking place on Wall Street; since the start of the Depression, the rich had, in fact, just been getting richer. While 45 million Americans went hungry, the financial community had been manipulating the market—and making a bundle. The outcry which resulted from the Senate investigation enabled FDR to fulfill another campaign promise: legislation to end the "callous and selfish wrong-doing" in banking and in business. To enforce the newly enacted regulations, a Securities and Exchange Commission (SEC) was established. And to head up the commission, Roosevelt appointed a man who had once manipulated the stock market better than anyone: Joseph P. Kennedy.

In spite of an uproar from his advisors, the president stuck by his selection. It was, he said, a case of setting "a thief to catch a thief." Journalists, too, were at first taken aback by the appointment. But Joe quickly headed off criticism in the press by telling a group of reporters, "Boys, I've got nine kids. The only thing I can leave them that will mean anything is my good name and reputation. I intend to do that and when you think I'm not doing so, you sound off." In July of 1934, with most of his skeptics disarmed, Joe Kennedy at last became a member of the Roosevelt administration—in the unlikely role as a reformer of capitalism.

A few months after his father entered public service, Jack, now a senior, wrote Joe from Choate that he had "definitely decided to stop fooling around. I really do realize how important it is that I get a good job done. . . ." He then proceeded to get into his worst trouble yet.

The Choate headmaster often used the derogatory term "muckers" when referring to those students who in some way had brought shame to the school's proud traditions. The temptation was too much to resist; Jack and a dozen of his friends decided to form a group called "the Muckers Club," whose purpose was, Jack said, "to buck the system more effectively." The Muckers defied curfews, played practical jokes, refused to straighten up their rooms, skipped chapel, came late to class, and in general behaved in ways unacceptable to Choate's standards for young gentlemen. The more the school tried to enforce those standards, the more the Muckers delighted in defying them.

The headmaster found his duties had split into two separate responsibilities: one, he said, was to run the school; the other was to run Jack Kennedy and his friends. By February the exasperated headmaster had had enough. Claiming the Muckers were "corrupting the morals and integrity of the other students"—a statement which made the group feel terribly important—he suspended Jack and asked Joe to come to Choate. President Roosevelt protested Kennedy's departure in vain. To Joe, not even the specter of the United States in financial crisis could compare to the threat of his son being expelled from prep school.

Jack was a bit overwhelmed that his own misbehavior had resulted in Joe's being summoned from the center of power in Washington to the rural backwater of Wallingford. Kennedy's influential presence managed to save Jack from expulsion, but the seriousness of the occasion was emphasized in a follow-up letter from Joe. "Don't let me lose confidence in you again," he wrote, "because it will be pretty nearly an impossible task to restore it. . . . You have the goods. Why not try to show it?" Jack did try—just enough to get through the rest of his senior year. He graduated in June 1935: sixty-fourth in a class of one hundred twelve.

To the bewilderment of the faculty, he was voted "Most Likely to Succeed." But students knew there was no mystery in his winning this distinction. Flouting Choate's prized integrity one last time, Jack had rigged the election.

3

PEACE IN
OUR TIME

In the fall of 1935, Joe and Rose, accompanied by Jack and Kathleen, sailed to Europe. Joe was on a vacation of sorts. Barred from investing in the stock market as long as he headed the SEC, Kennedy estimated he was losing one hundred thousand dollars a year. His salary, he said, barely paid the telephone bills. So after fourteen months in government service, Joe resigned to return to private life—and profit-making. First, though, came the trip abroad, during which he also acted as a kind of unofficial emissary from FDR, who had asked him to report on economic conditions in Europe.

The two children were off to school. Kathleen, whom the family called "Kick" because she reminded them of a high-spirited pony, was to be enrolled in a French convent. Joe had never pretended to be impartial about his children, and clearly Joe Jr. played the leading role in his father's grand plan. But among his daughters, Kick was the one Joe said was "especially special." Still, the girls counted for less in Joe's scheme, and he had no objection to sending Kick off to France for a year of Catholicism and culture.

Jack was to follow once again a trail blazed by his brother: this time at the London School of Economics, where Joe Jr. had spent a year before returning to the United States to take up his studies at Harvard. Very much his father's son, Joe Jr. had survived the school—as Joe knew he would—"untainted" by socialist thinking. During that year, he had made quite an impression. In addition to his enthusiasm and energy, Joe Jr. had not been at all shy about his ambitions. Professor Laski would often pose a question and then turn to his pupil, asking "Now, Joe, what will you do about this when you are president?" Unlike his brother, Jack had no chance to make an impression at the school; after only a month, he became ill and had to withdraw. The problem was said to be jaundice or hepatitis or, more vaguely, a "blood condition."

Although he had missed several weeks of classes, Jack insisted on returning home to enroll as a freshman at Princeton—a rare show of independence, since Joe wanted all his sons to go to Harvard. But shortly after Thanksgiving, Jack was sick again and forced to drop out of school. By now, his periodic illnesses were almost taken for granted by the rest of the family. "If a mosquito bit Jack Kennedy," his brother Bobby joked, "the mosquito would die."

After being hospitalized for two months in Boston, Jack recuperated on a ranch in Arizona during the winter and spring of 1936. He spent the summer months in Hyannis Port, and in the fall, bowing to his father's wishes, Jack enrolled at Harvard. Joe Jr. was already there, cutting his usual wide swath across the campus: serving on the student council, playing on the football team, grinning without embarrassment when classmates teased him about his ambitions by calling him "Prexy." Unlike Joe Jr., his younger brother had made no plans for a future he seemed unlikely to reach. Recurrences of the mysterious blood condition had become alarmingly frequent in recent years, and Jack looked thin and sickly. At the time he entered Harvard, he was six feet tall and weighed only 149 pounds.

In spite of his size, Jack's compulsion to play football drove him to try out for the team. He made little impression on the coaching staff, even though he regularly attended practice for several weeks. Finally, during a game in which Harvard had a big lead, Jack asked to be put into the lineup. The coach stared at him and said, "Who the hell are you?" That was as close as he ever got to playing college football. Joe Jr. knew his brother's efforts were doomed to failure, and tried to talk him into quitting the team: "You don't weigh enough and you're going to get hurt." Sure enough, at practice a few days later, Jack suffered an injury to a spinal disk, aggravating his chronic back problems and ending forever the dream of being an athlete. Yet he stubbornly refused to give up on sports. Next he attempted to make the varsity swimming squad, but once again his hopes were frustrated by illness. This time it was influenza, which kept Jack confined to the infirmary for a month—during which he would periodically sneak out to practice his backstroke.

As at Choate, Jack's energies were expended everywhere but in the schoolroom. He had campaigned for the office of class president, but did not even make the runoff election. He had failed at football and at swimming. His grades remained mediocre, but this, too, he accepted as a sign that he just didn't have what it took; no matter what he tried, he could never measure up to his brother. Still, Jack persisted in following in the older boy's footsteps. Leaving himself open to the inevitable unflattering comparisons, he moved into Joe Jr.'s residence and promptly told the housemaster, "I want you to know I'm not bright like my brother."

Blinded by his awe of Joe Jr., Jack couldn't see himself for what he was—an engaging young man whom many people liked and admired more than his confident older brother. Franklin D. Roosevelt, Jr., who was at Harvard with both of them, said, "Joe really had everything," but Jack was warmer, nicer, and "so much less self-centered." While others were always the target of Joe Jr.'s caustic sense of humor, Jack usually made fun only of himself. He had been spared the burden of his father's aspirations, a responsibility which meant, a friend said, young Joe was so absorbed by the future that he "could never fully enjoy the present." With little notion of what he wanted to do in life, Jack was free from the ambition which obsessed Joe Jr., making him more relaxed and fun to be with. Jack saw none of this. His patronizing, paternal brother simply outdid him in every way that counted. Or so it seemed.

Of course his failure as an athlete would ultimately matter not at all. And the ignominious loss of the class presidency would some-day seem very amusing. But at age twenty, Jack Kennedy thought he was a bit of a washout.

In the summer of 1937, Jack took off to Europe with Lem Billings, who had been his roommate at Choate. Feeling quite grown-up at being on his own, Jack decided to keep a diary of his impressions of the European political scene. His entries showed that he was rather naive about the situation on the Continent, but so too were many other, more sophisticated, observers in those last few years before the Second World War.

France was the first stop. Jack noted that the "general feeling seems to be that there will not be another war." Another entry stated that ". . . France is much too well prepared for Germany. The permanence of the alliance of Germany and Italy is also questionable." Jack found Italy lively and prosperous. "Fascism seems to treat them well," he wrote. A visit to Germany brought less optimistic thoughts about that particular form of government. The people were haughty and insufferable. Offers of friendly American handshakes were greeted with arrogant Nazi salutes of "Heil, Hitler."

The two young men had attended a Mussolini rally and regarded the Italian leader as a comic figure. But although they passed through Nuremburg only three days before Hitler was to speak, they decided not to delay their trip by waiting around to see him. Afterward, when Hitler's role in history became clear, they regretted having missed the mesmeric dictator; at the time, however, they just wanted to get out of the country. Amusing though Mussolini might have been, there was nothing humorous about the Nazis. Jack and Lem agreed that the tour of Germany had been an awful experience.

But there were many more agreeable memories to offset their unpleasant confrontations with the German people. As anyone who knew him was aware, wherever Jack Kennedy went there were bound to be notable encounters with women. Regardless of the academic and athletic failures during his freshman year at Harvard, Jack had been a great social success. He had written Lem that he could get women as often as he wanted, and that pattern continued in Europe. Even on board ship during the trip over, Jack noted in his diary, "Looked pretty dull the first couple of days, but investigation disclosed some girls." He went out with a young woman in France, only to discover, to his dismay, that local custom required the presence of a chaperone. Italy was better. "Very beautiful girls," he wrote, "although our not speaking Italian was a temporary damper."

Despite the fact that Jack was an abominable linguist, he managed to communicate very well wherever he traveled. No matter how inept his ability to speak the local language, no matter how skinny or sickly he might be, Jack had already learned that women, for some reason, found him irresistible.

His younger brother's attraction for women was a mystery to Joe Jr., and still another source of competition. But this was one area where Jack usually triumphed. "The girls really liked Jack," Lem later said. "Though Joe was bigger and better-looking, Jack knew better how to handle girls . . . he spent a lot of time thinking about girls and he was incredibly successful with them." Certainly Jack's grades seemed to indicate he was perhaps spending too much time "thinking about girls."

Back at Harvard in the autumn of 1937, Jack decided to major in government. He did not plan to enter politics since his father had already claimed that career for Joe Jr. Instead, Jack thought he might like to be a journalist, specializing in political and governmental issues. Jack had told his father that the trip abroad had given him the incentive to study more in his sophomore year. Then, just back from the continent of Europe, he proceeded to get a D— in a course on "Continental Europe." Failing to follow through on his hopeful statement to Joe, Jack's second year of college was no more distinguished than the first. As a freshman, he had maintained a C average, a lackluster performance he repeated as a sophomore after vowing to "study more." But for once, Joe Kennedy paid little attention to Jack's poor grades. By late 1937, he was far too preoccupied with leaving a job he hated for a new one which seemed too good to be true.

Joe had backed FDR's successful bid for reelection the previous year. He had even gone so far as to outline a book, *I'm for Roosevelt*, which was ghostwritten by his friend Arthur Krock, chief correspondent of the *New York Times* Washington bureau. The reward for his support of FDR was an offer to head up a new government agency, the Maritime Commission, which had been established to snap the American shipping industry out of a slump.

Faced with Joe's reluctance, Roosevelt finally persuaded him by implying that Kennedy's acceptance of the position at Maritime would lead to a more gratifying appointment in the future. The job proved to be just as frustrating as Joe had thought it would be. There was little doubt, Joe said, why the Merchant Marine was in "lousy shape." It just didn't have enough money behind it. After his first meeting with a group of shipowners, he impatiently threw up his hands. "Why, there wasn't a guy in that room," Kennedy said with disgust, "who could write a check for a million dollars."

But Joe's disdain didn't stop with the shortcomings of the maritime industry; he had also become less optimistic about the administration's economic policies. When he let the president know he was fed up with his own job in particular and with the way Roosevelt was running the country in general, FDR decided it was time to come through on his promise. The president was anxious to get Joe out of his hair. And there just happened to be an available post which would solve the problem nicely.

Almost all of FDR's friends, family, and advisers were horrified by the position he had in mind. Even the liberal Roosevelt administration was not without its snobs, and to them, Joe Kennedy was too critical, too crass, too crude—and too Catholic—for the job. But the president stuck by his choice. To those who objected politically, he explained his decision by saying, "Kennedy is too dangerous to have around here." To those who disapproved socially, FDR would laugh, saying the appointment was "the greatest joke in the world."

But to the son of a Boston saloonkeeper, to an Irish Catholic who had spent his life brooding over real or imagined slights which were the burden of his heritage, the joke was on the Protestant establishment. He had snared the most glittering prize of the American diplomatic scene. Joseph P. Kennedy was to become the United States ambassador to Great Britain.

The English were charmed with the first wave of Kennedys to reach their shores. By the spring of 1938 most of the children—only seven, Joe quipped, "so as not to complicate the housing problem"—had been installed in London. The press promptly dubbed Kennedy "the Father of His Country."

After Joe Jr.'s graduation from Harvard, he and Jack joined the family. The two young men spent the summer going back and forth between England and France, where the Kennedys had rented a house on the Riviera. In the fall, young Joe took on a temporary post, arranged by his father, at the American embassy in Paris. From there Joe Jr. traveled all over the continent on fact-finding missions, reporting back to the elder Kennedy that the deteriorating political situation was moving Europe closer to the brink of war.

Jack had begun his junior year at Harvard. Although he had been ill a good deal of the previous semester, he now wrote his parents that he was feeling much better. His grades were healthier as well. Whether brought about by maturity as a result of his travels, or by liberation from the intimidating presence of his older brother, Jack had at last begun to show the scholastic promise that had always been expected of him. In spite of taking extra classes during the first semester of his junior year, he maintained a B average and made the dean's list.

The additional courses meant Jack was able to go on a leave of absence at the beginning of his second semester, in order to spend the next seven months abroad. Joe Jr., who by the spring of 1939 saw himself as a seasoned diplomat, wrote a friend that Jack had come over "to begin his education." Although young Joe was being typically patronizing, he knew what the experience would mean to his younger brother. At that time and in that place, Jack's travels were far more educational than anything he could have been taught at Harvard. Political science learned in a classroom could never rival a chance to witness the drama of history in the making, and Jack was on the scene as the curtain began to rise.

In a letter to Lem Billings, he reported from France that talk of impending war was "so damned complicated that it is impossible to estimate the difficulties over there." Jack thought Russia was a "crude, backward, hopelessly bureaucratic country." While in Germany, his car, bearing English license plates, was pelted with bricks thrown by Nazi storm troopers. From Poland, Jack told his father, "The Poles will fight." Within a month of his return to London, the Poles were doing just that. World War II had begun.

It was a war few wanted to avoid more than Joe Kennedy, and he had backed those in the English government who had tried to placate Hitler at almost any humiliating cost. For all who had chosen that approach, appeasement proved to be a calamitous tactical decision as well as a grave political error. Although Joe would remain on as ambassador for another year, it was the beginning of the end of his career in public service.

Kennedy was not an immoral man, and the true evils of Hitler's reign were as yet unknown. Joe was awed by the industrial might of Germany, which the British could not hope to match. England's weakness meant that the United States would surely be dragged into the conflict, and America, with most of its military equipment left over from World War I, was unprepared to go to war. Even if Germany were to somehow be defeated, Joe believed another war would result in the destruction of European commercial centers, leading to the end of the capitalist system and the ultimate triumph of communism. But most frightening to Joe was the knowledge that if his country had to fight, so, too, would his sons.

Back in the United States in the fall of 1939, the Kennedy children scattered to various boarding schools, prep schools, and colleges. Joe Jr. enrolled at Harvard Law. Jack was now a senior. Having made the dean's list the year before, Jack was eligible to graduate with honors; in order to do so, he was required to write a thesis. As his subject, Jack chose to analyze the reasons behind the Munich pact, which the British prime minister, Neville Chamberlain, had signed with Hitler the previous September.

Heralded by Chamberlain as representing "peace in our time"— a claim for which Joe Kennedy thought he himself should be given credit since he had urged Chamberlain to sign it—the agreement instead made war inevitable. By promising England would do nothing while Germany pounced on the tiny nation of Czechoslovakia, the prime minister had convinced Hitler that the nations of Western Europe would not fight, and that the German dictator was free to unleash his army on the more defenseless countries to the east. "Peace in our time" was to last for exactly eleven months. On September 1, 1939, Germany invaded Poland. Chamberlain's agreement had resulted in the most devastating conflict the world had ever known.

Jack's thesis, written during the winter of 1939–40, was titled "Appeasement at Munich." The 150-page paper was completed, with the help of five stenographers, just under the wire of the March 15 deadline. In it Jack implied that the disastrous consequences of the pact were not the fault of England's rulers; instead the blame lay with the people of Britain, who had been unwilling to pay the taxes necessary to strengthen the country's armed forces. "Leaders are responsible," he wrote, "for their failures only in the governing sector and cannot be held responsible for the failure of a nation as a whole." The paper went on to further defend Chamberlain: "English public opinion was not sufficiently aroused to back him in a war."

Although the thesis was essentially a justification of his father's views, Jack differed with Joe in regard to one of the most important players in the tragic drama: Winston Churchill. Churchill had for years been a voice in the British wilderness, warning of the dangers of German rearmament after World War I, a position which had often brought him into conflict with Joe Kennedy. Now he had been vindicated. Jack acknowledged Churchill's foresight while at the same time somewhat contradicting his own theme: "In light of the present-day war, we are able to wonder at the blindness of Britain's leaders and the country as a whole that could fail to see the correctness of Churchill's arguments."

Joe Jr. read the thesis but dismissed it to his father, claiming "it seemed to represent a lot of work but did not prove anything." Jack's professors disagreed. The thesis received high honors.

The events of that spring proved just how wrong both Joe Kennedys could be. Jack graduated cum laude from Harvard University; he would eventually become its most famous alumnus. Winston Churchill became head of the British government; he would prove to be its most memorable prime minister.

In the summer of 1940, as his father's power and popularity dwindled away, Jack Kennedy was enjoying his first taste of fame.

Joe, whose own performance had become increasingly unsure, didn't miss a step as he moved to bring Jack into the spotlight. Jack had sent him a copy of the thesis, with the comment, "I'll be interested to see what you think of it, as it represents more work than I've ever done in my life." Joe immediately decided his son's thesis should be a book, and once again summoned the faithful Arthur Krock to turn amateurish Kennedy words into professional prose. Krock lined up a literary agent and even furnished the book with its title: *Why England Slept*. Not content to have a famous *New York Times* reporter polishing the manuscript, Joe asked Henry Luce, head of Time, Inc., to write a foreword. Luce agreed. He, too, had backed the British policy of appeasement, and Jack's theme seemed to put Chamberlain's supporters in a favorable light.

Joe's comments on the text, however, showed he had thought better of his own views and those of the British government—at least now that they were to be displayed before the reading public. "You have gone too far," he wrote Jack, "in absolving the leaders of the National Government from responsibility. . . ." Joe added that those leaders should have "thrown caution out of the window and attempted to arouse their countrymen to the dangers with which Britain obviously was confronted." Jack listened to his father and amended the manuscript to reflect Joe's comments. Thus, the published version contained a rebuke of Chamberlain's—and therefore Kennedy's—views, but to Joe, criticism of his own role was much less important than the fact that Jack was to be an author. "You would be surprised," Joe told his son, "how a book that really makes the grade with high class people stands you in good stead for years to come."

Joe arranged for Jack's publisher to send out 250 review copies, and the response was generally enthusiastic. The *New York Times Book Review* called it a work of "painstaking scholarship." The *Wall Street Journal* said it was "required reading for all who are sincerely concerned with maintenance of our institutions." The *Christian Science Monitor* praised its "sober, reliable, straightforward analysis of Great Britain's slowness in rearming to meet the Nazi menace." Others were less enthralled. The *Washington Post* claimed the book was superficial. A Harvard professor suggested a more accurate title might have been *Why Daddy Slept*. Harold Laski, to whom Joe had proudly sent a copy, responded by saying the book was immature and that he deeply regretted its being published. He added that as difficult as it was to tell Joe these things, his doing so represented "much more real friendship than the easy price of 'yes men' like Arthur Krock."

The critics, however, were very much in the minority. People on both sides of the Atlantic had become all too aware of the costliness of Britain's failure to properly rearm. *Why England Slept* was the right book at the right time—a time when everyone was seeking an explanation of the war's disastrous progress. The British might not be able to hold out against Germany's onslaught, and the public wanted to know why. They didn't mind, it seemed, that the answer came from a twenty-three-year-old college senior. The book sold forty thousand copies in America, the same number in England, and was a Book of the Month Club selection. *Why England Slept* was a best-seller and its author a celebrity.

Jack seemed unimpressed with the book's success, and said it would never have had a chance "except for luck." Harold Laski agreed with this view, although he pointed out that the only "luck" involved was the fact that Jack was the son of the American ambassador to Great Britain. Certainly Jack's fame as an author came less from his writing ability than from his father's importance. Yet Joe's position was by now very shaky. He had clung to his view that England would be beaten and that the United States should not waste men and material on a lost cause. "The British have had it," Joe said. "They can't stop the Germans and the best thing for them is to learn to live with them." The English people would have none of the defeatist views of the American ambassador and heeded instead the moving words of Winston Churchill: "What is our aim? I can answer in one word: Victory—victory at all costs, victory in spite of all terror, victory however long and hard the road may be."

Terror there was in abundance; having endured fifty-seven straight nights of air raids, Joe was convinced that in spite of the courage of its citizens, London could not hold out much longer. Since the embassy advised its personnel to find quarters outside the city, Kennedy rented a house near Windsor, thirty miles from the center of the capital. Londoners saw this as a strategic withdrawal, and began to refer to the American ambassador as "Jittery Joe." As he continued to warn that England's defeat was inevitable, Joe was taken less and less seriously. A British Foreign Office memo called him "undoubtedly a coward." The same source added Kennedy was "a very foul specimen of double crosser and defeatist." Official opinion at home was no less unflattering. "His mind is as blank as uninked paper," the secretary of state commented.

But Joe persisted in his criticisms. "I cannot impress upon you strongly enough my complete lack of confidence in the entire conduct of this war," Kennedy reported. To imagine, the ambassador added, "that the English have anything to offer in the line of leadership . . . would be a complete misapprehension." Churchill agreed that as prime minister he had nothing to offer—nothing, he promised the British, but "blood, toil, tears, and sweat."

The power of Churchill's eloquence was lost on Joe Kennedy. Germany had the greater military strength; its air force, the Luftwaffe, was systematically wiping out Britain's factories and railroads. Since bravery was no substitute for weaponry, England would be defeated. Although it was an opinion shared by many in the United States, it contradicted the views of both the British prime minister and the American president. All through the summer and fall of 1940, Kennedy found himself increasingly isolated from policymaking in Downing Street and on Pennsylvania Avenue. To be nothing but an "errand boy," as Joe described himself, was more than the proud Kennedy could endure. He wanted out—exactly what Roosevelt wanted for him. But although FDR cared nothing about Joe's bruised ego, he worried a great deal about the political impact of his ambassador's return.

Roosevelt was running for an unprecedented third term. A disgruntled Kennedy, back in the United States before the election, could possibly swing thousands of voters away from the president; Henry Luce and many other powerful isolationists were urging him to do just that. Joe himself had bragged to an acquaintance in London that he could "put 25 million Catholic votes" behind FDR's Republican opponent. The president, fully aware that he must find a way to both circumvent the political dangers and get Kennedy out of England, finally asked Kennedy to come to Washington "for consultation." But the sarcastic tone of FDR's cable left little doubt why the ambassador was being brought back to the United States: THE LIQUOR TRADE IN BOSTON IS NOW CHALLENGING AND THE GIRLS OF HOLLYWOOD MORE FASCINATING. I EXPECT YOU BACK HERE BY SATURDAY.

So Joe came home, ready for a showdown.

On the evening of October 27, 1940, the Kennedys dined at the White House. On their way there, Rose, steeped in the code of Democratic politics, cautioned Joe that a break with FDR would be seen as ungrateful and disloyal. Already disarmed by the advice of his wife, Kennedy was simply no match for the president, who bribed, flattered, and outmaneuvered his ambassador.

Joe's troubles, FDR said, were the fault of the State Department; the president had put up with its outrageous behavior only because he himself was so involved with the crisis in Europe. After the election, there would be a thorough housecleaning to rid State of those who had misused valued members of the administration such as Joe Kennedy. The ambassador would have Roosevelt's blessing if Kennedy eventually decided to seek the presidency for himself. Then FDR played his trump card: he would support Joe Jr. in a bid for the governorship of Massachusetts in 1942. Would Kennedy make a radio speech endorsing Roosevelt for a third term?

Within forty-eight hours, Joe was on the air to the American people. The United States would stay out of war, he said, and Roosevelt shared this conviction. Joe ended with an emotional appeal: "I have a great stake in this country. My wife and I have given nine hostages to fortune. Our children and your children are more important than anything else in the world. The kind of America that they and their children will inherit is of grave concern to us all. In light of these considerations, I believe that Franklin D. Roosevelt should be reelected president of the United States."

On November 5, FDR won his third term. In an amiable meeting two days later, he accepted Joe's resignation, asking that the news remain secret until a replacement had been found.

Kennedy did keep quiet about the fact he had resigned, the lone discretion he showed in an interview with a *Boston Globe* reporter early in November. "Democracy is finished in England," Joe stated, and might well be in America, too. It was a question of economics, and of "feeding people." The reporter asked Joe's opinion of the president's wife, Eleanor Roosevelt. She was a wonderful woman, "helpful and full of sympathy," he responded. Unfortunately Joe didn't stop there. Mrs. Roosevelt, he added, "bothered us more on our jobs in Washington to take care of the poor little nobodies who hadn't any influence, than all the rest of the people down there together. She's always sending me a note to have some little Susie Glotz to tea at the embassy." When the story was picked up by other newspapers, Joe's reasons for his pessimism about democracy, and his reference to Eleanor Roosevelt's kindness, were usually omitted. The interview cost Kennedy his chance to leave the administration with dignity, wiped out any gratitude Roosevelt felt for his last-minute help in the campaign, and sabotaged the hope that FDR would back him or Joe Jr. for future public office.

Joe Kennedy was now fifty-two years old. His service in government had ended ignominiously, and his uneasy friendship with FDR was ruined forever. Still, he was a millionaire many times over. And he had nine children, his "hostages to fortune."

In the eldest of these, Joe saw the certainty of reaching his impossible goal. He himself had accomplished more than he had dreamed, yet less than the "everything" he desired. But he would put the humiliations of 1940 behind him. As 1941 began, Kennedy looked only to the future, and there was no reason to doubt its outcome. With or without Roosevelt's backing, Joe Jr. would achieve *everything*.

Having finished his own political career, Joe wrote a friend, "I find myself much more interested in what young Joe is going to do than what I am going to do with the rest of my life." Kennedy was counting on a vow the president had made to the people of the United States: "To you mothers and fathers, I give you one more assurance. . . . Your boys are not going to be sent into any foreign wars!" No father in America wanted more desperately to believe those words than Joe Kennedy.

4

DID YOU
HAPPEN TO SEE

Jack Kennedy felt there was no point in setting goals or making plans for a career. Like many of his generation, Jack believed Roosevelt would be unable to keep his promise, and that the United States would soon be at war. His older brother didn't agree. Joe Jr. was at Harvard Law School, where he had formed the Committee Against Military Intervention. One of its first speakers was Joe Kennedy, who continued to sound the isolationist alarm. But few now paid much attention to Kennedy's familiar warnings—including his second son.

Jack was a continent away from his father and brother. Hoping that the warm California climate would improve his health, he had decided to audit courses at Stanford University as a way to pass the time until he was called into the service. Although Jack kept to a busy schedule of classes, swimming, exercising, and dating several young women, the threat of war was seldom forgotten. After the fall of France in June 1940, Congress had enacted into law the first peacetime draft in American history. On October 16, all men between the ages of twenty-one and thirty-five were required to register. College students were exempt until the end of the school year, but on July 1, 1941, they too would become eligible to be called up.

Although Jack had filled out the draft questionnaire stating he intended to go on with his studies, he was unable to finish even the first semester. Illness struck again, and he spent the next two months in a Boston hospital. Jack had continued to suffer both back and stomach problems, but the reason for his hospitalization was not disclosed. When he was finally discharged in February 1941, Jack headed south to recuperate. The house in Bronxville had been sold, and Joe had purchased property in Florida, a state which had no income tax. Home to the Kennedys was now Palm Beach during winter and Hyannis Port in summer.

In May, Jack accompanied his mother and sister Eunice on a trip to South America. While they were there the war situation worsened. That spring saw the most massive bombings yet inflicted on English cities, and it appeared the long-dreaded German invasion was about to begin. Japan, which had allied itself with Germany and Italy, seemed intent on conquering all of Asia. And if the Japanese turned their sights toward the southeast, they would be eyeing the home base of the United States Pacific Fleet at Pearl Harbor, on the Hawaiian island of Oahu.

On May 26, 1941, when President Roosevelt announced a state of national emergency, even Joe Kennedy began to have second thoughts about the possibility of war. If it was sure to come, then the United States must be prepared. The president's declaration, Kennedy said, was "a most historic and most solemn pronouncement" that required the unlimited loyalty of all Americans. Among the first of the "loyal Americans" to respond was Joe Jr. He decided to forgo his last year at Harvard Law and in June enlisted in the Navy's Aviation Cadet program. "My ideas haven't changed. I still don't think we should go into the war," Joe Jr. said. "But I thought I ought to be doing something and I'll do whatever they tell me to do." He began his preliminary training at a naval air base near Boston, an ideal location since it meant he could go to Hyannis Port most weekends. Joe was both frightened by and proud of his son's choice. "Wouldn't you know," he told everyone who cared to listen, "naval aviation, the most dangerous thing there is."

By the first of July, Rose, Eunice, and Jack had returned to Hyannis Port for the last time the Kennedys would all be together. Those months seemed typical of other carefree summers at the Cape. It was a time of sailing and swimming, of softball and tennis, of dancing and movies shown in the basement projection room. As usual, the most popular pastime was touch football. Visitors were taken aback and sometimes even alarmed by the intensity with which the Kennedy girls and boys alike played the game. There were no exceptions: to be a guest in Hyannis Port was to spend hours in ferocious football competition, and friendships were often made or broken in direct proportion to the passion one brought to the sport. That summer, as they did every year, almost all the children had invited friends to visit, and the house and lawn were filled with young people. One visitor described the Kennedys in July of 1941 as existing outside the usual laws of nature. "There was no other group so handsome, so engaged," he said. Their days were spent in constant activity, their nights in endless discussion. Much of the conversation, of course, was about the future—the threat of war hung over America like a black thundercloud. But there was another, strictly Kennedy, concern darkening Hyannis Port that summer: what to do about Rosemary.

From her earliest years, it was obvious to her parents that the eldest Kennedy daughter was different from the rest of the children. She was slow to learn to crawl, to walk, to talk. Doctors eventually confirmed their fears: Rosemary was mentally retarded. But Joe was adamant that his eldest daughter not be institutionalized. "What can they do for her that her family can't do better?" he said. "We will keep her at home." As always, Joe's word was law, and the Kennedys did their best not to let Rosemary know she was "different." Just like her brothers and sisters, she had been presented at court and taken skiing in Switzerland. She accompanied Rose on shopping trips and got her full quota of Joe's paternal pep talks. The children were no less attentive than their parents. Joe Jr. tried to teach Rosemary to play football and tennis, and she crewed for Eunice in sailboat races. Jack escorted her to dances, where he would arrange for his friends to cut in so Rosemary would feel popular.

But as the children matured and began to go their separate ways, Rosemary could not keep up. Surrounded by eight bright, energetic, and articulate siblings, it was obvious to Rosemary she was being left out—the only one of the children never allowed to go anyplace alone, the only one denied all those activities in which the others took part. A particular problem was her growing maturity as a woman. One of the most attractive of the Kennedy daughters, Rosemary was eager to begin dating, as her sisters had. But Rose feared Rosemary would be an easy victim for an opportunistic young man, and she was forbidden to attend social events alone.

As her frustrations grew, Rosemary started to regress. She became more uncoordinated, less able to converse, to remember, to concentrate. Her once docile personality changed, and she often threw tantrums. By the summer of 1941, her anger had turned to rage, then to violence. She began breaking objects and striking out at those around her, finally viciously attacking her seventy-eight-year-old grandfather Fitzgerald.

Even Joe realized it was probably impossible for Rosemary to continue to live at home. Yet there was one last chance: a neuro-surgical technique, prefrontal lobotomy. At the time, it was a new procedure for which there were high hopes and few qualms. The severing of nerves in the frontal lobe of the brain, doctors believed, would relieve violent tendencies and make the patient calmer and better adjusted. At Joe's instigation and without even Rose's knowl-edge, the surgery was performed on Rosemary—with disastrous results. Gone were her violent rages, but gone too was the ability to function at more than a childlike level.

In the fall, Rosemary was sent to a convent nursing home where, the Kennedys said, she had decided to devote her life to working with retarded children. It would be more than twenty years before even the sketchiest facts about Rosemary's condition were made public. In 1941, mental retardation in any family was regarded as shameful. To the Kennedys, the admission of such a problem would have been unthinkable. It was their secret to hide, their dis-grace to bear. The Kennedy family had suffered a tragic loss—and the war hadn't even begun.

Joe Jr. had beaten him into the service, and as usual Jack was deter-mined to follow his older brother. He attempted to enlist first in the Army, then in the Navy, but both turned him down because of his medical problems. Over the course of the summer, he followed a strict regimen of exercise and diet to improve his health. While Jack lifted weights, his father pulled strings. The naval attaché at the embassy during Joe's ambassadorship was now director of Naval Intelligence in Washington. On September 25, 1941, Jack Kennedy was sworn into the United States Navy, and assigned to the ONI: the Office of Naval Intelligence. He would be there just three months— a period later omitted from his official naval biography. During that time Jack, along with several other young ensigns, was responsible for the preparation of bulletins which summarized information from foreign intelligence sources. These bulletins were then sent to the secretary of the Navy and other key naval personnel.

By November relations between America and Japan had become critical. Japanese diplomats arrived in Washington to participate in last-minute negotiations to avoid war. But the discussions soon reached an impasse. The United States had broken Japan's diplomatic code, and messages being intercepted between Tokyo and Japanese embassies indicated the peace talks were a sham: Japan was preparing for war in the Pacific. But where would the Japanese strike? Pearl Harbor, the Office of Naval Intelligence concluded, was the least likely target. The Japanese would realize their huge armada could not steam halfway across the Pacific without being detected by U.S. Navy air patrols or by ONI sources.

By early December, however, the ONI had lost track of the Japanese fleet altogether. Naval intelligence had picked up no radio signals from Japanese aircraft carriers since November 16. The ONI decided that the lack of contact meant the carriers were in home waters. Instead, they were operating under radio silence; having taken a roundabout course through the North Pacific, they were now anchored 230 miles north of Oahu—biding their time until Sunday morning, when the U.S. fleet would be docked at Pearl Harbor.

At eight o'clock, December 7, 1941, Japan struck. Germany backed up its ally and also declared war on the United States. The years of waiting and doubt were over. It was no longer a "foreign war"; America was in it, too.

It was a winter of paranoia in the United States, and especially at the Office of Naval Intelligence. Failure to anticipate the attack on Pearl Harbor had been one of the worst intelligence blunders in history; those responsible would have to be disciplined, demoted, or reassigned. It seemed unlikely the housecleaning would extend into the tiny office in which Ensign Kennedy went about his duties. The material to which Jack was privy was not highly classified, and there was little chance he could have interpreted Japanese intentions. A long line of more important ONI personnel, reaching up to the secretary of the Navy, had ignored the clues which pointed to Japan's target. But post–Pearl Harbor hysteria meant that officials were taking a close look at the entire ONI staff. And one of the ensigns, it turned out, was having an affair with a woman suspected of being a Nazi spy.

In addition to his son's assignment at the Office of Naval Intelligence, Joe had arranged to get Kick a job in Washington. He once again called on Arthur Krock, who contacted a friend, the owner of an isolationist newspaper, the *Times Herald*. The paper's theory in hiring personnel was that pretty finishing school graduates with rich fathers were the most inexpensive source of labor, and Kick, who had attended Finch College for two years, qualified on every point.

She was not the only young woman Krock had placed at the paper. While serving on the Board of Trustees at the Columbia School of Journalism, he had been approached by a beautiful student who had asked him to find her a position in Washington. Like Joe Kennedy, Krock was always happy to oblige a pretty face, and he recommended the young woman to the *Times Herald*. Her name was Inga Arvad, a byline that began to appear on the paper's daily feature: a personality column called "Did You Happen to See . . ." Soon she became friends with her new co-worker, Kick Kennedy, and was introduced to Kick's brother.

Inga was unlike anyone Jack had ever met before. Although she was only four years his senior, she seemed to Jack the epitome of glamour, mystery, and sophistication. A native of Copenhagen, she had attended schools in Germany, France, and England, and had won the title of "Miss Denmark." When she was twenty-two, Inga decided to go to Germany, where she passed herself off as a newspaper reporter and managed to get an interview with Hermann Goering—head of the Luftwaffe and Adolf Hitler's closest friend. The interview went so well that a Copenhagen newspaper published it and hired Inga as its Berlin correspondent.

For a time, she moved in the highest circles of the Nazi government. Goering had been quite taken with the stunning young journalist, and invited her to his wedding, where Hitler served as best man. Like Goering, the German dictator was also captivated. Pronouncing her "the perfect example of Nordic beauty," Hitler granted Inga two exclusive interviews and asked her to accompany him to the 1936 Berlin Olympics. Having turned the heads of the two most powerful men in Germany, Inga then left the country—affronted, she said, because the Nazis had asked her to go to Paris as a spy. Inga returned to Copenhagen, where she had an affair with a journalist blacklisted by the U.S. State Department because of his friendship with Goering. Next she had shown up at Columbia University— and then in Washington, D.C.

Jack found this background intriguing. So did the Federal Bureau of Investigation.

Inga had been under government surveillance since November 1940, while she was still in journalism school. Her relationship with Jack Kennedy, who was serving in the Office of Naval Intelligence, soon came to the attention of the FBI, where a confidential file noted Ensign Kennedy was "playing around" with and "apparently spending the night" with Inga Arvad. On November 27, 1941, "Did You Happen to See . . ." was devoted to Jack. It gushed on about the young man's charm, intelligence, humility, and popularity, compared him favorably with his famous father, and praised his highly successful book. Eyebrows were raised throughout Washington. The glowing column made it obvious that Jack's involvement with the woman he had nicknamed Inga-Binga was a serious romance.

Ten days after the piece was published, Pearl Harbor had been attacked. Heads began to roll at ONI—including that of Ensign Kennedy. Even if his position was not important enough to compromise national security, his romance with a woman suspected of being a spy was an embarrassment. When Jack's immediate superior was ordered to inform the young man that his naval career was finished, Joe Kennedy was beside himself. Expulsion from Choate was nothing compared to a dishonorable discharge from the United States Navy! Joe's influence saved his son again. In January 1941, Jack was transferred to Charleston, South Carolina; his new assignment for the Navy was to instruct defense workers on what to do in case of a bombing.

Jack's boredom was relieved by visits from Inga-Binga, whom he continued to see in spite of her having caused his dismissal from the ONI. Although Jack was no longer doing intelligence work, official interest in Inga had not lessened. President Roosevelt himself had sent a memo to J. Edgar Hoover, director of the FBI, requesting that surveillance on Inga Arvad be intensified. As a result, the Charleston hotel room where Inga stayed had been bugged. Hoover now had in his possession—not for the last time—information that proved Jack's involvement with an inappropriate woman.

The president, the Navy, the FBI: Jack's affair had attracted some very high-level scrutiny. But no one was watching more closely than his father, and Joe Kennedy was all too aware of the ongoing romance. When Jack made the mistake of announcing he wanted to marry Inga, his father exploded. There was more string-pulling, and Jack suddenly found himself classified for sea duty. The Japanese, Joe had evidently decided, were less of a threat than Inga Arvad.

On July 27, 1942, Jack reported to the midshipmen's school at Northwestern University. As his officer training began, the affair with Inga came to an end. "As you probably haven't heard, Inga-Binga got married—and not to me," Jack wrote his friend Lem Billings. "She evidently wanted to leave Washington and get to N.Y.—so she married some guy . . . she didn't love. I think it would have been much smarter for her to take the train, as they have several a day from Washington to N.Y. Anyway she's gone—and that leaves the situation rather blank."

Jack was discouraged about much more than losing Inga. It was just like Choate all over again. He had so far pretty well fouled up his military career, and the fact that he was still in the Navy was due only to his father's influence. Joe Jr., in the meantime, had passed flight training and been named the outstanding cadet of his class. Joe had been present at the graduation ceremony and had pinned the golden wings of a naval aviator on his son's chest. Jack saw one last chance to redeem himself. After his own unheralded graduation, he volunteered for service in the Motor Patrol Torpedo Boats: the PTs.

In the early days of the war, patrol torpedo boats were thought to be very glamorous. When Japan attacked the Philippines, it had been a PT that evacuated General Douglas MacArthur, commander of the U.S. Army Forces in the Far East. Although he had left the Philippines from the relative safety of one of its most heavily fortified islands, MacArthur was anxious to give the impression he had departed under heavy fire. The general lavishly praised the PTs that had "rescued" him and his staff, and sent their commander back to the United States to lobby for a larger fleet.

With so little good news from the Pacific, the Navy enthusiastically went along with the welcome publicity and set up a PT training school in Rhode Island. There was just one catch. The public may have been fooled by tales of PT derring-do, but the men at Annapolis knew better. PTs were small, fragile, uncomfortable, and not very seaworthy. In spite of wide claims of their sinking enemy vessels, PT torpedoes were often defective and unlikely to put so much as a dent in the smallest Japanese ship. The 1942 Naval Academy class of 616 graduates yielded exactly twenty men who chose to go into PT-boat service.

To offset potential embarrassment—what good was a training school if there was no one to train?—the Navy began to look for volunteers in its officer candidate schools. Among the amateurs the Navy had better luck. To young men bursting with patriotism and an urge to get into the fight, PTs were an irresistible challenge. For Jack Kennedy, they also seemed an answer to his problems. By signing on for PT duty, Jack could show up his brother, impress his father, and please the Navy, all at the same time.

Joe Jr., still an ensign, was stationed in Puerto Rico and flying air patrols over a section of the Atlantic far from any war zone. In the PTs, Jack would have the rank of lieutenant junior grade and within a few months be fighting in the Pacific in command of his own boat. This was his chance to prove he had what it took. In a letter to

Lem, Jack mentioned that the fatality rate in PT service was ten men killed for every one that survived. In order to be accepted, Jack wrote, "You have to be young, healthy, and unmarried, and as I am young and unmarried, I'm trying to get in." Hidden from Navy brass was the fact that Jack had begun sleeping on a table instead of a bed to ease the severe pain in his back.

On October 1, 1942, Lieutenant (jg.) John F. Kennedy began his PT-boat training. When the course was completed two months later, Jack's plans hit a snag. Instead of being assigned to a combat unit, he was ordered to stay on at the school as an instructor. It was in a very unhappy state of mind that Jack went to Palm Beach in early winter. Joe Jr. was also there on leave, and the two shared their dismay over assignments which had kept them from seeing action. Joe Jr. however, had more to be upset about than his routine duty in the Caribbean. On Jack's uniform were the two gold braids of a lieutenant junior grade, while his own sleeve had only the single stripe of an ensign.

When their leaves were up, the two brothers said good-bye for what would prove to be the last time. Jack left Florida in mid-December to return to Rhode Island. But he was miserable in the new assignment and appealed to his father. Without being asked, Joe had often used his influence to get Jack out of a scrape. Ironically, he would now, at Jack's request, intervene to send his son into danger. The undersecretary of the Navy was a personal friend, and the arrangements were quickly made: on March 6, 1943, Jack shipped out to the South Pacific. He had gotten what he wanted. Freed from the tedium of training school, he was on his way into combat, finally scoring a victory over his big brother. It was the first time, Rose later said, "Jack had won such an 'advantage' by such a clear margin. I daresay it cheered Jack and must have rankled Joe Jr."

Within six months, tales of his brother's heroism would almost break Joe Jr.'s heart.

5

KENNEDYS
DON'T CRY

Once he got to the South Pacific, it didn't take Lieutenant Kennedy long to see the action he wanted. After an eighteen-day sea voyage from San Francisco, Jack landed in the New Hebrides Islands, fifteen hundred miles east of Australia. There on April 4, 1943, he boarded an LST, a durable Navy vessel capable of carrying both troops and cargo. Jack was bound for Tulagi, near Guadalcanal in the Solomon Islands, where he had been assigned to a PT-boat squadron.

The Solomons, a chain of several hundred large and small islands, were roughly split into two groups. One cluster lay to the north and one to the south of a body of water which American Marines had dubbed "the Slot." The Japanese used the Slot as a shipping channel. Their nocturnal forays, called "the Tokyo Express" by U.S. troops, ferried men and supplies to those of the Solomon Islands which Japan controlled. At the time of Jack's posting to Tulagi, some of the Solomons were in Japanese hands, a few were held by the Americans, while the majority were inhabited, if at all, only by natives.

The previous February, U.S. forces had finally captured Guadalcanal and Tulagi, in a battle that raged for almost six months. The Japanese had been constructing an airfield on Guadalcanal, which would have brought them within striking range of American-held Pacific islands farther to the south and east. If Japan had conquered these islands, planes based there, combined with battleships anchored at Tulagi, could have devastated shipping between the United

States and Australia. Without U.S. supplies and troops, Australia could not have held out against a Japanese offensive, and the main line of defense would have moved back to the North American continent. Thus, the victory, however costly, had been vital to the Allied cause.

On April 7, almost two hundred Japanese planes set out on the greatest air raid since Pearl Harbor in an effort to recapture Guadalcanal and Tulagi. Just off the northern coast of Guadalcanal, the ship in which Jack Kennedy was a passenger received the message "Condition Red": an air attack was imminent. The LST began circling. It was carrying a cargo of bombs and, if hit, would explode. A destroyer nearby received a direct hit and was sunk, but the LST managed to avoid the bombs that were landing all around it. A Japanese plane was downed near Jack's ship, and those aboard could see its pilot trying to swim away. A member of the crew threw him a rope, but the pilot pulled out a revolver and began to shoot. The LST responded with machine gun fire and the Japanese pilot sank from sight.

When Jack and his fellow passengers finally disembarked safely at Tulagi, they were greeted by a message on a large billboard near the harbor, placed there at the instigation of the area's chief of command, Admiral William F. "Bull" Halsey:

KILL JAPS. KILL JAPS. KILL MORE JAPS.

After only a week in the South Pacific, Jack was already aware that was what the war was all about.

By the end of April 1943, Lieutenant Kennedy had taken command of his own ship: PT 109. The unsuccessful Japanese bombing raid had been followed by a break in the fighting, and Jack took advantage of the lull in order to make his craft seaworthy. The boat, eighty feet long and, like all PTs, made of plywood, was dirty and in need of paint after months of service off Guadalcanal. Moored next to the heavy jungle typical of the Solomons, it had also become infested with cockroaches and rats. Jack Kennedy had come a long way from his trim sailboat in the waters of Cape Cod.

He was, for the first time, truly on his own—on the other side of the earth from his father and his older brother. He was not very pleased to learn that Joe Jr. was trying to get assigned to the South Pacific. In mid-May, with the world-weariness of one who had survived a bombing attack, Jack wrote his parents regarding Joe Jr.: "If I were he I would take as much time about it as I could . . . he will want to be back the day after he arrives, if he runs true to the form of everyone else." But the news that his seventeen-year-old brother intended to join the service was something else again. "As regards Bobby," Jack went on, "he ought to do what he wants. You can't estimate risks, some cooks are in more danger out here than a lot of flyers." The letter ended with a note dear to Rose's heart: "P.S. Mother: Got to church Easter."

When Bobby was sworn into the Navy, Jack wrote him:

The folks sent me a clipping of you taking the oath. The sight of you up there, just a boy, was really moving, particularly as a close examination showed that you had my checked London coat on. I'd like to know what the hell I'm doing out here while you go stroking around in my drape coat, but I suppose that what we are out here for, or so they tell us, is so that our sisters and younger brothers will be safe and secure—frankly I don't see it quite that way—at least if you're going to be safe and secure, that's fine with me, but not in my coat, brother, not in my coat.

While counseling Kennedy men on the home front, Jack was assembling a crew in the Solomons. The original crew had been transferred to another boat while PT 109 was in drydock, and Jack set about training his eleven recruits. By June 1943, PT 109 was shipshape and her crew had been drilled at sea in test firings and night patrols. Now, just in time, both the boat and the men were ready for action. The lull was over. The first major Allied offensive in the South Pacific began on June 30.

The Allied plan called for a simultaneous attack on New Guinea by General MacArthur and in the Solomons by Admiral Halsey. PT 109 was ordered into combat in mid-July, and moved eastward to the tiny island of Lumbari, just off the coast of the much larger island of Rendova. Over the next two weeks, the boat went out on seven night patrols. Japanese shipping was attempting to get through the Slot, and the mission of the PTs in the area was to intercept it. But they met with little success. The enemy had come up with a PT counterweapon—planes that dropped flares over the waters of the Slot. Illumination from the flares allowed the Japanese planes to bomb the PTs while warning Japanese ships that American vessels were in the area. In response to his mother's assurances that he was being remembered in the prayers of many, Jack replied, "I hope it won't be taken as a sign of lack of confidence in you all or the Church if I continue to duck." He even sent a letter to Inga. "If anything happens to me I have this knowledge that if I live to be 100 I could only improve the quantity of my life, not the quality," Jack wrote. "This sounds gloomy as hell but you're the only person I'd say it to anyway. As a matter of fact, knowing you has been the brightest part of an extremely bright 26 years."

PT 109 had already, on three occasions, been attacked by Japanese planes. In one attack, two of the crew were wounded by shrapnel—fragments of safety razors, faucets, car door handles, and other odds and ends of scrap which Japan had imported from America in the years before the war. The other crew members were unharmed, and the boat itself had been only slightly damaged. Then, on August 1, came word that a major Tokyo Express was expected that night. The message had no sooner arrived than eighteen Japanese dive bombers attacked the harbor between Rendova and Lumbari. Two PTs were destroyed. PT 109, which had been in the harbor refueling, returned fire at the planes.

The air raid was a sign that the Express was in the area, and fifteen PTs were sent out to meet it. Among the group was 109, with its crew of twelve, and an extra man, Barney Ross, who had come along for the ride. Ross had been assigned to another PT squadron, which had, on the night of July 20, been involved in a humiliating mix-up. American planes had gone out to search for the Express. They found instead PT boats, which they mistook for Japanese ships. The planes had bombed the boats, the boats had fired back at the planes. Three men had died, eleven had been wounded, and the squadron was temporarily out of action.

Now, reluctant to miss what promised to be a certain appearance of the Express, Ross asked if he could tag along on Jack's boat. The trip provided a lot more excitement than either man had bargained for. Four Japanese ships went through the Slot that night. None of them was destroyed. One suffered only slight damage—the one that rammed and sank PT 109.

A naval historian later described the next few hours as the most confused and least effective action in which the PTs ever took part. The Tokyo Express made its way through the Slot, unloaded its cargo of men and supplies at the Japanese base on Kolombangara, and made its way out again—unharmed by the fifteen PTs that were massed to stop it. The night had been one of complete chaos for the Americans. Since the Japanese destroyers were probing the darkness with searchlights and shooting at the U.S. vessels, some PTs took evasive action. Some seem simply to have gotten lost. Of the sixty torpedoes which the PTs carried into battle, only thirty-two were fired and, of these, not a single one hit a target. Several of the PTs, including 109, didn't fire any torpedoes at all.

Then, just after 2 A.M., as the Express was steaming out of the Slot, came the first and only contact of the battle. Lookouts on board 109 saw the wake of a ship and assumed it was from another PT boat. Suddenly, a huge shape, unquestionably that of a Japanese destroyer, loomed out of the darkness. Jack spun the wheel of his boat, but it was too late. The destroyer crashed into 109, almost splitting it in half. Its gasoline tanks were ruptured in the collision, and fire broke out. Fearing the tanks would explode, Jack ordered the crew overboard. But after a few minutes he realized the fires were burning gasoline on the surface of the water, and called out for everyone to climb back on the wreckage.

The most severely injured was Pappy McMahon, at thirty-seven the oldest member of the crew. McMahon had been in the engine room at the time of impact and was badly burned. Kennedy towed the older man to the boat, then went back in the water to check on the others. Bucky Harris, a gunner's mate from Massachusetts, had suffered a painful knee injury and was encumbered by a jacket and sweater. He attempted to swim to the hulk but finally gave up and began to drift. As Jack splashed toward him, Harris said he could go no further. "For a guy from Boston, you're certainly putting up a great exhibition out here," Kennedy snapped. He helped Harris out of the heavy clothes and they swam together back to the boat.

Two crew members were missing and never seen again. Throughout the night, the eleven survivors clung to the wreckage, waiting to be rescued. By sunup on the morning of August 2, help had not arrived, and the crew was terrified. They were two miles east of Kolombangara, where ten thousand Japanese soldiers were based. Four miles in the opposite direction lay the island of Gizo, site of another enemy garrison. And the wreckage was drifting southward, closer to several small islands which might also be occupied by the Japanese. Then, by midday, the situation got even worse. What little remained of PT 109 appeared to be sinking. They had no choice but to swim to one of the islands southeast of Gizo.

Selecting the most remote, they began to make their way toward it. Jack, clenching the strap of McMahon's life preserver between his teeth, towed the older man. The trip took almost five hours—in water infested by sharks, past islands bristling with Japanese. About 6 P.M., vomiting and exhausted, they crawled ashore on Plum

Pudding Island. Within two hours, Jack swam out again, hoping to encounter a PT boat on night patrol. But he was caught in a current and drifted, half-conscious, through the night. At dawn on August 3, he washed up on a sandspit and passed out. By noon he had awakened and managed to make his way back to Plum Pudding.

Jack found his crew to be in little better shape than he was. There was no fresh water. The only source of food was coconuts, but these were unripened and provided little moisture. Those who had been injured were suffering terribly from the lack of medicine or bandages. By the next day it had become imperative to move on to the nearby island of Olasana. It was now August 4, and they had had no water and nothing to eat but green coconuts since the first of August. Olasana was slightly nearer Japanese-held Gizo, but it was larger than Plum Pudding and might have fresh water.

This time the expedition took three hours, with Jack again towing McMahon. But the effort was for nothing. There was no water in the section in which they came ashore. The men stayed within a tiny area of heavy foliage, reluctant to explore the rest of the island for fear of encountering the Japanese. That night it rained, and the crew lay on their backs trying to catch raindrops in their open mouths. A few even licked at the foliage, but it was covered with bird droppings and they quickly gave up on the leaves as a source of liquid.

The next day, the fourth since PT 109 had been hit, Jack and Barney Ross set out to explore a larger island, Nauru. It was a half-mile still closer to Gizo, but the situation had become desperate. With no food, water, or medicine, able to sleep neither during the day because of the oppressive heat nor at night because of the terrifying sounds of the jungle, the men were growing weak and despondent. In spite of their physical condition, the short swim to Nauru seemed effortless compared to the previous ordeals. Jack and Barney crawled up on shore and looked around. There, in the distance, they could see Rendova, thirty-eight miles away. Still, Nauru offered more than the tantalizing glimpse of an American-held island. They came across a small canoe and a tin of fresh water, and a Japanese crate filled with crackers and candy. Jack tore a slat from the crate to use as a paddle, and loaded his precious cargo of food and water into the one-man canoe. Leaving Barney behind to swim back the next day, he set off late that night for Olasana. There he was amazed to find his men gathered around a fire, speaking pidgin English to two natives.

The pair was part of a network of spies established by an Australian, Arthur Evans. Evans was a "coast watcher" for the Allies: one of a few dozen spread out over the three thousand islands of the South Pacific. He lived in secret on Kolombangara, and from his hideout on the Japanese-held island, transmitted information to Rendova regarding enemy air and sea traffic. He had also radioed news of his sighting of the burning hulk of PT 109, and been asked to be on the lookout for survivors. When Jack learned that this was the natives' mission, he carved a message into the shell of a coconut:

NATIVE KNOWS POSIT
HE CAN PILOT
11 ALIVE
NEED SMALL BOAT
KENNEDY

On the morning of August 7, the two men, carrying the coconut shell, set off for Rendova in their canoe. By the next evening, a PT boat had picked up the survivors of 109. One of the boat's crew members immediately offered Kennedy some food. "No thanks," Jack replied, "I've just had a coconut."

As soon as naval officials learned that the eleven men, including Jack, were alive, they realized the story's potential. The survival and rescue of Joe Kennedy's son would make very good reading in newspapers back home. When the PT boat pulled out from Rendova on its rescue mission, two newspaper reporters were on board. Typical of the coverage of the event, which made the front pages of all the Boston papers and of the *New York Times*, was one story that began: "The luck of the Irish and some first class skill brought lanky Lt. JG John F. Kennedy, son of former ambassador Joseph Kennedy, and 10 of his torpedo boat mates back from a brush with the Japanese and death. . . ."

The story did indeed enhance the reputation of the U.S. Navy. It was also the beginning of the making of an American president.

On September 6, 1943, while Jack was still in the South Pacific, Hyannis Port was the scene of a fifty-fifth birthday celebration for Joe Kennedy. Friends and many of the family were present, including Joe Jr., who was at last en route to duty overseas. The group gathered around for the toast: "To Ambassador Joe Kennedy, father of the hero, our own hero Lieutenant John F. Kennedy, of the

United States Navy." The champagne in Joe Jr.'s glass must suddenly have seemed to go flat. That night a friend who was sharing a room with the eldest Kennedy son heard Joe Jr. crying. Suddenly, the young man sat up in bed, clenched his fists, and said, "By God, I'll show them."

By October he was in England, flying antisubmarine missions over the Channel. It was not a glamorous assignment. The patrols, which lasted as long as fourteen hours, were unpleasant and dangerous. The planes often took off and landed in rain and fog. While on patrol, they had to fly at a low altitude over water, and many of the bombers went down in fatal crashes. Still, for months, Joe Jr. never saw an enemy submarine, never dropped a bomb or fired a shot, never had an opportunity to "show them."

Kick was also in England, working for the American Red Cross and involved in a romance that was causing consternation on both sides of the Atlantic. Billy Hartington was the eldest son of the duke of Devonshire, whose family had belonged to England's ruling class for centuries. He would one day inherit his father's title, almost two hundred thousand acres, and eight great estates. He was considered a possible match for Princess Elizabeth. He was, of course, Protestant. Kathleen Kennedy was a member of one of the richest families in America. She was young, bright, pretty, and highspirited. Kick had become the toast of London while her father was ambassador. But she was also descended from Irish peasants. And she was, of course, Catholic.

The duke and duchess of Devonshire, like most of England's ruling class, disliked Catholics and felt superior to the Irish. The antagonism was mutual. After centuries of domination, the people of Ireland detested the English. In 1882, four Irish patriots had assassinated Lord Frederick Cavendish, Billy's great uncle. Marriage between Billy Hartington and Kick Kennedy was clearly out of the question—or so both their families believed. The duke, with aristocratic reserve, said all he thought need be said on the subject: "You can't expect an American girl to know how to run British estates."

Rose Kennedy was less restrained. The fact that her daughter had captured one of England's leading nobility paled beside what Rose called the heartbreaking and horrifying possibility that Kick might wed outside the Church. All through the winter, in a series of letters and telegrams, Rose begged her daughter not to enter into a marriage that would jeopardize her standing as a Catholic. Eunice and Bobby, as deeply religious as their mother, sent their share of correspondence as well. But her father and eldest brother were on Kick's side. Joe told his daughter she should "let all the rest of us go jump in the lake," although he added that if Rose learned about his advice to Kick, "I'd be thrown right out in the street." Joe Jr. was no less devout than Rose, and his squadron mates had been astounded to see him kneel by his bed every night to say his prayers aloud. Nevertheless, young Joe responded to the flurry of appeals from Palm Beach by pleading with the family to be more understanding. "I do know how you feel, Mother," he wrote, "but I do think it will be alright." Jack refused to be drawn into the fight. "In regard to Kick becoming a Duchess," he wryly commented in a letter to Lem Billings, ". . . it would be rather nice—as I believe it would give me some title or other."

By the end of April, when it became apparent she had lost the battle, Rose checked into a hospital for two weeks. The official explanation was that Rose was there for a routine physical, but the hospital room also formed an effective barricade against the unwelcome questions of reporters. On May 6, 1944, Rose received the news she had been dreading: Kick and Billy were married. Although the duke and duchess were present, trying hard to smile at the cameras, Joe Jr. was the only member of the Kennedy family to attend the ceremony. Her father, secretly pleased by Kick's spunk, sent a cable: WITH YOUR FAITH IN GOD YOU CAN'T MAKE A MISTAKE. REMEMBER YOU ARE STILL AND ALWAYS WILL BE TOPS WITH ME. From her mother, Kick received no message at all. Rose's only acknowledgment of the wedding was to request that her closest friends ask nuns to pray "everything would turn out all right."

By the time of Kick's wedding, Jack had returned from the South Pacific and had been assigned to a PT unit in Miami, Florida. Jack found the duty there boring. "Once you've got your feet upon the desk in the morning," he wrote a friend, "the heavy work of the day is done." But by the end of May, Jack was unable to do even that. Three weeks after Rose checked out of one Boston hospital, Jack checked into another. He had returned from the Solomons weighing only 125 pounds, weakened by malaria and nagging back problems. Since his back was growing steadily worse, doctors decided Jack must have an operation. Surgery was performed, but it failed to correct his disk condition and Jack was left in a great deal of pain. "In regard to the fascinating subject of my operation," he wrote a friend, "I should naturally like to go on for several pages . . . but will confine myself to saying that I think the doc should have read just one more book before picking up the saw."

His hospital ordeal was brightened on June 12, 1944, when Jack was presented with the Navy and Marine medal for "extremely heroic conduct as Commanding Officer of Motor Torpedo Boat 109 following the collision and sinking of that vessel in the Pacific war area on August 1–2, 1943." The commendation came as something of a relief. Jack had been concerned about how the Navy would react to the loss of his ship, aware that there had been a great deal of quiet criticism regarding his seamanship in allowing PT 109 to be rammed. There was even a rumor that MacArthur himself had said young Kennedy should be court-martialed. But the Navy had finally chosen to turn an official blind eye to events leading up to the collision and to concentrate instead on Jack's actions afterward. It would go along with what the press had already decided: Jack Kennedy was a hero.

During the same week in which Jack received his medal, a long, laudatory piece chronicling the saga of PT 109 appeared in *The New Yorker*. Jack was very pleased with the article and remarked, "Even I was wondering how it would all end." Joe, however, was not satisfied that the story of his son's heroics had appeared in a magazine of limited circulation. Once more bringing all his influence to bear, Joe arranged to have the article reprinted in *Reader's Digest*.

By August, when on an out-patient basis he was able to visit Hyannis Port, Jack was a celebrity. It was a happy occasion. Almost all the children were home, and the Kennedys thought the war would soon be over. In the Pacific, Allied forces were inexorably island-hopping toward Japan. Three years earlier, Hitler had doomed Germany's chances of victory by invading Russia. War on the Eastern front had finally enabled the Allies to land on the beaches of France early in the summer of 1944.

Joe Jr. had volunteered for a second tour of duty and had flown during the D-Day invasion of Normandy on June sixth. But his months in England had been filled with frustration. His own brother was not only a best-selling author, but now, it seemed, also the pride of the Navy—doing brave deeds, winning medals, being written about in newspapers and magazines. Joe Jr., on the other hand, had done nothing to distinguish himself, in spite of his desperate attempts. On one mission he had even disobeyed orders, flying so close to a German fortification that his plane was riddled with bullets and the crew had complained of his recklessness. But all his efforts at heroism had come to nothing. By July, his extended tour had ended; frustrated and disappointed, he was packed to go home.

Then a call went out from the Navy: experienced pilots were needed for an extremely hazardous top-secret project. It was Joe Jr.'s chance for glory, and he volunteered to fly one final mission.

Shortly after D-Day, Germany began its last effort to conquer England, devastating London with V-1 rockets. Intelligence sources had located their launch sites in France, and for months the Allies had tried to destroy the concrete bunkers through bombing raids, losing in the process 154 planes and almost 800 men. Yet despite the repeated raids, several sites were thought to still be operational. Finally, in desperation, Allied strategists came up with a plan: a radio-controlled pilotless bomber, filled with twelve tons of explosives, would be sent to crash on the launch sites. Because its electronic equipment was incapable of controlling a takeoff, a pilot and copilot would be aboard to get the heavy plane into the air and on course. Then they would bail out and an escort of "mother planes" would assume control of the bomber's guidance system to see it to its objective.

It was a foolish scheme, and a futile one; after the war it would be revealed that the bunkers had been abandoned early in the summer. But it was with high hopes for an Allied coup that the mission got under way on the evening of August 12. In one of the two escort planes was the president's son, Elliott Roosevelt, a photo-reconnaissance officer. Behind the controls of the bomber, code-named Zootsuit Black, was Joe Kennedy, Jr., who had been warned by an electronics officer that the explosives' arming mechanism might malfunction.

Just before takeoff, a friend teasingly asked young Kennedy if his insurance was paid up. Joe Jr. grinned and replied, "Nobody in my family needs insurance."

It was Sunday afternoon, August 13, 1944, in Hyannis Port. Two Navy priests came to the Kennedy home with the news: twenty-eight minutes into the mission, moments before its pilot and copilot were to bail out, Zootsuit Black had exploded. Elliott Roosevelt and others in the mother planes had been momentarily blinded by what was the largest nonatomic explosion of World War II. Then the bomber was gone.

Joe went to his room and locked the door. His eldest son was dead. So, too, was a part of Joe Kennedy.

The news of her brother's death brought Kick back to America, to be with her family, to reconcile with her mother. What she had known would be a depressing visit did not go well from the beginning. Jack, whom Kick had not seen in two years, met her at the Boston Airport. His skin was yellow from malaria; the back operation had left him in obvious pain and frighteningly thin. Shaken by Jack's appearance, Kick was dismayed by the reception she was given in Hyannis Port. In spite of their mutual grief, Rose had not forgiven her daughter for the controversial marriage, and her attitude toward Kick was aloof.

Kick's arrival was soon followed by a final letter from Joe Jr. He had written about the secret mission, explaining he was sure that when his parents knew the details, they would understand why he had volunteered. "Don't get worried about it," young Joe wrote, "as there is practically no danger." Years later Rose would recall that her husband "threw the letter on the table, and collapsed in his chair with his head in his hands, saying over and over again that the best part of his life was finished."

Still, the family was anxious to make things seem as they had been in the prewar summers at the Cape, and Jack invited some PT-boat friends as houseguests for Labor Day. But coming only three weeks after Joe Jr.'s death, there was no hope the party could re-create that once-carefree atmosphere, and the strain of the attempt soon became obvious.

The Kennedys traditionally served only one cocktail before meals—barely enough to wet the whistles of Jack's hard-drinking Navy buddies. After their parents had gone to bed, Jack and Kick decided to raid the kitchen for more scotch. Bobby was there, too, home on leave from the Navy. Nineteen years old and in uniform, he was still, where his father was concerned, an obedient little boy, terrified of Joe's reaction if he found out drinking had continued after dinner. Kick thought Bobby was ridiculous and, sneering at her younger brother to "get lost," took the scotch and joined the rest of the group on the lawn. Bobby, however, had read the situation very well.

Barney Ross was telling jokes and everyone was laughing and clapping when suddenly an upstairs window flew open. "Jack," his father's voice bellowed out, "don't you and your friends have any respect for your dead brother?" The next morning Barney approached Joe to apologize, but the older man turned away. The weekend was ruined.

For the Kennedys, the disagreeable conclusion of the holiday soon seemed unimportant. Less than two weeks later came news of still another death. While serving with his regiment in Belgium, Billy Hartington had been shot through the heart by a German sniper. Kick, who had spent only five weeks with her young husband, now prepared to return to England as a widow. For the next few days the whole family, even Rose, rallied around, trying to act as if their charmed circle had not again been shattered by tragedy. A friend, bewildered by the charade, wondered how Kick could possibly keep up the pretense. But that was the way they had all been raised: "Kennedys don't cry."

PART TWO

JACK

6

THE NEW
GENERATION OFFERS
A LEADER

Christmas 1944 was the Kennedys' first since Joe Jr.'s death. Rose had invited one of Jack's Navy friends, Paul "Red" Fay, then stationed in Florida, to spend the holiday with the family in Palm Beach. With little available cash, Red had arrived with a few dollars' worth of gifts for the entire family. Jack, whose surgery had left him unable to return to active duty, had filled his time planning his own Christmas gift for the family: a volume of tributes to Joe Jr. But, typically unable to stick to a schedule, he didn't have the book ready for the holiday, and there were no packages under the tree from Jack. After the gifts had been opened, Rose took her son aside. "Red Fay isn't even a member of the family, but he was thoughtful enough to give all those nice presents," Rose said of the trinkets Red had purchased at a local drug store. "It's your own family and you don't have the thoughtfulness to remember any of us at Christmas." Jack started to explain, but decided instead to keep the book a secret until it was completed. "You come down here with ten dollars' worth of drugstore supplies," he later told Red, "and you're the star of the day. What am I, an inconsiderate, selfish adult who doesn't love his family? Thanks, pal."

Jack's Christmas gift was finally completed in 1945. The book, called *As We Remember Joe*, was a privately printed collection of twenty essays written by friends and relatives, with an introduction by Jack. "It is the realization that the future held the promise of great accomplishments for Joe that has made his death so particularly hard for those who knew him," Jack wrote of his older brother. "His worldly success was so assured and inevitable," the introduction went on, "that his death seems to have cut into the natural order of things."

Just how hard his son's death had hit Joe Kennedy was obvious by his reaction to the book. In spite of Jack's loving care in compiling the volume, Arthur Krock later said that Joe opened the cover, closed the cover, and was never able to read a line in between. Still, the "natural order of things" about which Jack had written was very much on Joe's mind—as his son was well aware. "I can feel Pappy's eyes on the back of my neck," Jack told Red Fay.

In March 1945, Jack was discharged from the Navy "by reason of physical disability." After attempting to rebuild his health at an Arizona resort, Jack went to the Mayo Clinic for a checkup. While he was there, a telegram arrived from the executive editor of the *Chicago Herald-American*, asking one of the staff doctors to have Jack call. VISITED WITH HIS FATHER, the telegram read, AND ANXIOUS TO FIND OUT IF YOUNG JACK WILL COVER AN ASSIGNMENT. Joe had known William Randolph Hearst since his early days in Wall Street, and it was soon announced that Jack Kennedy, best-selling author and war hero, would become a special correspondent for two Hearst newspapers, the *Herald-American* and the *New York Journal-American*. His first assignment would be to cover, from a serviceman's viewpoint, the San Francisco conference on the founding of the United Nations.

With his introspective nature, Jack seemed well suited to be a writer. His closest friends had always commented on Jack's ability to remain detached in any situation, to look at events as if he had "an inner eye." That capability, along with his education and connections, would have made Jack an asset to any publishing enterprise. But Jack's undergraduate ambitions to enter journalism had died with Joe Jr. The position with Hearst was simply a way to keep his name before the public, which it did to an unusual degree. Instead of the normal byline given other reporters, Jack's articles were accompanied by his photograph and a brief biographical sketch. The purpose of the publicity was not to bolster the image of a fledgling Hearst journalist; the next Massachusetts congressional primary was only a year away.

From San Francisco, Jack filed pessimistic reports on the future of the United Nations. Along with British and American delegates, he was disheartened by the tough, unrelenting attitude of the Russians at the conference. Although the Soviets wanted peace, they believed their security could be achieved only through a massive military buildup. "There is a heritage of twenty-five years of distrust between Russia and the rest of the world," Jack reported, "that cannot be overcome completely for a good many more years." But in his personal journal, Jack's disillusionment was even greater. "Mustn't expect too much," he wrote. "There is no cure at all."

During the three-month UN conference there were major changes in the countries which had long directed the destinies of most of the world. Franklin Roosevelt died on April 12, 1945; Adolf Hitler committed suicide on April 30; Germany surrendered on May 8. Then in June, as the conference was winding down, Jack was off on a new assignment: to cover the parliamentary elections in England. He was one of the few journalists to consider the possibility that the British would vote their wartime leader out of office, a view that was confirmed by the defeat of Winston Churchill's Conservative Party at the polls in July.

With his assignment in England finished, Jack returned home to retire from his brief career in journalism. The war was over in Europe, and within days, would end in Asia as well. It was time to move on. Jack told Red Fay, who was going to work for his family's construction company in San Francisco as soon as he got out of the service, "When the war is over and you are out there in sunny California giving them a good solid five and a half inches for a six-inch pavement, I'll be back here with Dad trying to parlay a lost PT boat and a bad back into a political advantage. I tell you, Dad is ready right now and can't understand why Johnny boy isn't all engines ahead full. . . ."

Jack, of course, couldn't long hold out against his father's wishes, and at the time ruefully admitted Joe Kennedy's role in determining his future. "It was like being drafted," Jack told a reporter. "My father wanted his eldest son in politics. 'Wanted' isn't the right word. He *demanded* it. You know my father. . . ." Joe, too, was at first forthright in describing his role. "I got Jack into politics," he said, in an interview in *McCall's* magazine. "I was the one. I told him Joe Jr. was dead and that it was therefore his responsibility to run for Congress. He didn't want to. He felt he didn't have the ability and he still feels that way. But I told him he had to . . ."

The story became a legend in Massachusetts. Boston politicians delighted in telling how shortly after Joe Jr.'s death, his father had summoned Jack and announced that he must carry on the Kennedy/

Fitzgerald tradition of public service. With Joe's promise that the whole family would unite to help him, the young man reluctantly agreed to enter politics. Later, when Jack's sights turned toward the highest office in the land, both father and son tried to dismiss the scenario. It made Jack seem passive, without character or goals, his life controlled by an ambitious, domineering father. But by then it was too late to deny the legend. Statements made by both Joe and Jack, early in Jack's political career, confirmed that the story was accurate.

"I guess Dad has decided that he's going to be the ventriloquist," Jack wryly commented to Lem Billings, "so I guess that leaves me the role of dummy." During an interview with the author of a book about the Kennedy family, the patriarch made it clear that his son had run for office as little more than a stand-in. "Jack went into politics because young Joe died. Young Joe was going to be the politician in the family. When he died, Jack took his place." The son agreed with the father's dynastic view. "My brother Joe was the logical one in the family to be in politics," Jack explained in a magazine article. "If he had lived, I'd have kept on being a writer." Jack went on to say that if he died, Bobby would take over; if anything happened to Bobby, young Teddy would step in.

In 1946, it was Jack's turn.

It had been twenty years since Joe had packed his family into their private railroad car and left behind the "narrow-minded bigoted sons of bitches" who had accepted his wealth but not his religion. Yet Boston newspapers had continued to follow Joe's career as if he were one of their own. The wartime exploits of Joe Jr. and Jack had been reported as the heroic actions of two local boys, Kathleen's marriage as the social achievement of a hometown girl. After an absence of two decades, the Kennedys were still regarded as Boston's leading Irish-American family. Now that Jack was to enter politics, there was no question but that he would do so in a city he had left at the age of nine—a city, in which, just at the right time, a seat in the United States House of Representatives might become vacant. It was in the Eleventh Congressional District, the poorest in the state, an area heavily populated by Catholic voters. At the turn of the century, the district had elected a twenty-eight-year-old to represent it in Washington. The young man's name was John Fitzgerald: Honey Fitz.

The current congressman from the Eleventh was James Michael Curley, a Fitzgerald political rival of long standing. It was Curley who had won the mayoralty from Honey Fitz in 1914, when the incumbent chose not to stand for reelection. The Fitzgerald candidacy was quickly withdrawn after Curley threatened to reveal the mayor's relationship with Toodles Ryan by announcing the title of a proposed campaign speech: "Great Lovers in History from Cleopatra to Toodles." Having committed the one unpardonable sin in Boston politics—the threat to expose an opponent's private life—Curley had become political enemy number one to Fitzgerald and his family.

Now after several years in the House, Curley, although under federal indictment for mail fraud in connection with wartime defense contracts, had decided to return to Boston and run again for mayor. If he won the primary, the office in the heavily Democratic city was sure to be his, and he would have to resign his seat in Congress. The Kennedys and the Fitzgeralds found themselves in the uncomfortable position of hoping their detested rival would be victorious. In November 1945, when Curley took the primary with forty-five percent of the vote, the Eleventh District was up for grabs.

By the following April, ten candidates had announced for the Democratic primary to be held in June 1946. One of these was John Fitzgerald Kennedy. When he learned of Jack's candidacy, Curley commented, "How can he lose? He's got a double-barreled name. . . . He doesn't even need to campaign. He can go to Washington now and forget the primary and election." But Jack would need much more than his famous name to win this race.

One year after World War II had ended, the Irish concept of business-as-usual in Boston politics could suddenly no longer be taken for granted. Germany and Japan had been defeated, but there now loomed the chilling threat of the Soviet Union. Yet despite Russian hostility, the new president, Harry Truman, had demobilized 15 million servicemen and -women. Housing was at a premium, and many young vets were forced to live with their parents or in-laws. There was a scarcity of meat, tires, and other commodities which postwar Americans regarded as basic necessities. After years of sacrificing both raises and overtime pay, first during the Depression, then for the war effort, American workers wanted their slice of the economic pie. When management did not respond, a series of strikes brought about still more shortages and slowed industry's conversion to peacetime production.

A cold war, inflation, a lack of consumer goods, long lines at stores, a flourishing black market, a housing shortage—veterans returning from overseas found stateside reality far short of their vision of the American way of life. In spite of Curley's victory only the year before, there was, in Boston as in the rest of the country, a new electorate, eager to participate in the future of the nation for which it had fought, impatient to achieve the unfulfilled promise the nation had given. The time had come for a different kind of leadership.

Jack Kennedy's ability to be among those who qualified for that role was uncertain. Except for his college years, he had not lived in Massachusetts since he was a little boy; indeed, before the war he had given exclusive Palm Beach as his official residence. He came from immense wealth, had attended select schools, spoke with an upper-class accent. Jack's world of debutantes and nightclubs was as alien to the Eleventh Congressional District as its factories and slums were to him. Joe Kennedy himself wasn't confident Jack could win the primary. If Joe Jr. were the candidate, there would be no cause for concern. He had been, his father said, "altogether different from Jack, more dynamic, more sociable and easygoing." Joe Jr. could have gone into the tenements without showing distaste, could have talked and laughed with the hardworking longshoremen and truck drivers and waitresses, could have made them think he understood their lives of drudgery, could have made them believe he would change it all.

But Jack was another story. He was, Joe said, "withdrawn and quiet." Although Joe had gotten Jack into the race, neither he nor Rose could picture their son as a politician. Jack just didn't have the traditional backslapping, hand-shaking, baby-kissing qualities expected of those running for office—even, Joe was sure, by the unknown quantity of the post-war electorate.

Early in the campaign, Joe, expecting the worst, decided to go see for himself how his shy son, raised in wealth and privilege, went about soliciting votes in the tough Eleventh District. That day Jack was in East Boston, the area so well remembered from Joe's youth as the site of P.J. Kennedy's saloon. Now it had become an Italian ghetto, filled, Joe said, with "hard-boiled guys." From across the street, Joe watched his son approach a group of these men, who stared at the candidate without warmth or welcome. He saw Jack introduce himself, shake their hands, ask for their votes. Suddenly, to Joe's amazement, the men were smiling and chatting with the young candidate. "I never thought Jack had it in him," his father said. From that day on, Joe Kennedy felt much better about the campaign.

"THE NEW GENERATION OFFERS A LEADER." That was Jack's slogan and that was the veneer of his candidacy. But there were two Kennedy headquarters from which two very different campaigns were conducted. The more visible was in the Bellevue Hotel, which Jack used as both living quarters and as the base of operations for his youthful amateur volunteers—Lem Billings, Red Fay, and other college and Navy friends, all of whom had been personally screened by Joe Kennedy before being allowed to sign on. The real command post, however, was at the Ritz, where, behind the scenes, Joseph P. Kennedy was masterminding the show. There, Joe and the old hands he had recruited for the campaign made the professional decisions.

The first of these was that Jack would run as an Irish son of Boston, because the constituency of the Eleventh District was Catholic. Secondly, Jack would run as a war hero, because he had never done anything else—authorship of a best-selling book would cut little ice with the voters of the Eleventh. Joe Jr.'s heroism would also be stressed. He had posthumously been awarded the Navy Cross, a decoration higher in rank than the medal Jack had been given, so in death he had achieved one last victory over his younger brother. Now he would even be a part of Jack's campaign. Joe managed, through his pull in Washington, to get a destroyer named after his eldest son. The U.S.S. *Joseph P. Kennedy, Jr.* was christened by little sister Jean, with many of the family present, an event which received major coverage in all the local papers. Bobby, as a seaman, second class, was on its maiden voyage to Latin America. When it returned, Joe went on board for a well-publicized tour. Joe also managed to promote both elder sons through the establishment of the Joseph P. Kennedy, Jr., chapter of the Veterans of Foreign Wars, with Jack put in charge as its commander.

On no front would money be spared in bringing the Kennedy name before the public. Any expense was justified if it could turn Jack's slim qualifications to political advantage. "We're going to sell Jack like soap flakes," his father said. Joe's role went far beyond that of financier to the campaign. He also reserved for himself the right to select all its personnel, including someone to teach Jack the intricacies of Boston political warfare. Having long ago gone beyond the horizons of his hometown to the grander vistas of national and international affairs, Joe carefully studied the local scene for the man best qualified for the role of Jack's advisor.

But Jack, who a family friend said "didn't know ten people in Boston," had already gravitated to a familiar face: his eighty-three-year-old grandfather Fitzgerald. Although Honey Fitz had become a bit eccentric, as even Jack admitted, his grandson also imagined the legendary old man to be the epitome of wisdom regarding Massachusetts politics. Early in the campaign, the two attended meetings and rallies together, where Honey Fitz would usually make one of his traditional lengthy speeches—by now even more rambling than those which had once so annoyed P.J. Sometimes Jack would lean over and plaintively whisper, "Grampa, remember *I'm* the candidate." One day Honey Fitz took his grandson to City Hall, led all his old cronies in a chorus of "Sweet Adeline," and turned toward the door when he finished the song. On this occasion Jack was somewhat stern. "Gramp," he said, "notwithstanding the impression to the contrary, it is your grandson who is running for office, not the beloved former mayor. Do you think we could try and get that message over before we leave?"

Joe Kennedy was as little amused by Honey Fitz's shenanigans as his father had been before him. A politically astute old pro would have been one thing; a slightly senile elder statesman was quite another. Before things got out of hand, Kennedy enlisted his first cousin Joe Kane as a more appropriate choice to tutor Jack in the labyrinth of Boston politics. Most of Kane's adult life, it was said, had been spent drinking coffee in a cafeteria near City Hall. Now, at sixty-six, he was regarded as the shrewdest behind-the-scenes veteran of local Democratic warfare. Kane described himself as a "political engineer," and he soon began to shape young Kennedy's campaign. It was Kane who came up with Jack's slogan, Kane who put Jack in touch with the savviest young men throughout the neighborhoods of the Eleventh, and Kane who got rid of Honey Fitz.

In one of their first sessions together, he began by advising Jack in what he saw as the most basic of political fundamentals. "In politics," Kane was saying, "you have no friends, only coconspirators." At that moment, Honey Fitz, Jack's closest coconspirator to date, strolled into the room. Kane took one look at Boston's aging monument and yelled, "Get that son of a bitch out of here!" Jack couldn't believe his ears. *"Who? GRAMPA?"* Jack tried to protest, but Kane was adamant. "Either he goes, or I do." Honey Fitz went.

Among Kane's strategies was a plan for Jack, a stranger in the city from which he sought elective office, to meet almost everyone in the Congressional District. One of Jack's greatest assets was his appeal to women; it was regarded as a truism in the campaign that the older ones wanted to mother him, the young ones wanted to marry him. Since women made up more than half the registered voters, it was simply good politics for Jack to be seen by as many as possible. But to achieve maximum visibility within the Eleventh, he would need the right contacts in its three key areas: Cambridge, Charlestown, and a part of Boston that included the downtown North and West Ends, along with East Boston, across the harbor. Each of the three areas was low-income, each had its own local candidate, each looked to that candidate to improve its economy. Outside their own neighborhoods the individual candidates had little support, so that if Jack ran strongly enough to take second place in all three, his overall total might be enough to win the District itself.

The Boston/East Boston section, where Honey Fitz, Rose, and Joe had been born, was now more Italian than Irish, and considered a rough neighborhood. Charlestown was thought not to have a single Republican living within its boundaries. Still, it was the Democratic primary that was of concern, and this section had put up its own favorite son, John Cotter, who had served as Curley's administrative assistant. Although Charlestown was Irish, its population was strictly working class—the kind of electorate with which Jack had little in common except heritage. Cambridge, with thirty percent of the total vote, was by far the most important of the three. The candidate from this area, Mike Neville, would be Jack's strongest opponent, since Neville had both the greatest number of potential votes and the backing of almost all the local politicians. Jack had gone to school there, but the heart of the area lay outside the Harvard campus. This was East Cambridge, an Italian slum, a neighborhood totally unknown to Jack when he was in college, a neighborhood equally unaware of Jack Kennedy's existence as either student or candidate.

From these three sections, Joe Kane began to line up the support of Jack's contemporaries—those who had grown up on the lore of Boston politics, who had, in the years before Pearl Harbor, worked for one or another of the local politicians. These young men rallied to Jack, disregarding his unfamiliar background of Choate, Harvard, and Palm Beach, seeing beyond the facade of a spoiled rich kid trying to buy a congressional seat. They shared with him the greatest single experience of their generation: the war. But they were attracted by far more than the common bond of the past, for, in Jack Kennedy, they sensed the future.

One such vet was Dave Powers, a former Army Air Corps sergeant living in a cold-water flat with his widowed sister and her eight children. Through one of Joe Kane's connections, Powers had been suggested as a good contact in Charlestown, and on a bitter night in January 1946, Jack appeared alone at the door of the flat.

Dave was immediately taken with the thin young man, but he told Jack his support was promised to John Cotter. Jack persisted in asking Dave's advice: What would he do if he were running for Congress in the Eleventh? Jack was, Powers noticed, ill at ease and shy, but *aggressively* shy, and very appealing as he carefully took notes on all of Dave's suggestions. Then the young candidate said he had to give a speech in Charlestown and, knowing no one in the area, asked Dave if he would go along. Powers thought it was the least he could do, although he was amused to find, as he agreed to accompany Jack, that he felt sorry for the son of a millionaire.

The speech was to a group of Gold Star mothers, women who had lost sons in the war. Powers thought it was the worst speech he had ever heard and was relieved when Jack appeared to be ending it after only ten minutes. Then, awkwardly, but with some emotion, Jack said to the group. "I think I know how you feel because my mother is a Gold Star mother, too." All the women in the room stood up and flocked to the platform, surrounding Jack, shaking his hand, smiling, wishing him luck. Jack couldn't get away from them for more than half an hour. Powers had never seen anything like it. When they finally managed to leave, Jack asked how he had done. Dave told him he'd been terrific. Jack said, "Then do you think you'll be with me?" and Dave replied, "I'm already with you." Powers would remain with Jack for the rest of his life. Almost seventeen years later, he was riding in the car behind Jack's in a Dallas motorcade.

For all the enthusiasm of his college friends, his PT-boat chums, his young Boston vets, Jack had the support of yet another group even more committed to his candidacy: the Kennedys. As Joe had promised, the whole family had united behind Jack. Voters were surprised and flattered to open the doors of their tenement flats and find Pat or Jean smiling at them and distributing Kennedy brochures. Eunice worked in the main office in downtown Boston, where even fourteen-year-old Teddy ran errands and fetched coffee and sandwiches. Bobby, Lem Billings said, campaigned "as if his life and Jack's depended on it." Aged twenty and just out of the Navy, Bobby was assigned to one of the toughest areas, East Cambridge, where he endeared himself by eating endless plates of spaghetti and playing softball with the local kids. Rose, an old pro at campaigning, made charming little speeches in which she would tell the audience stories about the index cards she had kept on the children, and interesting anecdotes about life at the embassy. The chatty speeches, giving what audiences imagined to be a glimpse into Kennedy family life, were well calculated. Rose knew exactly what she was doing, and had, Dave Powers said in awe, a greater understanding of politics than anyone else in the organization.

Behind it all was Joe Kennedy's financial backing. The elder Kennedy was very much a subscriber to Joe Kane's motto: "It takes three things to win. The first is money and the second is money and the third is money." Joe thought that single ingredient in Kane's formula for success was too vital to be left to the whims of his son's amateurish volunteers. "Regardless of how many young guys were picked up by the Kennedys," one worker commented, "Joe always saw to it that every cent of campaign money was in the hands of old-timers." Although there was a lot more of it and a lot more of what it could buy, some of it was spent in the time-honored way of countless other Boston candidates—to ensure the support of key district politicians, who, it was said, went to bed with their hands outside the covers in case somebody was giving anything away while they were asleep.

The area was saturated with "New Generation" posters, leaflets, and billboards. Radios carried a steady stream of "Kennedy for Congress" commercials. Jack's war record gave his campaign an added bonus, and a hundred thousand reprints of the *Reader's Digest* article on the saga of PT 109 were mailed out within the District. There was even a story that after the wife of one of Jack's opponents read the article, she said she was going to vote for Kennedy. Supporters were asked to give house parties, at which local citizens could meet the candidate and his family—with dishes, silverware, refreshments, even flowers provided by Joe. He had spent enough in the campaign, Joe remarked, to elect his own chauffeur.

In June, Kennedy wealth and charisma were showcased in what was probably the most important event of the campaign, a formal reception and tea held in the ballroom of a Cambridge hotel. It was, Mike Neville's campaign manager said, "the clincher." Hand-addressed engraved invitations were sent to every registered Democrat in the area. Seasoned observers of the Boston political scene chortled at the notion of asking voters to dress up to meet a candidate. But over fifteen hundred guests, most of them women, many in rented finery, and all of them, Rose thought, looking as if they'd just had their hair done, showed up for the privilege of shaking the hand of a Kennedy. At the head of the reception line, wearing white tie and tails, stood Joe himself, making his first and last public appearance on Jack's behalf.

Observing her thin, sickly brother, whose skin had not lost its yellowish cast and who looked scarcely old enough to be out of high school, Eunice early in the campaign had asked, "Daddy, do you really think Jack can be a congressman?" Her father replied, "You must remember, it's not what you are that counts, but what people think you are." The reception seemed to indicate that people thought the Kennedys were Boston's version of a royal family.

The appealing idealism of the youthful volunteers, the pragmatic maneuvers of the old politicians, the lavish expenditure of his father's money, the unexpected elevation of the family to local aristocracy— all were vital ingredients in the campaign. Yet in the end, the candidate, driven by a real or imagined obligation to two Joe Kennedys, won it for himself.

It was Jack for whom the memory of Joe Jr. remained a persistent challenge. "I'm shadowboxing in a match the shadow is always going to win," he said to Lem Billings. Again and again Jack would tell his volunteers, "I'm just filling Joe's shoes. If he were alive, I'd never be in this." He compared himself constantly, knowing how effortlessly Joe Jr. could have met the people in the slums of Charlestown or the North End, how easily his brother could have withstood the physical rigors of the campaign. He resolved to try to "do the job Joe would have done." It was a job he really didn't want, but, he confided to a friend, "Sometimes we all have to do things we don't want to do." And what he had to do was win. Even more haunting than the shadow of his dead brother was the forceful living presence of his father. If there was one obsessive lesson Joe Kennedy had drilled into his children over and over again, it was that second place in anything, whether a sailboat race or a political race, was not acceptable.

It was Jack, driven by his father's passion for winning, who dragged his frail body, weighted down with a heavy back brace, up endless flights of stairs in endless tenements. Here he was admitted to slum flats, and here two different worlds confronted each other. One world had money, the other didn't, but both had good manners. Jack would be offered tea, the water drawn from the single tap of a cold-water flat, heated on a stove around which the occupants huddled. It was hard to know who was more taken aback by Jack's presence: the family, unable to conceal their pleasure that this handsome young man had come to their home to ask for their votes, or Jack himself, struggling to hide his dismay as he tried not to stare at the toilet which shared the room in which they sat sipping tea.

It was Jack who would return late at night to his own comfortable suite, recalling with guilt the poverty he had observed during the day, telling his advisers he now finally understood his "obligation as a rich man's son to help people who are having a hard time of it." Then, racked with exhaustion, he would soak in a hot bath to ease the pain in his back while nibbling at a bland meal to avoid aggravating his constantly upset stomach. Staff meetings were held as he bathed and ate, reviewing the schedule for the next grueling fourteen-hour day.

It was Jack who gave 450 speeches—shy, halting speeches in which he would often stumble over a word, then, as the member of one audience described it, "light up the room" with a self-deprecating grin. Rarely would he become angry with the taunts at his wealth or his carpetbagger status, but once when a heckler asked why he didn't run for office in Palm Beach, Jack replied, "Nobody asked me my address when the Japs sank my PT boat." More often it was his wit which saved a tense moment. At a rally with several rival candidates, the chairman pointedly introduced each of the others as having "come up the hard way." When Jack was finally called on to speak, he said, "I seem to be the only person here tonight who didn't come up the hard way. I hope you won't hold it against me." They didn't.

On the night of the primary, June 18, 1946, while Jack attended a Marx Brothers movie, the votes began to pour in. He had narrowly lost in Cambridge and Charlestown, but come in first in all the other areas. Joe Kane's strategy had paid off. With forty-two percent of the total vote, Jack was the Democratic nominee from the Eleventh District. At Kennedy campaign headquarters, Honey Fitz danced a jig and led the crowd in singing "Sweet Adeline." As its all-too-familiar chorus died away, a friend said, "Congratulations, John F. Someday—who knows?—young Jack may be Governor. . . ." Honey Fitz smiled. People might think he was in his dotage, but the old politician knew a winner when he saw one. "Governor?" he said. "Someday that young man will be president of the United States."

Despite his grandfather's confidence, the White House was a hazy vision in the distant future. Jack had yet to win the first stepping-stone, a seat on Capitol Hill. But victory in the general election seemed a foregone conclusion in Democratic Boston, and the next phase of the campaign proceeded at a more leisurely pace than the hurly-burly of the primary. Jack's platform was unremarkable. That he sought political office without any qualifications was daring enough, so the young candidate stuck to predictable topics, with a little something for everyone. He forthrightly declared he opposed "communism, fascism, nazism, and socialism." He was for low-income housing, veterans' benefits, and social security, against unemployment, inflation, and high prices. It was difficult for his Republican opponent to find anything to argue with Jack about.

His advisers, however, had a bone of contention with their own candidate, and that was the issue of Jack's wearing a hat. He hated hats, claiming they took away half his personality. Joe Kane contended that Jack would offend people in the local hat industry if he didn't wear a hat. Jack replied that his hair was his trademark and it appealed to women voters. But Kane persisted; a hat made Jack look more mature, more like a serious politician. Finally Jack gave in and agreed to wear one to a veteran's rally at which Rose was to introduce her son as the main attraction. Jack, typically, was late, and as the time passed, Rose had to drag out her opening remarks until finally Jack showed up. Walking up onto the stage, Jack pointed at his pet peeve and asked, "Well, Mother, how do you like my hat?" Rose had a pet peeve of her own. Glaring at her son, she said, "Dear, it would have looked a lot better two hours ago." It was Jack's only campaign appearance in a hat, but from then until the election he arrived on schedule.

In November, the minor aggravations of the campaign were forgotten when Jack defeated his opponent almost three to one. At twenty-nine years of age, he had become the representative of the Eleventh Congressional District of Massachusetts. He had never held a job, yet now Jack Kennedy was off to Washington to represent a working-class constituency.

7

WATCH THIS
YOUNG FELLOW

Shortly after the election, Jack and his sister Eunice, who had gotten a job with the Justice Department, rented a house in Georgetown. The three-story brick home soon became a sort of Washington branch office of the Kennedy household. Because her daughter's talents in the kitchen extended only to making mashed potatoes, Rose donated a cook to the new domestic establishment. Jack, no tidier now than in his days at Choate, was picked-up-after by a valet supplied by his father. One parent or the other seemed always to be dropping in to check up on the personal and professional lives of their son and daughter, while miscellaneous other Fitzgeralds and Kennedys were frequent overnight guests. So there they were, a twenty five year old sister and a twenty-nine-year-old brother, each with an annual unearned income of more than one hundred thousand dollars from trust funds established by their father; living together in a house paid for, staffed by, supervised by, and often occupied by their parents; just beginning careers for the first time in their lives.

Jack's job got under way on January 6, 1947, with the convening of the Eightieth Congress. It was an uneasy time for America. The country had emerged from World War II as the strongest nation in history, yet it seemed unable to take for granted its role as a superpower. Americans were starting to view the spread of communism as a threat not only abroad, but within the United States as well, and although that paranoia had not yet reached its peak, it had begun to develop. Jack's easy victory was an exception; Republicans had swept both houses of Congress the previous fall, many by insinuating their opponents were "soft" on communism. Among those who took congressional seats on the same day as Jack was a fledgling representative from California, Richard Nixon, who had made a modest impression nationally by defeating a well-entrenched Democratic incumbent. Another new face in Washington was that of the freshman Republican senator from Wisconsin, a dynamic man named Joseph McCarthy.

Jack himself had no set political philosophy. Refusing the label of either conservative or liberal, he insisted on being described simply as a "Massachusetts Democrat." Still he shared with his Catholic constituency a fear of what was beginning to be regarded as "the Red menace," and he was drawn to the two staunch anti-communists, McCarthy and Nixon. The Wisconsin senator often visited Jack's Georgetown home, and occasionally dated Patricia Kennedy. Jack and Dick Nixon established a friendly rivalry. Both newcomers to the House of Representatives were thought to have bright political futures, and they teased each other about which would be the first elected to the more prestigious Senate. The freshman from California admired the wit and intelligence of his Massachusetts counterpart. But Nixon, a meticulous dresser, was appalled—along with other members of Congress—when Jack regularly appeared on the floor of the House wearing khakis, mismatched socks, and sneakers. One of his aides could hardly keep a straight face when Jack returned to his congressional office one day and said that some visitors to the House had gotten "into the elevator and asked me for the fourth floor!"

Completely at ease with his own personal style, Jack was unselfconscious about wearing brown loafers with a tuxedo, or being seen in clothes which a staff member described as "god-awful." In spite of his wealthy background and a fashion-conscious mother, Jack cared as little for his wardrobe as he did for all possessions. He gave no thought to money, or to what it could buy. His physical condition was the dominant concern of Jack's life. He was always tired and continued to lose weight. His digestive condition had worsened to such an extent that it was necessary for the Georgetown cook to send specially prepared bland lunches to his office. Nevertheless, Jack seldom spoke of his stomach problems and never complained about his excruciating back pain.

In spite of the nagging mystery of his declining health, the Jack Kennedy who entered the House of Representatives in January 1947 was a very appealing young man: handsome, unaffected, bright, well informed. He had emerged from the domineering presence of his father and older brother with few apparent psychological scars—secure in his own worth, with a sense of humor he most often used to poke fun at himself, free from the neuroses which would eventually cripple his new friend, Dick Nixon. But now, at the beginning of their careers in Washington, Jack enjoyed another important advantage. Although Nixon had come to Congress on a wave of publicity after his upset victory in California, his political benefits did not include the support of a powerful father.

Just two weeks after being sworn into office, Jack was named one of the Ten Outstanding Young Men of 1946 by the U.S. Junior Chamber of Commerce. He had done little the previous year except be elected to office, but Joe Kennedy had engineered the award to put Jack in the company of well-known people such as historian Arthur Schlesinger, Jr., prizefighter Joe Lewis, and cartoonist Bill Mauldin. Although his son's inclusion on the list had been achieved solely through Joe's efforts, the *New York Times* reported that Jack had been selected "for civic responsibility and fighting for veterans' housing."

Low-income housing had been one of Jack's major concerns during the campaign. In Congress as a member of the Special Subcommittee on Veterans' Housing, he continued to organize veterans' groups to support a federal housing bill. Despite a sympathetic public, passage of the bill was not easily achieved. There was greater profit in constructing houses for the well-to-do, and real estate lobbyists had persuaded the American Legion to fight the legislation. During debate in the House, Jack startled other representatives by declaring that the leadership of the American Legion, widely regarded as one of the most patriotic organizations in the United States, had "not had a constructive thought for the benefit of this country since 1918!" Friends urged Jack to retract the statement, which they were sure would ruin his political future. But the official position of the American Legion did not reflect the views of its rank-and-file membership, and Kennedy's office received thousands of letters applauding his stand. When the housing bill was eventually approved, Jack had endeared himself to many supporters in Boston, where forty-two percent of the young veterans were unable to afford their own homes. Coverage in Massachusetts newspapers reflected the local enthusiasm for Jack's performance. "Watch this young fellow, Congressman John Fitzgerald Kennedy," one paper said, "for he definitely shows signs in more ways than one, of having moral courage, the most lacking thing in public life today."

Jack was called upon to show even greater moral courage—considering the loyalties of Boston Irish politics—on the issue of James Michael Curley. After eighteen months of legal maneuvers, the seventy-three-year-old mayor had finally been convicted of mail fraud. John McCormack of Massachusetts, the House minority whip and one of the most powerful men in Congress, drew up a petition to President Truman requesting a pardon for Curley, who was purportedly in failing health. All Massachusetts Democrats were asked to sign the petition, and only one, freshman John F. Kennedy, refused. Boston newspapers were agog. KENNEDY COURTS CURLEY VENGEANCE, DECLINES COMPROMISE WITH CONSCIENCE IN TRADITION OF INDEPENDENT FAMILY blared one headline. Just as his campaign had promised, Jack had shown himself to be a leader of the "new generation," those inclined to be unsentimental about aging political hacks. Statewide, many Republicans as well as Democrats were impressed with Jack's independence, no small achievement for a young congressman who might one day run for the Senate. Honey Fitz, too, was delighted with his grandson's refusal to do a favor for his ancient enemy, but other Irish voters in the Eleventh District were convinced Jack had, as one disgruntled supporter said, made "a hell of a mistake politically."

The Eleventh was not only pro-Curley but also overwhelmingly low-income working class, so Jack was again on thin ice when he was appointed to the House Education and Labor Committee, chaired by the antiunion Fred Hartley. While seeking to draft a bill that would restrain organized labor, which many Republicans thought had grown too powerful, the hearings soon also became an attempt to link unionism with communism. During questioning of witnesses, Jack proved eager to expose subversives who he felt threatened economic and political order in the United States. Yet when the committee approved a draft designed to curb the strength of the unions, Jack, along with five Democratic colleagues, signed a dissent claiming the proposed legislation was a "slave labor bill," because it jeopardized the right to strike and required management approval before a shop could unionize.

Jack found the wording of the minority report excessive, however, and to clarify his opinion, filed an additional statement of his own. This was regarded as another presumptuous move on the part of the junior representative, but Jack's comments managed to adroitly tiptoe between a position both anticommunist and prolabor.

Since this stance exactly reflected the viewpoint of his constituency, Jack, having weathered the storm over Curley's petition, was back in favor in the Eleventh District.

In April the Hartley bill came up for debate on the floor of the House, an occasion which marked Jack's first speech in Congress. "The grave error," of the Committee's recommendations, he claimed, was that "in seeking to destroy what is bad, they are also destroying what is good." Jack's middle-of-the-road comments, although well received in Massachusetts, had no effect on the conservative House, and the bill was overwhelmingly passed. The legislation then went for study by the Senate Labor Committee, which was chaired by Robert Taft.

A few days later two up-and-coming stars of the congressional freshman class, who had voted on opposite sides of the Hartley bill, met to argue its merits. The forum was held at the request of a Pennsylvania congressman in order to give representatives of the steel industry a chance to hear arguments on the proposed legislation. In a McKeesport hotel, before an audience of little more than one hundred, Richard Nixon and John Kennedy engaged in the first and least memorable of their public debates. Although Nixon later said that neither he nor Jack could recall much of what was said that evening, they greatly enjoyed their conversation following the debate. On the train back to Washington, the two discussed international affairs and the threat of communism, subjects dearer to their hearts than the antilabor issues of what was finally enacted as the Taft-Hartley Law.

Jack was especially interested in a major item pending before the Eightieth Congress: the first proposal of American foreign aid. President Truman and his secretary of state, George Marshall, were convinced that postwar economic chaos in Europe had left many of its nations vulnerable to communist takeover. They suggested a far-reaching program, eventually to become known as the Marshall Plan, in which money would be given outright, rather than lent, to the threatened countries. Jack's enthusiasm for the proposal was not at first shared by others in Congress. In spite of Truman's insistence that the measure be approved during the opening session, the Marshall Plan was too radical to be rubber-stamped by the House and Senate; many congressional members wanted to examine the situation in Europe firsthand before committing the United States to billions of dollars in economic aid. Jack, too, was eager to study conditions abroad, and made plans to join two other members of the Labor Committee in analyzing European labor problems and particularly communist infiltration of unions.

At the end of May, while the three congressmen were still planning their itinerary, Jack went to Hyannis Port for a birthday celebration. Although he looked like a teenager and was often mistaken for a page in the House of Representatives, Jack was now turning thirty. This major event was attended by most of the Kennedys, and was the occasion for many teasing and affectionate toasts to the family's up-and-coming politician. The celebration ended, however, when the youngest Kennedy reminded the group it was not Jack who had been destined for political fame. Asked by his father if he wished to say anything, fifteen-year-old Teddy lifted his water glass and said, "I would like to offer a toast to our brother who is not with us."

The opening session of the Eightieth Congress adjourned at the end of July 1947, and Jack, after a short vacation on the Cape, left for what was to be an extended tour of Europe. The first stop was in Ireland, where his sister Kick was staying at Lismore Castle, a magnificent structure which had been given to Sir Walter Raleigh for his efforts against Irish rebels, and which now belonged to Kick's father-in-law, the duke of Devonshire. Pamela Churchill, who had recently been divorced from Winston Churchill's son, Randolph, was also at Lismore. She agreed to accompany Jack on a journey back in time: a trip to the tiny village of New Ross, from which Patrick Kennedy had emigrated ninety-nine years before.

In the old Kennedy homestead—a farm cottage with dirt floors and a thatched roof—Jack had a wonderful day, "surrounded," he said later, "by chickens and pigs," and finally saying good-bye "in a flow of nostalgia and sentiment." Pamela Churchill, very much the English lady, had been less than delighted to find herself in the company of Irish farmers and their livestock. "She had not understood at all," Jack commented, "the magic of the afternoon." Kick, too, had become slightly grand. Having refused the invitation to accompany Jack and Pamela on their fifty-mile drive, she showed little interest in the details of the outing when the pair returned. Kick's only curiosity about her third cousins was to inquire if they had a bathroom. His sister, Jack wrote Lem Billings, had gone "completely English," even retaining her title as the marchioness of Hartington. "It's rather nice not having to be a Kennedy," Kick remarked to a friend. "Lord knows, there are enough of them as it is."

But Kick was less preoccupied with her aristocratic role than with a difficult romance, and confided her predicament to Jack. For the second time, she had become involved with a member of Britain's nobility. Kick was in love with one of the richest men in England, Peter Fitzwilliam, whose many family estates included the largest private residence in Europe. Set on twenty-two thousand acres, the house contained 365 rooms—one for every day of the year, it was said—and over a thousand windows. The house was so enormous that overnight guests were given wafers to be crumbled and left along the route to the dining hall, in order to find the way back to their rooms after meals.

Peter Fitzwilliam's personal wealth was no stumbling block in a relationship with Kathleen Kennedy, whose own family fortune was among the largest in the world. Nevertheless, the obstacles in their romance loomed much larger than in Kick's love affair with Billy Hartington. There was the now-familiar problem that Fitzwilliam was Protestant. But much worse was the fact that he was already married. The public scandal that would result if a British earl were to divorce in order to marry an Irish-American was the least of Kick's worries. Once she became Fitzwilliam's wife, she would be excommunicated from the Catholic Church. But more terrifying was the prospect of her mother's reaction. For all of Kick's bravura in claiming she didn't want to be a Kennedy, nothing troubled her more than the certainty that if she married a divorced man, Rose would banish her from the family.

Although Kick's dilemma seemed insoluble, Jack had a far greater worry than the prospect of his sister's unhappiness. During his visit at Lismore, he had not been feeling well. In England a few weeks later, ready to begin his European tour, he was seriously ill. At the suggestion of Pamela Churchill, Jack went to a London doctor for medical advice, and there the condition which had plagued him for so many years was finally diagnosed. It was Addison's disease. In a healthy person, the adrenal glands, located near the kidneys, produce hormones which help fight infection and provide extra strength in times of stress. But in those afflicted with Addison's, the glands begin to degenerate, causing weight loss, fatigue, stomach problems, and a yellowish skin tone. If the condition remains untreated, the body will have no resistance to infection, resulting in Addisonian crisis, coma, and, eventually, death.

By the time Jack reached London, he had entered this phase of the disease. He was rushed to a clinic and immediately given the only treatment then available for Addison's: injections of desoxycorticosterone acetate (DOCA). Jack's initial response to the medication was not promising. "That young American friend of yours," the examining doctor told Pamela, "he hasn't got a year to live."

On October 11, Jack sailed home on the *Queen Elizabeth*, where, in the ship's hospital, he received the last rites. But by five days later, when the liner docked in New York, the treatments of DOCA had begun to take hold. Jack, slightly improved but still very ill, was taken off the ship on a stretcher and flown by chartered plane to a hospital in Boston. There was extensive press interest in the condition of the well-known young congressman, and Joe Kennedy, ever mindful of his ambitions for Jack, refused to let the truth be known. It simply would not do for the public to learn that someone with high political aspirations was suffering from a serious disease, so once again the saga of PT 109 was trotted out. All the Boston papers, the *New York Times*, and *Time* magazine were told that Jack had suffered a recurrence of the malaria contracted in the South Pacific. Even though he had been too ill to make the tour, his Boston office gave out reports that the congressman's attack had come about "while studying labor conditions in Europe."

Unknown to the reporters and their readers was the fact that the carefully orchestrated press releases were just so much whistling in the dark. Joe had been making plans for Jack to take another step up the political ladder, a race for the Senate—yet now he believed his son would die within the next year. Jack himself was told he could not expect to live much past the age of forty.

When he returned to Washington in December 1947, Jack was a very different congressman from the active representative of the first session. A colleague in the House said he looked "decrepit"; another described him as "a frail, sick, hollow man." Frightened and depressed about his health, bored with the bread-and-butter needs of the Eleventh District, Jack spent less and less time in Congress, and more and more time in the only pursuit that held his interest: women. New York show girls, Palm Beach socialites, Capitol Hill secretaries, Hollywood starlets—who they were or what they did was unimportant, as long as they were attractive. In spite of his illness, Jack had not lost his charm, and so great was the number of responsive women that an acquaintance characterized them "a smorgasbord." Having a series of girlfriends seemed the only way Jack could forget that he had little time left to enjoy life.

In the early spring of 1948, Jack was temporarily distracted from his own affairs when his favorite sister came to Washington to discuss the problems in her troubled romance. Kick was on the way back to England after confronting Joe and Rose with the news of her affair with Peter Fitzwilliam. The encounter had been even worse than Kick had feared. If her daughter married a divorced man, Rose announced, she would never see Kick again. She also insisted that Joe cut off Kick's trust fund; should he refuse to do so, she would leave him and find a way to publicly embarrass him. Not even Joe's blatant womanizing had driven Rose to such a threat, but she vowed to take that drastic step in order to save her daughter from what she saw as certain damnation. Both Kick and Jack thought the only solution was an appeal to their father, who would soon be in France on a business trip. If the three of them were to meet, Kick was sure Fitzwilliam could win her father over, and that Joe, in turn, could find a way to placate Rose.

On the morning of May 14, the telephone rang in Joe Kennedy's Paris hotel room. Joe, who had already suffered the irreplaceable loss of his eldest son, now learned that his "especially special" daughter was gone, too. During a thunderstorm, Kick's plane had crashed on a French mountainside. She and Peter Fitzwilliam, the man for whom she had risked losing both the Kennedys and Catholicism, were dead.

As devastating as Kick's death was to the entire family, no one was more heartbroken than Jack. They had shared the same sense of humor, and were so much alike that strangers had often mistaken them for twins. Suddenly, within four years, both his awesome big brother and adored younger sister were gone. It was unfair and incomprehensible. Joe Jr. and Kick had been bright, handsome, and charming, with "everything," Jack said, "moving in their direction," while he was the sickly one, the one that should have died instead. Stricken with grief and guilt, and the constant concern of his own health, Jack told a friend he was living every day as if it was his last day on earth.

That fall Jack ran unopposed for his second term in Congress and returned, with little enthusiasm, to Washington in January 1949. "Well, I guess if you don't want to work for a living," he commented to some colleagues in the House, "this is as good a job as any." Jack was doing little more than going through the motions—at least to the extent his physical condition allowed. For his father, he would dutifully continue a political career as the stand-in for Joe Jr. For his constituents, he would conscientiously use that career to pursue prolabor and anticommunist goals. But for himself, there was little point in wasting his limited strength on much more than having a good time. Then in April something happened which changed Jack's life forever.

He had been undergoing the standard treatment for victims of Addison's disease: DOCA pellets implanted in the thigh, which gradually released the drug into the system. By replacing the pellets every three or four months, the need for daily injections was eliminated. At Joe's insistence, safety deposit boxes all across the country were kept filled with a supply of the drug so that Jack, on his frequent travels, would always have access to DOCA—thus lessening the chance of an Addisonian crisis, as well as the possible public exposure of his condition. But even with Joe's precautions, the risks were still there. Although the drug had reduced the mortality rate of those afflicted with Addison's, Jack was in great danger: fatigue, stress, a cold, or a minor infection could bring on a crisis and result in shock and even death. His back continued to deteriorate, but another operation was out of the question, since even the most minor surgery was thought to be too hazardous for an Addisonian.

In that bleak early spring of 1949, when Jack often wondered if there was much point to his existence, came the discovery of cortisone. A leading expert on Addison's disease said the effect of the new drug was "almost magical." From their first cortisone treatment, those who suffered from Addison's had more energy and endurance, an improved ability to concentrate, an increased appetite. Although cortisone wasn't a cure, and although surgery was still considered a gamble, Addisonians were, for the first time, able to lead normal lives.

Suddenly Jack Kennedy had a future.

8

BEATING
THE BEST

By the fall of 1949, Jack's attendance in the House had become so infrequent that the *New York Times* described his congressional record as being "notable chiefly for its high absenteeism." But now it was speaking engagements rather than illness that kept Jack from Congress. As his popularity in Massachusetts had grown, so, too, had requests for Jack's presence at affairs all over the state. In the past, distracted by his health or his social life, Jack had usually refused such invitations. Now there was a reason to attend all the functions for which he could find the time, especially those that would give him exposure outside the Eleventh District. Jack would, as he described it, "hustle for three years" to reach the next goal in his political career: the United States Senate.

The most immediate race, in the fall of 1950, would be for a third term in the House of Representatives. The outcome of that election was never in doubt; it appeared Jack Kennedy's congressional seat was safe as long as he wanted to stay in it. But intellectually and emotionally, Jack felt he must move beyond the domestic issues which were at that time the usual fare of a member of the House. Bored with the mundane needs of the Eleventh District, Jack longed to become more involved with the area which most held his interest: foreign affairs. He both agreed with and resented the superiority with which much of official Washington regarded representatives. "We're worms over in the House," Jack said. "Nobody pays much attention to us nationally." And remaining a "worm" just wasn't Jack Kennedy's style. He had no desire to improve the status of those in the lower congressional body; he simply wanted to join the more select group in the Senate. The next opportunity to do so would be in 1952, and with the energy and enthusiasm which had come with his new lease on life, Jack was already running hard to make sure he got there.

His friend Joe McCarthy was also anticipating the 1952 election. After an undistinguished first term, the Republican senator was looking for a campaign gimmick that would bolster his popularity in Wisconsin. By opting to cash in on the growing concern over communism, McCarthy found an issue that would succeed beyond his wildest dreams. On February 9, 1950, at a Republican dinner in Wheeling, West Virginia, McCarthy delivered a speech that touched off years of communist witch hunting and caused a disgraceful era in American history to bear his name. "While I cannot take the time to name all the men in the State Department who have been named as active members of the Communist party and members of a spy ring," he said, "I have here in my hand a list of 205, a list of names that were made known to the secretary of state as being members of the Communist party and who nevertheless are still working and shaping policy in the State Department."

McCarthy's startling charge had originated from a 1946 State Department report on federal employees being considered for transfer from wartime agencies to State. After the workers had been screened, it was recommended that 285 be let go. Seventy-nine people had already been dismissed, and a simple mathematical error had led McCarthy to the conclusion that 205 remained employed. The report, which was a matter of public record, was almost four years old. It did not list specific names and did not mention membership in the Communist party. McCarthy had absolutely no proof of his charges, did not have a single name, and later said the piece of paper he had waved before the audience had been "an old laundry list." Nevertheless, he had touched the nerve of national paranoia. Since the end of World War II, Americans had watched Russia establish communist, pro-Soviet governments in most East European countries. Then a few months before McCarthy's speech in Wheeling, two events had shocked a country already wary of the Red menace.

The huge population of America's wartime ally, China, had come under Communist domination when Mao Tse-tung finally won the control he and his followers had sought for almost three decades. More terrifying was the discovery of radioactivity over the Pacific Ocean—fallout that had not come from U.S. atomic tests. Years before American experts had thought it technically possible, the Soviet Union had an atom bomb of its own. In what would prove to be the beginning of the arms race, the United States began stockpiling atomic weapons. But increasing at a much greater rate than its nuclear arsenal was the hysteria of its citizens. Communism was on the move abroad, and to many Americans, its success seemed impossible without the help of subversives from the public and private sectors of the mightiest nation on earth.

In this fertile soil, Joe McCarthy had sown the seeds of suspicion: Communists lurked within the U.S. government, and treason, he had implied in Wheeling, reached as high as even the secretary of state, Dean Acheson. Without any substantiation of McCarthy's charges, several newspapers across the country reported his accusations as fact. Within a week McCarthy went from being a little-known senator to a star of national headlines. Among the first of his supporters was Joe Kennedy, who became McCarthy's friend and frequent host in Hyannis Port—where the Wisconsin senator even suffered a cracked rib in one of the legendary Kennedy touch-football games. In spite of his lifelong affiliation with the Democratic party, Joe contributed to McCarthy's cause, as well as to the campaign fund of Republican Richard Nixon, who was seeking a senatorial seat in California.

In the months before the 1950 elections, "McCarthyism" spread throughout the United States. In every race in which it was an issue, the candidate who could sling the most red mud won the election. No one had to be proven a Communist; it was enough to simply hint that he was.

Americans, already apprehensive about domestic subversion, the "loss" of China, and the threat of atomic attack, became even more alarmed in the summer of 1950, when the first major military conflict of the Cold War began. On June 25, North Korean Communist forces, equipped with Russian-made artillery and tanks, invaded the Republic of Korea. Within a few days, American combat troops were ordered into Korea, joined by the soldiers of a few other members of the United Nations. President Truman called their deployment a "police action," but Americans recognized the move for what it was. Five years after the end of World War II, United States servicemen were fighting again—this time against Communist troops. The long-dreaded confrontation had begun, and most of those who had predicted it were swept into office in November.

Shortly after the elections, Jack Kennedy appeared at a Harvard Graduate School seminar, where he made remarks that would come back to haunt him in later years. Proving once again his independence from the Democratic party if not from the views of his father, Jack commented that he knew Joe McCarthy fairly well and thought the Wisconsin senator "may have something." He also expressed his pleasure at Richard Nixon's victory in California.

Jack, too, had won his election that fall. Although he was by now a leading member of the congressional "Tuesday to Thursday Club," made up of those who usually spent only three days in Washington and four days in their home state, Jack's continued absenteeism from the House seemed to make little difference to his constituency. Having beaten four opponents for the nomination with five times the combined total of their votes, he had gone on to trounce the Republican nominee by a margin of five to one.

Just after Christmas, with an eye toward the 1952 senatorial race, Jack left for a tour of Europe, in an effort to acquire a reputation as an authority on foreign policy. During the trip he visited West Germany and Spain, conferred with General Dwight D. Eisenhower, commander of the recently formed North Atlantic Treaty Organization, and toured NATO installations outside Paris. Jack also had an interview with Marshal Tito, head of the Yugoslav government, and an audience with the pope. Back home, Joe made sure his son's conferences with important men in Europe were well covered in Massachusetts newspapers, and Jack himself delivered a radio report on the trip when he returned in February.

To further impress the voters with his grasp of international affairs, Jack was off on another long trip in the fall of 1951—this time to the Far East. Asia had become a hotbed of revolution, with many of its countries attempting to gain freedom from the colonial domination of European nations. The American government assumed that all Far East revolutionary movements were Communist in origin, with every action directed by Moscow. Jack wanted to judge the situation for himself, and was not very pleased when Joe Kennedy decided the trip would be a useful learning experience for Bobby as well. Prep school, college, and military service had kept the two brothers from getting to know each other, and Bobby's life had followed a much more traditional path than that of his thirty-four-year-old bachelor brother. The previous summer he had married Ethel Skakel, Jean Kennedy's college roommate. The newlyweds had spent their first year together in Charlottesville, where Bobby had graduated from the University of Virginia Law School in the spring of 1951. In July the young couple had presented Joe and Rose with their first grandchild, Kathleen. Considering Bobby's strict religious views and the fact that he was now a lawyer, a husband, and a father, Jack was not looking forward to his brother's company on the long trip, and complained to Lem Billings that Bobby would probably be "a pain in the ass."

But to Jack's surprise, he discovered that Bobby, although eight years his junior, was mature and clearheaded, often instrumental in helping him form his own views on the people and places they visited. Bobby, for example, was quick to recognize that, in contrast to the rabid anticommunist mood in the United States, many countries of the Far East regarded communism as less menacing than a continuation of colonial rule under France, Britain, or the Netherlands. In New Delhi, he and Jack listened carefully as the head of the Indian government, Jawaharlal Nehru, commented that the United States had no moral right to insist that unaligned countries choose between it and the Soviet Union. America, Nehru said, preached freedom and independence while continuing to support European colonial empires. Communism would thrive, the Indian leader went on, in an atmosphere of discontent; it was a cause "to die for." Democracy must somehow be given that same aura, Bobby later noted in his journal. "We have only status quo to offer these people. Commies can offer a change."

Within a week, Jack and Bobby were observing the reality of Nehru's warning in the little-known country of Vietnam, where a Communist leader, Ho Chi Minh, had proclaimed his nation's independence from French colonial rule. Vietnam's Declaration of Independence, modeled on that of the United States, began "All men are created equal. . . ." But France, the country that had proclaimed its own eighteenth-century revolution with the stirring sentiment, "Liberty, Equality, Fraternity," met Vietnam's noble words with a brutal show of military force, partially supported by American financial aid. Ho Chi Minh, the U.S. State Department announced, was "an agent of world communism." In contrast, the French were "an integral part of the world-wide resistance by the Free Nations to Communist attempts at conquest and subversion."

Both Kennedys were skeptical about France's chance of victory. In a letter to Joe, Bobby wrote, "As it stands now we are becoming more and more involved in a war to a point where we can't back out." Seventy percent of the Vietnamese, he felt, were behind Ho Chi Minh; and the United States, because of its support of the

French, was "quite unpopular." Bobby concluded his letter with a thought which would become ever more true over the next two decades: "It doesn't seem to be a picture with a very bright future."

The Asian trip made a major impression on Jack. In a radio address given after his return, Jack's comments showed he had learned a great deal in the twenty-five thousand miles he had traveled. Having witnessed what he was sure would be the futile outcome of French military efforts in Vietnam, Jack said, "Communism cannot be met effectively by merely the force of arms," and added that the task was "to build strong non-Communist sentiment" rather than relying on a military solution. To achieve that goal, however, America would have to reexamine its priorities. The United States, he commented, was "too ready to buttress an inequitable status quo." Jack deplored American diplomats who were aligning themselves "with the 'haves' and regarding the action of the 'have-nots' as not merely the effort to cure injustice but as something sinister and subversive."

In an appearance before the Boston Chamber of Commerce, Jack continued to display his new authority on foreign affairs. "We cannot reform the world," he said. "We should not impose upon the Eastern world our values, institutions, or customs. However much we may value our concepts, our mechanical well-being, even our bathtubs, the East may think little or nothing of them." Jack suggested that America should think in three categories: "The things we cannot and must not do; the things we are doing that should not be done; and the things we are not doing that we should be doing."

The speech was typical of those Jack was giving with greater frequency throughout the state. During the two years he had been making public appearances across Massachusetts, his staff systematically arranged for Jack to speak over and over again in every one of the state's 39 cities and 312 towns. A large map of the state had been tacked to a wall in Jack's Boston apartment, with pins stuck into each place where he had given a speech. Jack told Dave Powers he would announce for the Senate race as soon as the map was completely covered with pins.

Jack was already planning his strategy for that contest. As he traveled throughout Massachusetts, his aides compiled an index card file of young people with whom he was impressed, and who volunteered to work for him in future campaigns. The cards formed the nucleus of what would become known as the "Kennedy machine"—Jack's own organization of new faces with which he could dissociate himself from the tired old hacks of the state Democratic party and show his candidacy to be a break from the past. In April 1952, when the map bristled with pins, Jack announced for the Senate. He would face a seemingly invincible Republican incumbent, a man whose family had always won out against the repeated efforts of Massachusetts Democrats: Henry Cabot Lodge, Jr.

Lodge was a product of the social class that had historically excluded the Kennedys and other prominent Irish-Americans from acceptance in the loftier reaches of Boston society. He was a descendant of two of the oldest, wealthiest, and most aristocratic Massachusetts families. His great-great-great grandfather, a friend of George Washington and Alexander Hamilton, had been the first senator from Massachusetts. The marriage between a Lodge and a Cabot, the current senator's great grandparents, had produced not only the first Henry Cabot Lodge but an ongoing political rivalry with aspiring Irish Catholics, in which the Protestants always prevailed.

The disdain Henry Cabot Lodge, Sr., had for the Irish was well known; he had once characterized them as "inferior peoples whose prolific issue threatened the very foundations of Anglo-American civilization." In 1916, he had run for the Senate against one of the "inferiors": Honey Fitz. Their campaign reflected the mutual antagonism, Rose later said, between the world of "ancestral portraits and mahogany sideboards and silver tea services" and that of the less well established and less distinguished ethnic groups. "Do you think," Lodge had once asked Honey Fitz, "Jews and Italians have any right in this country?" "As much right as your father or mine," Honey Fitz shot back. "It was only a difference of a few ships." In the 1916 senatorial election, that difference still mattered, and Honey Fitz lost by thirty-three thousand votes. Yankee dominance continued over the next two decades; in the 1936 Senate race, Henry Cabot Lodge, Jr., won out over the legendary James Michael Curley. Sixteen years later, this was the formidable candidate Jack would have to defeat.

Not only did the Lodges have traditional supremacy, but in 1952 their political power seemed to be at its peak. It had been Henry Cabot Lodge, Jr., who persuaded the popular World War II commander Dwight D. Eisenhower to resign his NATO post and return to the United States to seek the presidential nomination. Given the mood of the country, which blamed the Democratic administration for America's having lost ground to communism, the stage seemed set for a nationwide Republican sweep. "Tell Joe not to waste his money on Jack," Lodge told Arthur Krock, "because he can't win. I'm going to win," he added, "by three hundred thousand votes." In spite of Lodge's apparent advantages, Joe had faith that his son would triumph. "When you've beaten him," he told Jack, "you've beaten the best." In fact, he assured the family, Jack would "knock Lodge's block off."

Joe was envisioning another campaign of all-out Kennedy involvement, the strategy which had worked so well in the 1946 congressional race. But this time Bobby was reluctant to sign on. He had taken a job with the Criminal Division of the Department of Justice, and was working on his first important case before a Brooklyn grand jury. Since it was impossible to completely dissociate himself from the race, Bobby asked a college friend, Kenneth O'Donnell, to join Jack's campaign and keep him posted on how it was going. Soon Kenny telephoned with a dismaying report. Joe Kennedy had taken personal charge and had recruited old political pros to run the show, while the card files of youthful statewide volunteers remained unopened. Jack preferred to stay out of the everyday details of running for office—that was not his job, he said. Still less did he want to confront his father.

The campaign, O'Donnell told Bobby, was floundering. Joe knew nothing "about politics in this day and age," Kenny said, but he was "such a strong personality that nobody could—nobody dared—fight back." If Jack himself wouldn't set his father straight, there was only one person who could. Bobby had to leave Brooklyn and come to Massachusetts to run the campaign. But Bobby, as wary as Jack at the prospect of taking on their father, decided he was much better off where he was. "Don't drag me into it," he begged. Bobby explained all the reasons for his reluctance. He loved his job, he dreaded the arguments with Joe, he knew nothing of politics. O'Donnell persisted; the campaign was heading toward "absolute, catastrophic disaster." Protesting he would "screw it up," Bobby finally agreed to go. No matter what his personal feelings, family loyalty came first. O'Donnell's judgment was soon proven right. In spite of his unwillingness to take charge, Bobby had, within days, gotten the campaign back on track.

Another addition to the staff at the same time as Bobby was Larry O'Brien, one of the few newcomers with political experience. He had worked for a prominent local politician of Italian descent; when O'Brien left to join Jack's organization, his former boss was furious and refused to support the Kennedy candidacy. Jack was concerned. "In return for one Irishman, I lose all the Italians," he commented, "and I need another Irishman around here like I need a fur hat." The press, too, was well aware of the ethnic makeup of Jack's staff, and dubbed O'Brien, O'Donnell, and Powers his "Irish Mafia." But O'Brien had much-needed organizational skills, and Jack soon realized he was a valuable asset to the staff.

Not even O'Brien, however, could rival Bobby's importance to the campaign. Jack had never before been aware, Lem Billings later said, "that Bobby had all this tremendous ability." Soon after his younger brother came on board, Jack knew there was no longer any reason to worry about the disaster O'Donnell had predicted. Bobby got results. Under his direction, the "Kennedy machine" became a reality. Caring not at all about whom he offended in the process, he showed political pros the door. That group, who had done nothing but sit in Kennedy headquarters giving endless advice, got little respect from the new campaign manager. "If you're not going to work, don't hang around here," Bobby told one who had refused to address envelopes. So many of the old-timers went off in a huff that a soon-to-be-famous image in American politics was born: Bobby Kennedy was "ruthless." His own reputation was of no interest. "I don't care if anybody around here likes me, as long as they like Jack," Bobby said.

It was his intention to stay behind the scenes, doing the dirty work, leaving Jack with a spotless reputation while he himself took responsibility for offending other members of the Democratic party. The governor of Massachusetts, aware that his own reelection campaign was stumbling, met with Bobby to discuss merging their efforts. He was given such short shrift Joe soon received a telephone call: "I know you're an important man around here and all that, but I'm telling you this and I mean it," the governor said furiously. "Keep that fresh kid of yours out of sight from now on." Another candidate for office, eager to associate himself with the Kennedy campaign, was also the target of Bobby's disapproval. "I don't want my brother to get mixed up with politicians!" Bobby had yelled at the startled man.

When no other family member was available, Bobby occasionally had to make a public appearance, where he was much less formidable than in shouting matches with local Democrats. Once he was pressed into service to make a speech at a function Jack had been scheduled to attend. Clearly frozen with embarrassment, Bobby managed to mumble seven uninspired sentences. "My brother Jack couldn't be here. My mother couldn't be here. My sister Eunice couldn't be here. My sister Pat couldn't be here. But if my brother Jack were here, he'd tell you Lodge has a very bad voting record. Thank you."

Bobby's shy recitation of names was a reflection of how the campaign was being waged. Since Jack himself couldn't appear all over the state at the same time, his mother and sisters made it possible for a Kennedy to be almost everywhere in Massachusetts on any given day. Although Teddy was overseas in the Army and couldn't participate, the family was kept at full strength by the addition of Ethel Kennedy to their ranks. Heavily pregnant, she campaigned with enthusiasm and energy up to the last possible moment before giving birth to a son, Joseph Patrick Kennedy II. But sixty-two-year-old Rose was the most skilled campaigner of all. She "wowed them everywhere," Dave Powers said. In poor neighborhoods, simply dressed in a skirt and blouse, she once again gave her intimate chats about Kennedy family life and displayed the index-card file she had kept on her nine children. Then, back in the car, Rose would put on expensive jewelry, wrap a mink stole around her shoulders, and be off to tell the ladies of Beacon Hill about the newest fashions she had seen in Paris that spring.

Rose didn't hesitate to campaign even during her cab trips from one appearance to the next, and for a time always asked her drivers who they thought would win the election. She stopped that practice when one driver, learning his passenger was Rose Kennedy, announced that "Your son owes me one dollar and sixty-five cents." Well aware of Jack's reputation for never carrying money, she decided not to risk bringing up the subject of politics in her taxi rides for the rest of the campaign. It was the only detail she chose to overlook. Thirty-five-year-old Jack would often receive one of his mother's ubiquitous notes, suggesting he keep his hands out of his pockets when he was standing, or pointing out that Lodge's striped neckties made a better impression than the solid-colored ones Jack favored, or adamantly insisting he should never wear anything but black shoes.

The role played by Jack's family went further than advice or public appearances. In addition to the huge amount of money spent by Joe, all his children involuntarily chipped in as well. During the 1952 campaign, and in all the Kennedy campaigns that followed, each received a smaller than usual check from their annual trust funds, with a note enclosed: "Greetings. You have just made a political contribution." But in varying amounts, Joe's was by far the most enormous expenditure. The owner of the financially strapped *Boston Post,* initially in favor of Lodge, gave Jack a front-page endorsement three weeks before the election, and subsequently received a half-million-dollar loan from Joe Kennedy. Joe McCarthy, running for reelection while riding the crest of his anticommunist crusade, got a three thousand dollar contribution. Despite his many avid admirers in Massachusetts, the Wisconsin senator declined to campaign for fellow Republican Henry Cabot Lodge. Perhaps Joe knew more about politics than Kenny O'Donnell gave him credit for.

In addition to his generous financial aid to a Boston newspaper and a United States senator, Joe also paid for almost a million copies of an eight-page tabloid, which featured a familiar theme. Under the headline "John Fulfills Dream of Brother Joe Who Met Death Over the English Channel" were a photograph of Joe Jr. and drawings of Jack rescuing his shipmates in the Solomon Islands. Inserted in each paper was a reprint of the *Reader's Digest* article on PT 109. In the midst of the campaign, a bit of Irish luck brought the Democratic candidate a letter from Kohei Hanani, commander of the Japanese destroyer that had rammed PT 109. Having read an article about Jack in the August issue of *Time,* Hanani wrote that he hoped for Jack's election not only as a way of promoting "genuine friendship between Japan and the United States, but also to the establishment of universal peace." Joe, of course, made sure the letter was well publicized.

Voters were given another reminder of Jack's World War II service. His back condition, often attributed to his ordeal in the Solomon Islands, was worsening, and for much of the campaign he was forced to use crutches. He attempted to keep them concealed in the car, gritting his teeth in pain as he made his way to the platform at a speaking engagement. Once in the room, Jack would stand erect, smiling, looking fit and healthy. But back in the car, he leaned against the seat, closing his eyes in agony, until arriving at the next function, where he forced himself to go through the whole torturous process all over again. Still, there were times when the pain was just too great and the crutches were there for all to see. But even when they had to be used, Jack, knowing full well his appearance was a large part of his appeal, managed to project an image of youth and energy.

As in 1946, Kennedy strategy was for the candidate to meet as many voters as possible, since few seemed able to resist his personal charm. Even Henry Cabot Lodge admitted Jack was "extraordinarily likable." Lodge said that in most of his political races, he had found his opponents' faults and campaigned on them. But in Jack's case, he ruefully added, that just wasn't possible. Since there were few ideological differences between the two candidates, the campaign came down to one of personalities rather than issues, and here Lodge was at a disadvantage. Tall, dignified, and handsome though he was, Lodge had to fight not only Jack's charisma, but the glamour of the whole Kennedy family. Having initially taken his victory for granted, Lodge had spent most of the pre-election months campaigning across the country for the national Republican ticket. Too late, he realized the entire state of Massachusetts was under siege by the Kennedys. By the time Lodge returned to his own campaign, members of the Kennedy family had shaken the hands of more than two million voters. But the fatal blow to Lodge's hopes for reelection was the teas.

No one who had worked for Jack's candidacy in his first congressional race had ever forgotten the astonishing success of the famous formal tea reception, which his leading opponent had proclaimed "the clincher" in Jack's victory. Since one tea had worked so well in 1946, why not give several more in 1952? "Reception in honor of Mrs. Joseph P. Kennedy, Sr. and her son, Congressman John F. Kennedy," read the invitation. Much to Republican dismay, the women of Massachusetts went wild. To the hairdresser, to the seamstress, off to the reception, just for a chance to shake the hands of Rose and Jack Kennedy. Such was Rose's effect that a veteran newspaper reporter covering one of the events said, "It was all they could do to keep those old gals who came to the affairs from curtsying." As his mother was enchanting the matrons, Jack was dazzling the young ladies. "What is there about Jack Kennedy," a bewildered Republican asked, "that makes every Catholic girl in Boston between eighteen and twenty-eight think it's a holy crusade to get him elected?" But Jack's appeal went beyond Boston. In thirty-three statewide receptions, he had shaken hands with more than 70,000 women. And on election night, when the votes were tallied, Kennedy had defeated his opponent by 70,737 votes. Lodge knew exactly what had hit him: "It was those damned tea parties!"

Democratic triumphs were a rarity across America that fall, and Massachusetts was no exception. Dwight Eisenhower, with Richard Nixon as his vice-presidential running mate, had taken the state by 208,800 votes, making Jack's election all the more remarkable. A great deal of the credit and even more of the satisfaction belonged to Rose. "At last," she said serenely, "the Fitzgeralds have evened the score with the Lodges." The moment was no less sweet for Joe, whose bitterness toward Boston's ruling class matched that of his wife. The only dark cloud in Jack's upset victory was that his grandfather couldn't be there to see the downfall of Yankee dominance. Honey Fitz had died in October 1950, never to know of the ancestral revenge achieved by his grandson. But the old man was in Jack's thoughts. In an uncharacteristic display of emotion, John Kennedy honored John Fitzgerald in a most fitting way. As soon as he knew he had won, the new senator-elect sang "Sweet Adeline."

THE SENATOR
GOES A-COURTING

When Jack returned to Washington in January 1953, he was a more eligible bachelor than ever. Being elected to the Senate had moved Jack into the select company of its ninety-six members, and his new status caught the attention of even more women, who were determined to snare the best catch in the nation's capital. For those who weren't already aware of Jack's existence, a national magazine made it clear he was everything a young woman could hope for. A frothy article in *The Saturday Evening Post* described Jack's "bumper crop of lightly combed brown hair," told of his dashing around Washington in a "long convertible, hatless, and with the car's top down," said he was frequently "photographed with a glamour girl in a nightclub," and proclaimed Jack Kennedy "just about the most eligible bachelor" in the country.

This was not the impression Jack wanted to make. He was now thirty-five years old, and anxious to be perceived as a dignified United States senator. Yet Jack's ambitions already reached beyond that exclusive group. Even before the election in the previous fall had been won, his father was seen wearing a necktie with the inscription "Kennedy for President." The giant step from Capitol Hill to the White House would be impossible, however, if the nation's voters saw Jack as an aging boy whose only interests were his hair, his car, and his girls. It was time to put the playboy image behind him, to show Americans he was a mature man who had given serious thought to the future of the United States.

People also expected their country's leader to be a family man. The 1952 Democratic presidential nominee, Illinois governor Adlai Stevenson, had gone into the election with three strikes against him. He had faced the hopeless task of representing a party which had fallen from favor nationally. He had run against a popular World War II hero. And he was divorced. As far as the American electorate was concerned, any man who wanted to occupy the White House had better plan to live there with a wife or forget the plan of living there at all. For Jack, who had the added burden of being Catholic in a country traditionally ruled by Protestants, any future political aspirations would be derailed if he continued to remain a bachelor. The decision was obvious: the Senate race had been a necessary stepping-stone to the presidency, but even more important was the selection of a perfect wife. The first goal had been accomplished; now Jack was well on his way to taking care of the second. He had waged two campaigns the previous year— one to defeat Henry Cabot Lodge, the other to win Jacqueline Bouvier.

Jacqueline's parents, Janet and Jack Bouvier, were socially prominent New Yorkers. Growing up on Park Avenue and in the Hamptons, a fashionable summer resort on Long Island, Jackie had known only the world of wealth and status which the Bouviers had enjoyed through four generations in America. Her great-great grandfather, a French Catholic, had fought with Napoleon at the Battle of Waterloo in 1815. After that defeat, he fled to Philadelphia, became a cabinetmaker, and eventually went into the mass production of furniture. By 1848, when Patrick Kennedy was bound for Boston and his life of poverty, Michel Bouvier had become a rich man by buying up vast amounts of West Virginia coal land. In 1929, the year of Jacqueline's birth, her father was estimated to be worth seven and a half million dollars, all made in the stock market—just about the same amount Joe Kennedy had amassed through bootlegging, real estate, and the movie industry. But by the 1930s, the Kennedy fortune far surpassed that of the Bouviers. Through bad investments and the strict regulations imposed by the SEC under Joe Kennedy, Jack Bouvier's money had been all but wiped out. The strain of their financial problems, along with Jack's fondness for women and drink, took its toll; in 1938 the Bouviers were divorced, with Janet getting custody of their two daughters, Jacqueline and Lee.

Four years later, Janet married again—this time to Hugh Auchincloss, a man of considerable wealth and an even more impeccable background than that of her first husband. Given the snobbishness of her New York contemporaries, it seemed Janet Lee Bouvier Auchincloss had achieved two remarkably good marriages for one whose heritage was completely Irish. Janet's great grandfather Lee had left Ireland during the potato famine. Her mother's mother, a more recent immigrant, still spoke with a brogue. But when James Lee, Janet's father, began to compile a fortune in banking, he carefully concealed the family's background. His mother-in-law was never allowed to meet guests, for fear her Irish accent would reveal the family's immigrant beginnings. Janet, whose marriages had brought her farther up the social ladder, followed her father's example. If asked, she would say she was descended from "the Lees of Maryland," implying these nonexistent ancestors were somehow related to the fabled Lees of Virginia. Having been admitted to the rarefied world of Auchincloss wealth, Janet was going to allow nothing to endanger her standing in society.

Marriage to Hugh Auchincloss brought with it two large estates: Merrywood in McLean, Virginia, and Hammersmith Farm in Newport, Rhode Island. Jacqueline's teenage years were spent in an endless round of travel. Her exclusive prep school, Miss Porter's, was in Farmington, Connecticut. She often went from there to New York, to visit her father. Summers and holidays were spent in Virginia or Rhode Island with Janet and Hugh. In the fall of 1947 she enrolled at Vassar College, in Poughkeepsie, New York. Her junior year was spent abroad, studying French history and literature at the Sorbonne in Paris. As a senior she attended George Washington University in Washington, D.C., from which she graduated in 1951. That summer Hugh Auchincloss approached a friend about the possibility of getting a job for his stepdaughter, who had shown a flair for writing. The friend was Arthur Krock. Ten years after he had sent Inga Arvad to the *Washington Time-Herald*, Krock found a position on its staff for Jacqueline Bouvier.

One evening at a Washington dinner party given by journalist Charles Bartlett, a handsome politician "leaned across the asparagus," as he later described it, and asked the beautiful woman on the other side of the table for a date. It was the beginning of what Jacqueline called a "spasmodic courtship," since Jack spent so much time in Massachusetts. "He'd call me from some oyster bar up there, with a great clinking of coins," she said, "to ask me out to the movies the following Wednesday in Washington." In May 1953 the *Times-Herald* sent Jacqueline to England to cover the coronation of Elizabeth II. When Jack telephoned her in London, it was not with an invitation to the movies, but with a marriage proposal. In a glare of publicity carefully engineered by Joe, the engagement was announced in June. Jack and Jacqueline were even featured on the cover of *Life* magazine, with an accompanying caption, "The Senator Goes A-Courting."

Jacqueline had been worried that Joe's relentless drive to keep Jack in the spotlight would repel her mother, and that her father would object to the Kennedys on principle. But to her relief, neither parent was against the marriage. With some reservations, Janet Auchincloss approved of Jack, although, he told Red Fay, she "has a tendency to think I'm not good enough for her daughter." The Kennedys were a step down socially: both Irish, which Janet had been taught was a heritage better kept under wraps, and Catholic, which was far more déclassé than the Episcopal religion to which she had converted early in her social climb. Nevertheless, the Kennedys were rich and Jack was ambitious. The marriage would bring Jacqueline immediate wealth and, given Jack's prospects, perhaps eventual prestige. All in all, in spite of her qualms about the Kennedys' background, she thought her daughter had made a good match.

Of much greater concern to Jacqueline was the possible reaction of Jack Bouvier. She worshiped her dashing, sophisticated father, who was so handsome he was often mistaken for Clark Gable. Jacqueline thought he and Jack Kennedy would have a lot in common—if one major stumbling block could be overcome. Because of his role at the SEC, her prospective father-in-law was the very man on whom Jacqueline's father blamed his reduced financial circumstances, and she had learned at an early age that "Kennedy" was a dirty word in the Bouvier household. Yet when Jack Kennedy and Jack Bouvier met for dinner in New York, the two hit it off quite well. "They talked about politics and sports and girls," she said, "what all red-blooded men like to talk about." Joe Kennedy was not mentioned. Once Jack had been found acceptable, it was Jacqueline's turn to win over the Kennedys. She endured her trial-by-fire one weekend in Hyannis Port.

For all their money, the Kennedys had a complex about their social status. To them, Jacqueline Bouvier's background was not unlike that of the Boston establishment, whose snubs had resulted in the creation of the Kennedys' own slightly defensive closed society. Jacqueline was no less careful than her mother in concealing her Irish background, and, because of her association with the Auchinclosses, gave an illusion of personal wealth. Jack's family saw her as rich, French, and aristocratic. Having aroused all their insecurities, Jacqueline was a prime target, and the Kennedy children gave her a brutal welcome.

The sisters, whom Jacqueline would privately call the "rah rah girls," treated her, she said, as if the visit were "a sorority hazing." Anxious to make a good impression, she had brought stylish outfits; the girls thought she was overdressed and dubbed her "The Debutante." When she said she preferred to be called "Jacqueline," with the name given a French pronunciation, Eunice muttered "rhymes with queen"—and persisted, along with Jack and most of the family in using the nickname "Jackie." The worst ridicule of all came from Ethel, who prided herself on being more Kennedy than the Kennedys. When Jacqueline remarked that she once hoped to be a ballet dancer, Ethel looked down with a sneer and said, "With those feet of yours? You'd be better off going into soccer, kid."

Through the whole merciless weekend Jacqueline held her temper, but she later enjoyed sarcastically recounting the experience to her sister Lee, and took special pleasure in describing the touch-football games, in which the Kennedys, she said, "fell all over each other like gorillas." Yet in spite of the girls' sniping, the family had accepted "Jackie." She had withstood the first round of their relentless teasing, which the Kennedys initially employed to test a person and then continued to use as an expression of affection. They also realized Jackie gave the Kennedys a touch of class; as a member of the family, she would enhance their social image as well as further Jack's political career. Nevertheless, there was some private Irish gloating when Jack Bouvier, descendant of a prominent French-American family and pillar of New York society, was too drunk to show up at the wedding.

The event, which Joe made sure was well publicized as the "Wedding of the Year," took place in Newport on September 12, 1953. Before eight hundred notable guests, Hugh Auchincloss escorted his stepdaughter down the aisle, because, it was reported, the father of the bride had been taken ill. Although bitterly disappointed by her father's absence, Jacqueline was delighted by the flawless reception at Hammersmith Farm. The weather was perfect, and the three-hundred-acre estate, which overlooked Narragansett Bay, was an ideal setting for twelve hundred friends and acquaintances who watched the newlyweds with an awe usually reserved for movie stars. Jackie looked beautiful in an ivory silk dress. Jack, one guest said, appeared "too tanned and too handsome to be believed," although his face was scratched from falling into a rose bush during a touch-football game before the wedding.

The newlyweds made a difficult adjustment to married life. Jacqueline wanted to spend several weeks of their honeymoon in Acapulco, but Jack insisted they move on to see Red Fay and other Navy buddies in California. From there, the couple went to Hyannis Port for a visit with the Kennedys. When Jack returned to his Senate duties in October, the two stayed first at the Auchincloss estate at Merrywood, then rented a small house in Georgetown, and finally bought their own home, Hickory Hill, in McLean, Virginia. Jackie did a great deal of redecorating, and Jack, a wealthy man with absolutely no comprehension of money matters, tried to make up for his financial innocence by being frugal. After Jackie had new wallpaper put up in the kitchen for the third time in as many months, Jack complained about the cost and said the constant changes made him feel like "a transient." But he was hardly more than that; Jack's crowded personal and professional schedule left him little time at home.

As the wife of a well-known senator with national ambitions, Jackie soon realized the role she was to play. She should remain slightly in the background: supportive, decorative, unthreatening, uncomplaining, taking part in activities which were beyond reproach. The public seemed interested in almost everything Jackie did, and she was photographed going horseback riding, painting watercolors, playing bridge, on her way to attend an American history class at Georgetown University. But beneath the surface of this appealing portrait, Mrs. John F. Kennedy was confronting the reality of having a husband who found women irresistible. Jackie was, in many ways, as stoic as Rose, and like her mother-in-law, she would need every bit of her self-discipline.

Jackie thought she had gone into the marriage with her eyes open. "I don't think there are many men who are faithful to their wives," she told a friend. "Men are such a combination of good and evil." Still, their first few months together were a shock. At thirty-six, Jack had come to married life later than most, and, perhaps taking his cue from the marital style of Joe Kennedy, he continued to behave much as he had during his celebrated bachelorhood. Jack was, a friend said, "so disciplined in so many ways."

Discipline was, after all, the secret of his success. But when it came to women he was a different person. It was Jekyll and Hyde." Occasionally, Jackie was left alone at parties while her husband went off with a woman who had caught his attention. One Washington observer noted Jackie seemed miserable at social events and once even "took a chair, turned it towards a corner and sat there for the entire evening without bothering to talk to anybody."

Jackie's refusal to cultivate important people was a source of annoyance to her political husband. At a party he was overheard saying, "The trouble with you, Jackie, is that you don't care enough about what people think of you." She snapped back, "The trouble with you, Jack, is that you care too much about what people think of you." On another occasion, bystanders heard an argument about their age difference. "You're too old for me," Jackie bitterly told her husband. "Well, you're too young for me," he replied. When an interviewer asked Jackie her theories for a successful marriage, she grimly responded, "I can't say I have any yet." Before long, twenty-four-year-old Jacqueline Kennedy was, an acquaintance said, "wandering around looking like the survivor of an airplane crash."

It wasn't just the relentless socializing or other women. The pressures of his political career made the company of his friends and family all the more important to Jack, and Lem Billings or some other pal seemed always to be hanging around. When Jack and Jackie went out, it was often to have dinner with Ethel and Bobby. If they left Washington, it was usually to go to Hyannis Port or Palm Beach. Although Jackie had become very fond of Joe and Bobby, she resented that of her little time with Jack, so much was spent with the Kennedys. Occasionally Jackie was even sent off to visit the family by herself, as Jack, involved with speaking engagements across the country, began to enter the arena of national politics. In this effort, he was assisted by a young man whose brilliant prose would come to symbolize the Kennedy style.

One of Jack's first acts as a senator had been to hire, on a trial basis, a new legislative aide. Given their differences in age and ideology, the relationship had worked out better than either of them could have imagined. Theodore Sorensen was a twenty-four-year-old liberal lawyer from Nebraska, a registered pacifist and civil rights activist years before either cause was popular. He was also a skilled writer, and had published articles in several progressive journals. Sorensen had doubts about going to work for someone whose political philosophy seemed much more conservative than his own. Jack, he said later, must have thought he was "an odd duck"; during their second meeting, Ted had questioned his prospective employer's positions on Joe Kennedy and Joe McCarthy. Intrigued by what he sensed would be Sorensen's ability to help him move beyond Massachusetts politics, Jack was almost apologetic for the less-than-liberal views he had taken so far in his career. "You've got to remember," he told Ted, "that I entered Congress just out of my father's house." Jack survived the interview, and Sorensen signed on, it was announced, "to work on the legislative program for Massachusetts."

Ted quickly became an expert on issues of importance to a region he had at first known little about, which led to a Kennedy/Sorensen collaboration on a plan to help expand New England's lagging economy. Jack's first speech in the Senate, on May 18, 1953, outlined the problems. In two subsequent speeches he suggested federal aid to attract new industry to the region, and concluded with a program to increase its commercial activity.

Although Jack's presentation was enthusiastically received in Massachusetts and surrounding states, Boston newspapers soon dubbed him "The Suicide Senator" for his support of the proposed St. Lawrence Seaway—a series of canals, dams, and locks through the Great Lakes that would provide passage for large oceangoing vessels into the central section of North America. The project had come up before Congress over and over again for twenty years, and throughout that time every senator and representative from Massachusetts had voted against it, fearing that the establishment of new ports would eventually destroy the Boston shipping industry. By early 1954, the Canadian government announced it would build the Seaway with or without the participation of the United States, and President Eisenhower again sent the proposal to Congress. Jack felt what was good for any area of the American economy would ultimately benefit the country as a whole, but his constituents didn't see it that way.

Jack was particularly vulnerable to the criticism that his support of the Seaway was influenced by his father's business interests. In 1945, Joe Kennedy had purchased the Chicago Merchandise Mart, then the largest commercial building in the world and by far the greatest source of income to the Kennedy fortune. Since ships traveling the Seaway would bypass East Coast ports en route to the upper Midwest, the *Boston Post* accused Jack of "ruining New England" for his father's sake, claiming the Seaway would lead directly to the front door of the Merchandise Mart. Nevertheless, Jack addressed the Senate to declare his support of the project, in a speech which Sorensen said was "a turning point in the Seaway debate as well as in the Senator's career."

When authorization to begin construction on the Seaway was passed by Congress, Jack knew he had played a leading role in that outcome, and from then on, saw himself as a national rather than regional political figure. To emphasize the fact that his expertise went far beyond New England, articles dealing with broader issues, such as social security or foreign policy, were drafted by Sorensen. These began appearing, under the byline of Senator John F. Kennedy, in magazines such as *The Atlantic Monthly* and *The New Republic*.

The printed page, however, could not convey Jack's personal magnetism, and that, he had learned while campaigning, was his greatest political asset. As a senator, Jack was still a member in good standing of the "Tuesday to Thursday Club"; now, however, his travels took him far beyond the familiar path which had led from Washington to Massachusetts and back again. In an effort to make a national reputation, Jack accepted invitations to speak all over the country, frequently calling attention to a subject of special interest to him: colonialism in Southeast Asia. Since his 1951 trip to Indochina, Jack had continued to question France's conduct there, and to express pessimism that the Communists could be defeated. By 1954, it had also become apparent to the French that they couldn't hope to win without intervention by the United States. With President Eisenhower considering the possibility of sending U.S. troops to Vietnam, Americans began to pay attention to Jack's apparent expertise about a place of which few had even heard.

At a speech in Chicago, Jack commented on a suggestion from Vice-President Nixon that the United States become militarily involved in Southeast Asia. The administration, he thought, was naïve to even consider the possibility. Making such a commitment, Jack said, would be "to enter the jungle to do battle with the tiger." In April 1954 he told the Senate that "no amount of American military assistance in Indochina can conquer an enemy which is everywhere and at the same time nowhere, an 'enemy of the people' which has the sympathy and covert support of the people." To a Brooklyn audience, Jack commented that the Vietnamese wished only for independence from the French, and saw Ho Chi Minh and his Communist forces as liberators from oppression. Speaking in

Los Angeles, Jack reflected on optimistic official reports of conditions in Southeast Asia, and said Americans were being "deceived for political reasons on the life and death of war and peace." Eventually, Eisenhower decided to send only military "advisers" to Indochina, but in the meantime, Jack's speeches on the subject had brought him considerable attention. "Keep your eye on young Democratic Senator John Kennedy," wrote a columnist in the *Brooklyn Eagle*. "He's been getting a build-up for a nationwide campaign such as a Vice Presidential candidate."

Even with his growing reputation nationally, Jack was still very much under the watchful eye of his mother. Rose had gratefully turned over to Jackie the task of trying to get Jack to upgrade his wardrobe. Jackie's efforts were successful, and Jack—who a staff member once said, "couldn't tie his own tie"—had become an immaculate dresser. Still, Rose didn't quite trust her son to maintain Jackie's standards while on the road. Dave Powers often went along on the speaking tours, assisting in a variety of ways—from giving political advice to carrying the luggage in order to avoid strain on Jack's back. Dave was never surprised to find one of Rose's famous little notes inside a suitcase, with a suggestion such as "Make sure the socks Jack wears do not have holes in them."

But in spite of Dave's careful attention to his friend's appearance and well-being, Jack paid a high price for the political points he earned during his constant travels. The back condition continued to deteriorate, and the pain was unbearable. By late May, he weighed only 140 pounds and was once again using crutches. It was obvious surgery couldn't be postponed much longer, and although the procedure was potentially fatal for an Addisonian, Jack said he would rather die than go on the way things were. The gamble of having surgery at all was bad enough; but in terms of his career, the operation couldn't have come at a worse time. It would be years before many liberal Democrats would forgive Jack Kennedy for checking into a hospital in October 1954—and thus ducking the issue of Joe McCarthy.

10

TOO MUCH PROFILE, NOT ENOUGH COURAGE

No question in Jack's political life was ever as sticky as the one that confronted him over the Republican senator from Wisconsin.

From the time of his reelection, Joe McCarthy had been on a tear against the "Red Menace." At the start of his crusade he was probably no more anticommunist than much of his generation, which had seen ideology brought to the extreme under Nazism, and which viewed communism as a potentially equal threat. But McCarthy had made the issue his own, and his name had become synonymous with the vigorous pursuit of subversives. As chairman of the once insignificant Committee on Government Operations, established to look into government fraud and corruption, McCarthy appointed himself to head its investigating subcommittee as well. But there was only one topic he wanted to "investigate," and the minor chairmanship soon became the focus of national attention as McCarthy went on a rampage.

The Wisconsin senator had a genius for sniffing out communists in even the most unlikely places: government printing plants, General Electric, the Federal Communications Commission, Bethlehem Steel, the Voice of America, the nation's colleges, the Westinghouse Corporation, and, of course, his personal favorite, the State Department. He was not even reluctant to condemn an entire administration: President Truman's, he said, had been "crawling with Communists." The inflammatory rhetoric surprised absolutely no one. Where the Red Menace was concerned, McCarthy could be counted on to make the most outrageous accusations, and so far nobody had dared to shut him up. By mid-1953, Joe McCarthy was at the height of his power, the public ravenous to learn in what new woodpile subversives lurked. Most Democrats kept quiet; to criticize McCarthy might be construed as being "soft" on communism—the surest way to end a public career. Republicans saw the Wisconsin senator as a political asset. As scandalous as his methods were, much of the country seemed to agree with his views, and he could undoubtedly do a great deal for the Republican ticket in the 1954 congressional elections. Just when it seemed he was unstoppable, Joe McCarthy bit off more than he could chew.

To keep in the public eye, McCarthy had to make new and even more shocking discoveries of subversion, and after years of giant-killing, no target seemed sacred. In October 1953, his subcommittee announced it would begin investigating Communist infiltration of the United States Army. This was a direct slap in the face of the Republican president, who had spent his entire life in military service. But Eisenhower kept silent, saying he refused to "get into the gutter with that guy."

It was in the Senate and not the White House that the phenomenon of McCarthyism was finally destroyed. Republicans and Democrats alike saw McCarthy's latest move as an embarrassment. World War II had ended little more than eight years before, and an armistice had been signed in Korea only the previous July. Americans were proud of their armed forces, and it was psychologically the wrong time to attack that hallowed institution. In April 1954, the Senate ordered a hearing to uncover the truth of McCarthy's allegations. The investigating subcommittee itself would review the charges, and its members serve as judges in what was virtually a trial of Joe McCarthy versus the United States Army. For thirty-five days, a fascinated American public watched the televised proceedings, as Joe McCarthy's reign came to an end.

Self-restraint had never been one of the Wisconsin senator's virtues, and heavy drinking had added to his recklessness. McCarthy's accusations were outlandish and unsubstantiated, delivered in a manner the viewers found rude and repellent. His temper, his scowling face with its heavy five o'clock shadow, his grating voice, combined, an observer said, to make him seem "the perfect stock villain." In an effort to help his fellow Republican, Senator Karl Mundt of South Dakota, who was chairing the hearings, usually allowed McCarthy to speak whenever he wanted. The ploy backfired. McCarthy constantly broke into the proceedings with the cry "Point of order, Mr. Chairman, point of order." His often irrelevant interruptions soon produced giggles among the audience and the expression "Point of order, Mr. Chairman . . ." became a national joke. Suddenly McCarthy's power was gone; fear had been replaced with laughter.

When the hearings ended in June, McCarthy's allegations against the Army were shown to be unfounded. Now it was McCarthy who was vulnerable to attack. One month later, a Senate resolution was drafted censuring his behavior, and a committee, under Utah Republican Arthur Watkins, was established to hear the charges. The object of all this attention responded in character; McCarthy denounced the new committee as the "involuntary agent" of the Communist party. Even his remaining admirers in the Senate couldn't sit still for the accusation that some of their fellow legislators were Communist stooges, and at the end of September, the Watkins Committee recommended censure. The next step would be for the full Senate to vote on the resolution, a move which was postponed until after Election Day. There was no point in taking any chances.

Although McCarthy's popularity had dropped dramatically, he still had a number of zealous supporters. At a rally for his cause held in Madison Square Garden in New York, one speaker said that for the Senate to vote censure would be "the blackest act in our whole history." Feelings in the audience ran high. A woman who was photographing the event for *Life* magazine, scarcely a left-wing publication, was led out amid cries of "Hang the Communist." Many Democratic candidates across the country found themselves the target of McCarthy-like smears. One radio commercial featured a voice with a Russian accent saying, "Defeat the Republican congressional candidates in 1954! That is an order from Moscow!" Vice-President Nixon, campaigning nationwide, sounded McCarthy's familiar warning that Democrats tolerated internal subversion. The tactic didn't work, and on November 2 Republicans lost control of the House and Senate. True to form, McCarthy said the Democrats had won because of the failure of their opponents to speak out against Communist infiltration of the government. The people of America, however, had spoken loud and clear on their ballots. And since the nation had apparently renounced McCarthyism, the Senate would finally act in the matter of McCarthy himself.

WANTED—A good, reliable woman to take the care of a boy two years old, in a small family in Brookline. Good wages and a permanent situation given. No washing or ironing will be required, but good recommendations as to character and capacity demanded. Postively no Irish need apply. Call at 224 Washington street, corner of Summer street.

6t   jy 28

The infamous "NINA" ads were designed to keep the immigrants in their place. But two young Irishmen found a way around the Yankee barricades: P.J. (left) with a slow and steady climb to power that began behind the bar of his saloon, Honey Fitz in a frontal assault on Boston political institutions.

Rose Fitzgerald spurned suitors such as Thomas Lipton, the wealthy tea magnate, in order to marry Joe Kennedy. Although their wedding united two of the city's most powerful families, it received little coverage in local papers. Irish social events were not considered suitable for inclusion among the activities of proper Boston society.

This dreamy photograph of Rose with Joe Jr., Jack and Rosemary does not reflect her mental anguish at the time. Depressed by Joe's absences because of work, and by gossip about his womanizing, Rose moved back in with her parents for several weeks. Only after Honey Fitz gave her a stern lecture on honoring her commitment to Joe and the children did Rose return to Brookline.

After Jean's birth, Joe gave Rose a diamond bracelet. Although he teasingly told his wife he would "give her a black eye" if they had a ninth baby, Teddy was born four years later. This time Rose got a trip to Europe.

Rose's famous index cards. When she was a young mother, the file helped her keep track of nine children's vital statistics. Years later, it lent a homey touch to her campaign speeches.

The heir apparent with the rival to his throne. Years after the older boy's death, Jack admitted that the only problem of his childhood had been Joe Jr.'s "pugnacious personality."

Rose must surely have had a conniption when she saw that the "Most Likely to Succeed" in Choate's class of 1935 had posed for his graduation picture in saddle oxfords.

Jack and Lem Billings during their 1937 tour of Europe. The trip ended with Jack's violent illness — this time an allergic reaction to the little dachshund he and Lem had bought in Germany.

The Kennedys. Seated: Eunice, Jean, Teddy, Joe, Pat,
Kick. Standing: Rosemary, Bobby, Jack, Rose, Joe Jr.
Of these nine children, one would be mentally retarded,
one would die in a freakish wartime accident, one in an
airplane crash, and two by assassination. When Teddy
was almost killed in a 1964 plane crash, Bobby said,
"There's more of us than there is trouble." Four years
later, he himself was shot to death.

On September 3, 1939, Joe Jr., Kick and Jack hurried to the House of Commons to hear Prime Minister Chamberlain declare war on Nazi Germany. Joe Kennedy encouraged his children to observe history in the making — and to make history themselves.

Jack donated most of the royalties from his 1940 best-seller to assist the bomb-ravaged city of Plymouth, England. He also used a portion of the earnings to buy a green Buick convertible. The book — and the car — made him Big Man on Campus during his brief stay at Stanford.

Jack in the Solomon Islands, 1943. Even then, Red Fay and Barney Ross were making bets that their friend would one day be President of the United States. The officers in Jack's PT boat squadron would meet in his quarters to hear him talk about the war, international affairs, and politics. "We enjoyed it more than playing poker," Fay said.

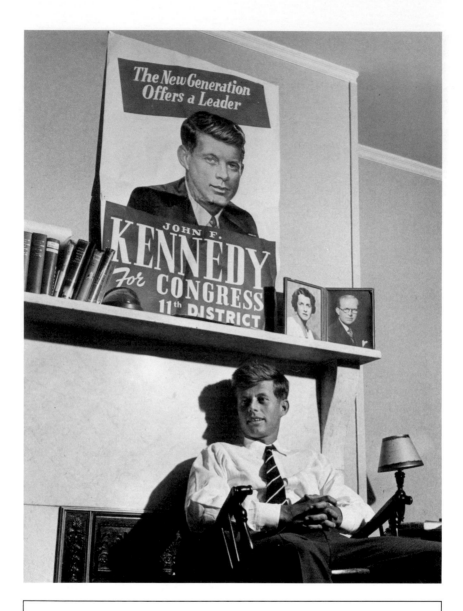

In 1946, Jack's political career began in a typically disorganized fashion. Ninety minutes after the deadline, an aide realized that Jack had never filed his papers. The leader of the new generation charmed — and bribed — a clerk to open the filing office, thus enabling the candidate's name to appear on a ballot for the first time.

Under the watchful eye of Rose Kennedy, her son makes a campaign appearance on crutches. Jack seldom complained about his agonizing back pain. "It all depends on the weather," he would say, "— political and otherwise."

Jack's 1952 Senate campaign included commercial broadcasts called "Coffee with the Kennedys," featuring the candidate with his mother and three youngest sisters. The family brought a new sophistication to politics by using opinion polling, specialized advisory personnel, and television. But as Eunice demonstrates, the cornier gimmicks were not overlooked.

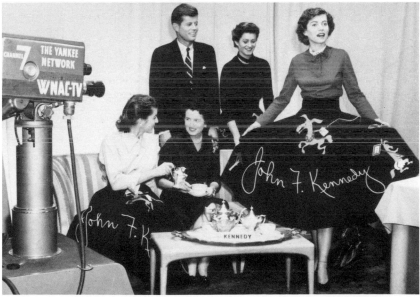

As a child, Jacqueline had predicted she would grow up to become *"queen of the circus"* and marry *"the man on the flying trapeze."* Her wedding proved to be something of a circus, as the smiling and radiant bride gave not a hint that she was heartbroken over Jack Bouvier's absence. Much of Jacqueline's adulthood would be spent concealing her emotions.

1956
DEMOCRATIC
NATIONAL

Chicago, 1956. This was the moment, an observer said, when Jack Kennedy passed through a kind of political sound barrier and into the American consciousness.

Bobby and Jack, shown at a meeting of the "Rackets Committee," found themselves increasingly in the news during the late 1950s. The committee's hearings also led to a great deal of publicity for its chairman. When Bobby was asked if he would support Senator McClellan for president, he smilingly replied that McClellan would be his second choice.

When asked the best site for the 1960 Democratic national convention, Jackie suggested "Acapulco." Hoping to avoid another miscarriage, she did not attend the convention in Los Angeles, where — as this newspaper headline shows — her husband easily won the nomination. Some observers thought Jackie wasn't really pregnant, and that instead, the Kennedys were afraid she was too chic to expose to the American public. She offered to stuff a pillow in her dress to convince the doubters.

Although they realized there would be many advantages to a Kennedy/Johnson ticket, few of JFK's supporters wanted LBJ (left) to accept the vice-presidential nomination. When Jack told his brother, "You won't believe it. He wants it!" Bobby exclaimed, "Oh my God! Now what do we do?"

In early December 1954, a resolution condemning his conduct was passed, with twenty-two Republicans voting for the measure, twenty-two against. McCarthy himself simply voted "present." Of the forty-four Democrats in attendance, all supported the resolution. Jack Kennedy did not take part in the proceedings. He was in the New York Hospital for Special Surgery.

After his statement four years earlier that Joe McCarthy might "have something," Jack had begun to reconsider that view. Since then, he had neither given the Wisconsin senator public encouragement nor expressed any of the beliefs held by McCarthy's supporters regarding patriotism or civil liberties. Jack had voted against McCarthy protégés nominated for government appointments, and had backed those of whom McCarthy disapproved. Yet in spite of their ideological differences, Joe McCarthy was a subject on which Jack was vulnerable.

There was the fact that his brother had briefly worked for McCarthy's subcommittee, an appointment engineered by Joe Kennedy. Bobby had resigned after only a few months, sure that the Wisconsin senator was "headed for disaster." But although Bobby had left the subcommittee, there remained the problem of their father. Joe's own views had put Jack on the spot more than once, and his friendship with McCarthy compounded the dilemma. The two were very much alike: affable men who often behaved abominably and were surprised when someone took it personally. After a lifetime of exposure to his father, Jack not only understood McCarthy but had great fondness for him—no less so when he was under fire. Although Jack condemned McCarthy's methods, he would never renounce the man himself.

For those of liberal beliefs, it had once been prudent to keep a low profile on the subject of Joe McCarthy; now it had become safe and even fashionable to openly despise him. People of such varying political philosophies as Eleanor Roosevelt and President Eisenhower likened McCarthy to Hitler. Yet the Kennedys would never turn their backs on a man who had been their friend. Although condemnation by the Senate carried no penalty, the humiliation alone had been enough to turn McCarthy from a heavy drinker into an alcoholic. When McCarthy eventually died of cirrhosis, Bobby was at the funeral in Wisconsin, and both Jack and Bobby stayed in touch with McCarthy's widow. Even after his death, no Kennedy would renounce the senator. "In case there is any question in your mind," Joe defiantly told an interviewer, "I liked Joe McCarthy." The Kennedy attitude wasn't very smart politically, but it showed the family's fierce loyalty—even to a person who would haunt Jack for the rest of his life.

Yet at the time, McCarthy's role in Jack Kennedy's future seemed insignificant. In late October 1954, political controversy was of no importance when compared to the fact that Jack apparently would not live to pursue his ambitions.

Surgeons had been reluctant to perform the back operation, since Jack ran a high risk of shock or infection. But although he was warned his chances of survival were fifty-fifty at best, Jack had insisted on going ahead. The spinal fusion itself appeared to be successful; then, as the doctors had feared, a urinary tract infection developed and Jack slipped into a coma. Shortly afterward, Joe Kennedy went to the office of Arthur Krock, where he broke down. It was the only time, Krock later commented, that Joe had shown an emotion that equaled his response to the death of Joe Jr. Now it appeared certain the Kennedys would lose their second son as well. On two occasions, the family was summoned and Jack received the last rites of the Catholic Church.

But gradually, Joe said, Jack "fought his way out of it" and began to hold his own. The Kennedys' mood changed to one of cautious optimism and then to joy. The gamble had evidently paid off. Still, there was a long recuperation ahead, and Jack would be in the hospital for another two months. A friend described his room as coming to resemble one in a college dormitory. There was a tank of tropical fish on the windowsill, a Howdy Doody doll on the bed, a poster of Marilyn Monroe on the wall. Jackie dropped in every few hours to play checkers or Monopoly, bringing news and gossip, blowing up balloons which Jack used as targets for the popgun she had bought him. Although his Washington office announced Jack was too ill to confront the issue of Joe McCarthy, he was apparently well enough to have company. He was visited by a succession of young women, all of whom, Jack told the bemused hospital staff, were "cousins."

In mid-December, Jack was released to go to his parents' Palm Beach home. By then, McCarthy's Senate condemnation was over. If Jack had been present, he could certainly not have stood alone as the only Democrat to support the Wisconsin senator, so the hospital stay had seemed the most graceful way to avoid casting a vote. But Jack was well aware no one was fooled by the timing of the operation. Even though he was leaving the hospital on a stretcher, Jack knew reporters would be waiting to question him. "When I get downstairs I know exactly what's going to happen," he told a friend. "There's going to be about ninety-five faces bent over me with great concern, and every one of those guys is going to say, 'Now Senator, what about McCarthy?' You know what I'm going to do? I'm going to reach for my back and I'm just going to yell 'Ow,' and then I'm going to pull the sheet over my head and hope we can get out of there."

With Jacqueline walking alongside his stretcher, Jack made his escape and was flown to Florida. It was not a merry Christmas. The Kennedys spent the holidays anxiously watching for some improvement in Jack's back. He was in a great deal of pain, and as weeks passed, it appeared the operation had not only failed to do any good but that Jack might never walk again. There was even talk that he might have to give up his seat in the Senate. Lem Billings took a month's leave of absence from his job to be with Jack. "It was a terrible time," Lem said. "We came close to losing him. I don't just mean losing his life. I mean losing him as a *person*." Yet for all of Jack's pessimism about the future, he didn't often let others see his despair. Joe likened his son to Rose. "I don't think I know anyone who has more courage than my wife," he reflected. "In all the years that we have been married, I have never heard her complain. Never. Not even once. That is a quality that children are quick to see."

Jack needed the strong example set by his mother when he learned that a second and equally risky surgical procedure was necessary. A silver plate which had been put in his back during the previous operation had obviously made his condition worse. Now doctors had decided to remove the plate and do a bone graft instead. By February 1955, Jack was in the hospital again. Jackie tried everything she could to cheer her husband. On one occasion she asked actress Grace Kelly to wear a nurse's uniform and feed Jack his meal. Jack was so ill he barely noticed her, and the beautiful movie star told Jackie, "I must be losing it."

For two weeks the Kennedys were again afraid their son wouldn't pull through. Then he began to get better, and Joe was ecstatic. "I know nothing can happen to him now," he told Dave Powers, "because I've stood by his deathbed three times and each time I said good-bye to him, and each time he came back stronger." But mending was a slow process. A hopeful bulletin, released when Jack left the hospital, announced he planned to return to the Senate late in March. It would actually take two months longer, and in Palm Beach part of the house was converted to something like a hospital wing to accommodate Jack's lagging recovery. It was set back even further when a loose screw in one of his crutches resulted in a bad fall. For several weeks Jack was in such pain that he could sleep for no more than an hour or two at a stretch, so he used the time to study. "That's where the book came from," Joe proudly explained. The book was *Profiles in Courage.*

When Jack got back to Washington at the end of May, he publicly revealed he had spent his convalescence writing a collection of biographies about eight senators who had listened to their consciences instead of their constituents in supporting unpopular causes. During the long months in Palm Beach, Jack's room had been piled high with reference works from the Library of Congress. When he was too tired or in too much pain to write, Jackie read aloud to him. Writing itself was an exhausting process, since Jack had to work lying on a board with another board propped up in front of him which he used as a desk. From this uncomfortable position, he had roughed out his theme on legal pads. But the final result would not be the effort of a single author.

From the beginning of Jack's first draft, Ted Sorensen had done research in Washington and worked on the manuscript in Palm Beach. Historians such as Arthur Schlesinger, Jr., were consulted for suggestions. Dr. Jules Davids, the professor who had taught Jackie's American history course at Georgetown University, was brought in to contribute his ideas. By the end of the summer, the book had been revised, reworked, and rewritten by several people. Leaving Ted Sorensen to pull it all together, Jack and Jacqueline went to Europe in August.

So far, 1955 had been a difficult year for both of them. During Jack's convalescence, Jackie had seldom left his bedside. She changed his dressings several times a day, put on his socks and slippers, played games with him, helped him in and out of bed, and slept in a small room next to his. Jackie paid a high price for the months in which she served as a round-the-clock nurse and companion to her husband. As Jack had begun to improve, Jackie had suffered a miscarriage. The trip, it was thought, would do them both a lot of good. But almost immediately, the back problem flared up again. In Rome, where Jack had an audience with the pope, he was photographed on crutches. He had used them, Jack quipped, because he was afraid he couldn't kneel gracefully enough. In spite of the pain, his office announced Jack would go on to Warsaw, to study "conditions in Communist Poland." From there, the Kennedys visited Paris and Dublin before returning home in mid-October.

As soon as they arrived, Jack saw a doctor, who prescribed massive injections of novocaine to relieve his discomfort. The treatment seemed to work, and for the first time since the sinking of PT 109, Jack was free from pain. But he had no sooner given up his crutches than Jackie was on crutches herself. In November, she retired without regret from her brief career in touch football after suffering a broken ankle on the lawn in Hyannis Port. When the Kennedys went to Palm Beach for the holidays, the couple agreed they were glad to see 1955 coming to an end.

The new year began with the publication of *Profiles in Courage*. Its preface made note of Ted Sorensen's "invaluable assistance" and of Jacqueline's "help during all the days of my convalescence." The book, also dedicated to Jackie, was an instant success. The *New York Times* marveled that a politician had written so thoughtfully and persuasively "about political integrity." The review concluded that Jack had restored "respect for a vulnerable and much abused profession." In Boston, *Profiles in Courage* was made required reading in the city's schools. Just as with *Why England Slept*, Jack had come up with the right book at the right time.

A frightened nation needed reassurance that at least some of those in government could find a way to stand tough against the Communists. Jack had taken up that very theme, stating in his first chapter that "In the days ahead, only the very courageous will be able to take the hard and unpopular decisions necessary for our survival in the struggle with a powerful enemy." Many had also been dismayed by the reluctance of politicians to speak out against the extremes of McCarthyism, so Jack's closing stuck just the right note for the future: "A man does what he must—in spite of personal consequences, in spite of obstacles and dangers and pressures—and that is the basis of all human morality." His stories of historical bravery could not "supply courage itself. For this," the book concluded, "each man must look into his own soul." The American reading public, delighted to be reminded they did, after all, live in a country with brave and decent leaders, made *Profiles in Courage* a best-seller. A year later, to complete Jack's triumph, the book was awarded the Pulitzer Prize.

The literary success of *Profiles in Courage* seemed quite a coup for its ambitious author, but in the long run Jack might have been better off if the book had received a little less attention. During the period in which it was written, Jack Kennedy had been first a very sick and then a very busy man. To many who were aware of Jack's schedule, it seemed unlikely he could have undergone two life-threatening operations, made a long and difficult recovery, reestablished himself in Washington, toured Europe, kept up his political obligations in Massachusetts, accepted a number of speaking engagements, and still have found time to write. Then the charge was made publicly. On the *Mike Wallace Show*, ABC Television broadcast an allegation that the book had been written by someone else, and although the program didn't come right out and say so, most people believed the "someone else" was Ted Sorensen.

Jack was irate. *Profiles in Courage* was a tribute to integrity, and now the honesty of its author was being questioned. Obviously such a charge had to be answered. Sorensen made a sworn statement that he had not been the author, and ABC apologized on the next *Mike Wallace Show*. To make sure the retraction said exactly what Jack wanted it to say, it had been written for ABC—by Ted Sorensen. But questions of the book's authorship would continue to hound Jack throughout his career. When he was asked about the matter more than twenty years later, Sorensen chose his words carefully and replied, "The concept of the book was Kennedy's. The responsibility for the book was Kennedy's. The decision as to which individuals, which individual stories should go in the book were all made by Kennedy." He concluded by saying, "the philosophy expressed in the opening and closing chapters" was Kennedy's.

Jack's difficulties with the book went beyond the question of who had written it. No one had dreamed that its title would make Jack the butt of a joke about his handling of the matter of Joe McCarthy. But Eleanor Roosevelt made a pun which would be repeated over and over again whenever Jack seemed to dodge a difficult problem. By avoiding the vote of censure, she said, Senator Kennedy had shown "too much profile and not enough courage." Yet Jack displayed plenty of both when he moved to take over the Massachusetts Democratic party.

11

THE HERO
OF THE HOUR

As the 1956 national convention in Chicago drew closer, Jack announced he would support the second presidential candidacy of Adlai Stevenson. To some extent, this decision was influenced by the fact that Stevenson was considering Jack as his vice-presidential running mate. A Stevenson/Kennedy ticket would have advantages for both men. The vice-presidential nomination would bring Jack national prominence, while Stevenson thought Kennedy would appeal to young voters and attract conservative Irish Catholics who disagreed with his own liberal philosophy. Since Stevenson was divorced, having a Catholic on the ticket would take some of the sting out of that issue. But the religious factor could backfire: traditional political wisdom had it that a Catholic could not win national office. For Jack, there was a further problem which might influence Stevenson against him. The Democratic party in Massachusetts, with powerful House Majority Leader John McCormack as its head, was anti-Stevenson. In order to deliver his state to the candidate of his choice, Jack needed to control its delegates.

Joe Kennedy had no enthusiasm for Jack's becoming involved with either the local fight or the national ticket. "Leave it alone and don't get into the gutter with those bums up there in Boston," Joe told his son. He was adamant that Jack should not seek the vice-presidency. Eisenhower was immensely popular, and "Adlai," Joe said, is "going to take a licking." His loss might be blamed on a Catholic running mate, which would make Jack's chances of someday winning the presidential nomination for himself all the more difficult. In four years, however, Eisenhower would step down at the end of his second term; not until then, Joe thought, should Jack seek higher office. Uncharacteristically, Jack ignored his father's advice and went ahead with his own plans. Although he cautioned aides Kenny O'Donnell and Larry O'Brien not to "mention my name to anybody," he told them to lay the groundwork for taking over the Massachusetts State Democratic Committee.

In 1952, Joe Kennedy had given the *Boston Post* a half-million-dollar loan to guarantee the paper's support of his son's senatorial candidacy. But in spite of Kennedy's financial assistance, Jack had since fallen from favor with its publisher, John Fox, an ardent anti-communist. Jack's lack of enthusiasm for McCarthyism and his support of the St. Lawrence Seaway had finished him off with the publisher. When Jack came out for Stevenson, Fox used a tactic learned from his idol, Joe McCarthy: in one front-page editorial after another, the *Post* said both Kennedy and Stevenson had social-ist tendencies. Fox didn't stop there. Massachusetts Democrats were able to indicate their preference of a presidential nominee in the April 1956 primary, and the paper mounted a write-in campaign for John McCormack, who ended up with ten thousand more votes than Stevenson. Jack's venture into the local political battle seemed to be headed for disaster. While the *Post* was still relishing its Primary Day triumph, "Onions" Burke was the next to be heard from.

Burke was an onion farmer, a friend of John McCormack and James Curley, and the chairman of the Democratic State Committee. Riding the crest of McCormack's strong showing against the liberal Stevenson, Burke went a little too far for his own good and publicly implied that Senator Kennedy was soft on communism. This was too much for Jack, who quickly changed his mind about keeping his name out of the power play. "The gloves," Kenny O'Donnell said, "came off." And the fight got just as messy as Joe Kennedy had predicted it would. Getting a new chairman was Jack's first priority; Burke responded by saying he would have Kennedy's brains knocked out. Jack counterattacked by telling a reporter he intended to have Burke removed from the chairmanship. Curley announced Jack had offered him a bribe to resign from the Democratic National Com-mittee, but said "he hasn't got enough money to buy me." McCormack said he was behind Burke "one thousand percent," and added he would consider it a personal affront if Onions did not stay on as chairman.

Local newspapers were fascinated. Jack's "sudden entry into an intra-party dispute is a major change of character," said the *Worcester Telegram*, "and once having taken the plunge, it is difficult to see how he can withdraw." If Burke did win out, Jack Kennedy was going to look like a fool—a Massachusetts senator with no influence in Massachusetts politics. Jack had unenthusiastically put up a candidate for the chairmanship, John "Pat" Lynch, a typical Irish politician of the sort Jack had always taken pains to avoid. But the committee, Kenny O'Donnell said, would only accept a regular like Lynch. "They don't want you pushing one of your bright new faces down their throats," Kenny told Jack. "They want an old familiar face."

The date of the showdown was May 19, 1956, and its timing could not have been less convenient for Jack. That morning, his sister Jean was being married to Stephen Smith, a wealthy business executive. The wedding would be held at St. Patrick's Cathedral in New York City, followed by a reception at the Plaza Hotel, and Jack simply couldn't duck the major family event. But Kenny O'Donnell told Jack he had to stay in Boston, to woo the delegates before their meeting at the Hotel Bradford. Jack decided he would somehow do everything expected of him. Early in the day he flew to New York, where he served as an usher at the wedding. By mid-afternoon he was back in Boston, charming delegates. Just before the start of the meeting, he returned to New York and joined Jacqueline at the reception. As Jack sipped champagne at the Plaza, the battle raged at the Bradford.

Two off-duty policemen had been hired to keep order, but there was still shoving and pushing, which threatened to disintegrate into an Irish free-for-all. When the smoke cleared after what Jack called "a brawl of monumental proportions," Pat Lynch had won by sixteen votes. As soon as Jack heard the news, he asked O'Donnell to have Lynch issue a statement that the day had been "a great victory in Massachusetts for Adlai Stevenson." Lynch quickly dismissed that idea. "Let's not try to kid anybody. This is no victory for Adlai Stevenson," he told Kenny. "This is a victory for John F. Kennedy and nobody else."

Jack followed up on his triumph in the state committee by calling a meeting of the delegates to the national convention, who elected him their leader. Realizing the importance of making peace with John McCormack, he agreed to let the influential majority leader be nominated as a "favorite son" on the first ballot, after which Massachusetts would switch to Stevenson, if a second ballot was necessary. With everything under control in his home state, Jack took off for California to work on a project that would play an important part in his becoming the new political star of 1956. He had been chosen to narrate the convention's opening event, a documentary on the history of the Democratic party. Dore Schary, the film's producer as well as a delegate, was delighted with Jack's contribution. "All of us who were in contact with him immediately fell in love with him," Schary said, "because he was so quick and so charming and so cooperative and obviously so bright and so skilled." Having wowed them in Hollywood, Jack moved on to Chicago and more rave reviews.

The convention in mid-August was the occasion for a gathering of much of the Kennedy clan. Confident that Jack would heed his warning to stay out of the vice-presidential race, Joe departed with Rose for their annual summer vacation on the Riviera. But most of Joe's children were in Chicago, and all of them, it turned out, were more than ready to ignore their father's advice. Only sister Pat, now married to movie actor Peter Lawford, and eight months pregnant, was missing. Although Jackie, too, was expecting, she had come along to be part of the excitement. Jackie spent the week with Eunice and her husband of three years, Sargent Shriver—Jack's old friend from Canterbury who now oversaw his father-in-law's financial plum, the Chicago Merchandise Mart. Kenny O'Donnell was also part of the entourage, and roomed with Bobby at the Ambassador East Hotel. Jack, sharing a suite with Ted Sorensen, had started the week at the Drake in downtown Chicago; when it soon became obvious he was going to play one of the leading roles at the convention, Jack moved to another hotel nearer the site of the action.

The documentary had been a smash hit, although not in the way convention organizers had intended. The viewers, expected to swell with pride at the film's glorification of the Democratic party, had instead noticed only the charisma of its narrator. "Kennedy came before the convention tonight as a movie star," reported the *New York Times*. Jack received a huge ovation from the delegates, who were immediately abuzz with speculation about his appeal as a vice-presidential candidate.

The impact of Jack's appearance, however, went far beyond the impression he made on the delegates. Before 1956, television had had only minimal use in American politics. That year marked its beginning as a national political tool, and no candidate for office was ever better suited to the medium than Jack Kennedy. Millions watching on television saw for the first time a charming, handsome Massachusetts senator, so different from their image of politicians who made deals in smoke-filled back rooms. Still, politics were usually conducted in just that way, and Jack wasn't reluctant to take part in wheeling and dealing behind the scenes.

Until he came to Chicago, Jack was unsure whether or not he would press for the nomination as vice-president. But when he saw how the delegates responded to him, he began to get more intrigued. "I think he just wanted to put his foot in the water," Bobby said later, "and see how cold it was, but he hadn't made up his mind to swim." Jack decided he would first test the waters of Democratic power on a visit to one of his toughest critics, Eleanor Roosevelt. Mrs. Roosevelt was a fervent supporter of Adlai Stevenson, and her approval would assure Jack of a chance to get his name on the ticket. That hope soon died when Mrs. Roosevelt used the meeting as an opportunity to chide Jack on his attitude toward Joe McCarthy. Then Bobby suggested Jack plead his case to Stevenson himself. That didn't work out either. Instead of an offer of the vice-presidency, Stevenson asked Jack to give the speech placing his name in nomination. The request meant Stevenson wasn't going to choose Jack as his running mate, since convention protocol held that the person who gave the presidential nominating speech was never selected for the second spot on the ticket.

Jack was annoyed. Stevenson had been dangling the vice-presidential bait for months; now he had obviously decided to choose someone else. An aide later commented that the last-minute decision caused the Kennedys to regard Stevenson with "an attitude of coolness and irritation" that would persist long after 1956, and ultimately do little for Stevenson's public aspirations. But that August, Adlai Stevenson was in charge, and Jack had to abide by his decision.

Still, the nominating speech was no small consolation prize. It was a chance to further impress the delegates as well as the national television audience, and Jack wasn't going to waste the opportunity by giving a speech Stevenson had already had prepared. By the next day, Jack and Ted Sorensen were ready with their own version. The speech proved to be another great success. Delegates and journalists alike were enchanted, and one reporter summed up the reaction of many by describing Jack as "terribly thin, terribly tired, and terribly handsome."

After being nominated on the first ballot, Stevenson made an unusual request. He had been persistently criticized throughout his career for being indecisive, and Stevenson proved the critics right once again when he addressed the convention. Trying to conceal uncertainty behind high-minded sentiment, he announced that instead of selecting his own running mate, he would leave the decision to the delegates. "The choice will be yours," Stevenson said. "The profit will be the nation's." It was too great a temptation for the young senator who had spent the week being mobbed in his hotel lobby, on the streets, and at the convention; Jack decided to defy his father and fight for the nomination. Surrounded by advisors new to national politics, and with little more than twelve hours to get organized, Jack nevertheless was going to "swim."

Although his name was not as well known as the other vice presidential aspirants—senators Estes Kefauver and Albert Gore of Tennessee, and Hubert Humphrey of Minnesota—Jack felt there was cause for optimism. Within a few days he had not only dazzled people at the convention but throughout the city of Chicago as well. Even Bobby, en route to a strategy session on how to get the nomination, was asked for his autograph because he was "Jack Kennedy's brother." Bobby's elation at that request did not survive past the first few minutes of the meeting.

As soon as he arrived, Jack asked Bobby to call their father in France: "Tell him I'm going for it." The news sent Joe Kennedy into a rage. He thought he had already made it clear why the nomination could hurt Jack's career, and he thought Jack had seen the wisdom of his arguments. Now, six thousand miles away, Joe learned otherwise. Kenny O'Donnell, who was in the room while Bobby phoned, said even he could hear Joe's "blue language." Joe's gentlest comment was that Jack was "an idiot," which, Rose later commented, he said "vigorously." When they were accidentally cut off, Bobby made no attempt to get his father back on the line. "Whew!" he shakily told O'Donnell. "Is he mad!" Although there was nothing Joe Kennedy hated more than losing, he was relieved when word reached him that Estes Kefauver had been selected as the vice-presidential candidate.

On the other side of the Atlantic, however, there was bitter disappointment. Jack had been within thirty-eight votes of the nomination when, on the second ballot, Albert Gore threw his support to his fellow senator from Tennessee and put Kefauver over the top. Jack had silently watched the outcome on television in his hotel room, then turned to Ted Sorensen and said "Let's go." When he arrived at the convention, the delegates greeted his appearance with a roar, which grew louder as Jack made his way to the rostrum. "Ladies and gentlemen of this convention," he said, "I want to take this opportunity to express my appreciation to Democrats from all parts of the country, north and south, east and west, who have been so kind to me this afternoon." Jack then asked the delegates to make Kefauver's nomination unanimous—an appeal for Democratic unity which delighted the crowd and which for television audiences was, a reporter said, "a moment of magic they would never forget."

In spite of Jack's graciousness, he was angry and frustrated. Commenting to a friend, he compared himself to "the Indian who had a lot of arrows stuck in him . . . It only hurts when I laugh." Coming from a state with a large Catholic vote, Jack was surprised that the issue of his religion, as Joe had warned, seemed to be a factor in his loss. The only good thing about it was that the defeat had taken place in Chicago, rather than in the nationwide disaster Joe had feared. When Jack finally got up the nerve to call his father, he quickly assured Joe, "We did our best. I had fun and I didn't make a fool of myself." Joe, however, wanted to know all the details, and requested that his son join him in France. He also suggested that Bobby accompany Stevenson around the country to get an insider's view of a presidential campaign.

Bobby made the most of the six weeks he spent traveling with the Democratic candidate, and what he observed, the young man decided, was that Stevenson did everything the wrong way. "You wouldn't believe it," Bobby confided to Kenny O'Donnell. "This is the most disastrous operation you ever saw. He gives an elaborate speech on world affairs to a group of twenty-five coal miners standing on a railroad track in West Virginia." Bobby had begun the tour admiring Stevenson. He ended it by dismissing the candidate with ten damning words in his private journal: "Stevenson was just not a man of action at all." That, to a Kennedy, was possibly the worst thing one could say about a person. By contrast, Bobby thought admiringly, Jack had taken action in Chicago. And although he lost the vice-presidential nomination, even Joe had to admit his son had emerged a winner. "Don't feel sorry for young Jack Kennedy," the *Boston Herald* reported. "Despite his second ballot defeat, he probably rates as the one real victor of the entire convention. . . . His charisma, his dignity, his intellectuality, and, in the end, his gracious sportsmanship . . . are undoubtedly what those delegates will remember. So will those who watched it and heard it via TV and radio."

The story was not just the wishful thinking of Jack's hometown newspaper. Even Adlai Stevenson had immediate misgivings about not naming Jack as his running mate. "I have a feeling that he was the real hero of the hour," Stevenson said, "and that we shall hear a great deal more from this promising young man." Although Stevenson realized too late Jack's potential value to the national ticket, he was quick to recognize what an asset it would be to have the "hero of the hour" working for his candidacy. When Jack returned from France, he obliged by giving 150 campaign speeches across the country—an exhausting effort made more on his own behalf than Adlai Stevenson's. By selecting key states in which to make his appearances, Jack seemed a selfless campaigner while ingratiating himself with the most powerful leaders in the Democratic party. Although Stevenson was buried by an Eisenhower landslide on Election Day, no one could say Senator John F. Kennedy hadn't done his best to prevent it.

After a decade of staying out of party politics, Jack had at last gotten into the thick of it. He had taken control of the state committee in Massachusetts, he had galvanized the delegates in Chicago, he had befriended important Democrats all across the country. And somewhere along the way he had emerged from the shadow of Joe Jr. Commenting to a reporter on the events of that summer and fall, Jack had begun with the seemingly obligatory recognition of his older brother's superiority. "Joe was the star of our family. He did everything better than the rest of us. If he had lived, he would have gone on in politics and he would have been elected to the House and Senate as I was. And, like me, he would have gone for the vice-presidential nomination at the 1956 convention, but, unlike me, he wouldn't have been beaten. Joe would have won the nomination." Jack paused and grinned. His brother's spell was broken. "And then he and Stevenson would have been beaten by Eisenhower, and today Joe's political career would be in a shambles and he would be trying to pick up the pieces."

Jack Kennedy faced no such dilemma. Instead of the fragments of a shattered career, Jack told Dave Powers, he was going to pick up "all of the marbles." Flirtation with the vice-presidency had come and gone. Only one office interested Jack now, and that goal seemed within reach. But the road to the White House could be blocked by a personal problem: Jack's marriage was in real trouble.

Both Jack and Jacqueline had left Chicago on August 18, completely worn out from the tension and excitement of the convention.

But more than fatigue was troubling Jackie; after having a miscarriage the previous year, the thought that the same thing could happen again was very much on her mind. Despite the fact that the baby was due at the end of September, the Kennedys went their separate ways: Jacqueline to Rhode Island to stay with her mother, Jack to France to see his father. The convention had not turned out so badly, after all, and although he was exhausted, Jack was in a good mood. "I see Dad's roughing it again this year," he said wryly as he entered Joe's rented mansion with its staff of servants. The brief visit went well. Newspaper coverage of the convention had by then reached the Riviera, and Joe's anger at Jack's defiance in seeking the vice-presidency had been replaced with giddy optimism that the ultimate prize would be won in 1960. After spending two days reviewing events in Chicago and conferring on plans for the future, Joe told his son good-bye—all but patting Jack on the head as he said, "God is still with you and you can still be president if you want to and if you work hard."

Having received his father's blessing, Jack went off to spend the rest of his vacation on a yacht with his brother Teddy, Florida senator George Smathers, and other friends. As Jack cruised the Mediterranean, Jackie went into premature labor. She was admitted to a Newport hospital on August 23, where she gave birth to a stillborn baby girl. When Jackie regained consciousness, Bobby was sitting by her bed. "You knew that if you were in trouble, he'd always be there," Jackie later said of her brother-in-law. The same could not be said of her husband, whom the family was unable to reach. Not until the yacht put into port at Genoa, Italy, on August 26 did Jack learn that Jackie had suffered another miscarriage. Even then he seemed in no hurry to leave the yachting party, but George Smathers convinced Jack that his future political hopes would go right down the drain along with a broken marriage, advising him to get "back to your wife if you ever want to run for president." Two days later, Jack came home.

Although Jackie had stayed by her husband's bedside for months following his surgery, he had been five thousand miles away when she most needed him. But just three weeks after he returned, Jack again left his wife at Hammersmith Farm and spent the next two months on the road, campaigning for Adlai Stevenson. Even Charles Bartlett wished that, for Jackie's sake, he had never introduced her to Jack. Bartlett said Jack was "a lousy husband" who had inherited not only his father's brains but Joe's "love for women" as well. And that, he added, "doesn't really go to make a very happy marriage."

Gossip was an integral part of political life, so almost no one was surprised when a Washington columnist broke the news that Senator and Mrs. John F. Kennedy had separated.

Knowing full well what effect a divorce would have on Jack's plans for the presidency, Joe flew back to the United States to negotiate a reconciliation. Jackie was close to her father-in-law; they had become good friends during Jack's convalescence in Palm Beach and she found it easy to confide in him. Next to her husband and her own father, Jackie said of Joe, "I love him more than anybody— more than anybody in the world." It was probably her fondness for Joe that convinced Jackie to stay in the marriage, although a rumor soon began making the rounds that even Joe Kennedy could not persuade his daughter-in-law until he had offered her a million-dollar bribe.

Whatever Joe did, it worked. After the election in November 1956, Jack and Jackie took a vacation together in Europe. When they returned to Washington, the couple agreed that two miscarriages seemed to make their chances of having children very slim. The Virginia home, where Jacqueline had fixed up a nursery, now seemed too large and rambling, so the Kennedys again rented a house in Georgetown and sold Hickory Hill to Bobby, whose own family had grown to include two daughters and three sons. Then, early in 1957, Jackie learned she was pregnant for a third time. When Caroline Bouvier Kennedy was born in November, Jack was ecstatic. He had turned forty the previous May and had given up hope of ever being a father. In that role people saw a whole new Jack Kennedy. His well-known detachment, his habit of always seeming a little removed, vanished when he was around his daughter. After a long period of frustration and illness, everything had finally started to go right in 1957. But Caroline's birth in November was what made it a perfect year.

THE RISE
OF THE
BROTHERS KENNEDY

Nineteen fifty-seven was personally and professionally the most exciting time Jack had ever known. He was now regarded as the front-runner for the Democratic party's 1960 presidential nomination. After two years of strain, his marriage had begun to work, and Caroline gave him and Jackie renewed hope for their future together. That same year Jack was awarded the Pulitzer Prize for *Profiles in Courage*, and, in an accomplishment that most impressed his father, was chosen to sit on the Harvard Board of Overseers. "Now I know his religion won't keep him out of the White House," Joe told Kenny O'Donnell. "If an Irish Catholic can get elected as an Overseer at Harvard, he can get elected to anything." For a first-term senator, Jack was also the focus of an amazing amount of national press coverage. Everyone, it seemed, was avid for information about the man who had come to such enthusiastic public attention through the televised convention the previous summer.

He was featured in a *Time* magazine cover story, which stated that "Jack Kennedy has left panting politicians and swooning women across a large spread of the U.S." *The Saturday Evening Post* reported that Kennedy admirers "confidently look forward to the day when Jack will be in the White House, Bobby will serve in the Cabinet as Attorney General, and Teddy will be the Senator from Massachusetts." A member of the Democratic National Committee said that if a convention was to be held that year, the presidential nomination would go to "Kennedy, period." Jack's office was inundated with twenty-five hundred speaking invitations from all across the country, a number which grew to more than one hundred a week by the following spring. Jack accepted one hundred forty-four of these in 1957, using his travels to establish a card file modeled on the one he had set up in Massachusetts, so that a nationwide organization would already be in place for a presidential campaign.

Jack was also getting a great deal of publicity from his work in the Senate. He was assigned to the prestigious Foreign Relations Committee, an appointment that put him in an official position from which to speak out on international events. Because of Jack's new political prominence, his comments on foreign policy were given wide press coverage. This led to a few sour grapes among other committee members, and the chairman, Democrat J. William Fulbright, said Jack's only role was to sit at the end of the table "autographing pictures of himself."

In July, however, Jack turned to a foreign policy issue that brought the wrath of the entire Republican administration down on his head. The subject was a logical extension of his interest in Vietnam: colonialism. In the first of two Senate speeches intended to examine "America's role in the continuing struggle for independence," he called for an end to French rule in Algeria. The United States, Jack said, should use its influence with France to "shape a course of political independence" for Algerians. The address had been calculated to get publicity, and the resulting hue and cry was everything Jack could have wanted. His position contradicted that of the American government, for whom friendship with the French was more important than the self-determination of a little-known African country. Jack was accused of jeopardizing NATO unity as well as advocating revolution in a nation which, the Eisenhower administration said, would form a Communist government if it achieved independence. The fuss which followed the speech earned Jack so much attention that he told aides he was afraid of becoming known as "the Senator from Algeria."

The second of Jack's two speeches took him onto somewhat less controversial ground. It was wrong, he believed, to deplore the policies of a friend while overlooking the similar policies of a foe, and Jack felt he could not logically condemn French colonialism in Algeria while ignoring Soviet treatment of nations behind the Iron Curtain. In August, he introduced a bill proposing American economic assistance to Poland, a country in which Jack had taken considerable interest since his visit there in 1955. Criticizing Russia was always a reasonably safe tactic, and this speech was more warmly received than his Senate address the previous month. Still, there were some conservatives who denounced even that idea, claiming that U.S. aid to the Poles would only help the country's Communist regime. Jack saw things differently. "Hunger has never been a weapon of American foreign policy," he stated, "and if we can score these 'cold war' advantages only by turning a deaf ear to Polish hunger and misery, then we will have won only a 'dubious' victory at best."

Foreign affairs was the area that Jack loved most, and he thrived on the controversy surrounding his speeches on imperialism. Yet it was in domestic issues that Jack, as a member of the Senate labor committee, received the greatest amount of publicity over a two-year period, much of it as a result of work done by his younger brother.

Bobby had returned as chief counsel to the Government Operations Investigating Subcommittee, now chaired by Democratic senator John McClellan of Arkansas. Having dropped from the headlines since the fall of Joe McCarthy, the subcommittee had quietly returned to its original function of looking into fraud and mismanagement. The discovery of underworld involvement with the labor movement had been made in the spring of 1956, when a review of governmental purchasing of military uniforms revealed New York gangsters were muscling in on unions in the East. A few months later, investigation of that situation was broadened to explore the extent of mobster influence within labor nationwide.

The previous year, labor's two largest factions, the American Federation of Labor and the Congress of Industrial Organizations, had merged into the AFL-CIO, with George Meany as president. The new organization had done little to curb wrongdoing in the individual unions within its ranks, and there were no effective laws to police union behavior. Neither the AFL-CIO nor Congress had pursued the problem, but journalists who followed up on it discovered that the International Brotherhood of Teamsters seemed to be concealing the worst abuses. The Teamsters, with almost a million and a half members and a quarter of a billion dollars in welfare and pension funds, was the largest, wealthiest union in the country. The organization was composed primarily of workers in the trucking industry, and was headed by President Dave Beck and Vice-President Jimmy Hoffa.

As chief counsel of the Government Operations subcommittee, responsibility for researching organized crime's role in the labor movement fell to Bobby Kennedy. He began his study in November, knowing almost nothing about labor itself and still less about the Teamsters, which soon became the focus of the inquiry. By the time Bobby concluded his initial study at the end of 1956, he had found that Teamster management was not only involved in illegal financial dealings but employed members of the underworld to violently enforce its policies. Although there was more than enough evidence to bring Dave Beck up on charges, Bobby encountered no little resistance. Leading the opposition was his father. Joe thought the investigation would turn labor against the Kennedys and ruin Jack's chances for the presidential nomination. Christmas 1956 was spent in a furious nonstop argument between Joe and Bobby. The whole idea made Jack a little nervous, too. He told a reporter that he had "some apprehensions about this from the standpoint of what it does to me with organized labor. But," he added, "Bobby wants to do it so badly." Bobby was aware of the danger, and asked Kenny O'Donnell to sign on as his administrative assistant. The situation was the reverse of four years earlier, when Kenny had pleaded with Bobby to come to Massachusetts for Jack's first senatorial campaign. Now Kenny wanted to stay in Boston to begin work on Jack's campaign for reelection, and this time it was Bobby who insisted. "If the investigation flops it will hurt Jack in 1958 and in 1960, too," he told Kenny. "A lot of people think he's the Kennedy running the investigation, not me. As far as the public is concerned, one Kennedy is the same as another Kennedy."

Next Bobby tried to get labor officials to cooperate. But George Meany thought the subcommittee was attempting to discredit the entire labor movement, and said the AFL-CIO would oppose any Senate hearings. Bobby replied that Dave Beck was "a crook," and that the investigation would take place with or without cooperation by the AFL-CIO. In January 1957, over Beck's objections, Meany agreed to go along. Since the proposed hearings involved issues of interest to both the Senate Labor Committee and the Investigating Subcommittee, members from each were selected to sit on a new committee. Jack was appointed from Labor; McClellan and Bobby moved over to take the same positions they had held on the subcommittee. The new panel was officially called the Senate Select Committee on Improper Activities in the Labor or Management Field. That awkward title was soon shortened to the McClellan Committee, although it eventually also became known as the Rackets Committee, because of the many underworld figures that would appear before it. Its public hearings, which opened in February, turned into what The *Saturday Evening Post* called "the biggest, most spectacular congressional investigation in recent years."

After a prolonged "vacation" out of the country, Dave Beck finally made his first appearance before the committee in March. He sailed through questioning by the senators, but the chief counsel destroyed him. Bobby's detailed interrogation was, a writer for the *Chicago Daily News* said, "the finest job I've ever seen done on Capitol Hill." Beck was indicted, convicted, and sent to prison for larceny and income tax evasion. And that left Jimmy Hoffa in charge.

When hearings on the new Teamster head began in August 1957, Bobby Kennedy and Jimmy Hoffa soon became obsessed with trying to outdo each other. One night Bobby and staff member Pierre Salinger left the office after midnight. Driving past Teamster headquarters, Bobby noticed a light on in Hoffa's window. "If he's still at work," Bobby said, "we ought to be." Turning around, they went back to the office for two more hours. After Hoffa heard the story, he started leaving his light on all night. The Teamster leader regarded Bobby as a "spoiled jerk," a rich kid who knew nothing about the problems of working people, while Bobby thought Hoffa was a bully and a crook who had abused the trust of his union members, misused almost $10 million in union funds, and hired gangsters to beat or murder those who opposed his leadership. By now Bobby knew enough about labor to realize that financial wrongdoing or violence during strikes could probably never be entirely done away with. But for the country's largest union to be involved with organized crime was, he told a reporter, "far more sinister" than fistfights or minor finagling of union funds.

A parade of well-known underworld figures, all with some connection to Hoffa, were subpoenaed to appear before the committee. Among the gangsters called to testify was Sam Giancana, a friend of Frank Sinatra and leader of organized crime in Chicago, who had used the local Brotherhood of Electrical Workers to take over vending machine operations in that city. Also appearing on the stand was Red Dorfman, who became head of the mob-dominated Scrap Iron and Junk Handlers Union in Chicago after its president was murdered. One person the police questioned in that case was Jack Rubenstein, a Junk Handlers organizer, who later moved to Dallas and changed his name to Jack Ruby. The committee learned very little from their unsavory witnesses, all of whom answered most of the questions put to them by invoking the Fifth Amendment— declining to answer to avoid self-incrimination.

Hoffa proved as elusive as his underworld buddies. Since the AFL-CIO had passed a resolution against labor leaders taking the Fifth, he instead simply pleaded a bad memory. When queried about Teamster connections with the mob, he responded, "To the best of my recollection, I must recall on my memory, I cannot remember." Answers like these made him a little hard to pin down. Bobby was also exasperated with the FBI, which, he said, worried so much about domestic subversion that it ignored the problem of organized crime, and with the Justice Department, which refused to file any indictments, claiming there was not enough hard evidence of wrong-doing.

In spite of the hearings, Hoffa was elected president of the Teamsters and Dave Beck was given a fifty-thousand-dollar annual pension. Although the union was expelled from the AFL-CIO, Hoffa pointed out that the McClellan Committee had changed nothing: he was still in charge of the Teamsters, and Bobby was still trying "to elect his brother president."

Although Bobby was convinced that Jimmy Hoffa was the personification of evil, the more conservative committee members didn't agree. Hoffa supported Republican candidates and bragged about his "close family life." His union seldom called strikes, and he himself staunchly declared his belief in free enterprise. Under questioning by Senator Barry Goldwater of Arizona, Hoffa had condemned union leaders who attempted to use their organizations to bring about social and economic changes. "We both recognize that in the writing in the clouds today there is an individual who would like to see that happen in this country," the Arizona senator responded. "For the good of the union movement, I am very hopeful that your philosophy prevails." The "individual" to whom Goldwater referred was Walter Reuther, head of the United Auto Workers. The huge membership of the UAW made it the closest rival to the Teamsters, and Hoffa claimed the Kennedys had set out to destroy his organization in order to get UAW support for Jack's presidential candidacy.

With the exception of the liberal Irving Ives of New York, Republican committee members had little fondness for Reuther, whose union leadership they suspected of having Communist ties. Hoffa deliberately played on this fear, and called Reuther "the leader of Soviet America." Conservatives on the committee, resentful of Bobby's pursuit of the Teamsters, were quoted in *Newsweek* as saying that Robert Kennedy had "ignored continual demands for an investigation of Reuther" and instead concentrated on union leaders "who had stood in the way of Reuther's domination of American labor." The Republicans were particularly eager to look into a UAW strike against the Kohler Company, a manufacturer of plumbing fixtures, which had been deadlocked for almost four years. Both

Jack and Bobby were anxious to avoid offending Reuther, and said the issue was more appropriate for bargaining-table negotiation between labor and management. But conservative committee members were determined to push an inquiry, and there seemed no way the Kennedys could stop it without appearing partial to the UAW.

Early in 1958, Bobby flew to Wisconsin to look into the situation at the Kohler plant. The report on his findings led Kenny O'Donnell to characterize the problem as management's "fourteenth century attitude toward labor unions." One item of dispute was the union's demand for a thirty-minute lunch period. Under existing conditions, employees worked eight straight hours in the one-hundred-degree heat of an enamel shop. They were allowed to remove their face shields and eat lunch while the enamel was hardening in the oven: a break of two to five minutes. The Republicans' own investigator, Jack McGovern, saw the situation differently. McGovern said he had uncovered "sensational developments" that would discredit the UAW. One was the charge that in 1956 the union had hired a man named Brotz to bring in a gang of thugs to attack strikebreakers. Further examination by O'Donnell proved that Brotz had died in 1951. McGovern also claimed that one hundred thousand dollars was missing from the UAW treasury. Bobby's staff accountant soon discovered that McGovern had simply looked for the money under the wrong column of figures in the union's books. The Republicans, realizing they had little ammunition to use against the UAW, began to stall, and finally Senator Goldwater said he no longer wanted to call Reuther before the committee.

Up to that point, Jack had kept a low profile in what was essentially Bobby's show. But the longer the committee waited to summon Reuther, the more newspapers claimed it was Jack himself who was trying to protect the UAW leader. One typical comment was that of a syndicated columnist who reported Jack was hoping to help Reuther "build his United Auto Workers from the ruins of the Teamsters Brotherhood." It seemed increasingly obvious to Jack that conservative committee members were dragging their feet not only because they had nothing on Reuther, but also to make sure the Democratic front-runner took the blame for the delay. Jack was furious, and after five heated closed sessions with his Republican counterparts, finally succeeded in having Reuther called before the committee in late March 1958.

The conservatives made a poor showing against the head of the UAW. When Barry Goldwater read aloud from a newspaper clipping which mentioned thirty-seven deaths during the Kohler strike,

Reuther pointed out "that all the dead people were strikers." Gold-water finished the article and admitted, "Oh, my God, you're right." Not having learned his lesson, the Arizona senator went on to say it was "strange" that both the Communist party and the UAW employed violent tactics. Jack quickly ridiculed that innuendo by pointing out "My brother's name was Joe and Stalin's name was Joe, but this should scarcely support an argument that they had anything in common."

At the conclusion of Reuther's appearance, Committee Chairman McClellan announced there was no evidence of corruption in the UAW. The Kohler Company was eventually found guilty of unfair labor practices, and its workers were awarded the largest back payment sum in American history. But the outcome was a victory for more than Walter Reuther and the United Auto Workers. It was Jack Kennedy, Kenny O'Donnell later said, who, through his penetrating questioning of witnesses, had been the "star" of the televised hearings. As he had on the Labor Committee during his first term in the House, Jack had again walked a fine line—this time upholding the rights of workers while opposing union corruption. Most important to his political future, he had also won a powerful friend. Jack Kennedy, Reuther said, was a "saint towards the UAW."

While Jack's involvement with the McClellan Committee had been limited, it paid off handsomely in winning the support of one of America's most important unions. But his work with labor didn't stop there. While Bobby had been pursuing Jimmy Hoffa, Jack had spent much of the previous year involved with other labor issues. As chairman of the Senate Labor Committee's Subcommittee on Labor Legislation, Jack had fought for higher minimum wages and the strengthening of unemployment insurance. These proposals were in keeping with his own philosophical movement leftward, a direction in which both political expedience and a growing independence from his father were moving him. Now when Jack spoke out on immigration quotas, substandard wages, welfare, civil liberties, or health care for the elderly, it was from a position much further to the left than in his first congressional term a decade before.

After years of following a somewhat conservative course, Jack had begun taking attitudes more in tune with the liberal elements of his party. They were the people Jack Kennedy needed to woo for the support of his presidential candidacy: the active intellectuals and professionals who, although not great in number, played a disproportionate role in both Democratic finances and nationwide public opinion. It was a group largely committed to Adlai Stevenson, but one which Jack was gradually winning over. "All those men who had once been quite snotty about the Kennedys were coming around," Lem Billings said. "We considered it quite a coup to have taken them into camp. But they changed things: weekends at the Cape were no longer as much fun as they'd been before." The liberal intellectuals were indeed not a lighthearted group, and one area they took most seriously was civil rights, a topic that had been increasingly in the news since the 1954 Supreme Court decision that racial segregation in schools was unconstitutional.

Jack's record on the subject was mixed. He had been the first member of Congress from New England to appoint a black person to his staff, and he had given the money from his Pulitzer Prize award to the United Negro College Fund. Yet hiring one black and donating $500 for black scholarships was mere tokenism. Taking a stand on the civil rights legislation pending before the Senate throughout the spring and summer of 1957 was far more important, and Jack seemed to avoid a commitment either for or against the measure.

Integration was a subject about which most Americans had strong feelings one way or the other, and Jack's failure to establish a clear-cut attitude toward the bill reflected the difficulty of his position. As his party's leading candidate for the presidential nomination, he needed the support of Democrats throughout the country. To identify with his party's moderates, Jack had to come down firmly on the side of civil rights, which meant he would probably sacrifice support in the South. If he continued to avoid the issue, he risked losing the backing of liberal Democrats in the North.

The proposed bill would, if passed, create a Civil Rights Commission with authority to investigate voting irregularities, which had long prevented many southern blacks from taking part in the electoral process. Jack's first action on the pending legislation caused consternation among the liberals. Under normal procedure, the bill would be sent for study by the Judiciary Committee, where, under the chairmanship of James Eastland of Mississippi, Southerners hoped it would be buried. Jack voted against a proposal to bypass committee consideration, and Senator Eastland immediately announced he would support Kennedy for the presidency. Liberals were outraged at what they saw as blatant courting of segregationists. But they were somewhat mollified when Jack did an about-face and supported a section of the bill that gave the attorney general broad powers to seek injunctions against those who violated the civil rights of others. Now it was the Southerners' turn to be disgruntled.

Then in August Jack again sided with the South in voting for an amendment that would require a jury trial for violators of the bill, thus leaving enforcement up to local jurors who would undoubtedly be sympathetic to the defendants. Jack's waffling on the subject did not go over well in Massachusetts. Liberals accused him of trying "to be on both sides at the same time," and wondered if Jack considered it "more important to his career to vote in line with his principles and wishes of his home state voters, or to compromise and curry favor with Southern interests." A Salem newspaper said his quest for the nomination had "received a terrific shock by the integration question."

If Jack had moved slowly on civil rights, so too had many of America's educational institutions. Since the Supreme Court decision three years before, those schools which were not already integrated had taken advantage of the Court's vague ruling that desegregation must proceed "with all deliberate speed." Gradually, however, school after school gave in, some with much less grace than others. On September 2, the attention of the nation was on Little Rock Central High School, where Governor Orval Faubus had called out the Arkansas National Guard to prevent enrollment of nine black students. Three weeks later, Faubus withdrew the Guardsmen, allowing a white mob to take control of the streets outside the school. Finally, President Eisenhower ordered troops of the 101st Airborne Division to Little Rock to assure the safe admission of the students. That defiance of states' rights by the federal government brought Southern fury to a level not seen since the days of Reconstruction.

Naturally, the entire Democratic party was interested in what Jack would say when, a few weeks later, he spoke before the Mississippi Young Democrats in Jackson. This time he angered the Southerners. Announcing that he endorsed the Supreme Court decision, Jack added he was sure almost everyone there agreed it was necessary "to uphold law and order in every part of the land." The young audience responded warmly to Jack's personal presence, but throughout the state, reaction was frigid. "Thank you, Mr. Kennedy," said one caustic newspaper editorial. "You have told us all we need to know."

Once again Jack had sided with the moderates on a subject that dominated American schools that fall. But in October, even the divisive issue of integration was eclipsed by an announcement that rocked the U.S. educational system. An already troubled nation learned the Soviet Union had entered the space age by launching the world's first satellite: *Sputnik*. A few weeks later, *Sputnik II*, with a dog on board as passenger, was, the Russians announced, paving the way for eventual human space flight. Although President Eisenhower had promised the United States would send up a small unmanned satellite in late 1957, the project seemed stalled. And now Americans learned that with *Sputnik II*, the Soviets had launched a satellite fifty-two times heavier than the one planned by the U.S.

Then came still another shock: Russia had also developed an intercontinental ballistic missile—a self-propelled space vehicle capable of carrying a nuclear warhead within a range of several thousand miles. Warnings of a "missile gap" began to be heard, and a country which had complacently regarded itself as the mightiest on earth had to admit the loss of its military supremacy. The knowledge of Communist technological achievements created what Eisenhower called a "wave of near hysteria." Something had gone wrong with the American dream, and suddenly the nation was questioning its schools, its character, its leadership, and even its ability to survive in a nuclear world.

Jack was among the first to publicly fault the educational system —and, by implication, the Republican administration—for America's failure to produce scientists capable of matching Soviet accomplishments. Addressing a group of teachers in Fall River, Massachusetts, he deplored the shortage of school funding that had resulted in a "lack of high quality education," and which might ultimately lead to "the undoing of our nation." In a Senate address, Jack spoke of the loss of American "superiority in nuclear striking power," and said the missile gap presented "a peril more deadly than any wartime danger" the United States had ever known. With Jack leading the way, Democrats soon made Russia's advances in science and technology a major political issue. Senate Majority Leader Lyndon Johnson took a swipe at the administration by suggesting that Bobby Kennedy be put in charge of investigating ways to close the missile gap, while the *New York Times* commented that the country was seeking "more dynamic leadership."

It did not escape the attention of many Americans that in sharp contrast to the grandfatherly president was the youthful vitality of the Kennedy brothers.

By early 1958, both Jack and Bobby were increasingly in the public eye. In March, Jack began drafting comprehensive labor-reform legislation to implement the findings of Bobby's work on the McClellan Committee. George Meany, head of the AFL-CIO, was alarmed; he felt the proposed regulations went beyond Jack's stated intention to clean up corruption and were too restrictive to unions. Recognizing the validity of Meany's criticism, Jack agreed to adjust his proposals. By May, with the help of an AFL-CIO lawyer, Arthur Goldberg, and a group of labor relations experts headed by Archibald Cox from Harvard Law School, the legislation had been redrafted to a form that met the requirements of both Jack Kennedy and George Meany.

The next month, under the bipartisan sponsorship of senators Kennedy and Ives, and backed by every important national labor figure except Jimmy Hoffa, the bill passed the Senate and was sent to the House. There it languished throughout the summer. Finally, a lack of administration support, along with the opposition of business and the Teamsters, led to its defeat. "Jimmy Hoffa can rejoice at his continued good luck," Jack said. "Honest union members and the general public can only regard it as a tragedy that politics has prevented the recommendations of the McClellan Committee from being carried out this year." Although the bill had been voted down in the House, the Kennedys benefited greatly from their efforts over the previous eighteen months. Bobby's investigation had led to important friendships with editors and reporters all across the country. In addition to cultivating valuable ties to labor, Jack had also established his reputation as a serious legislator. His career, a journalist said, "really took off" with his work on the two committees.

The labor reform hearings also resulted in a great deal of gratifying publicity. *Look* magazine published an article on "The Rise of the Brothers Kennedy," which included sixteen photographs of Jack and Bobby. In a *Saturday Evening Post* lead article titled "The Amazing Kennedys," Jack was described as "trustworthy, loyal, brave, clean and reverent, boldly facing up to the challenges of the Atomic Age." One reporter said Jack Kennedy was Washington's "hottest tourist attraction." But there was a flip side to all the attention; some people regarded Jack as a celebrity rather than someone worthy of consideration for the presidency. A *New York Post* columnist expressed the concern of many Democrats: "Month after month, from the glossy pages of *Life* to the multicolored cover of *Redbook*, Jack and Jackie Kennedy smile out at millions of readers; he with his tousled hair and winning smile, she with her dark eyes and beautiful face. We hear of her pregnancy, of his wartime heroism, of their fondness for sailing. But," the column concluded, "what has all this to do with statesmanship?" Adlai Stevenson also appeared lukewarm to Jack's candidacy. Kennedy, he was quoted as saying, "has three strikes against him: religion, too young, too rich."

His 1958 campaign for reelection to the Senate was one way Jack could prove himself to those who still doubted his credentials as a heavyweight politician. Joe Kennedy saw the election as crucial: if Jack could win by a large margin, he said, "they can't stop us for the presidency." Joe had little doubt Jack would be reelected by a landslide. Proving his lack of concern, Joe insisted that twenty-six-year-old Teddy be named campaign manager and that son-in-law Steve Smith be brought in to learn a little something about politics. The rest of the staff was not quite as blasé as Joe. That Jack would win was never in doubt, which meant, his aides thought, there would be very little for the electorate to get excited about. But in order to get the kind of record-breaking showing Jack needed to impress national Democratic leaders, voter turnout would have to be much larger than usual in a contest that held no suspense. The candidate himself, sensitive to Adlai Stevenson's remark about Kennedy wealth, didn't help matters by insisting that there be much less spending than in other elections.

Jack, however, benefited from a new asset which he had not had in the four previous campaigns: his wife. Jackie proved to be more valuable than any billboards or radio spots Joe Kennedy's money could buy. "When Jackie was traveling with us," Kenny O'Donnell said, "the size of the crowd at every stop was twice as big as it would have been if Jack was alone." Jackie's presence also meant there was no longer a need for the famous tea parties; the staff realized fewer women would turn out to see Jack now that he was a married man. Still, Jack never neglected the ladies. On the day before the election, he was riding through South Boston when he saw an elderly woman about to cross the street. Asking his driver to stop the car, Jack got out, introduced himself, took the woman's arm, and helped her across. When he got back into the car, one of his aides stared at him and said, "You really want *all* of the votes, don't you?"

Even the Republicans cooperated in helping Jack get "all of the votes." At first they couldn't find anyone who would agree to be a candidate against him. Finally Vincent Celeste, whom Jack had trounced in the 1950 election, volunteered as the sacrificial lamb. One reason for Republican defeatism was that almost everyone in the state had taken personal pride in Jack's performance at the 1956 convention. Now, no matter what their politics, most of the Massachusetts electorate wanted Jack Kennedy to be nominated for president. Since they were aware this would first require a good showing in his senatorial race, a record-breaking 2 million voters turned out. Jack received 73.6 percent of the total, winning by the greatest landslide by either party for any office in the history of the state. Jack even carried the area which, he said, "I proudly call home," as the first major Democrat to ever win on traditionally Republican Cape Cod. All across the country, other Democratic presidential hopefuls were forced to agree with Joe Kennedy. Probably nothing could stop Jack now.

At the end of 1958 Joe Kennedy was on top of the world. For more than four decades he had dreamed of seeing his son in the White House, and in two years that grand ambition would undoubtedly become a reality. But just as important to Joe was the fact that he had kept the loyalty of his family to a degree almost unknown in American life. Hyannis Port was now the site of what journalists called "the Kennedy compound." Bobby and Ethel had purchased a house next door to that of Joe and Rose; Jack and Jackie had bought a house directly behind Bobby's, and the three backyards adjoined. Jean and Steve Smith and Eunice and Sargent Shriver all had houses within a few minutes' walk; Teddy and his new wife, Joan, were only a mile away. The Lawfords and their children visited frequently, staying with Pat's parents. The family spent all of their holidays and most of their vacations with each other.

Joe was confident that even after he was gone, nothing would change. In Jack, the Kennedys would realize all of Joe's ambitions. And in Bobby the family had an emotional center. He was the one, his father said, who would "keep the Kennedys together in the future." By Christmas 1958, Joe and Rose had thirteen of what would finally become twenty-nine grandchildren. Looking around at his large, loving, happy, and successful family, Joe allowed himself a little bit of Irish emotion when he said, "This is the most exclusive club in the world."

13

THE FIVE-RING CIRCUS

The inevitable backlash began as soon as Jack seemed guaranteed the presidential nomination. As Adlai Stevenson had pointed out, Jack was vulnerable in three areas, and critics from all sides of the political spectrum began taking pot shots at his religion, his wealth, and his comparative youth. When he had suddenly risen to national prominence in 1956, few people were aware that Jack was Catholic. But the barrage of publicity over the two and a half intervening years had made that fact common knowledge, and it was an aspect of Jack's fitness for the presidency that made many people uncomfortable. From the Founding Fathers on down, America had been ruled by Protestants, and many feared a Catholic in the White House would be accountable to the ultimate Catholic authority of the pope. Jack would have to face that charge over and over again, as he did in an interview published in *Look* early in 1959. Whatever an officeholder's religion, Jack said, "nothing takes precedence over his oath to uphold the Constitution and all its parts—including the First Amendment and the strict separation of church and state."

The subject was so worrisome and aroused such bitter controversy that Jack was delighted when, at a speaking engagement in Los Angeles, a member of the audience facetiously asked if a Protestant could be elected president in 1960. "If he is willing to answer questions on his views concerning the separation of church and state," Jack replied, "I see no reason why we should discriminate against him." But lighthearted moments were few and far between.

Jack was surprised that many liberals were against a Catholic president, although members of that group were less honest about admitting it than were their counterparts on the right. The redoubtable Eleanor Roosevelt was an exception; she made no secret of her belief that in the presidency Jack Kennedy would follow the generally conservative philosophy of his Church's hierarchy, and was therefore unacceptable to one of her liberal beliefs.

Mrs. Roosevelt remained the one woman Jack was unable to charm. She couldn't stomach Joe Kennedy, she had loathed Joe McCarthy, and Jack was suspect because of his relationships with both. She continued to goad Jack with the title of his Pulitzer Prize-winning book, and with what she imagined to be the behind-the-scenes machinations of his father. Jack Kennedy, Mrs. Roosevelt said in a December 1958 television appearance, was "someone who understands what courage is and admires it, but has not quite the independence to have it." She added that Joe Kennedy was spending "oodles of money all over the country" in an effort to assure his son's nomination, and that he "probably has paid representatives in every state by now."

Although Jack wasn't anxious to take on the grande dame of the Democratic party, he knew the accusation couldn't go unanswered, and challenged her to name "one such example of any spending by my father around the country on my behalf." She replied that many people had told her about it, and that it was "commonly accepted as a fact." Jack somewhat gleefully responded by letter, with an unstated but obvious reference to the tactics Mrs. Roosevelt had so despised in Joe McCarthy: "I am disappointed that you now seem to accept the view that simply because a rumor or allegation is repeated it becomes 'commonly accepted as fact.'"

Another venerable member of the Democratic party soon chimed in with his opinion of Joe Kennedy. "I like Jack. He is a nice person," Harry Truman told a writer. "But I don't like his daddy and never did." To Truman, Jack's religion wasn't the problem. "I'm not against the Pope, I'm against the Pop," he said. Jack didn't think the line was nearly as funny as the former president did. But he took in much better humor the kidding of Washington journalists at their annual Gridiron Club dinner. One skit presented by the group took aim at the popular theory that Joe Kennedy's money was responsible for Jack Kennedy's political success, and performers trilled out the lyric "We send all our bills to Daddy 'cause Daddy pays them so well." When Jack got up to speak, he charmed the assembly of seasoned reporters by announcing, "I have just received the following wire from my generous daddy: 'Dear Jack—Don't buy a single vote more than necessary—I'll be damned if I'm going to pay for a landslide.' " It was one of the increasingly rare instances when the subject of Joe Kennedy was a laughing matter.

Joe was reluctant to concede he played a controversial role in Jack's quest for the White House. "Let's not con ourselves," he remarked to a reporter. "The only issue is whether a Catholic can be president." He described himself as just an "average guy" and couldn't quite understand the animosity he aroused. But in a career which spanned almost five decades, Joe had stepped on plenty of toes. The upper class was still offended that an Irish Catholic upstart had become a rich man through bootlegging and the dubious enterprise of making movies. Members of the business community would never forgive the SEC chairman who imposed regulations to restrict their incomes while his own fortune continued to grow. Liberals had not forgotten the isolationist ambassador to Great Britain. Depending on one's point of view, Joe Kennedy was a cutthroat, a reactionary, a traitor to his class, or someone who didn't know his own place. And that added up to a lot of enemies. Now, in the most important drama of his life, Joe had to watch from the wings. "I have withdrawn completely from public life," he said in an interview with the *Boston Herald*. Toward the end of the decade, Ted Sorensen commented, Joe was never present—although his presence was never absent.

And the money was always there, to be used where it would do the most good. Joe formed a company called the Ken-Air Corporation, purchasing an airplane which was leased to the as yet unofficial Kennedy campaign. The plane, which Jack named the *Caroline*, gave him a significant advantage over other potential presidential candidates. While they traveled by bus or wasted time waiting for commercial flights, Jack could cover more territory at less expense. In 1959 and 1960, the *Caroline* logged a total of 110,000 miles in trips back and forth across the country.

Joe also made other less tangible but equally important contributions. By calling in his many political markers, Joe knew how to get a favor without spending the "oodles of money" for which his critics were constantly on the lookout. He was also mindful of the tapes of Jack and Inga Arvad which were in the possession of the FBI, so J. Edgar Hoover, the Bureau's director, became the willing recipient of nonstop flattery and attention. Hoover had little fondness for Jack and still less for his brother. He also was well aware that Bobby might one day be attorney general and therefore in charge of the FBI. Nevertheless, the existence of the tapes, which could have doomed Jack's chances for the presidency, was not made known during the campaign. In turn, the director felt certain that after thirty-six years with the Bureau, his job would remain secure in a Kennedy administration.

Then there were Joe's influential contacts in the press. William Randolph Hearst had died in 1951, but Henry Luce, head of Time-Life, and Arthur Krock, Washington bureau chief of the *New York Times*, were still going strong, and both were happy to oblige an old friend by keeping his son's name in print. In this endeavor, Joe also got plenty of cooperation from the American people.

Interest in Jack and Jackie had continued to grow, and now the public had an overwhelming curiosity about even Caroline. In 1959 alone, stories about the Kennedys appeared in *Life, Redbook,* the *Ladies' Home Journal, Look, Coronet, Reader's Digest,* and the *Washington Post.* The ongoing publicity offered both advantages and disadvantages. Jack knew that many Democrats, heeding the criticisms of Eleanor Roosevelt, Harry Truman, and Adlai Stevenson, had begun to consider him a more appropriate vice-presidential candidate. When a friend asked Jack if he was perhaps "getting sick" of all those magazines reporting the same facts over and over again, he replied, "These stories about me do have one effect. They help take the 'v' out of the 'v.p.' " But the constant spotlight also heightened the public's perception of Jack as some sort of celebrity rather than a serious contender for the nation's highest office. It was important to emphasize his legislative duties in Washington, and an article about Jack in the *New York Times Magazine* reported that he did "not intend to sacrifice his Senate career on the altar of his presidential ambition."

Accordingly, in early 1959 Jack reintroduced the labor-reform bill. Its original Republican cosponsor, Irving Ives, had retired, and this time the legislation was cosponsored by another Democrat, Sam Ervin of North Carolina. The bill passed the Senate with only Barry Goldwater voting against, but it again ran aground in the House, where Democratic representative Philip Landrum of Georgia and Republican Robert Griffin of Michigan had drafted a much stiffer labor bill of their own. Jack was named chairman of a Senate-House conference to work out a compromise between the two proposals. He was once again in the headlines as a congressional leader determined to end union corruption, but he was also vulnerable to the loss of labor support if the final legislation was considered too harsh. It was, an observer remarked, a "political banana peel."

Finally a restrictive form of the bill, backed by the Teamsters and big business, was assured passage when President Eisenhower went on television to attack the Kennedy-Ervin version and to urge acceptance of the tougher Landrum-Griffin proposal. Although Jack had needed no urging to seek the presidency, passage of the Landrum-Griffin Act in September 1959 reinforced his desire to move on from the Senate. "I have realized more and more that the real source of power is the Executive Branch, the White House," he said. "I work on a labor bill for two years, and nothing happens, but the president makes a fifteen minute speech and the bill is passed." Although the final legislation contained most of Jack's union-reform provisions, the end product was also essentially the one originally proposed in the House, and Jack had asked to have his name removed from the bill.

Nevertheless, he had kept the act from being a total disaster for labor. The AFL-CIO called the new legislation worse than the original Taft-Hartley Law, but praised Jack for his efforts. A *New York Times* editorial also complimented Jack, saying he had "outstandingly provided" skill in the art of compromise. In his ticklish position as head of the Senate-House Conference Committee, Jack managed to give the impression he had done the best he could against great odds. A witness to the proceedings said that Jack Kennedy could fall into a well and come up dry with two watches running—one on daylight and one on standard time.

Legislative duties had kept Jack in Washington throughout much of the summer. As a result, his Senate office became what one writer called a "five-ring circus," since Jack was functioning simultaneously as United States senator, Massachusetts politician, chairman of a joint Congressional committee, potential presidential candidate, and author. While he was trying to bring about acceptable labor reform, requests poured in for Jack to make speeches and personal appearances, and to write articles, book reviews, and guest editorials. Constituents constantly dropped into the office, other senators were often there for conferences, the phone never stopped ringing. Things were only a little quieter at home. The Kennedys had purchased a three-story brick house in Georgetown, where Jacqueline hoped to provide her husband with a restful setting to which he could return from the chaos of his Senate office. But visitors and phone calls intruded even there. The Kennedys' personal life was one of nonstop activity. Friends were amused that among Caroline's first six words were *Daddy, airplane*, and *car*; even at the age of eighteen months, his daughter was aware that Jack was always either leaving or arriving.

In the fall, with the unhappy conclusion of the labor legislation, Jack began a big push to campaign for the nomination. On October 28, he presided over a meeting in Hyannis Port, where he amazed fifteen advisors with a state-by-state political analysis. Speaking without notes for three hours, Jack reeled off places, names, and dates. His knowledge, political adviser Larry O'Brien said, was "remarkable." Jack knew every important person in every state. He listed who could be counted on for support, who could probably be won over, who would oppose his candidacy. He ran through sixteen primaries, specifying which were important and which should be skipped. He was aware of every delegate situation: areas that were controlled by party leaders in which the delegates would vote as a bloc; local politicians who might themselves be delegates or who would influence the delegates from their areas. Jack didn't overlook a single important national political statistic, and the combined wisdom of all those in the room, Ted Sorensen commented, couldn't "match his knowledge of detail."

An unofficial campaign headquarters, with only Steve Smith's name on the door, was already quietly operating in Washington. Here Smith, Kenny O'Donnell, Larry O'Brien, and Ted Kennedy had divided the country into regions, each directing the efforts of his own area with the help of the more than forty thousand supporters Jack had collected on his travels. Four secretaries handled correspondence to and from politicians and voters, and sent letters of thanks to everyone of any importance in the cities Jack visited across the country. Rows of filing cabinets held press releases, newspaper clippings, and polls; the walls were covered with state maps showing counties and congressional districts. All this activity had a dual purpose: to win delegates and to coordinate Jack's awesome schedule. While his Washington headquarters hummed with behind-the-scenes activity, Jack stepped up his nationwide appearances. In October and November, he spoke in Kansas, New York, Illinois, Colorado, Massachusetts, Wisconsin, West Virginia, Nebraska, Delaware, Louisiana, Ohio, Oregon, Iowa, Oklahoma, and California. Before the year was over, Jack had visited twenty-two states.

People meeting him for the first time were always amazed at Jack's boyish appearance, and everywhere he went there was concern about his age. For two years, Americans had been contemplating the specter of Russian long-range missiles; now some who had supported a Kennedy candidacy began to have second thoughts, wondering if a more mature president would have greater skill in confronting the challenge of a nuclear enemy. Newspapers never failed to comment on Jack's youthful features, and a columnist brought shudders to the Kennedy staff when he commented that Jack "still looks like a Harvard graduate student out to get his Ph.D. in political science." Jack's office even received a suggestion that his current publicity photo should be scrapped and replaced by one in which he appeared older.

At a 1959 speaking appearance in Arizona, Jack was, as usual, asked about his age: "Do you think a 42-year-old can meet the demands made on the president?" This time Jack smiled at the wording; after all, the election wasn't until the following year. "I don't know about a 42-year-old man, but I think a 43-year-old can." Questioned about the rumor that Bobby, who had just turned thirty-four, would be named campaign manager, Jack said he thought his brother was old enough for the job. But if it turned out he needed someone more mature, Jack added, "There's no need to go outside of the family. I can always get my father." When a New York Democrat told Joe Kennedy that Jack was too young to be president, Joe showed he could be no less charming than his son. "He is," Joe agreed. "But I'm seventy-two and I want to be around to enjoy it."

Joe had little doubt that everything would turn out fine. One son would be the Democratic candidate. "Jack is the greatest attraction in the country today," he said in an interview. "The party leaders around the country realize that to win they have to nominate him." And one son would be the campaign manager. Joe thought the competition was completely outclassed in that regard, too. The best organizational men had good jobs they didn't want to quit, he explained. "And the others—the ones you *can* hire," Joe said with disdain, "aren't any good." But Bobby was the best, the "first and only choice," as Ted Sorensen put it, because he could be "trusted more implicitly, say 'no' more emphatically, and speak for the candidate more authoritatively than any professional politician."

Bobby joined the campaign late in the year. In September, he had resigned from the McClellan Committee, and spent the next few months writing *The Enemy Within*, a book about the spreading influence of the underworld. With the completion of his manuscript, Bobby moved on to the challenge of securing the Democratic nomination for Jack.

At a December meeting in Palm Beach, Bobby made no secret of his opinion that, while he had been busy writing, his brother had obviously been goofing off. "All right, Jack, what has been done about the campaign? What planning has been done?" he demanded. While Jack paused, considering how to summarize his progress, Bobby impatiently went on. "Jack, how do you expect to run a successful campaign if you don't get started? A day lost now can't be picked up on the other end. It's ridiculous that more work hasn't been done already." Jack glanced over at his friend Red Fay, who was visiting the Kennedys. "How would you like looking forward to that voice blasting into your ear for the next six months?" he asked Red. Since Jack had been running hard since his reelection the previous year, he smilingly reassured his brother that "we've been able to do a few things in your absence."

In spite of his belief that Jack had been wasting valuable time, Bobby allowed his candidate to take a few days off just after Christmas, when Jack, Jackie, and two-year-old Caroline flew to Jamaica for a vacation. It was the last opportunity they would ever have for privacy, and during that brief time the three were an almost ordinary family, swimming, sailing, walking together on the beach. But by New Year's Eve, Jack was on the telephone making last-minute arrangements with Pierre Salinger, Bobby's aide from the McClellan Committee, who was soon to become the campaign press secretary. Jackie felt no resentment that politics had intruded even in Jamaica. She too had caught presidential fever, and thought that life in the White House might, as a journalist put it, "compensate for a lot of other things." Jackie was almost as excited as her husband when, on the first day of the new year, the Kennedys returned to Washington to begin a quest that would change their lives forever.

It had been only fourteen years since a shy young man, not at all sure he would like politics, had hesitantly become a candidate from the Eleventh Congressional District in Massachusetts. It had been little more than a century since Patrick Kennedy had landed in Boston and learned that "No Irish Need Apply." Now his great grandson intended to find out if that same notice hung on the door of the White House. On noon on January 2, 1960, John F. Kennedy walked into the Senate Caucus Room, pushed back a lock of his famous hair, and told reporters, "I am announcing today my candidacy for the presidency of the United States."

14

PICKING UP
ALL THE MARBLES

"If I were Protestant, fifty-five, and the governor of a large state," Jack said, "I could sit back and let the nomination come to me." Instead, he was Catholic and only forty-two years old. The Senate had seldom proven a good springboard to the presidency, and Massachusetts was, at best, a medium-sized state without major influence or a great number of delegates. The only way Jack could prove he was a viable candidate was to enter seven of the most important primaries and win them all. New Hampshire, on March 8, was considered a must. It was the first primary in the nation and as a result always received extensive press coverage. Jack's victory there was never in doubt; since the state bordered on Massachusetts, no other major Democratic candidate wanted to take him on in what was regarded as strictly Kennedy territory. Jack received forty-five thousand votes, more than twice the previous record in that primary. Although it was a rather meaningless triumph, it did result in a lot of national publicity.

The next primary loomed very large: Wisconsin, on April 5. There Jack would face Senator Hubert Humphrey of Minnesota, who was to date his only serious Democratic rival. Wisconsin was Humphrey country, and by beating the popular Protestant candidate in his own backyard, Jack felt he would have the nomination wrapped up. Both men campaigned hard all over the state, much of which was rural and, in the early spring, still covered with snow. Jack's growing fame had evidently not reached some of the more remote areas. In one small town, he shook a man's hand and said, "My name is John Kennedy and I'm running for president." The man stared back. "President of what?"

By early April, Jack had covered Wisconsin so thoroughly that he claimed to know "the difference between the kinds of farms" from one congressional district to another. Any place Jack missed, some other member of his family was sure to show up. It was a Kennedy blitz. "They're all over the state, and they look alike and sound alike," Humphrey commented. Bobby or Teddy or Eunice or Jean seemed to be everywhere. Sister Pat was a major attraction, since Peter Lawford was the star of a weekly television show and therefore of more interest to the people of Wisconsin than her brother.

Jacqueline had just learned she was pregnant again, but she, too, braved the snow and wind in one town after another, shaking hands and talking to the voters. As his wife greeted people on one side of the street, Jack would do the same on the other. He didn't fail to notice "Jackie's drawing more people than I am, as usual." She even charmed the manager of a Kenosha supermarket into letting her interrupt his recitation of sale items over the store's loudspeaker system. Customers were astonished to hear a soft voice say, "Just keep on with your shopping while I tell you about my husband, John F. Kennedy." She went on to talk about his career in the Navy and in Congress, spoke of how deeply he cared for his country, and ended by saying "Please vote for him." All the while Jackie was speaking, an observer said, "you could have heard a pin drop" in the busy store. Even seventy-year-old Rose joined the campaign, making speech after speech over the course of her twelve-hour days. Between the Kennedy family and the Kennedy fortune, Humphrey said he felt like "a corner grocer running against a chain store."

On primary day, Jack got 56 percent of the overall vote, more than any other candidate in the state's history. He carried six of its ten congressional districts. But the other four were predominantly Protestant, which meant his victory was not decisive enough. By failing to prove he could win in an area with few Catholic voters, Jack had not succeeded in "wrapping up the nomination" in Wisconsin. That goal would have to be achieved in West Virginia on May 10. There he would again be going head-to-head with Hubert Humphrey, and a loss in that Protestant state would probably derail his candidacy once and for all.

Humphrey was optimistic. He claimed a moral victory in Wisconsin and said he would take Jack outright in West Virginia. His biggest concern, however, was money; no one could match the

Kennedys when it came to campaign spending. "Maybe," Humphrey gibed, "I can hitch a ride down there on Jack's private plane."

To Bobby, on the other hand, it soon seemed that all the money in the world wouldn't assure the necessary outcome. At his opening meeting with local Democrats, Bobby began by asking, "Well, what are our problems?" A man in the group stood up and shouted back, "There's only one problem. He's a Catholic. That's our God damned problem!" For the Kennedy campaign manager, West Virginia was not off to a very good start. Jack's initial reception wasn't much more encouraging. On his first appearance in the state, people shied away, watching him from the other side of the street. Those that had to pass Jack shrank back, "as if they were afraid," Kenny O'Donnell commented, "of being touched by him." Finally two men approached to shake his hand. The pair, Jack told Kenny, "must have been a couple of visiting Catholics from Pennsylvania."

Religious prejudice was much more deeply ingrained than even the most pessimistic of Jack's staff had anticipated. The population of West Virginia was 95 percent Protestant, and one woman voiced the opinion of many when she said, "We've never had a Catholic president and I hope we never do. Our people built this country. If they had wanted a Catholic to be president, they would have said so in the Constitution." Initially, even those who wanted to support Jack seemed ashamed to admit it. Pollster Lou Harris was startled when a woman called him into her home, pulled down the blinds, and confessed she had decided to vote for the Catholic candidate. "We have enough trouble in West Virginia, let alone be called bigots, too," she explained.

The state's "trouble" was poverty. Coal mining had once been the leading industry, and people revered the memory of Franklin Roosevelt for pushing through legislation which had allowed miners to unionize in order to achieve better wages and working conditions. But automation and the use of alternate fuels had lessened the demand for coal and led to high unemployment; the number of miners had fallen from almost 117,000 at the end of World War II to about 43,000 in 1960.

With a large percentage of the population on relief, Jack's advisors were afraid his wealth would offend West Virginians. But an encounter Jack had with one voter made them feel somewhat more optimistic that, however troublesome the religious issue, the Kennedy fortune wouldn't play a role in the campaign. Jack was standing at the entrance of a mine shaft shaking hands when a miner asked, "Is it true you're the son of one of our wealthiest men?" Jack hesitantly replied he guessed he was. "Is it true," the miner went on, "you've never done a day's work with your hands all your life?" Jack nodded his head. "Well, let me tell you this," the miner said. "You haven't missed a thing."

Joe's greatest contribution to Jack's successful candidacy was not his money. Although he continued to remain out of public view, Joe never stopped thinking about ways to assure his son's victory. One of his suggestions was to bring Franklin D. Roosevelt, Jr., into the campaign—a stroke of genius, considering the affection West Virginians felt for the late president. In spite of his mother's opposition to a Kennedy candidacy, Roosevelt introduced Jack at speaking appearances throughout the state by holding up two tightly entwined fingers and telling the crowds, "My daddy and Jack Kennedy's daddy were just like that!" It didn't matter that nothing could have been further from the truth; audiences loved it.

As in Wisconsin, the Kennedy clan turned out in force. Ethel, Jean, and Joan went door to door distributing campaign literature. In the very coal mining areas where the Bouvier fortune had begun, Jackie visited miners' wives in their tiny company houses. Nothing seemed to faze her. Noticing a group of railroad workers eating lunch alongside the tracks, Jackie asked her driver to stop the car and spent the next thirty minutes chatting with the men. Teddy got up every morning in time to shake hands at factory gates before dawn. "In the pitch dark, it's sort of like a hold-up," he said. At twenty-eight, Teddy proved to be such an impassioned campaigner that Jack teasingly reminded him he wasn't old enough to meet the constitutional age requirement for the presidency. Outside of Joe's voluntary absence, only Jack's mother, as she herself put it, "wasn't invited." Since her strong religious beliefs were well known, Bobby suggested she might better serve the campaign in Nebraska, which was also holding its primary on May 10, or in Maryland, where the primary was May 13.

Against Bobby's advice, Jack finally decided to meet the issue of his Catholicism head on. In a paid telecast, FDR Jr. interviewed Jack about his religion, using questions supplied by Ted Sorensen. Jack closed with an emotional reference to the presidential oath of office. In the swearing-in, with his hand on the Bible, a president was vowing to support the separation of church and state, Jack explained. "And if he breaks his oath," Jack went on, "he is not only committing a crime against the Constitution, for which the Congress can impeach him—and should impeach him—but he is committing a sin against God." Jack paused dramatically and then softly repeated, "A sin against God, for he has sworn on the Bible." It was, one journalist said, the finest TV broadcast any politician had ever made.

Emphasizing service in World War II proved to be another way to offset the religious problem. West Virginians were very patriotic; their state had proportionately contributed more men and women to American armed forces than any other state in the Union. Bobby, who since 1952 had become a more confident speaker, sensed the subject of Joe Jr.'s war heroism would be emotionally appealing. But the first time he tried to talk about it in a speech, he broke down and was unable to continue. "Bobby must be tired," Jack commented, and decided to try the approach himself. It was so effective he continued to use it throughout the campaign. Jack would ask audiences if 40 million Americans had lost their right to run for the presidency on the day they were baptized Catholic. "That wasn't the country my brother died for in Europe," he said, "and nobody asked my brother if he was a Catholic or a Protestant before he climbed into an American bomber plane to fly his last mission." Then, to remind the crowd that a genuine World War II hero stood before them, Jack went on, "Nobody asked me if I was a Catholic when I joined the United States Navy." It was an area in which Hubert Humphrey, who had never served in the armed forces, couldn't even compete. "To listen to their stuff," one of his workers groused, "you'd think Jack won the war all by himself."

No matter how much it disgusted the Humphrey forces, West Virginians lapped it up. On election night, while Jack and Jackie attended a movie in Washington, D.C., the returns showed Kennedy had carried all but seven of the state's fifty-five counties. When Jack got home, there was a message to call Bobby. "Get your ass down here," his brother said. "You're winning by a landslide." Shortly afterward, Kennedy headquarters in Charleston received Humphrey's telegram conceding the election. "This must be awful for poor Hubert, ending up this way after working so hard," Bobby told Kenny O'Donnell. A few minutes later, Bobby made his way alone through the rainy night to pay a call on the defeated candidate. Humphrey read an announcement to his workers that he was withdrawing from the presidential race, and began to cry. Bobby cried with him; then, putting his arm around Humphrey, the two walked together back to Kennedy headquarters to greet Jack when he flew in from Washington.

Jack Kennedy had won the Indiana primary unopposed the previous week. On the same day as his victory in West Virginia, he also carried Nebraska in the largest Democratic victory there since FDR's election twenty years before. Three days later, he took Maryland four-to-one. In Oregon on May 20, he got more votes than all the other candidates combined. By the time the national convention rolled around, there was no longer much doubt who would represent the Democratic party in the presidential election of 1960.

The next several weeks were spent, Kenny O'Donnell said, in "putting together the political bits and pieces." From the day of the Oregon primary to June 27, when Jack addressed the Montana state convention, the *Caroline* crisscrossed the nation several times. Some of the travel involved nothing more than a routine check to make sure already-promised delegate support was holding. But the far more vital task was to win over the political bosses in the large industrial states who had not made public their choice of a candidate. Those leaders had only one consideration in determining that choice: whose name at the top of the ticket would bring in the most votes for local candidates. After Jack's smashing victories in West Virginia and Oregon, the governor of Michigan, a state with 51 convention votes, announced he was backing Kennedy. New York, where Joe had quietly been putting pressure on the party professionals, soon after pledged a majority of its 114 delegates to Jack.

By the end of June, Kennedy forces had the announced support of 550 of the total 1,520 delegate votes; Jack would need a minimum of 761 to win the nomination. Four large states were as yet publicly uncommitted. The governor of New Jersey, Robert Meyner, held firm against giving Jack his 41 delegates until after the second ballot. Meyner was a favorite-son candidate, and told a reporter he intended to have his "twenty-five minutes on television." The governors of two important states, California and Pennsylvania, were Stevenson loyalists. Although Stevenson refused to announce he was running, Governor Pat Brown of California held back his state's 81 votes, waiting for a sign of encouragement from the former presidential candidate. Pennsylvania Governor David Lawrence finally bowed to the influence of local Democrats and pledged his 81 delegates to Jack.

The powerful Mayor Richard Daley of Chicago, a political realist, also decided to throw his considerable support to Jack. Those 69 delegate votes would bring Jack's total to 700—still 61 shy of a majority. One Illinois delegate was a holdout: Adlai Stevenson. Jack had visited Stevenson's home in Libertyville, trying to get a commitment from the man for whom he had campaigned four years earlier. But Stevenson, hoping for a miracle when the convention opened in Los Angeles on July 11, refused to endorse Jack. Many in the Democratic party had strong affection for Stevenson. Now, although he would not play the role of an active candidate, Stevenson held out on the slim chance that Jack could be stopped. Others shared that hope.

Although Jack arrived in Los Angeles confident of victory, he was also aware that four of the most influential members of the Democratic party were against him. There was the wife of one of the most popular presidents in history, whose heart belonged to Stevenson; she too yearned for a miracle. Eleanor Roosevelt urged those liberals who had signed on with Jack not "to accept anyone as second best until you have done all you can to get the best." Then there was a former president, who claimed the country needed "a man with the greatest possible maturity and experience," and urged Jack "to be patient." Believing his own favorite candidate, Missouri senator Stuart Symington, didn't have a chance against the Kennedy bandwagon, Harry Truman chose not to attend the convention.

There was also, of course, the two-time presidential candidate who had refused to come out for Jack, saying he had promised the other candidates he would "remain neutral." Instead, Adlai Stevenson was secretly hoping for a deadlock, so the delegates would, for a third time, turn to him. And finally, there was the man who had an outside chance of getting the nomination: the Senate majority leader. While Jack had been winning primaries and rounding up votes, Lyndon B. Johnson had bided his time in Washington, somehow expecting to translate his mastery of the Senate into national influence in Los Angeles. Stevenson and Johnson had the same plan: stop Jack Kennedy on the first and second ballots and the convention would have to arrive at a compromise choice. Johnson had even confidently told Stevenson, "If I don't get it, it will be you."

Jack had won 134 firmly committed delegates in his primary victories, but some states, such as Indiana, were compelled to back Kennedy only on the first ballot and could not be counted on to stay with him for the second. Every vote for Stevenson, LBJ supporters reasoned, would be a vote taken from Jack. Yet Stevenson, they thought, could probably not win the nomination; to do so, he would have to get almost all of Jack's first-ballot commitments. But

Johnson, with considerable support from southern and western states, could take the nomination by wooing away about half of Jack's delegates.

The style of the two aspirants was very different. While Stevenson stayed above the battle, stubbornly clinging to his dignity while refusing to withdraw his name or endorse any other candidate, Johnson played rough. There were the predictable digs at Jack's youth: the Democrats, Johnson said, needed a candidate "with a touch of gray in his hair." There were slaps at Jack's father: "I never thought Hitler was right." At Jack's wealth: "I haven't had anything given to me. Whatever I have and whatever I hope to get will be because of whatever energy and talent I have." And at Jack's attendance record in the Senate: "Jack was out kissing babies while I was passing bills."

For the first time, the question of Jack's health also became an issue. Johnson supporter John Connally told a press conference that Jack had Addison's disease and was physically unfit to be president. Bobby was incensed when he learned that in private conversations with reporters, Johnson was even more vicious, hinting that Jack's disease was terminal, saying outright that a Kennedy presidency meant Joe would run the country. Bobby unleashed his fury on one of LBJ's aides. "You Johnson people are running a stinking damned campaign," he said, "and you'll get yours when the time comes."

As always, Jack remained more detached than his emotional brother. Johnson suggested "young Jack" debate him before the Texas delegation, a notion that caused Bobby to have a fit and which got little more enthusiasm from his father. Jack would be "a damned fool," Joe said, to go into that lion's den. His daughter Jean, who was with Joe at the time he got the news, was unperturbed. "But Daddy, how can Jack say no? That man *challenged* us." A few minutes later Joe heard that Jack had accepted the invitation, with the stipulation that the debate be held before a joint meeting of Texas and Massachusetts delegates. Joe liked the sound of that, and said Jack "will absolutely take this fellow apart." He did. Johnson spent much of the debate contrasting his leadership in the Senate with the frequent absenteeism of "some people." When Jack rose to speak, he said he assumed LBJ "was talking about some other candidate," hailed the Texan's "wonderful record" in the Senate, and concluded, "So I come here today full of admiration for Senator Johnson, full of affection for him, strongly in support of him . . . for Majority Leader."

Jack spent most of his time before the nominating process began addressing delegates from one state or another. On Monday, July 11, the opening day of the convention, he spoke to representatives of Nevada, Pennsylvania, Michigan, North Carolina, Arkansas, New York, South Carolina, Florida, and Alaska. On Tuesday, he met with delegates from the northeast states, and from Wyoming, South Dakota, and California. It was the day before the convention would nominate its presidential candidate, and Jack was fairly confident. Both he and Bobby calculated they were, with what now seemed to be 740 certain votes, just 21 short of a majority. Bobby said they were "dead" if they didn't make it on the first ballot. Jack thought they would be all right if they took it on the second. It would be then, he said—or never.

All the Kennedys except Jaqueline were in Los Angeles. Since the excitement and tension of the 1956 convention had been followed by a miscarriage, Jackie, now four and a half months pregnant, had decided to stay in Hyannis Port. Rose and Joe were at the Beverly Hills home of Marion Davies, longtime mistress of their late friend William Randolph Hearst. Although they were eleven miles from the convention site at the Sports Arena, Joe kept in touch with the action by telephone. The Kennedy command post was in the Biltmore Hotel, where Jack also had taken a suite. But he and Dave Powers were actually staying in a rented apartment in Hollywood owned by Jack Haley, who had played the Tin Man in *The Wizard of Oz*. There Jack could get some peace and quiet during the tumultuous week and still be near the convention site at the Sports Arena.

On Wednesday morning, Dave fixed Jack his favorite breakfast of bacon and eggs. Jack was in a good mood. "Does your wife know you can cook like this?" he teased Dave. "No, and don't tell her," Dave replied. But a moment later, Dave reminded Jack that in spite of the pleasant banter, it was only a few hours until the most momentous event of their lives would take place. "Well, this is the day you've been waiting for four years," he said, recalling their 1956 conversation. "This is the day you'll pick up all of the marbles." Jack smiled. "Let's hope the breakfast tastes as good as this tomorrow morning." They left for the convention site, where Jack met with delegates from Indiana, South Dakota, and Colorado before going to the Biltmore to confer with Bobby. Later that afternoon, Jack went to Beverly Hills to have a meal of Irish stew with his parents. The television set was on, and the nominations had begun.

Symington. Johnson. Kennedy. Then Senator Eugene McCarthy of Minnesota rose to offer the name of Adlai Stevenson.

"Do not reject this man who has made us all proud to be Democrats," McCarthy said. "Do not leave this prophet without honor in his own party." Four thousand of the Stevenson faithful in the galleries went wild. It was a last hurrah for the man from Libertyville. That morning, Stevenson had phoned Chicago's Mayor Daley to test the waters. No, Daley informed him, there was no widespread delegate support. Stevenson persisted: was there no support, period, or no support because people thought he wasn't a candidate? No support, period, Daley replied, not even in Stevenson's home state of Illinois. Jack, with his constant checking and rechecking of the delegates' positions, knew that just as well as Daley. While television showed the emotional demonstration going on and on, Jack was unconcerned. "Don't worry, Dad," he assured his father, "Stevenson has everything but the votes."

After dinner, Jack returned to his rented apartment to watch the balloting. Seated in front of the television set, armed with pencil and paper, Jack was ready to keep score. The roll call began. "Alabama casts twenty votes for Johnson, three and a half for Kennedy, and—" The lights went out. "God Almighty!" Dave heard in the darkness. "I slave and knock my brains out for four years to get this nomination, and now I can't even sit here and see it." Jack ran to the floor below and knocked on the door of William Gargan, a television actor. "Do you mind, Bill?" he asked, explaining that the electricity was out in his apartment. The startled Gargans, both in their nightclothes, had also been watching the convention on TV. "Please don't worry about your pajamas," Jack told the astonished couple. "Sit down and be comfortable." The roll call continued, and by the time Jack heard Connecticut cast its twenty-one votes for him, the electricity had been fixed.

Back upstairs, Jack continued to calmly mark the state totals on his informal scorecard. By Illinois, he was over 100. With Iowa, he went past 200. His home state brought Jack above 300. New York made the total just short of 500. Pennsylvania brought it to 650. By the time the state of Washington was called, he had 710 votes—51 to go for a majority. West Virginia made it 725, Wisconsin 748. The television cameras moved on to the Wyoming delegation, in the center of which Jack saw his brother Teddy standing. As campaign manager of the Rocky Mountain states, Teddy had previously reported Wyoming's vote to be split, with Jack certain of only 8½. But just before the state was called, Teddy shoved his way through to reach its chairman. Wyoming could nominate the next president of the United States, he shouted over the roar of the crowd. "Such support can never be forgotten by a president." Intently watching the TV screen, Jack saw a big smile spread across his brother's face. "This may be it," he said to Dave.

For four years, no one had cultivated more members of the Democratic party, had spoken in more places throughout the nation, had supported more local candidates, had become more familiar with the power structure of every state, than Jack Kennedy. He had kept a card file on every delegate and every person of any importance, from precinct leaders on up. In the first six months of 1960, he had flown sixty-five thousand miles, visited more than half the states, made 350 speeches. That exhausting effort was finally paying off. "Wyoming," the chairman called out, "casts all fifteen votes for the next President of the United States, John Kennedy."

After Jack phoned his wife and his father, he was driven to the Sports Arena, which little more than an hour before had been filled with the shouts of Stevenson supporters. Now the delegates were on their feet screaming for Jack as the band began to play an Irish song, "Toora-Loora-Loora." On the platform were Rose, Jack's brothers and sisters, their wives and husbands. Only Joe, still avoiding the public eye for the sake of his son, had stayed behind at the Davies home. After a few brief words of thanks, Jack returned to the apartment. He was worn out, and celebrated by drinking a single beer. Then, although it was very late, he glanced through a few congratulatory telegrams. One of the most cordial messages was from Lyndon Johnson: "LBJ now means Let's Back Jack." A few minutes later Jack sent a note to Johnson's suite at the Biltmore, requesting a meeting the next morning.

The first three days of the convention had been spent in the frantic activity of winning the presidential nomination, and there had been no chance to think seriously about the vice-presidential candidate. Suddenly Jack realized he had only a few hours in which to make that decision. There were many reasons to consider Lyndon Johnson. He was a Protestant with voter appeal in the southern, western, and border states, where Jack was less popular. His work in the Senate had also given Johnson national recognition, and his legislative skills could be a useful liaison between the White House and Capitol Hill. He had been the runner-up in the nomination balloting, with 409 votes compared to Jack's final total of 806.

But there were disadvantages as well. Since Johnson had supported Landrum-Griffin and, as a Texan, was considered a Southerner who could not be counted on to push for civil rights legislation, both labor and liberals regarded him with suspicion. With so little time to consider an alternate choice, Jack reluctantly made a decision which those two important factions, newly enthusiastic about his own candidacy, would see as betrayal. Next he had to face his own staff: from Bobby on down, Jack's closest personal aides detested Johnson. Kenny O'Donnell told Bobby that the selection of LBJ would be "a disaster," and when Jack arrived at the Biltmore early Thursday morning, Kenny let him have it. "This is the worst mistake you ever made," he told Jack. "You come out here to this convention like a knight on a white charger, the cleancut Ivy League college guy who's promising to get rid of the old hack machine politicians. And now, in your first move after you get the nomination, you go against all the people who supported you. Are we going to spend the campaign apologizing for Lyndon Johnson and trying to explain why he voted against everything you ever stood for?" Kenny asked furiously.

Jack was pretty mad himself. "Wait a minute. I've offered it to him, but he hasn't accepted it yet and maybe he won't. If he does accept it, let's get one thing clear," Jack replied. "I'm forty-three years old and I'm the healthiest candidate for president in the United States. I'm not going to die in office, so the vice-presidency doesn't mean anything." Kenny was somewhat mollified. Of course liberal Democratic goals would be safe with Jack in the White House for the next four or eight years, no matter who his running mate was. And it was unlikely Johnson would relinquish his power as Senate majority leader for the largely ceremonial position of vice-president. But to the astonishment of almost everyone, and the dismay of some, LBJ accepted.

Despite rumblings of rebellion on the convention floor, the name of Lyndon Johnson was placed in nomination Thursday morning. To head off the possibility of a liberal revolt, Jack's staff made arrangements to have the nomination declared unanimous. When the roll call reached Massachusetts, John McCormack moved that Johnson should be accepted by acclamation. Although historian Arthur Schlesinger, Jr., later said he thought the ayes and nays were in equal proportion, the motion, it was announced, had carried. That night, Jack and Bobby had dinner with their parents. Bobby, who would never forgive Johnson for the smear tactics he had used against the Kennedys, was in despair. "Yesterday was the best day of my life," he had confided to a journalist. "Today is the worst." His father, however, was a realist. Just forty-eight hours before, Johnson had been calling Joe a pro-Nazi. Joe could take that in stride. Jack's decision had been good politics, and that's what counted. "Don't worry, Jack," he told his son. "Within two weeks they'll be saying it's the smartest thing you ever did."

On Friday, Jack appeared before the delegates to formally accept the nomination. Although haggard and exhausted, he summoned the nation to follow him into his vision of the future. "We stand today on the edge of a New Frontier, the frontier of the 1960s, a frontier of unknown opportunities and perils, a frontier of unfulfilled hopes and threats," he told the convention. "The New Frontier of which I speak is not a set of promises, it is a set of challenges. It sums up, not what I intend to offer the American people, but what I intend to ask of them." Jack ended by saying it had been a long road to the convention. "Now begins another long journey, taking me into your cities and homes all over America. Give me your help." The crowd cheered. "Give me your hand." More cheering. "Your voice and your vote." With those final words, John F. Kennedy accepted his party's nomination for president. The delegates gave him a standing ovation.

Less than two weeks later, Vice-President Richard Nixon became the candidate of the Republican party, with Henry Cabot Lodge as his running mate.

15

LET'S GET THIS COUNTRY MOVING AGAIN

The American people had been lulled throughout almost two terms by the benign leadership of Dwight Eisenhower, but at the decade's end, international events conspired to make the choice of his successor critically important. Because of his experience in foreign affairs, Richard Nixon appeared to have an edge over Jack Kennedy.

In July 1959, Eisenhower sent his vice-president to Russia on a goodwill mission, a curtain-raiser to Soviet premier Nikita Khrushchev's upcoming September visit to the United States. In Moscow, the two men toured the American Exhibition, part of a U.S.-USSR exchange designed to show the latest technological advances in both countries. One section of the exhibit was the "Miracle Kitchen," and sneering at its array of appliances, Khrushchev launched into a tirade about American consumerism which escalated into a condemnation of U.S. foreign policy. Photographs of the vice-president answering back, shaking his finger in Khrushchev's face and apparently holding his own against the Russian leader, were published in almost every newspaper and magazine in America. "The Kitchen Debate" made Nixon look like a statesman who could stand up to the Communists. *Time* said he was "the personification of a kind of disciplined vigor that belies tales of the decadent and limp-wristed West." Adlai Stevenson admitted Nixon's performance would apparently make him "a formidable candidate" in 1960, a thought, Stevenson added, which filled him with "nausea."

The Russian premier's subsequent tour of the United States went well enough for the leaders of the two nations to plan a summit meeting in Paris the following spring, after which Eisenhower would visit the Soviet Union. But on May 1, 1960, relations between the superpowers suddenly turned very chilly when a young American, Francis Gary Powers, was shot down while flying a Central Intelligence Agency U-2 plane over Russia. When word first reached Washington that the high-altitude plane had been downed, the administration, assured by the CIA that it would be "impossible" for Powers to be captured alive, tried to give the impression the U-2 had been flying a weather reconnaissance mission. But the "impossible" had happened: both the plane's pilot and its espionage equipment were in the hands of the Soviets, and now the new "American Exhibition" was the wreckage of the U-2 on display in Gorky Park. Khrushchev demanded an apology; Eisenhower refused. Violation of Russian air space by a CIA plane meant, the Soviet government then announced, that Eisenhower's proposed visit would not be received with "proper cordiality." The summit meeting, which began on May 16, had also been "torpedoed" and should be postponed six to eight months, to a time when Eisenhower would no longer be in office.

Khrushchev was keeping an eye on the upcoming presidential election. Kennedy, whom he had met and rather liked when he had visited the Senate the previous fall, was an unknown quantity. Stevenson, the Russian premier thought, would be the most agreeable American leader. Nixon would be a disaster, and Khrushchev hoped the disrupted conference would harm the vice-president's chances to be elected. In the United States, polls showed that Eisenhower himself was more popular than ever; there was little question that, had he been constitutionally permitted to do so, the president could easily have won a third term in the White House.

Criticizing Eisenhower was always politically dangerous. When, during the Oregon primary, Jack said a Kennedy administration would have expressed "regret" over the U-2 affair in order to save the summit, his office was deluged with angry telegrams, all with the same theme: YOU'RE UNFIT TO BE PRESIDENT. Nixon denounced Jack as "naive and inexperienced." While political rhetoric in the United States heated up, the Cold War got even frostier.

Test-ban talks, seeking an agreement to end above-ground nuclear explosions which were poisoning the atmosphere with radioactive fallout, had been under way in Geneva, but in June the Russians walked out. Two months later in Moscow, Francis Gary

Powers was found guilty of gathering state secrets for a foreign government and sentenced to ten years' "deprivation of liberty," with the first three years to be served in hard labor. Then, in September, both Khrushchev and the head of the Cuban government, Fidel Castro, came to New York for the opening of the General Assembly of the United Nations.

Castro especially seemed to arouse American animosity, and there was so much concern about protecting the life of the Cuban leader that 258 members of the police department were assigned to guard him. Ironically, only a few days before Castro's arrival in New York, another, very different conference had taken place at the Plaza Hotel in that same city. As if the CIA hadn't already done enough harm by allowing its U-2 flight over Russia just two weeks before the Paris summit, it had now dreamed up an even more inflammatory scheme. The get-together at the Plaza included James O'Connell, chief of the Agency's Operational Support Division; Robert Maheu, a former FBI officer now on a monthly retainer to the CIA; and Johnny Roselli, an underworld figure who had once been in the Al Capone organization. The group had met as the result of an internal CIA memo written the previous month, regarding "a sensitive mission requiring gangster-type action." The mission: "the liquidation of Fidel Castro." Even the CIA, however, thought better of murdering the head of a foreign government visiting an American city, so it was decided that the attempt would be made after Castro returned to his own country. But the huge population of the metropolitan area included any number of ardent right-wingers who might try to assassinate the Communist leaders, and for their own safety, President Eisenhower announced that Castro and Khrushchev would be confined to the island of Manhattan. On the campaign trail, Jack pointed out that the administration had not been able to confine them "in Latin America or around the world."

The electorate found the duo's high jinks so entertaining that, in the middle of the campaign, public attention focused more on the pair of Communist leaders than on the two men who were seeking the presidency. During the twelve days Castro remained in New York, Khrushchev made a pointed effort to emphasize Russia's "solidarity with Cuba." The Soviet leader had sought Castro out at his hotel, where the Communist odd couple met for the first time. As photographers snapped away, Castro, tall, bearded, and wearing combat fatigues, swooped down to hug Khrushchev, who was considerably shorter, less hairy, and, as he himself admitted, "broad abeam." The display of mutual affection continued at the United

Nations, where they made a great show of repeatedly embracing for the cameras. At the second day of the UN session, Khrushchev spoke for three hours, demanding that the General Assembly debate the U-2 incident and calling America a "disgrace to civilization," while Castro beamed his approval. When Castro addressed the group for four and one-half hours, denouncing U.S. "aggression," Khrushchev smiled and applauded throughout the speech.

Khrushchev particularly seemed to enjoy the furor his presence caused in New York, and stayed on for two weeks after his Cuban counterpart had departed. He dined at the Plaza, where he was booed; the Russian premier booed back. When British prime minister Harold Macmillan addressed the General Assembly and denounced the Soviet Union for destroying the Paris summit, Khrushchev tried to shout Macmillan down, called the UN a spitoon, and pounded first his fist and then his shoe on the table in front of him. When he left New York, Khrushchev said he would have nothing further to do with the United States until it had chosen a new leader.

With the increasing tension between Russia and their own nation, Americans began to take a good hard look at the two presidential candidates. Jack felt he could claim that under the Republican administration, the country had lost ground politically and militarily. Nixon thought his greater experience in international affairs made him the logical choice to lead America through dangerous times. By contrast, he said, Jack was "the kind of man Mr. Khrushchev will make mincemeat of." Early in September, the voters seemed to agree: Jack trailed Nixon in the Gallup poll 53 to 47 percent.

There were other reasons why the poll showed Jack behind. One of the most important was his religion. "I'm getting tired of these people who think I want to replace the gold at Fort Knox with a supply of holy water," Jack told Kenny O'Donnell. He had a chance to confront the problem on September 12, when he addressed the Ministerial Association of Houston, Texas, in a meeting which almost everyone on his staff advised against. "We can win or lose the election right there in Houston on Monday night," Ted Sorensen remarked to a friend during the weekend before Jack's appearance. Although the speech was to be televised statewide, it was not shown nationally, so Jack was spared his mother's certain criticism had she been able to watch. Somberly attired in a dark-blue suit, blue shirt, and blue and white striped tie, Jack discovered at the last minute that his black shoes had accidentally been left on the plane. Don't worry, Dave Powers assured him; most of the men in America wear brown shoes. "Do you realize that tonight, by wearing these shoes, you'll be sewing up the brown-shoe voters?" Although Jack had been nervous about his speech, Dave's remark made him laugh, and he went in to face the difficult situation in a much better frame of mind.

The ministers, too, had been on edge before Jack began to speak, but the tension soon lessened. He believed, Jack said, in an America "where religious liberty is so indivisible that an act against one church is treated as an act against all. . . . Today," he told the group, "I may be the victim, but tomorrow it may be you." He reassured them by saying he would resign the presidency rather than violate the national interest in order to avoid violating his conscience—a statement carefully thought out to convince Protestants that Jack would be above Vatican pressure, while reassuring Catholics that he would be true to his faith. He appealed to the pride of Texas ministers by saying, "side by side with Bowie and Crockett died McCafferty and Bailey and Carey, but no one knows whether they were Catholics or not, for there was no religious test at the Alamo." Jack received heavy applause from the spectators. "It was the best speech of his campaign," Ted Sorensen said, "and one of the most important in his life."

Another "most important" event followed two weeks later, with the first of four televised debates between Jack and Richard Nixon. The networks had offered the candidates free time, a chance for unprecedented national exposure that neither of the two parties could have afforded to buy. Ten years before, television had been little more than a curiosity; now there were TV sets in 88 percent of American homes, every one of which was turned on for an average of four or five hours a day. In this, what the country had come to regard as a crucial election, it was a sure bet that many of the nation's forty million sets would be tuned in to the debates.

Jack accepted the network's offer immediately; Nixon, with much more to lose, saw no way out but to agree as well. The Republican candidate went into the debates leading in the polls, and after holding national office for almost eight years, was thought to be better-known, more experienced, and more mature. Eisenhower had advised him not to accept; it was television that had brought Jack Kennedy stardom. But Nixon was confident. His popularity had greatly increased after the "Kitchen Debate," and he expected the TV match-up to show he was a more skilled speaker than his opponent. The difference was that this time he wouldn't be going against the short, stocky, balding leader of the despised Soviet Union.

There was now also his own appearance to consider. Earlier in the month, Nixon had been in the hospital because of an infected knee; fuming about the lost time, he had spent the intervening weeks in an exhausting round of campaigning, during which he caught a cold. By the evening of the first debate in Chicago on September 26, Nixon appeared gaunt and haggard. Although he was clean-shaven, the paleness of his face accentuated the heavy shadow of his beard; nervous and perspiring heavily, the vice-president projected an almost sinister image. By contrast, Jack seemed vigorous, relaxed, and clean-cut. He was also better prepared. Kennedy aides had put every conceivable question and statistic on index cards, and used them to drill Jack for two days. Before leaving for the TV studio, he had taken a long nap, piles of index cards scattered around him on the bed.

Jack had the opening remarks, and began by speaking of his hopes for the nation. "This is a great country, but I think it could be a greater country." He touched on themes which had become his favorites: Soviet superiority in science and technology, the failure of the American educational system, hunger, unemployment, racial tension. He concluded with an appeal which he would use constantly throughout the campaign. It was time, Jack said, to get the country "moving again." Nixon's response sounded weak. "I know Senator Kennedy feels as deeply about these problems as I do, but our disagreement is not about the goals for America but only about the means to reach those goals." As he continued to speak, the camera occasionally turned to show his opponent. Jack looked calm, listening to Nixon with an expression of respect—under which there was, perhaps, a slight hint of boredom and amusement. During the question-and-answer session which followed the opening statements, Nixon directed his responses at Jack as if his opponent was the judge in a high school debate. Jack, however, knew who the real judge in the contest was, and addressed his self-assured comments to the camera. Suddenly, with six weeks to go until the election, there was a reversal in the polls: Jack had now taken the lead.

Although three more debates followed in October, the first was by far the most consequential. Seventy million viewers had watched; many of whom recognized that John F. Kennedy was presidential quality. His youth and inexperience, the Republicans' two major weapons against him, now seemed absurd; Jack appeared mature and well versed in domestic and foreign affairs. And although Richard Nixon was an extremely earnest and sober candidate, Jack generated excitement—somehow combining, one senator said, "the best qualities of Elvis Presley and Franklin D. Roosevelt." That combination was particularly in evidence on the road, where Jack abandoned the cool, self-contained image that worked best on television and threw himself into fiery political rhetoric. Almost every speech ended with the same imperative: "Let's get this country moving again!"

In spite of the grinding exhaustion of the campaign, Jack's self-deprecating humor remained intact. During one address, which he presented without notes and with little sleep, he realized he had repeated the same phrase three times in a single sentence. The crowd laughed, and Jack joined in, saying that perhaps he should set the speech to music. When an admiring member of an audience asked how he had become a war hero, Jack responded, "It was strictly involuntary. They sank my boat." On one of the *Caroline*'s flights, the plane, filled with its usual contingent of reporters, made a sudden drop. Musing with the journalists about how a crash might have been covered in newspapers, Jack said, "If we'd really gone down, I just want you fellows to know that your names would have been in very small type."

Jack was always comfortable talking to members of the press, but a group that made him ill at ease was farmers. He had difficulty understanding agricultural problems: "Where I grew up, we were taken out on a bus to see a cow," he confided to one staff member. In some farm areas he would tell crowds, "We have not had much manure on our shoes up to now, but we're catching up fast." Speaking at a rally in Sioux City, Iowa, Jack posed a question in his Boston accent: "So I ahsk what's wrong with the American fahmah today?" While he paused for effect, a voice in the audience yelled out, "He's stahving!" No one laughed louder than Jack. He was more relaxed with young people, and enjoyed the signs they held up for him to read: WHEN I GROW UP, I'M GONNA VOTE FOR YOU, promised one. IF I ONLY HAD A VOTE, YOU'D HAVE IT, said another. Jack suggested that the voting age be lowered to nine. Jack hadn't lost his appeal to a slightly older age group, either. Reporters entertained themselves counting empty shoes along the routes of his motorcades. "Women," one said, "literally leaped out of them" when they saw Jack. They also tore at his clothes, ripped off his cuff links, pulled out his hair.

Yet he almost never lost his temper, even when being heckled. After a man in Brooklyn had interrupted several times, Jack said, "Let me speak first, then you. Okay?" In Milwaukee, a drunken woman threw whiskey at him. Wiping off his face, Jack handed back the tumbler and calmly said, "Here's your glass." While he was trying to speak at New York University, some students kept chanting

"We want Nixon, we want Nixon." Jack at last acknowledged the group: "I don't think you're going to get him." But once, after being harassed by an overweight Teamster member who had been following the campaign for several hours, Jack finally snapped. "Get lost, Fatso," he told the man.

Most of the campaign dialogue was much more high-toned. There were serious issues involved, and Jack's appearances were not confined to bantering with audiences. Nixon always defended Republican leadership, America's military strength, and the nation's economy. Those were the very topics, Jack said, that separated the two candidates. The election was, he explained, a contest "between the comfortable and the concerned." His speeches reflected a conviction that the United States should be doing better. "I don't run for the office of the presidency to tell you what you want to hear," Jack said to a crowd in Portland, Maine. "I run for the office of the presidency because in a dangerous time we need to be told what we must do if we are going to maintain our freedom and the freedom of those who depend on us." He concluded: "You cannot be successful abroad unless you are successful at home."

Jack worried a great deal about America's prestige, which he thought had fallen to a new low under the Republican administration. "I want a world which looks to the United States for leadership, which does not always read what Mr. Khrushchev or what Mr. Castro is doing. I want them to read what the President of the United States is doing." The Soviets, he claimed, "have made a spectacle before the world of the U-2 flight and the trial of our pilot, and have treated this nation with hostility and contempt." In an effort to get Jack to stop criticizing American defense policies, Eisenhower asked that Jack be briefed on the status of U.S. military strength. Jack was not convinced he was being told the full story, and said he had access to more information as a member of the Senate Foreign Relations Committee. The Joint Chiefs of Staff, Jack thought, seemed a little too complacent with America's state of preparedness, and after one session in Washington, asked if there were no doubting Thomases in the Pentagon. Unwilling to accept the administration's view, he continued to label Republicans as "the party which gave us the Missile Gap."

The campaign moved into the critical last three and one-half weeks. An unwritten political law was that the full attention of the electorate couldn't really be captured until the baseball season was over. On October 13, the second baseman of the Pittsburgh Pirates hit a home run and gave his team its first successful World Series since 1925. A few hours later, the New York Police Department breathed a collective sigh of relief: Nikita Khrushchev had stopped pounding his shoe and gone home. Now the United States could finally get down to the serious business of electing a president. The latest Gallup poll showed Jack holding his lead: 49 percent for Kennedy, 46 percent for Nixon, 5 percent still undecided.

A few days later, on October 19, Martin Luther King, Jr., was arrested during a sit-in at an Atlanta, Georgia, restaurant. By October 24 all the other demonstrators had been released, but King was sentenced to four months hard labor and sent to a state penitentiary. The black leader was so hated in the South that there was fear for his life; his wife was convinced he would be lynched in prison. Three Southern governors had already told Jack not to have anything to do with King or his cause. If he did so, they warned, the Democratic national ticket would lose the entire region below the Mason-Dixon line. Nevertheless, on October 26 Jack telephoned King's wife, Coretta, to express his concern. The next day Bobby took things one step further.

Although he didn't consult with his brother, Bobby did call Lyndon Johnson, who was campaigning in the South, to warn the vice-presidential candidate of what he intended to do. "Tell Jack that we'll ride it through down here some way," LBJ responded. "At least he's on the side of right." Then Bobby picked up the phone and called the judge who had sentenced King, requesting that the black leader be released on bail. "I made it clear," Bobby explained later, "that it was not a political call, that I am a lawyer who believes in the right of all defendants to make bond."

King was a hero to his people, and now so were the Kennedys. King's father, a Baptist minister, announced he would use his influence with other blacks to get them to support the Democratic candidate. "I've got a suitcase of votes and I'm going to take them to Mr. Kennedy and dump them in his lap," Martin Luther King, Sr., said, although he told journalists he had previously thought he could never vote for a Catholic. When Jack heard the comment he was amused. "Imagine Martin Luther King having a bigot for a father. Well," he added, "we all have fathers, don't we?"

Joe Kennedy continued to be a campaign issue himself. Republicans wisecracked that he had promised Jack, "Don't worry, son, if you lose the election I'll buy you a country." Another wit on the opposition had come up with the rhyme, "Jack and Bob will run the show, while Ted's in charge of hiding Joe." But although the

Kennedy patriarch was rarely seen publicly, he was still wheeling and dealing behind the scenes. Her husband, Rose said serenely, was working "in his own way." Joe's "own way" included political savvy, millions of dollars, and powerful contacts that reached from Harvard to Hollywood.

En route to Election Day, Joe was also not reluctant to let some old friendships fall by the wayside. After Arthur Krock dared to criticize the Democrats' platform as being too liberal, Joe—who had always shared Krock's conservative views—phoned him to end their twenty-eight-year association. When Cardinal Spellman of the New York Archdiocese rode with Nixon in a Fifth Avenue parade, Joe refused to ever speak to him again. Although some of his advisors warned Jack that Joe might be doing more harm than good, he replied, "Look, I can't control my father. He's an old man and he's having the time of his life going around helping me. Do you think that I can do anything about that, or that I'd want to?"

Joe wasn't the only member of the family enjoying himself. There were Kennedys campaigning all over America, and bumper stickers began to appear: BE THANKFUL ONLY ONE CAN WIN. Jack had a sister living in each of three key states: Jean in New York, Eunice in Illinois, Pat in California. But the Kennedy women made appearances everywhere in the country, at such a frantic pace that at one point Eunice called campaign headquarters to ask, "Where was I yesterday?" Ethel pitched in with her usual enthusiasm, and even managed to win over a group of Republican women in Aberdeen, South Dakota, when she told them her husband's instructions: "Whatever you do, don't speak!" Joan was working in the Rocky Mountain states, where Teddy was again in charge. Pregnant for the first time, she had borrowed clothes from Jackie so that she could accompany her husband on public engagements. "We went around by car," Joan said, "with me bumping in the back with my fat little figure."

Because her own baby was due in November, Jackie's participation was limited. She didn't really mind. "Thank God I get out of those dreadful chicken dinners," she told a friend. "Sitting at head tables where I can't have a cigarette, and listening to some gassy old windbag drives me up the wall." Jack also thought it was just as well his wife was not participating in the national campaign. She had, he liked to say, too much status and not enough quo. Jackie was chic and glamorous, and not at all in the typical image of a politician's wife. "The American people just aren't ready for someone like you," Jack told her.

But there was one U.S. city cosmopolitan enough to accept and admire Jacqueline Kennedy. With only a few weeks left before Election Day, Jack was scheduled to appear in New York, and asked his wife to join him. "If he lost, I'd never forgive myself for not being there," Jackie said, and against her doctor's advice, she went. They drove through the Garment District in one of the wildest scenes of the campaign. A motorcycle patrolman had a sleeve torn off his uniform; he said it was worse than Omaha Beach on D-Day. Jackie, eight months pregnant, later commented that she had felt the sides of the car bending in. Dave Powers estimated the crowd, which stretched for twelve blocks, to be one million people. Jackie did her bit before slightly smaller audiences as well. In different ethnic neighborhoods, she made speeches in French, Italian, and Spanish. "I assure you that my wife can also speak English," Jack told reporters.

Back in Hyannis Port, Jackie gave occasional interviews. When asked if her husband was different since becoming a presidential candidate, she replied, "I don't think Jack has changed much, I really don't. He still thinks nothing of answering the door at home when he's wearing his shorts." Somebody mentioned it would be good politics to have her baby on the eve of the election. "Oh, I hope not," Jackie replied, "I'd have to get up the next day to go and vote."

Jack must often have wished he could gag both his wife and his mother. Rose was inimitable. Nixon, she thought, was doing well "without the advantages of a powerful family." When Teddy asked her to come west to speak, Rose bemused a Cheyenne audience by announcing she loved everybody in "little Wyoming." Still a powerhouse in spite of her age, the appearance was one of forty-six Rose made in fourteen different states.

Bobby seemed to be everywhere, telling everyone what to do. Kennedy staff members groused to each other, "Little Brother Is Watching You." But Bobby didn't care whom he offended as long as the job got done. "I don't give a damn if the state and county organizations survive after November," he told an astounded group of New York big shots, "and I don't give a damn if you survive. I want to elect John F. Kennedy." The one thing Bobby wouldn't permit was criticism of the family. When a *Time* correspondent mentioned he thought Eunice was a stodgy campaigner and that Pat was too flippant, Bobby snapped. "If you say anything more I'm leaving."

Although the strain was beginning to show in the Kennedy camp, their candidate was thriving. The harder Jack worked, the better he got. He loved to taunt his opponent, and where humor was concerned, it was strictly no contest. Nixon frequently used his well-publicized confrontation with Khrushchev to prove his ability to stand tough with the Communists. "Mr. Nixon may be very experienced in kitchen debates," Jack said, "but so are a great many other married men I know." To a crowd in the Bronx, Jack mentioned his opponent had "called him an ignoramus, a liar, a Pied Piper, and all the rest. I just confine myself to calling him a Republican." But, he added, Nixon thought that was hitting too low.

The vice-president often spoke glowingly of the wisdom he had gained in two terms in national office, so Jack said "the worst news for the Republicans" was that Casey Stengel, longtime manager of the New York Yankees, had been fired. "It must show that perhaps experience does not count." In the week before the election, Nixon called Jack a "barefaced liar." Jack responded by making fun of his opponent's five o'clock shadow, which had been so obvious in the television debates. "Having seen him four times close up in this campaign, and made-up, I would not accuse Mr. Nixon of being barefaced," he told an audience in Albuquerque. "But I think the American people next Tuesday can determine who is telling the truth." Suddenly the election was only a week away.

The Kennedy staff was completely worn out from working eighteen-hour days. Checking into a small-town hotel one morning at two-thirty, Dave Powers and Kenny O'Donnell left an early wake-up call. "We do things for this guy that we wouldn't do for our own mothers," Dave commented. There were mornings when Jack himself had a little trouble getting out of bed, but Dave could always get him up by asking, "What do you suppose Nixon's doing while you're laying there?" Jack commented to one crowd that his schedule usually showed there were "five minutes allotted for the candidate to eat and rest." By November 3, near the end of the week before the election, Jack told his audience: "I am going to last about five more days, but that is time enough." It was almost too much.

In the last several days of the campaign, public sentiment seemed to be swinging back to Nixon. One factor was that the topic of Jack's religion had reared its head again. A joke began making the rounds that Jack was collecting bowling balls in order to string a rosary for the Statue of Liberty, which would be renamed Our Lady of the Harbor. Jack responded with some humor of his own, telling a New York audience he had sent a letter to Harry Truman, who had finally gotten into the campaign in a typically salty-tongued fashion: "Dear Mr. President," Jack pretended to read, "I have noted with interest your suggestion as to where those who vote for my opponent should go. While I understand and sympathize with your deep motivation, I think it is important that our side try to refrain from raising the religious issue."

Republicans, of course, wanted to keep the subject alive. There was the ongoing rumor, quietly but carefully encouraged by the Nixon forces, that a Catholic president would be ruled by the Vatican. Even the pope himself responded to that notion. He told an American bishop he had been trying to learn English, but smilingly added that no one should expect him "to run a country with a language as difficult as yours." To the Kennedy organization the religious problem was no laughing matter, and Nixon supporters were counting on it to be an important ingredient in their candidate's victory. "I have a deep and abiding faith," a Republican party leader said cheerfully, "in the fundamental bigotry of the American people."

Jack's opponents also thought they could rely on "the American people" to be seduced by an eleventh-hour TV blitz. And to add to the magic of television, the Republicans finally brought out their most powerful weapon of all: Dwight Eisenhower. Nixon advisors had kept the president out of the campaign, because they claimed Jack would otherwise charge that their man was riding on Eisenhower's coattails. There was actually more to it than that. Earlier in the year, a reporter had asked the president what Nixon ideas had been adopted during his administration. "If you give me a week," Eisenhower had replied, "I might think of one." That statement and others equally unenthusiastic caused some embarrassment in the Nixon camp, and as a result, the president had been excluded in the first weeks of the campaign, when the polls still showed the Republican candidate to be ahead.

But a few days before the election, that strategy was changed. Nixon needed the president in order to win. Eisenhower wanted his vice-president to be elected, both as an endorsement of his own two terms in office, and a confirmation that U.S. citizens believed in everything his administration had tried to accomplish. As Tuesday, November 8, drew closer, television viewers were inundated with Republican faces at Republican rallies in several large cities. Nixon, Cincinnati; Eisenhower, Pittsburgh; Nixon, Eisenhower, and Lodge, New York. The president, with his irresistible grin, the vice-president standing alongside. Finally, for four straight hours: Nixon, Detroit. Now the polls said the election was "too close to call."

Jack went into a last-minute blitz of his own. He was tired, but, his father reminded him, he'd be a lot tireder if he didn't win. On November 5, Jack gave a rousing speech to a New York audience, making fun of both the symbol and the candidate of the Republican party. "You've seen those elephants in the circus. They have a long memory but no vision. When they move around the ring, they have to grab the tail of the elephant in front of them, so they'll know where to go. Dick Nixon grabbed the tail of the elephant ahead of him in 1952 and 1956, but now, in 1960, he's the one who is supposed to be running, not President Eisenhower." The crowd roared.

Early on Sunday, November 6, Jack took his campaign home to New England. He arrived in pouring rain at Bridgeport, Connecticut, at twelve-thirty in the morning. From there, he was driven to Waterbury, just twenty-seven miles away, on a trip that lasted two hours. The whole state, it seemed, had turned out to line the highway, greeting the appearance of his car with torchlights and flares and cries of "We love you, Jack!" At 3 A.M. he reached Waterbury, where he was met by thirty thousand people. Jack made a short speech from his hotel balcony and then told the crowd he had promised their mayor he would send them home. They refused to let him go. He made a few more brief remarks and tried to leave. But they called him back again and again. Jack finally went to bed at four o'clock, but he was up again at seven. There were only two days left.

In those last frantic forty-eight hours, Jack traveled from Connecticut to Long Island to New Jersey to Maine. Arriving in Lewiston at one thirty in the morning, he found twenty thousand people awaiting him in the cold. "My God, isn't this unbelievable?" Jack happily asked Kenny O'Donnell. From there, he flew to Rhode Island, on to Massachusetts, back to Connecticut, to Vermont, to New Hampshire. In Manchester, Jack shared a stage with his three sisters, who were worn out from appearances in forty states. Introducing his sister Pat, seven years younger than he, Jack said, "Somebody asked her last week if I was her kid brother, so she knew it was time this campaign came to an end." Within a few hours the polls would begin to open.

The Kennedys moved on to Boston, the city in which it had all begun. Jack was greeted by a screaming hometown mob. He had planned an hour's sleep before giving his final two speeches of the campaign, but the streets of the North End, birthplace of Honey Fitz and Rose, were jammed. The crowd swarmed around the car, breaking its windows. Men and women alike were screaming, "I love you,

Jack!" slowing his progress until finally he gave up hope for a rest and went directly to the Boston Garden. After a fifteen-minute ovation, Jack had time for only a few brief remarks, which he ended by asking the audience to join him in "picking this country of ours up and sending it into the sixties." Then, at 11 P.M., he made a national television address from Faneuil Hall, the "Cradle of Liberty," where almost two centuries before, American patriots had begun to plot a revolution. "I come back to this old city," he said, "with the strongest possible confidence in the future of the United States, in the ability of its people to meet their responsibilities."

Less than an hour later, at midnight, the citizens of New Hampshire cast the first votes of the 1960 American presidential election.

Tuesday, November 8, 1960, was a very long day in Hyannis Port. There would be little news until evening, with many hours to fill before the returns started coming in. Jack had breakfast with most of the Kennedy family at the home of his parents. Back in his own house later in the morning, he gave Caroline a large bag of toys he had collected for her during his travels. At noon, photographers arrived for a session of picture-taking. Jack, usually at ease with members of the press, was tense and irritable, so the group left after a few minutes. He was no longer the youthful candidate of ten months before. Early in the campaign he had agreed to a shorter haircut, in order to seem less boyish. The rigors of the last two months had taken care of the rest, and now his face was puffy from exhaustion and lined with new wrinkles. Although his right arm was inflamed, scratched and swollen from the ordeal of shaking millions of hands, Jack couldn't resist joining his brothers on the lawn, where they were tossing a football.

After lunch with Jacqueline, he cut across the three backyards in what would be the first of many visits to Bobby's house. There a command post of thirty telephones and four wire-service teletypes had been set up; Democratic headquarters across the country had each been assigned a special Hyannis Port number to call with news from ninety key districts nationwide. In the afternoon the phones were still quiet, and Jack returned home to take a nap. But by early evening he was back at Bobby's to hear the first scattered returns. Those calling with information from the East reported that voting seemed to be going well for the Democratic ticket. Eunice, who assumed good news from Connecticut and Pennsylvania indicated a trend, began to sing "When Irish Eyes Are Smiling."

Then came a sobering shock. At seven-fifteen, a bulletin from CBS: its computer was predicting the odds for a Nixon victory at 100 to 1. Jack said the computer was "nuts," and CBS soon agreed. By eight o'clock, the network estimated Jack would win with 51 percent of the vote. NBC refused to forecast the outcome, and called the election a "cliff-hanger." Between nine o'clock and midnight, Jack restlessly paced back and forth from his own home, to his parents', to his brother's. Up until ten-thirty, the news was encouraging; then returns began to trickle in from the center of the country. Jack was losing in Wisconsin, Kentucky, Tennessee, the farm-belt states. Lyndon Johnson called to say Texas was holding, and Jack managed to laugh when the vice-presidential candidate added, "I see *we* won in Pennsylvania, but what happened to *you* in Ohio?" The loss of that midwestern state made Jack especially bitter. He had toured there on six separate occasions throughout the campaign, and now, staring at his red, infected hand, he commented, "Ohio did that to me."

As the night dragged on, the command post grew very quiet. By 3 A.M., it was clear that the final result of the election hinged on just four states: Michigan, Minnesota, Illinois, and California. Richard Daley phoned Kenny O'Donnell to report that, in spite of Jack's diminishing lead, Illinois would go Democratic. One of the precincts outside of Peoria, "where there are only fifty voters," Daley said, "just announced five hundred votes for Nixon." Nevertheless, the Chicago mayor assured Kenny, late returns from his city would wrap up the state for Jack. A few minutes later, a TV announcement: Nixon was going to appear on television. Jack came into the room, munching a sandwich, and asked, "Is there any milk in the house?" No one paid the slightest attention to the presidential candidate; everyone was too intent on watching the television screen.

Nixon looked awful, as if he already knew how the contest would finally end. But his few brief remarks stopped just short of a concession, and at 4 A.M., with the outcome still hanging in the balance, Jack decided to go to bed. Bobby stayed on, checking returns from those areas in which the result of the election depended, running up a phone bill which, it was estimated, came to ten thousand dollars for a single night. There was bad news from the other side of the continent: California was going for Nixon. Hearing the discouraging report that Jack had lost one of the four key states, Bobby's concern was for his other brother. "I'm worrying about Teddy," he told Kenny. "We've lost every state that he worked in out west. Jack will kid him and that may hurt Teddy's feelings."

But even if Teddy was disappointed by election results in the far West, he and the rest of the family awoke to joyful news. Although Jack had lost twenty-seven of the fifty states, he had taken Illinois, Minnesota, and Michigan. In the electoral college total, Jack would receive 303 votes to Nixon's 219. In the popular vote, the Democratic national ticket had won by the narrowest of margins: one-tenth of one percent. Out of a total of 68, 832,818 votes cast, Jack had beaten Nixon by only 112,881. But that was enough to make him the next president of the United States.

By 7 A.M. Secret Service agents had surrounded the Kennedy compound.

Jack awoke at 9 o'clock on Wednesday and learned from Ted Sorensen that the decision of American voters was no longer in doubt. Almost immediately, the phone rang. It was Janet Auchincloss, the woman who wasn't sure Jack Kennedy was good enough for her daughter, calling with congratulations. When Jack went downstairs for breakfast, Caroline greeted him with "Good morning, Mr. President." She was rewarded with a piggyback ride on the lawn, while Jackie, somewhat dazed by events, went for a walk alone on the beach. Jack went to get her, and when the couple walked through the front door of Joe Kennedy's home, the entire family burst into applause.

By one o'clock, Richard Nixon had conceded, so Jack could acknowledge his victory. He and the rest of the Kennedys were driven to the local National Guard armory, where the press was waiting. Jack read aloud congratulatory telegrams from Eisenhower and Nixon, made a few brief remarks, and concluded, "So now my wife and I prepare for a new administration—and for a new baby." Then Jack introduced family members to the journalists. He came at last to his father.

Earlier, as he started to get in the car for the drive to the press conference, Jack had glanced toward the house. Joe Kennedy, who thought he should continue to remain out of the limelight, had been standing alone in the shadows of the porch. Turning back, Jack had gone to his father and insisted that Joe take his place with the family.

Now, one hour later, as dozens of flashbulbs went off, cameras recorded a rare public display of emotion. There on the stage of the armory, the president-elect of the United States hugged the man who had made it all possible.

PART THREE

JFK

16

THE TORCH IS PASSED TO A NEW GENERATION

"I thought this part of being president was going to be fun."

Even before he reached the Oval Office, Jack was getting some idea of how awesome his new job was going to be. Forming a government meant trying to find qualified people for a dizzying number of positions in the Cabinet, the White House, the regulatory agencies. For the last few years, Jack told former secretary of state Dean Acheson, he had spent so much time getting to know those who could help him *become* president that he knew very few who could help him *be* president. "People, people, people!" Jack said. "I don't know any people. I only know voters. How am I going to fill these twelve hundred jobs?"

Choosing his White House aides was the easiest part. On the Thursday following the election, Jack made his first appointments. Ted Sorensen would become special counsel to the president, a position in which he would be responsible for drafting legislative programs, researching and writing speeches, and helping to formulate government policies. Kenny O'Donnell was named appointments secretary, which meant he would supervise Jack's daily schedule, as well as all travel and security arrangements; Dave Powers would serve as Kenny's assistant. Pierre Salinger would remain press secretary, the function he had performed during the campaign; now he would be the president's link with the outside world. An early Salinger request to journalists was that after taking office, the president be referred to as JFK. Eisenhower had often been called by the familiar nickname "Ike" in newspaper headlines. But his successor, thirty-seven years younger, thought initials seemed more mature and presidential than the less-dignified "Jack."

The president-elect's first press announcement also included the information that J. Edgar Hoover, director of the FBI, would stay on in that position. Jack's motivation went beyond the explosive Inga Arvad tapes in the Bureau's files. He knew his slender victory required a gesture of continuity and political balance—so only two days after the election, Hoover and CIA director Allen Dulles were reappointed to the most sensitive positions in government. Since both men symbolized the kind of Cold Warriorism which liberals had not expected to be part of the New Frontier, the announcement caused dismay among many of Jack's supporters.

Another sop to conservatives was Jack's courtesy call on Richard Nixon—a further indication that he intended the transfer of power, the first from a Republican to a Democratic administration since 1933, would be without rancor. When a *New York Times* reporter asked what he and Nixon had discussed, Jack replied, "I asked him how he took Ohio, but he did not tell me. He must be keeping it secret for 1964." Privately, Jack had a grimmer assessment, and told Kenny O'Donnell, "It was just as well for all of us that he didn't quite make it."

During the weeks following the election, Jack was back and forth between Washington, New York, and Florida. Because of her pregnancy, Jacqueline remained at their home in Georgetown, which Jack used as a base from which to announce many important appointments. Since the house was not large enough to accommodate the frenzied activities of the transition, Jack also took a spacious two-story suite at the Carlyle Hotel in Manhattan to use as a temporary headquarters. When things got too hectic, he retreated to his parents' home in Palm Beach. After a week there in late November, Jack flew to Washington to have Thanksgiving dinner with Jackie and Caroline. But on his way back to Florida that night, a radio message brought word that Jackie had gone into premature labor. Jack was restless and upset on the return trip to Washington; four years earlier, his absence during Jackie's miscarriage had almost ruined their marriage. Now he told O'Donnell, "I'm never there when she needs me."

Jack spent most of the flight in the pilot's cabin, wearing radio earphones. Suddenly he removed them and smiled. Jackie had given birth to a baby boy, and "both mother and son," Pierre Salinger announced over the intercom, "are doing well." Everyone on the plane burst into applause, and the president-elect took a bow. For the next two weeks, Jack stayed close to home, visiting the hospital several times a day. The little boy, whom his parents named John F. Kennedy, Jr., had been born almost a month prematurely and had to spend nine days in an incubator. By early December he was well enough to travel, and Jack took his family to Palm Beach to stay through the Christmas holidays.

In spite of the distraction of young John's birth, the business of forming a government continued. Even before the election, Jack had prepared for the contingency of his victory. Washington lawyer Clark Clifford was asked to anticipate the problems of a presidential transition, and compiled a fifty-page handbook which was given to each new appointee. The report helped, Salinger said, serve as a guide through the "twilight zone" of the weeks before Jack was sworn into office. In return for his help, the president-elect joked, Clifford had asked for nothing except the right to advertise his law firm on the back of one-dollar bills.

Jack wanted his appointments to be as apolitical as possible. "I want the best men we can find," he told Sargent Shriver and Larry O'Brien, who were organizing the talent search. "If they've been our friends, fine, but primarily I want the best men." One person who met both standards was Harvard faculty member Arthur Schlesinger, Jr., who was appointed special assistant to the president. The historian would undoubtedly write a book about the Kennedy government, Jack pointed out, and might as well do it as a coconspirator.

Jack's alma mater would eventually be well represented in his administration. The key post of national security adviser was given to McGeorge Bundy, Harvard's dean of arts and sciences at the time of his appointment. When Archibald Cox was hired as solicitor general, his Harvard faculty slot was then offered to lawyer Willard Wirtz. Wirtz had to turn down the job; he had already accepted a position as undersecretary of labor. The New York Times noted, "There's nothing left at Harvard except Radcliffe," and the dean of Harvard Law School said he was going to try to arrange a "no raiding pact" with the new government. One of the most important Cabinet positions, secretary of defense, went to Robert McNamara, a Harvard Business School graduate. McNamara was at that time president of the Ford Motor Company, and it was thought quite a coup for the Kennedy administration to get him. Yet Jack, mindful of journalistic teasing about the "Irish Mafia," wouldn't even consider the appointment until reassured that, in spite of his name, McNamara was a Protestant.

The most urgent positions, those of the Cabinet, were gradually being filled. On the afternoon J. Edward Day, a Harvard Law School graduate, was appointed postmaster general, Jack said he had received a letter which had taken eight days to get from Boston to Washington. He hoped that Day, with a background in government and business, would bring some efficiency to the antiquated Post Office Department. Minnesota governor Orville Freeman, who had placed Kennedy's name in nomination at the national convention, was designated secretary of agriculture—a position Jack said was high on his own personal list of "ten dullest jobs." Freeman, however, was pleased with the appointment and said he thought he had gotten it because "Harvard does not have a school of agriculture."

A Harvard diploma did not necessarily assure a prospect's being named to the position he wanted. Jack had been under a great deal of pressure from liberals to appoint Adlai Stevenson as secretary of state. But Stevenson's waffling over Jack as the vice-presidential candidate in 1956, and his refusal to endorse a Kennedy presidential candidacy in Los Angeles four years later, had doomed that hope. Stevenson, still another graduate of Harvard Law School, instead reluctantly accepted the ambassadorship to the United Nations, with cabinet rank. To head the State Department, Jack chose Dean Rusk, a Rhodes Scholar and head of the Rockefeller Foundation.

Jack's front steps in Georgetown were a very busy place during the first two weeks of December, as announcements of the Cabinet appointments continued. AFL-CIO lawyer Arthur Goldberg, with whom Jack had worked on the union reform legislation, was named secretary of labor. Abraham Ribicoff, the governor of Connecticut and an early JFK supporter, became secretary of health, education, and welfare. To give the Cabinet geographical balance, North Carolina governor Luther Hodges was appointed secretary of commerce, while Stewart Udall, an Arizona congressman, was designated secretary of the interior.

Secretary of the Treasury was regarded as one of the most important Cabinet positions, and Jack was determined to make the best possible choice without regard to party affiliation. That selection turned out to be another Harvard graduate, Douglas Dillon, a Republican. Liberal Democrats were suspicious of a man whom Richard Nixon might well have chosen for the same post, but the naming of Dillon, a former investment banker, reassured Wall Street that the incoming administration did not intend to pursue radical economic policies.

Jack had originally expected Joe Kennedy's help in choosing a man for the Treasury job, but when he asked his father to give suggestions, Joe replied, "I can't." The elder Kennedy intended to use his influence to determine only one Cabinet appointment, that of attorney general. In all of the president-elect's visits to Palm Beach, his father had been much in evidence, and Joe told a journalist he could now appear with Jack "anytime I want to." Yet there was still the awesome knowledge that his son was soon to be president. "Jack doesn't belong anymore to just a family," Joe said in a *New York Times* interview shortly after the election. "He belongs to the country. That's probably the saddest thing about all this. The family can be there, but there is not much they can do for the President of the United States." Joe thought, however, that one thing the family *could* do was contribute a Cabinet member.

It had long been Joe's dream that if one son was elected to the presidency, another would be designated attorney general, and the third would become a senator. Now Jack was on his way to the White House, and arrangements had been made for the appointment of Ben Smith, a former mayor of Gloucester, to finish out Kennedy's term in the Senate. Smith had been Jack's Harvard roommate, and it was understood he was merely to keep the Senate seat "warm"— because twenty-eight-year-old Teddy was two years short of meeting the constitutional age requirement for a U.S. senator. That left only Joe's plan for Bobby to be finalized. Jack was at first very uncomfortable with the idea of appointing his own brother to the Cabinet, and asked Clark Clifford to try to change Joe's mind. It wasn't possible. Kennedy heard Clifford out and then replied, "Thank you very much. I appreciate that. Now we'll turn to some other subject because Bobby is going to be attorney general."

Joe's reasons went beyond personal ambition for his sons. Kennedy felt the new young president would need someone in the Cabinet he could completely trust, and to achieve that, the family would just have to face down the inevitable charges of nepotism. Jack finally came to agree with Joe's point of view, and in turn eventually convinced his reluctant brother—although Bobby had agonized over the decision, telling a friend, "I changed my mind five times today alone." When journalist Ben Bradlee asked Jack how he intended to make the controversial announcement, he replied:" Well,

I think I'll open the front door of the Georgetown house some morning about 2 A.M., look up and down the street, and if there's no one there, I'll whisper, 'It's Bobby.' "

When the appointment was finally announced at a more traditional hour, both Kennedys tried to cover up their nervousness. Just before they went out to face the press, Jack glanced at his brother and said, "Damn it, Bobby, comb your hair." Bobby cracked up at the idea of a president-elect worrying about his attorney general's hair. "Don't smile too much," Jack cautioned him, "or they'll think we're happy about the appointment."

Absolutely no one but Joe Kennedy seemed "happy about the appointment." A *New York Times* editorial commented, "If Robert Kennedy was one of the outstanding lawyers of the country, a preeminent legal philosopher, a noted prosecutor or legal officer at Federal or State level, the situation would have been different." The *Wall Street Journal* said Bobby could turn out to be an "unqualified disaster." But despite his own initial misgivings, Jack appeared unperturbed and said he didn't see anything wrong in giving Bobby "a little legal experience before he goes out to practice law."

Because Jack had not previously met some of the appointees and had only a slight acquaintance with several others, one staff member joked that the new Cabinet was made up of "nine strangers and a brother." Strangers or not, with the addition of UN ambassador Adlai Stevenson to the Cabinet, the leader of the New Frontier had appointed eleven white males—five of them with degrees from Harvard.

By January 19, 1961, the day before the inauguration, John F. Kennedy thought he was well prepared to assume the presidency.

He had selected almost one hundred people to serve on twenty-nine task forces, set up to study domestic and foreign policies. Ted Sorensen had also prepared a checklist of administrative, budgetary, and legislative issues, which he and Jack reviewed at a marathon session in Palm Beach. As a result, a Kennedy program was defined even before there was a Kennedy presidency—which would enable Jack, Sorensen said, "to take the legislative initiative immediately."

There had been two meetings at the White House with President Eisenhower. The first took place soon after the election, and Jack, anxious to be punctual, left home so early he had to be driven around Washington to kill time. The solemnity of the occasion was reflected in the fact that Jack had brought along a hat, although he didn't actually wear it. The session began awkwardly: the youngest man ever elected to the Oval Office greeted its oldest occupant with "Good morning, Mr. President." Eisenhower, who privately called Jack a "young whippersnapper," replied by pointedly addressing his successor as "Senator." But as always, Jack was well prepared, and after their long meeting, Eisenhower said he was "tremendously impressed" with Kennedy's "understanding of the world problems, the depth of his questions, his grasp of the issues and the keenness of his mind."

Both men were more relaxed at their second get-together. Eisenhower delighted in demonstrating that, by merely pushing a button, a helicopter would suddenly appear on the White House lawn. "I've shown my friend here how to get out in a hurry," he smilingly told the others at the meeting. There were no smiles, however, during a long, serious discussion about Southeast Asia, where Communist troops were threatening the entire area. "This is one of the problems I'm leaving you that I'm not happy about," Eisenhower told Jack. "We may have to fight." The president-elect confided to Sorensen that he wished whatever was going to happen "would happen before we take over and get blamed for it." In spite of the cordial conversation, Jack was worried, and told Kenny O'Donnell "things were really just as bad as I had said they were during the campaign."

Another new burden was the constant presence of the Secret Service. Even when Jack was sitting on the patio at his parents' home in Florida, four agents dressed in business suits and ties watched him from behind the palm trees. When he swam in the ocean, a Coast Guard cutter patrolled the water. "Are they expecting Castro to invade Palm Beach?" Jack asked Kenny. But he was grateful for their vigilance when the Secret Service arrested a would-be assassin, carrying seven sticks of dynamite and a note which said, "The Kennedys bought the Presidency and the Whitehouse."

Not all preinaugural events were as grim. Christmas was spent in Palm Beach, where a reporter noted stockings hung over the fireplace: "Grandpa," "Grandma," "Mommie," "Daddy," "Caroline." Jack and Jackie's gift for Bobby was a leather-bound copy of *The Enemy Within*. Jackie's inscription read, "To Bobby, who made the impossible possible." Jack's reflected typical Kennedy sarcasm: "For Bobby—the Brother Within—who made the easy difficult." Jack was in good humor and feeling well. Busy as he was, he still managed to spend a lot of time in the Florida sun and was deeply tanned. He had even gained fifteen pounds, and a journalist noted that Jack was beginning to get a spare tire around his waistline. Rose was delighted. Her son, she said, had "lost that lean, Lincolnesque look," but had "gained something I liked better: he looked entirely healthy."

The handsome president-elect gave some New Yorkers a thrill when, just before closing down his temporary headquarters at the Carlyle, he decided to attend a Broadway show. Since Jack was characteristically late, management held the curtain, then held it even longer as he received a five-minute standing ovation from the audience. When a woman in the balcony climbed up on her seat for a better view, her foot got stuck and a carpenter had to be called to extricate it. Jack appeared unconcerned at intermission, during what a *Time* reporter called "one of the most observed trips to the men's room in modern history."

Included in Jack's travels before the inauguration was a brief trip to Boston, where he attended a meeting of the Harvard Board of Overseers and told cheering students, "I'm here to go over your grades." He also gave an address to the Massachusetts state legislature, which included the words of St. Luke Rose had often recited to her children: "For of those to whom much is given, much is required." Although Joe had no idea what his son intended to say in the inaugural address, he was sure it would be overshadowed by Jack's eloquent speech in Boston.

January 19, Inaugural Eve, was a memorable night in Washington. A heavy snowstorm slowed the pace of the city, and although most of the scheduled events took place, nothing went quite as planned. The streets were filled with abandoned cars, but the Kennedys' limousine managed to get through to Constitution Hall, where a pre-inaugural concert was being given by those members of the National Symphony who were not stuck in snowdrifts.

Yet in spite of the weather, the mood in the nation's capital was one of excitement. Bonfires had been lit along the main avenues, and floodlights around the base of the Washington Monument shone through the falling snow. As the Kennedys were driven toward the National Armory, where Frank Sinatra was staging a gala, stranded motorists recognized the car's occupants and began to wave and applaud. Jackie looked beautiful in a white gown, and her husband instructed the driver to turn on the interior lights so people could see her. Jack, reading the concert program in which Thomas Jefferson's inaugural address had been reprinted, shook his head. "It's better than mine," he told Jackie.

At midnight, exhausted, Jackie left the Armory to rest up for the next day's long events. But Jack stayed to the end, then went on to a party his father was hosting at a downtown restaurant. At three-thirty, Jack stopped by the table where Kenny O'Donnell was sitting. "I suppose you'll be laughing it up here for another three hours after I go home and get into bed with my inaugural address," he said. Kenny watched him leave and noticed his wistful expression. It was the end, Kenny thought, of Jack's "last carefree night on the town, the last time he would be able to enjoy himself in a public restaurant for years to come."

To the cheers of the crowd waiting outside, Jack and Jackie left Georgetown late the next morning and were driven to the White House to have coffee with the Eisenhowers. In spite of his aversion to hats, Jack had requested that men wear formal attire for the inauguration, and although he carried it throughout much of the day, Jack occasionally put the top hat on his head. Just before noon, the Kennedys and the Eisenhowers set out on the mile drive between the White House and the Capitol, both men wearing self-conscious grins along with their hats. At 12:51, Jack placed his hand on a Bible that had belonged to Honey Fitz and his father before him, and recited the presidential oath. Then the new president began his inaugural address.

Jack had been thinking about the speech ever since the election, and seeking advice from friends, politicians, and journalists. He had asked Ted Sorensen to read the addresses given by previous presidents and to "study the secret" of Abraham Lincoln's Gettysburg Address. Sorensen commented that Lincoln had "never used two or three words where one word would do," and set out to model the inaugural address on that principle. Jack wanted the text to be brief, optimistic, and unpartisan; without Cold War rhetoric, yet strong enough so that Khrushchev could not ignore his resolve.

"Let the word go forth from this time and place, to friend and foe alike, that the torch has been passed to a new generation of Americans. . . ."

That one era was giving way to another was evident in the contrast between the two presidents on the inaugural stand. Dwight Eisenhower was seventy years old. He had grown up as a poor boy in the Midwest, gone to West Point, become a hero when he commanded the Allied forces on D-Day, led his country through two terms of uneasy peace and unequaled prosperity. But the small-town

America of Eisenhower's youth on the Kansas plains was gone forever. Young people were flocking to urban centers, learning new skills and becoming part of a burgeoning technology which had made the United States the mightiest industrial nation on earth. Eisenhower would also be the last of a long line of folk-hero generals to reach the White House. Proliferation of atomic weapons made conventional warfare between the superpowers seem impossible, and instead the threat of nuclear holocaust hung over the planet. It was time for a different kind of leadership.

Jack Kennedy was forty-three years old, the product of a wealthy family, a sophisticated city, an Ivy League school. Yet he was far more than the sum of those parts, and the rich complexity of his life was reflected in the audience which had gathered to hear him speak: the duke and duchess of Devonshire, the first members of British aristocracy ever to attend the inauguration of an American president; members of the crew of PT 109, and Kohei Hanami, commander of the destroyer that had sunk it; Harvard intellectuals and Irish politicians from Boston's North End; Hollywood celebrities and Palm Beach socialites; representatives of labor and of management.

Also in the crowd were the men of the new administration—old enough to remember the Depression and Munich, Hiroshima and Joe McCarthy; young enough to believe a better future was possible, confident they would be a part of the government that would achieve that goal. But the two most remarkable people in the audience, the proudest of those who sat listening, were thinking of the past. Looking at her son, without a coat in the twenty-degree weather, Rose remembered the little boy who always forgot to put on a sweater when he ran out to play. Joe forgot his own rule that "Kennedys don't cry," and his eyes glistened with tears.

"And so, my fellow Americans, ask not what your country can do for you; ask what you can do for your country."

Back inside the Capitol building after the speech, Jackie touched her husband's face. "Oh, Jack, what a day," she said softly.

The day's next event was the inaugural parade. Wearing his top hat, Jack got into a limousine to be driven to the reviewing stand in front of the White House, where the Kennedy family was seated. As the car approached, Rose and Joe stood up, applauding their son.

Jack stood up as well, and tipped his hat in a salute to his parents.

17

WHY COULDN'T
THIS HAVE HAPPENED
TO JAMES BOND

Although January 21 was a Saturday, the new president was eager
to get started, and asked his aides to report at nine o'clock that
morning. As the staff began to arrive, they found JFK already in his
office, testing the buttons and buzzers on his telephone.

But soon the president got down to business, and by ten-thirty
had signed his first executive order—doubling the quantity of surplus food to be distributed to needy people nationwide, a pledge he
had made during the West Virginia primary. Most of the day was
spent in general activities much like those of anyone starting a new
job: talking with staff members, opening mail, making telephone
calls, poking his head into other offices.

It seemed odd to settle into a routine work schedule. After years
in the Senate and on the campaign trail, JFK commented to Sorensen
that the White House was "awfully quiet." Although he and his
aides had worked since 1956 to get there, it was still a little hard to
believe they had made it. On Sunday morning after mass, the
president brought his brother Teddy and Red Fay, newly appointed
under secretary of the Navy, over for a visit. Spinning around in the
chair behind his desk, Kennedy asked Red, "Do you think it's
adequate?" His old friend replied, "I feel any minute somebody's
going to walk in and say, 'All right, you three guys, out of here.'"

JFK, however, quickly adapted to his new role, and nowhere
more easily than when facing reporters. The first of his presidential

press conferences took place on January 25. Since he was masterful on television, Kennedy had accepted Pierre Salinger's innovative suggestion that this and all his conferences be televised live, something no other president had ever attempted. JFK also defied another presidential custom that had, in the past, required journalists to submit their questions in advance. In this and the sixty-one press conferences to follow, he beguiled the nation with his spontaneous wit and grasp of the issues, no matter how broad or complex.

But there were few newsworthy events during the first weeks of the Kennedy presidency, and the Washington press corps, famished for information about the New Frontier, constantly badgered Salinger. At one of his twice-daily briefings with the press, a reporter complained, "You never give us hard news, just tidbits." Salinger replied he had a story of major importance, and paused for effect. "The cat is here." "What cat?" "Caroline's cat." "What's the cat's name?" "Tom Kitten." The reporter who had accused Salinger of handing out tidbits drew closer. "What color is this cat? I came here for news. I've got to leave with something."

There was nothing lighthearted about Kennedy's first State of the Union address on January 30. "I speak today in an hour of national peril and national opportunity," the president said. The state of the economy was "disturbing." He was concerned about unemployment, inadequate housing, lack of health care for the elderly, the educational system, organized crime, juvenile delinquency, and defense. JFK felt that at home the "national household" was "cluttered with unfinished and neglected tasks," while abroad "weapons spread and hostile forces grow stronger." But the greatest challenge, he said, was in "the world beyond the Cold War."

In a tough, self-congratulatory speech given two weeks before Kennedy's inauguration, Premier Khrushchev had predicted communism would eventually achieve global supremacy through "wars of national liberation." This warning made a deep impression on the president, confirming his view that, unlike the Eisenhower administration, his government should concentrate on the countries of the Third World. The battleground of freedom, he said, was in "Asia, Latin America, Africa, and the Middle East—the lands of rising peoples. Their revolution is the greatest in human history. They seek an end to injustice, tyranny, and exploitation. More than an end, they seek a beginning." To assist these new nations, Kennedy proposed a Food for Peace program, in which U.S. surpluses would be used to meet specific nutritional needs of poorer countries; a

Peace Corps of volunteers to help Third World nations develop their natural and human resources; and an alliance with the countries of Latin America to encourage economic and social reform.

The Peace Corps, which would exemplify American generosity and idealism to the nations of the Third World, captured the imagination of many who responded to the president's inaugural request that they ask what they could do for their country. Under the direction of Sargent Shriver, it would tap, Kennedy said, an "immense reservoir of dedicated men and women willing to devote their energies and time and toil to the cause of world peace and human progress."

On March 13, the president announced his formal proposal for the Alliance for Progress: *Alianza para el Progreso.* "Call forth your strengths and let each devote his energies to the betterment of all," Kennedy said at a White House reception for Latin American diplomats, "so that your children and our children in this hemisphere can find an even richer and freer life." Although the purpose of the Alliance was to transform the Western Hemisphere "into a vast crucible of revolutionary ideas and efforts" through peaceful means, there was another, less benign, plan in the works to demonstrate U.S. influence in Latin America.

To Americans, not even Nikita Khrushchev was as annoying as Fidel Castro. When he came to power in Cuba in January 1959, Castro seemed a fascinating revolutionary figure who had triumphed over the corrupt regime of dictator Fulgencio Batista. That idealistic image soon changed.

Cuba had once been a U.S. playground, an island of nightclubs and gambling casinos. The most valuable real estate belonged to Americans, while Cubans lived in poverty. Batista had resisted all efforts at reform, but Castro, in what he called the "beginning of a new era," soon seized almost a billion dollars' worth of U.S. property in Cuba, returning the land to his people. He announced, "We will take and take, until not even the nails of their shoes are left." By the following summer, the Cuban leader had formed an alliance with Russia, leading the Eisenhower Administration to believe Castro meant to instigate communist revolutions throughout Latin America.

Hoping to bring about Castro's fall, the CIA came up with an array of devices in an attempt to discredit him. Its Technical Services staff suggested a powder which, if sprinkled on Castro's shoes, was supposed to make his beard fall out; a chemical substance to be put in his cigars that would cause him to become disoriented before giving a speech; an LSD-type spray to be used in his broadcast studio. None of these plans were successful, so the Agency secretly decided on an "Executive Action"—a euphemism for murder. Because of organized crime's expertise in that area, CIA officials turned to the underworld to carry out the plan. Their first recruit, Johnny Roselli, had contacted two other gangsters for help with the assignment. One was his boss, Sam Giancana, head of the Chicago syndicate; the other was Santos Trafficante, former mob chief in Havana, new crime boss in Florida. Both men were enthusiastic about the scheme.

In spite of their importance to his country's economy, Castro had closed down the extensive gambling, prostitution, and drug interests from which organized crime had once made an annual multimillion-dollar income in Cuba. Syndicate attempts to depose the premier had been unsuccessful, although mob members such as Jack Ruby were rumored to be running guns to the island in order to achieve Castro's overthrow. Now the underworld saw a chance to reclaim its lucrative Cuban empire. In Miami in October 1960, Roselli, accompanied by Trafficante and Giancana, met for a second time with CIA officials Robert Maheu and James O'Connell to discuss their common goal: getting rid of Fidel Castro.

O'Connell wanted a gangland-style killing, in which Castro would be gunned down by a Cuban. But Giancana said it would be too difficult to find someone for such a dangerous assignment, and suggested poison be used instead. Technical Services went to work on the problem. First its staff developed poison pills to be dropped into Castro's water glass, but the pills, they discovered, wouldn't dissolve. A second batch, containing botulism toxin, was tested on monkeys and worked efficiently. Four months after the Miami meeting, the pills were passed on to Roselli, who in turn got them to a Cuban official. The man returned the pills several weeks later, saying he had lost his position and no longer had access to Castro. Botulism toxin was put into a box of Castro's favorite cigars, which was entrusted to another syndicate pal in Havana. The Cuban was never heard from again. Technical Services then offered poison pens, poison capsules, poison powders, and poison dart guns. But even with their extensive Cuban contacts, the three mobsters had no luck in finding anyone to employ the devices.

The CIA began to have second thoughts about their hired help. In addition to a lack of efficiency, there was also an alarming chance of a security leak. Both Giancana and Trafficante were on the FBI's list of ten most wanted criminals and under close surveillance. The Bureau sent Richard Bissell, CIA deputy director of plans, a memo warning that Giancana had told "several friends" he was involved in the assassination plot, and that Fidel Castro "was to be done away with very shortly." Worse yet, the memo added, President Kennedy himself was involved with Giancana's girlfriend, Judith Campbell. Frank Sinatra had introduced the woman to JFK in February 1960, and records of phone calls to and from the White House showed Campbell and Kennedy were in frequent touch. Because Giancana was a braggart, the possibility of a scandal that could both smear the Agency and destroy the presidency was all too real.

Since it seemed the CIA would be unable to achieve Castro's fall through "executive action," it proposed an alternative course that would bring about the same result: an invasion of Cuba. At the time JFK took office, that most recent Agency operation was being handled almost as clumsily as the assassination attempts.

During the summer of 1960, Cuban exiles had been training at a farm south of Miami, where nearby residents heard Spanish drills being given over loudspeakers and watched the Cubans marching. In August, neighborhood teenagers tossed firecrackers into the camp and the trainees, thinking they were under attack, started shooting. Although one of the youngsters was wounded and several Cubans were arrested, Miami officials dropped the case at the request of federal authorities. There was another CIA camp in Central America, a fact which the *New York Times* disclosed on January 10, 1961, under the headline, U.S. HELPS TRAIN AN ANTI-CASTRO FORCE AT SECRET GUATEMALAN AIR GROUND BASE.

Volunteers from the Alabama Air National Guard were in Nicaragua instructing Cuban pilots, frogmen were training near New Orleans, and landing craft exercises were under way at Vieques Island off Puerto Rico. A covert plan conceived during the Eisenhower administration as a small guerilla operation had, by March 1961, become both an ill-kept secret and a major military undertaking of tanks, ships, planes, and a brigade—*La Brigada*—of almost fifteen hundred men. And the decision to proceed with the invasion had been inherited by Eisenhower's successor.

On November 27, 1960, less than three weeks after the election, Allen Dulles and Richard Bissell had gone to Palm Beach to brief Kennedy on the CIA's invasion proposal. Because of his interest in decolonization, JFK had long been intrigued with the romantic appeal of revolutionaries such as Castro, Mao Tse-tung, and Ho Chi

Minh. Although it was impossible for the president of a superpower to play a similar role in the international drama, Kennedy yearned to capture the world's imagination in the daring fashion of those Third World leaders. "He wanted the dignity of Harold Macmillan," Adlai Stevenson said, "but he also wanted to ignite the passions that Castro did." Now when presented with a plan for an invasion of Cuba, Kennedy was quick to see the appeal of this venture, which combined clandestine action, guerilla warfare, and a chance to score a major Cold War victory. At the time, however, JFK expressed neither approval nor disapproval; he had hundreds of other things to think about while forming his administration. The operation was not seriously discussed again until January 19, when at their White House meeting, Eisenhower recommended that Kennedy agree to the project and do whatever was necessary to make it successful.

JFK realized there were many good reasons to give his consent. He was the youngest man elected to the presidency, and he had won that position by the narrowest of margins. A spectacular blow against communism during his first few months in office would prove to Americans he was neither immature nor inexperienced. Yet Kennedy was in fact a bit of both, and the junior-grade lieutenant of World War II was reluctant to challenge the military expertise of those who favored the plan. Eisenhower himself had been the supreme commander of Allied Forces in Europe; he urged that the operation be "continued and accelerated." When Kennedy requested that the Pentagon review the proposal, a Joint Chiefs of Staff memorandum predicted the invasion could be expected to achieve "initial military success," although, it added, "ultimate success" would depend on further action by anti-Castro elements within Cuba. Because of that qualification, the Joint Chiefs and JFK were given to understand that the CIA anticipated an organized Cuban uprising as soon as a beachhead had been secured.

Although Kennedy instinctively harbored doubts about the undertaking, he felt backed into a corner. At a meeting on March 11, Dulles told him, "Don't forget we have a disposal problem." If the troops of La Brigada were demobilized, they would spread word that the United States had canceled the invasion, a sign of weakness which, Dulles warned, could lead to further communist takeovers throughout Latin America. The Republican party, under whose sponsorship the plan had originated, would make sure JFK's withdrawal was well publicized, a fact that could have disastrous political consequences for the president. Against his better judgment, Kennedy tentatively gave his approval, but he specified there was to be no U.S. military intervention. America would assist but not directly participate; the invasion force was to be made up only of Cuban exiles, who would be on their own in the battle to win back their homeland.

Kennedy heard from just two dissenters. In a memorandum to the president, Arthur Schlesinger pointed out that an invasion would "fix a malevolent image of the new administration in the minds of millions." JFK reassured Schlesinger that he had agreed to the operation on a contingency basis only. "I've reserved the right to stop this thing up to twenty-four hours before the landing." J. William Fulbright, chairman of the Senate Foreign Relations Committee, also sent Kennedy a memo. "To give this activity even covert support is of a piece with the hypocrisy and cynicism for which the United States is constantly denouncing the Soviet Union in the United Nations and elsewhere," Fulbright wrote. "This point will not be lost on the rest of the world—nor on our own consciences. . . . Remember always," the memo concluded, "the Castro regime is a thorn in the flesh; but it is not a dagger in the heart."

Sensing that Schlesinger and Fulbright were correct, JFK continued to hesitate: postponing the invasion date, arguing about the landing site, fussing over details. His complicity in the plan would be impossible to deny, and the invasion of another country was blatant intervention which could lead to widespread criticism at home and abroad. If it failed, the president would suffer a humiliating defeat after only three months in office. "It was a sort of orphan child JFK had adopted from the Republicans—he had no real love or affection for it," Allen Dulles later said. Well aware that Kennedy was "only half sold," Dulles and Bissell stepped up their pressure on the president. "You can't mañana this thing," Bissell told him. Both gave the impression, which they later denied, that the invasion brigade could count on the active support of at least one-fourth of the Cuban people.

And if the worst happened, if the troops were defeated on the beach, then, Kennedy was assured, they could easily "melt away" into the mountains. Nothing could really go wrong. The joint chiefs backed the CIA, and Defense Secretary Robert McNamara accepted their military judgment. Secretary of State Dean Rusk and his two top Latin American advisors gave approval. Rusk even expressed an opinion that the operation wouldn't make the front page of the *New York Times*. On April 8, after seventy-eight days in the White House, Kennedy made up his mind: the invasion was on. The Cuban Brigade would land on the beaches of a place called the Bay of Pigs.

At six o'clock on the morning of April 15, 1961, two B-26 planes with Cuban markings bombed and strafed a landing strip near Castro's command post. Two other strikes took place simultaneously at air bases outside Havana and Santiago. Although Agency propagandists said the planes were flown by Cuban air force pilots attacking their own bases, they were actually CIA bombers which had taken off from Nicaragua. Because of his insistence that American involvement be as minimal as possible, Kennedy ordered the Agency's original scenario be scaled down. It had requested sixteen planes for the mission, but the president cut that number back to six. Still, the strikes destroyed five Cuban aircraft, leaving Castro's tiny air force with only seven pilots and eight operational planes.

On the afternoon of Saturday, April 15, Cuba requested an emergency session of the UN Political Committee, at which the Cuban foreign minister denounced both the attack and the CIA cover story as an American plot. From Washington, an assistant secretary of state phoned to inform Adlai Stevenson, U.S. ambassador to the United Nations, that the CIA had assured him the story was true: the pilots were genuine defectors. Confident he had been told the facts, Stevenson gave an eloquent rebuttal to the Cuban charges. By the next day, when he learned he had been duped into lying before the UN committee, Stevenson was furious. So was Dean Rusk, who thought the clumsy deception could compromise U.S. diplomatic policies throughout Latin America.

It was now too late to cancel the invasion, but Kennedy felt foreign policy risks overruled military necessity and called off any additional bombings. If the operation had ever had any chance of success, both Castro and the CIA would later agree, the lack of air support doomed it. Before dawn on Monday, General C. P. Cabell, the Agency's deputy director, begged JFK to give the landing craft air cover from the U.S. carrier *Essex*. The president refused Cabell's plea, reiterating there was to be no direct participation by the United States. Nevertheless, as the invasion got under way on the morning of April 17, the first shots were fired by a CIA agent, and the first frogmen to come ashore at the Bay of Pigs were American.

The little news received in Washington was all bad. There had been no anti-Castro uprising, and CIA predictions had been wrong in several other catastrophic ways as well. U-2 reconnaissance photographs had shown a dark mass underwater just offshore, which Agency experts interpreted as seaweed. It turned out to be a coral reef. Landing-craft engines hit the reef and stopped, so the men had to either abandon their boats full of supplies or try to push them onto the beach. The CIA told the Brigade that the Bay of Pigs was occupied by Cuban construction workers, who would be asleep as they came ashore. Instead, the area was brightly lit and its armed occupants wide awake. Agency intelligence thought the area was without communications; in fact, it had a radio station.

Richard Bissell later admitted the CIA had also underestimated "Castro's capability in certain specific respects, mainly his organizational skill, speed of movement, and will to fight." He expressed surprise that Cuba's three jet trainers were armed. The joint chiefs too had not considered the jets' combat capabilities, so none of the president's advisors had been warned about the dangers they might pose. Castro also had two other planes equipped with rockets, which strafed the invasion ships. Under heavy attack, the ships were forced to steam out of the bay and into open waters, making evacuation impossible. Because of JFK's specific instructions, U.S. airmen from the *Essex*, standing by offshore, were allowed to make observation flights only. The Navy pilots had little information about Cuban landmarks; security on board ship was so tight that the *Essex* yielded only one out-of-date road map of Cuba. Yet they could plainly see the battle was going badly for the invasion forces, and they themselves were being fired on. Again and again the pilots, some in tears, requested permission to return fire or to bomb Castro's troops. The answer was always the same: "Negative." Helplessly, they watched the defeat of the nearly thirteen hundred men stranded on shore.

La Brigada had no escape. The mountains to which Dulles and Bissell promised the invaders could, if necessary, "melt away" were eighty miles from the Bay of Pigs. Absolutely nothing went according to plan. From Washington, Admiral Arleigh Burke, chief of naval operations, sent desperate queries to the *Essex* to find out the battle's progress. For two days, the ship's communications officer was bewildered; Burke kept asking questions he had already answered. Each time a reply was sent, the officer asked if the message was received, and each time he was assured it had been. Finally he asked who had received it. The reply: "Londonderry, Ireland." A new high-frequency radio on board the *Essex* had malfunctioned.

In spite of the fouled-up communications, President Kennedy had learned enough to realize the invasion was floundering. And as always when he was in trouble, JFK phoned his father—the first of several calls he would make to Palm Beach that week. The president was despondent, but Joe would have none of it. "Oh, hell," he told his son. "If that's the way you feel, give the job to Lyndon!" Joe, along with almost everyone in the administration, blamed the CIA for the fiasco. "I know that outfit," he said, "and I wouldn't pay them a hundred bucks a week." As the news worsened, President Kennedy was in complete agreement, telling Arthur Schlesinger, "We will have to do something" about the CIA. He needed, JFK commented, someone to head the Agency whom he could completely trust. Before the invasion he had planned to eventually replace the aging Dulles with Richard Bissell. But the credibility of the deputy director of plans had plunged to zero. "I made a mistake in putting Bobby in the Justice Department," he said. "Bobby should be in the CIA."

By the afternoon of April 19 it was all over. Castro's troops had captured almost twelve hundred members of *La Brigada*, and the fingerpointing began. Many in the Agency saw Kennedy's refusal to order a second air strike as betrayal. "It was inconceivable," Bissell said, "that the President would let the operation fail when he had all this American power." General Cabell, whose dislike of JFK was reciprocated, called Kennedy a traitor. Eisenhower said the story of the Bay of Pigs was "a Profile in Timidity and Indecision." Richard Nixon said the president had "turned chicken."

The administration was just as eager to lay the blame elsewhere, and White House staff members began to brief journalists on what had gone wrong. The plan had been conceived under Eisenhower; the joint chiefs had selected the landing site; the CIA had promised a Cuban uprising which never materialized. Publicly, however, Kennedy took the blame. "There is an old saying," he said at a press conference, "that victory has a hundred fathers and defeat is an orphan." But he was, JFK added, "the responsible officer of the government and that is quite obvious." As such, the president knew he had to show a decisive response to the catastrophic events in Cuba. "An error doesn't become a mistake until you refuse to correct it," Kennedy commented—and set about making some corrections. Dulles, Bissell, and Cabell were asked, after a "decent interval," to leave the Agency. "If this were the British government," he told Bissell, "I would resign and you, being a senior civil servant, would remain. But it isn't." Bobby refused to accept the position of CIA director; it was, he said, "a bad idea" because he was "a Democrat, and brother." But he agreed to serve as a member of a fact-finding committee set up to investigate the Bay of Pigs, and quietly took on the responsibility of serving as the president's unofficial watchdog over the Agency.

JFK felt he had done all he should in the aftermath of the operation. Although he was heard to quip, "Why couldn't this have happened to James Bond?" privately Kennedy was angry. "How could I have been so far off base?" he asked Ted Sorensen. "All my life I've known better than to depend on the experts. How could I have been so stupid, to let them go ahead?" Both the Central Intelligence Agency and the Pentagon had proven to be fallible. The Soviet Union would view the U.S. failure as weakness on the part of the new administration, and that could lead to a crisis in Berlin or Southeast Asia or perhaps again in Cuba. At this vulnerable time, Khrushchev suddenly accepted an invitation Kennedy had issued two months earlier. The Russian premier agreed to meet the American president for a summit conference in Vienna.

18

A WORLD
FULL OF TROUBLE

Since February, President Kennedy had been thinking about a meeting with Khrushchev as a way to open "channels of communication" and "lessen the chance of danger." The Bay of Pigs fiasco made all the more urgent JFK's need to prove his ability to stand firm against the Russian leader. "I have to show him that we can be just as tough as he is," Kennedy said. "I'll have to sit down with him, and let him see who he's dealing with." Cuba was only one area of concern the president wanted to discuss with Khrushchev. True to Eisenhower's prediction, the situation in Southeast Asia was worsening. Using armaments supplied by the Soviet Union, Communist troops seemed close to a victory in Laos, and Kennedy was under pressure from the Pentagon to launch a major military counteroffensive in that country.

In late April, JFK visited Douglas MacArthur at the retired general's home in New York City, to review the Bay of Pigs and conditions in Indochina. The eighty-one-year-old MacArthur made quite an impression on the young man he had once thought should be court-martialed. No doubt one reason the two got along so well was their willingness to blame Kennedy's problems on the previous occupant of the White House—the man who had also been MacArthur's rival for fame during World War II. "The 'chickens are coming home to roost' from Eisenhower's years," the aging general told JFK. "You happen to be in charge of the chicken house." MacArthur thought it "would be a mistake to fight in Laos," and instead recommended a small "rear-guard action" farther to the southeast, in Vietnam.

The leader there was Ngo Dinh Diem, a man of right-wing views who was attempting to resist both Communist aggression and meaningful reform within his country. Unfortunately, the United States was committed to Diem's repressive rule. In 1954, at the urging of the CIA, America had handpicked Diem to be president of the newly independent South Vietnam. Throughout the next seven years, a determined leftist guerrilla movement, in an attempt to unify the nation, threatened to oust his unpopular regime. In response, Eisenhower had sent several hundred military advisors to assist the South Vietnamese in opposing the insurgent efforts. Initially reluctant to expand that number, Kennedy decided instead on a goodwill gesture to reassure Diem of continued American support, and in late 1961 asked Lyndon Johnson to visit Saigon.

The vice-president, leery of possible danger in the volatile region, was reluctant to go, but JFK jokingly promised him that if anything happened, LBJ would be given "the biggest funeral Austin, Texas, ever saw." When Johnson returned safely a month later, he reported to Kennedy that Diem "is remote from the people, is surrounded by persons less admirable than he." Publicly he hailed Diem as "the Winston Churchill of Southeast Asia." But when a journalist asked Johnson what he really thought of Diem, the vice-president was more realistic: "He's the only boy we got out there." And the important thing to do "out there" was to stop the communists—no matter what the Vietnamese people might want.

Kennedy had also put Johnson in charge of another area of competition with the Soviets. Determined to revitalize the space program, the president asked for an increase in its budget and named LBJ to chair the National Space Council. It was obvious how far America was behind when, on April 12, Russia announced that cosmonaut Yuri Gagarin had become the first person in space, orbiting the earth in one hour and forty-eight minutes. The day after news of that Soviet triumph reached Washington, the head of the National Aeronautics and Space Administration came to the Oval Office with a desk model of the capsule designed to send up an American astronaut. A dismayed President Kennedy later told Ted Sorensen the model looked as if it had been purchased in a toy store. But on May 5 there was a breakthrough in the U.S. space program when Captain Alan B. Shepard, Jr., made a fifteen-minute suborbital flight and was recovered by helicopter from the Atlantic Ocean.

On May 25, President Kennedy appeared before Congress to give his second State of the Union address. Although the speech was usually delivered only once a year, JFK said "this tradition has been broken in extraordinary times," and that the spring of 1961 was certainly an extraordinary time. Encouraged by the successful flight of astronaut Shepard and the National Space Council's optimistic reports for the future, Kennedy made a bold proposal. "I believe that this nation should commit itself to achieving the goal, before this decade is out, of landing a man on the moon and returning him safely to earth."

But there was another, much more urgent concern which had finally begun to confront America that same month: the question of equality for all its citizens. Blacks and whites together had started "Freedom Rides"—traveling by bus throughout the Deep South in an attempt to integrate restaurants, waiting rooms, and restrooms. They were prepared to die for that cause, and many in the group made out wills before leaving on a trip across Alabama. It soon became apparent that the Riders were indeed risking their lives. In Anniston on May 14, a white mob overturned and burned a bus. Some of the riders had to be hospitalized; others went on to Birmingham in a second bus. There the Ku Klux Klan, armed with chains, pipes, and baseball bats, awaited them. Eugene "Bull" Connor, Birmingham police commissioner, had promised the Klansmen fifteen or twenty minutes before interceding, at which time, he told the Klan, he hoped the Riders would look "like a bulldog got a hold of them."

Among the Klan members was an FBI informant, who got word to J. Edgar Hoover that the Klan was planning an attack. Unfortunately for the Freedom Riders, Hoover had become increasingly disenchanted with the president. The puritanical Bureau director disapproved of JFK's private life, and thought the administration was neglecting Hoover's own obsession, domestic subversion. He admittedly "hated" Bobby, who as attorney general was his direct superior in the government hierarchy. Everything about Bobby annoyed the Bureau director: his youth—Bobby had been born the year after Hoover became head of the FBI—his working in shirt sleeves, his bringing the family dog to the office, his habit of throwing darts at a dart board during meetings, and most of all his refusal to kowtow to Hoover's position. Now, hoping to embarrass the Kennedy's, Hoover did not let the attorney general know of Connor's plan. Instead, FBI agents stood watching as the Riders were brutally beaten. There were no policemen at the scene. It was Mother's Day, Connor explained, and he had let his men go home.

In spite of the violence which they encountered at every stop, the Freedom Riders were determined to continue. After Bobby threatened to send in federal marshals, Alabama governor John Patterson promised the Riders would be protected as they made their way to Montgomery. The next problem was finding someone willing to drive them. The attorney general called the Greyhound Company and insisted that "the government is going to be very much upset if this group does not get to continue their trip." Bobby said that the Riders were lawfully entitled to transportation and "somebody better get in the damn bus and get it going and get those people on their way." The trip proceeded, but Patterson went back on his word. In Montgomery, the Riders were attacked again, while FBI agents watched and took notes. There were no police in sight, and onlookers were screaming, "Get 'em, get 'em," to those beating the Riders with ax handles and chains.

Bobby ordered five hundred U.S. marshals to the city, but only fifty had arrived by the time Martin Luther King, Jr., rose to address an audience in the First Baptist Church, outside of which a menacing throng of one thousand people had assembled. Bobby spent the night alternately phoning Patterson and King. The governor claimed some of King's group were known communists, and that the affair would politically ruin both him and the Kennedys. "Now, John, don't tell me that," Bobby replied. "It's more important that these people survive than for us to survive politically." Trapped in the church all night, King and the others were finally allowed to leave at dawn when the governor belatedly ordered in the National Guard.

The young civil rights movement was, in 1961, a long way from becoming a popular cause, and the demonstrators got little support from the American people. A Gallup poll showed 63 percent disapproved of the Freedom Riders, and even President Kennedy, who during the campaign had committed his administration to move forward in the field of human rights, requested the Rides be stopped. The summit conference in Vienna was only a few days away, and a lecture by Khrushchev on segregation in America was the last thing JFK wanted to hear.

The first stop on the European trip was in France, where Kennedy was to meet with President Charles de Gaulle. Just before departing, JFK celebrated his forty-fourth birthday in Hyannis Port. As he left the Kennedy home to begin the trip that would take him to the Vienna summit, there was a typical father–son exchange. "Oh, Dad, I don't have a cent of money," the president of the United States said, patting his pockets. After being handed a large packet of bills, he promised, "I'll get this back to you, Dad." Watching his son depart, Joe said quietly, "That'll be the day."

Having said good-bye to his father on Cape Cod, he was greeted by his mother on the other side of the Atlantic. Rose, in Paris on her annual visit to view the spring collections of French fashion designers, was included among the official party assembled to meet President and Mrs. Kennedy when they arrived at Orly Airport on May 31. Although she later wryly noted, "a U.S. President is not under obligation to have his mother nearby while consulting with other heads of state," Rose managed to be in on most of the events of the Kennedys' four-day stay in Paris. Yet in spite of her ease and elegance, Rose was for once completely upstaged.

France went wild over Jackie. During the motorcade into the city, a million people lined the route and the streets rang with cries of "*Jacqui. Jacqui. Jacqui. Vive Jacqueline!*" Her maiden name, her fluency in their language, and her knowledge of their culture made the French welcome her as a native daughter. Jackie's beauty and style overwhelmed everyone—including both presidents. When she appeared in a pink and white gown and wearing a regal hairdo to go to the first state dinner, JFK said, "Well, I'm dazzled." Throughout the meal, de Gaulle hardly touched his food; he was too busy talking to Jackie. "Your wife knows more French history than any Frenchwoman," de Gaulle told Kennedy. Among the dinner guests, women murmured, *Elle est plus reine que toutes les reines*: "She is more queenly than all the queens." Although Kennedy had been warned de Gaulle would be aloof, their talks went well, "probably because," JFK remarked to Kenny O'Donnell, "I have such a charming wife."

On the Kennedys' last evening in France, they were given a dinner in the Hall of Mirrors at Versailles—a rare honor, since by the twentieth century the ancient palace was seldom used for state occasions. Again de Gaulle was so absorbed in conversation with Jackie that he ate little. De Gaulle's interest did not go unobserved, and a French cartoonist depicted him sharing a canopied double bed with his wife but dreaming about Jackie. Kennedy was so delighted he ordered the cartoon framed for his desk. Speaking at a press luncheon on the day following the dinner, JFK began by saying he thought it would be appropriate to introduce himself: "I am the man who accompanied Jacqueline Kennedy to Paris."

Two extremes of a presidential campaign. In early 1960, Jackie and Jack, along with Dave Powers, were greeted by four people at an Oregon airport. Ten months later, their car was almost overturned by a crowd of more than one million New Yorkers.

Accompanied by Raggedy Ann and Caroline, Jack makes a rare visit to Hyannis Port during the presidential campaign. He commented that during his long absences, his daughter's vocabulary had expanded to include the words New Hampshire, Wisconsin, and West Virginia.

The two 1960 presidential candidates just after their first televised debate. Rose thought Jack had looked, sounded, and acted "like young Lincoln." Mrs. Nixon, on the other hand, phoned her son to ask if anything was wrong, because he "did not look well."

Rose had been praying. Early in the evening, Bobby feared the Democratic ticket might get "clobbered." Jackie called it the "longest night in history." At 1.30 a.m., Eisenhower sent premature congratulations and then withdrew them. At 3:30, Nixon refused to admit defeat. Thirty minutes later, Jack went to bed, saying it was too late to change any votes.

When Richard Nixon finally conceded, Joe decided the whole family should pose together to record the moment he had been dreaming of for almost half a century. Here, at Hyannis Port on the afternoon of November 9, 1960, are: Eunice, Rose, Joe, Jacqueline, and Teddy (seated); Ethel, Steve Smith, Jean, Jack, Bobby, Pat, Sargent Shriver, Joan, and Peter Lawford.

JFK is sworn into office by Chief Justice Earl Warren. Little more than a thousand days later, Warren would head up the commission investigating the president's death.

This photograph seems to demonstrate the burdens of the Oval Office. Actually, Kennedy was reading a newspaper column that criticized his administration. Moments after the picture was taken, JFK turned and said, "That goddamned Arthur Krock."

Kennedy admirers included the Soviet head of state, Nikita Khrushchev, and former movie star, Princess Grace of Monaco.

Most journalists were also Kennedy fans, due in part to his witty repartee during live press conferences. One typical exchange took place when a reporter asked JFK to comment on a Republican National Committee resolution that declared him a failure. The president quickly replied, "I assume it passed unanimously."

Perhaps the most memorable symbol of the vigorously youthful Kennedy administration was, improbably, that of a rocking chair. JFK began using a rocker during his senate years, to ease the pain in his back. He erased forever the image of "Whistler's Mother," and rocking chair sales soared in the early 1960s.

One hour after this photo was taken at the Palm Beach airport, Joe suffered the massive stroke that left him paralyzed and unable to speak.

On his next visit to the Oval Office, Joe began to cry. Pretending not to notice his father's tears, JFK moved Joe's wheelchair next to his rocker and said, "Well, Dad, it looks as though we both need special chairs."

JFK and Teddy at a 1963 Democratic fund-raiser. Although his younger brother was considered by both LBJ and Bobby to be the best politician in the family, the president liked to joke that Teddy was determined to make it on his own and had considered changing his name . . . to Roosevelt.

Like a fascinated little boy, the president peers into John Glenn's space capsule, Friendship 7. *When Glenn (standing behind JFK) returned from his historic flight, Kennedy told him, "You're doing pretty well for someone who's not in the family."*

Foo-Foo Head and the Bunny Rabbit

Photographers claimed wars, firing squads, and secret police were less terrifying than Jackie's anger over unauthorized pictures of her children. But she agreed to pose with her family for this windblown photo taken on the Cape in the summer of 1962.

Endearingly human, seductively elegant . . . the Kennedys brought a style to American political life that will probably never be recaptured.

WANTED

FOR

TREASON

THIS MAN is wanted for treasonous activities against the United States:

1. Betraying the Constitution (which he swore to uphold):
He is turning the sovereignty of the U. S. over to the communist controlled United Nations.
He is betraying our friends (Cuba, Katanga, Portugal) and befriending our enemies (Russia, Yugoslavia, Poland).

2. He has been WRONG on innumerable issues affecting the security of the U.S. (United Nations-Berlin wall-Missle removal-Cuba-Wheat deals-Test Ban Treaty, etc.)

3. He has been lax in enforcing Communist Registration laws.

4. He has given support and encouragement to the Communist inspired racial riots.

5. He has illegally invaded a sovereign State with federal troops.

6. He has consistently appointed Anti-Christians to Federal office: Upholds the Supreme Court in its Anti-Christian rulings. Aliens and known Communists abound in Federal offices.

7. He has been caught in fantastic LIES to the American people (including personal ones like his previous marraige and divorce).

Despite the right-wing antagonism reflected in handbills distributed in Dallas on the morning of November 22, welcoming crowds at the airport and along the motorcade route convinced even the wary Secret Service that "Lancer" and "Lace" — its code names for the Kennedys — were in no danger. At 12:30, an agent turned with relief to the Dallas chief of police and said, "Five minutes more and we'll have him there." Then there was a sudden sharp noise ...

Flanked by his wife and a stunned Jacqueline Kennedy, Lyndon B. Johnson becomes the thirty-sixth president of the United States. The photographer carefully angled his camera so the bloodstains on Jackie's clothes could not be seen. Kennedy aides remained in the corridor of Air Force One, *reluctant to take part in a ceremony they felt LBJ had arranged with unseemly haste. But when Johnson insisted on Jacqueline's presence in the plane's sweltering stateroom, she agreed, saying "In the light of history, it would be better if I was there."*

Jacqueline Kennedy
John F. Kennedy, Jr.
November 25, 1963

In spite of his pleasure that the brief stay in France had gone so well, the president had an all-too-familiar concern: he was in a great deal of pain. In mid-May, JFK had visited Canada, where he addressed Parliament and later took part in planting a red oak which was to serve as a lasting symbol of his visit. As Kennedy bent over, he felt a sudden sharp twinge in his back. That problem, which had not bothered him for years, had suddenly reoccurred— and at the worst possible time. For the next two weeks, the president used crutches in private, and received a series of novocaine injections. Publicly, he refused to admit his agony, and he would not even consider meeting with de Gaulle or Khrushchev while on crutches. On June 3, with JFK still in wrenching pain, the Kennedys boarded the presidential plane, *Air Force One*, to fly eastward.

JFK went to Vienna with the idea that he wanted to meet the Russian premier "at the summit, not the brink." Kennedy's greatest concern was that a miscalculation on the part of the leadership of either superpower would result in nuclear war. But when the president expressed this view during their first session together, the word "miscalculation" seemed to annoy Khrushchev; it suggested, he said, that America wanted the Soviet Union to sit like a schoolboy with its hands on top of a desk. Kennedy pointed out he meant nothing more than the danger of one side erroneously predicting the next move of the other. He himself, JFK admitted, had misjudged the situation at the Bay of Pigs. Although that American debacle was in everyone's thoughts, Khrushchev appeared indifferent to pursuing a discussion of Cuba; he simply commented that U.S. policy had made Fidel Castro turn toward communism.

At the luncheon which followed their morning meeting, Kennedy asked about two medals Khrushchev was wearing. Told they were Lenin Peace Medals, JFK responded, "I hope you get to keep them." So far, he thought, the session had been somber; he was unable to find any "area of accommodation." Things went somewhat better in the afternoon, when Kennedy brought up the subject of Laos. Because it was a small country of no strategic importance to either Russia or the United States, the president stated a way should be found to secure a cease-fire and to establish a neutral government acceptable to all sides. Laos was simply not worth the danger of either superpower becoming more involved.

To this, Khrushchev agreed. The Soviet Union, he said, had no obligation or vested interest there, and he would support an effort to seek a satisfactory negotiated settlement. Khrushchev felt leftist forces would win out in Laos no matter what he or Kennedy decided. That country would, he had previously promised the American ambassador in Moscow, "fall into our lap like a rotten apple." In Southeast Asia and throughout the world, communism would triumph. "Ideas cannot be stopped," he told JFK.

Talking to Khrushchev, Kennedy later commented to Lem Billings, was like "dealing with Dad—all give and no take." The Soviet premier also felt the generation gap: at sixty-seven, he was facing a man younger than his own son. Yet Khrushchev had absolutely no problem communicating with Kennedy's wife.

When photographers asked him to pose shaking hands with JFK, he smiled and pointed at Jackie: "I'd rather shake hands with her." At a dinner held for the two heads of state, Khrushchev moved his chair closer to Jackie, complimented her on her dress, and began telling one joke after another. It was, Arthur Schlesinger said, like sitting next to Abbott and Costello. When the Russian leader turned serious and began to speak of the number of teachers in the Ukraine, Jackie said, "Don't bore me with statistics," sending Khrushchev into gales of laughter. They talked about the space programs of their two countries, and the dogs which Russia had sent into orbit. When Jackie learned one had given birth to a litter of puppies, she casually said, "Why don't you send me one?" Two months later, a fluffy white puppy named "Pushinka," accompanied by the Soviet ambassador, showed up at the White House. When the president asked what it was doing there, Jackie confessed. "I'm afraid I asked Khrushchev for it in Vienna. I was just running out of things to say."

Khrushchev himself had plenty to talk about on the second day of the conference, when the summit ended on a very chilling note. His good mood of the previous evening had vanished, and he again showed little interest in the subject Kennedy wanted to discuss.

The president had hoped the morning meeting would lead to agreement on a nuclear test ban, but Khrushchev argued that such a treaty should come only as a part of complete and total disarmament. JFK responded that general disarmament was complex and long-range, and that a test ban would at least be a start. He quoted a Chinese proverb, "A thousand-mile journey begins with a single step," and urged Khrushchev to take that step with him. But the Russian leader refused to budge; he felt on-site inspection would be little more than an excuse for espionage. The Soviet Union and the United States had observed a moratorium of nuclear testing for the past three years, and his country, Khrushchev promised, would not be the one to break it. After brushing aside Kennedy's dream that their conference would lead to a test ban, Khrushchev turned to the grim topic he had come to Vienna to pursue: Berlin.

At the end of World War II, Germany was partitioned into four military zones, with the eastern part of the country controlled by Russian troops and the western section under the authority of France, England, and the United States. Berlin itself, landlocked more than one hundred miles within the East German border, was administered by the governments of all four nations. In 1948, much to Soviet alarm, the West German Republic had been established. The specter of a revived German nation, from whom the Russians had suffered more than 20 million deaths during the war, was not their only cause for concern. All of western Europe had drawn closer to the United States through the Marshall Plan, and the Soviet Union felt threatened both by its former enemy and by those countries which, a few years before, had been its allies. In response to what it saw as a new menace, Russia blockaded the Autobahn, the highway leading to Berlin, in the hope of forcing both an American pullout and subsequent loss of face with other European nations.

Instead, President Truman ordered a massive airlift of supplies to West Berliners. By the time the blockade was lifted in May 1949, and Americans were again allowed to travel on the Autobahn, the city had become a lasting symbol of the struggle between the Soviet Union and the United States. With Berlin a powderkeg in the heart of the continent, ten nations of western Europe joined with Canada and the United States to form the North Atlantic Treaty Organization in the spring of 1949—agreeing that an attack against one would be an attack against all. That same year, Russia announced the creation of the German Democratic Republic, thus formalizing the dilemma: two Germanys, two Berlins. America refused to recognize the new nation, and the predicament continued to exasperate the leadership of both superpowers.

Upon assuming office in 1958, Khrushchev had called West Berlin a "bone in the throat." Now, three years later, he told President Kennedy the situation was intolerable. Russia, he said, intended to sign a treaty with East Germany which would change the occupied status of Berlin to that of a "free city"—meaning that in reality, all of its citizens would come under total Communist domination, and that members of NATO would have access only by negotiating their own treaties with the German Democratic Republic. Since the United States did not acknowledge the existence of that nation, Khrushchev knew Kennedy could not enter into any agreement with it. But if the president wouldn't accept the validity of the separate Soviet treaty, "I'll step on your corns any time I want," Khrushchev promised.

His earthy language did not disguise the seriousness of the threat, and Kennedy responded accordingly. Berlin was not Laos; it was of vital concern to the United States. Americans had fought their way there in World War II, and intended to stay. Should the United States abandon West Berlin, commitments to its allies would be regarded as nothing more than scraps of paper. His country would defend Berlin, the president said, "at any risk." Khrushchev refused to back down. America had perhaps six months in which to work out an agreement with East Germany. But in December, the Soviet Union would sign the treaty with or without U.S. approval. With the treaty in effect, any American presence inside East Germany would mean a violation of its borders, and that violation would be met with force. "If that is true," the president replied, "it will be a cold winter." Instead it proved to be a heated summer and fall.

JFK reported on Vienna in a nationally televised address on June 6. The summit had been, he said, "a very sober two days." Soviets and Americans had "wholly different views of right and wrong, of what is an internal affair and what is aggression, and above all, we have wholly different concepts of where the world is and where it is going." Several days later, Khrushchev made his own report to the Russian people. "A peace treaty with Germany cannot be put off any longer," he claimed, and warned that any American effort to cross East German borders would be viewed as "aggression" which would be "duly repulsed."

In a press conference at the end of the month, Kennedy commented that the Russian premier's statements were "apparently designed to heighten tension." So were his actions: by early July, the Soviets had announced a one-third increase in their national defense budget. As Khrushchev tightened the screws, backing the United States into a corner where, JFK said, the only alternatives would be "holocaust or humiliation," a strong response seemed imperative. "That son of a bitch won't pay any attention to words," the president remarked. "He has to see you move."

On July 25, Kennedy addressed the nation to explain the direction in which he intended to "move." It was one of the grimmest speeches ever given by a United States peacetime leader. "We cannot and will not permit the Communists to drive us out of Berlin," JFK said, "either gradually or by force." To back up his words, the president announced that the American defense budget would be increased by $3.25 billion; U.S. long-range nuclear bombers would go on a fifteen-minute alert; the number of draftees would be doubled and then tripled; a quarter of a million reservists would be activated; air-raid warning and fallout-detection systems would be improved; widespread construction of fallout shelters was recommended. "We seek peace, but we shall not surrender. That is the central meaning of this crisis, and the meaning of your government's policy."

Khrushchev thought the speech was belligerent, and said Kennedy's moves were military hysteria. By mid-August, the situation was nearing flashpoint. Thirty thousand refugees had poured out of East Berlin during the previous month alone, part of a steady stream seeking economic opportunity and freedom from oppression in the thriving capitalistic city to the west. The communists were facing a serious shortage in their work force and a loss of prestige as East Berliners made obvious to the world which system they preferred. Khrushchev's response to the problem was the Wall—a twenty-eight-mile-long barricade of cinder blocks, concrete, and barbed wire, which, when completed, sealed the border between the two Berlins.

Having anticipated almost every other possible response to the president's speech, everyone in the White House was completely surprised by the Wall. But there was no discussion about halting its construction; however repugnant it might be, the Wall stood within Soviet territory. Kennedy thought it was an indication that Khrushchev no longer intended to sign a treaty with East Germany. "There wouldn't be any need of a wall if he occupied the whole city," JFK told Kenny O'Donnell. "This is his way out of his predicament." But among the countries of NATO, and especially within West Berlin, there was less optimism. The Wall was regarded as only the first step in some sinister long-range Soviet plan. To reassure America's worried Allies, the president decided the "brutal border closing" called for still another forceful response.

Fifteen hundred U.S. troops, traveling in armored trucks, were ordered to move through East Germany to West Berlin. On Sunday morning, August 20, while the world held its breath, they began the 110-mile journey across the Autobahn. In Berlin itself, Russian and American tanks lined up to face each other along the border.

Ted Sorsensen later described it as the "most anxious moment" of the crisis, but the anxiety actually dragged on for hours. It was Saturday night in Washington, D.C. The president had forgone his usual weekend visit to Hyannis Port; it would be, he commented to a staff member, an "inappropriate place from which to start World War III." Everyone in the White House was on edge. "Talking to Kennedy then was like talking to a statue," an aide recalled. "There was the feeling that this mission could very well escalate to shooting." Privately, JFK admitted the odds were one in five that Russia and the United States would soon be at war—nuclear war.

But one by one, the American trucks cleared Soviet checkpoints along the Autobahn, and by Sunday evening, the last one had arrived safely in West Berlin. The confrontation between U.S. and Russian troops, which both sides had dreaded since the end of World War II, had been avoided. Soviet tanks pulled back from the border; Khrushchev withdrew his six-month deadline for the signing of a separate Russian treaty with East Germany. It seemed a turning point had finally been reached in U.S.-Soviet relations.

Then on August 30, Khrushchev went back on the promise he had given Kennedy in Vienna, and Russia resumed nuclear testing in the atmosphere. In early September, the president ordered the resumption of underground tests; "We have no other choice," he said. By the following spring, America, too, was conducting atmospheric tests. The Cold War showed no signs of a thaw after all.

As 1961 drew to a close, John Kennedy regarded the future with mixed feelings. "It's been a tough first year, but then they're all going to be tough," he told a journalist. "We're in better shape now, but there are so many chances for trouble because the world is full of trouble." From Asia to Europe, the planet seemed to be in upheaval. Leftist guerrillas continued to violate the Laotian cease-fire, and bit by bit were winning over most of the country's territory. Under the corrupt regime of President Diem, the situation in Vietnam was deteriorating. Describing that problem as "the worst one we've got," JFK in December pledged continued American aid but withheld his approval for the commitment of combat troops. A show of U.S. military force, Kennedy believed, would lead to an escalation of the nation's involvement. "It's like taking a drink," he commented to Arthur Schlesinger. "The effect wears off and you have to take another." Yet despite JFK's determination to avoid the trap into which the French had fallen a decade earlier, the five hundred U.S. military personnel in Vietnam at the time of his inauguration had, by the end of 1961, been increased to more than three thousand.

But it was Cuba that continued to be JFK's own "bone in the throat." That autumn, at the suggestion of presidential assistant Richard Goodwin, Kennedy authorized Operation Mongoose—the code name given a plan designed to coordinate intelligence activities, propaganda, and guerrilla strikes against Cuba, which, it was hoped, would eventually result in Castro's overthrow. Interpreting the scheme as one meant to revive their assassination attempts, the CIA not only assigned four hundred officers to work on Mongoose full-time, but also renewed its contacts with mobsters Roselli and Giancana.

A more positive plan of action for Latin America was the Alliance for Progress. In mid-December JFK and Jackie visited Venezuela and Colombia, where they took part in ceremonies inaugurating *Alianza* housing projects. On their return trip, the couple stopped in Palm Beach to visit the president's parents.

Back in Washington the next afternoon, Kennedy received a call from Bobby. When he hung up the phone, JFK looked stunned. "Dad's gotten sick," he told Pierre Salinger. At age seventy-three, Joe had suffered a massive stroke. Although his mind was alert, the once-commanding Joe Kennedy was left speechless and with his right side paralyzed. Trapped in a wheelchair, he would live for eight more years: long enough to see another dream realized when Teddy was elected to the Senate in November 1962, long enough to learn Teddy was his only surviving son.

19

READING MORE BUT ENJOYING IT LESS

At a press conference on March 29, 1962, Kennedy was asked, if he had it to do over again, whether he would run for the presidency and whether he would recommend the job to others. JFK smilingly responded, "The answer is to the first 'yes' and the second is 'no.' I don't recommend it to others—at least for a while." Despite his father's illness and the continuing crises that were a part of the job, JFK was optimistic about the future. The long-stalled American space program had finally moved ahead in the previous month, when on February 20, Lieutenant Colonel John Glenn successfully completed a five-hour, three-orbital flight. Kennedy was firmly committed to the space program, well aware of its public relations value in a world that had in recent years seen the decline of U.S. prestige. "We have a long way to go. We started late," he said. "But this is the new ocean, and I believe the United States must sail on it." Among the congratulatory telegrams was one from Nikita Khrushchev, suggesting that America and Russia cooperate in space research and exploration—an idea Kennedy had proposed in Vienna, and which the Soviet leader at that time declared "impossible."

JFK got more good news just before his forty-fifth birthday, when, on May 24, Lieutenant Commander Scott Carpenter became the second American to orbit the earth. The president had also enjoyed an early birthday celebration at a Democratic fund-raising event in Madison Square Garden. The climactic moment of that evening came when Marilyn Monroe, with whom Kennedy was rumored to have had an affair, appeared onstage. Attired in what she called "skin and beads," the movie actress gave a breathy and slightly off-key rendition of "Happy Birthday, Mr. President." In thanking her, JFK said with a grin that he could now retire from politics after having had "Happy Birthday" sung to him "in such a sweet, wholesome way."

But for Kennedy, lighthearted occasions had again become increasingly rare.

The president hoped his administration could play a role in keeping prices down, both to prevent inflation and to promote exportation of American goods. One key product of concern was steel. "As goes steel, so goes inflation" was an economic truism. Steel was used in so many products that a price hike in that industry always led to corresponding cost increases throughout the nation. Accordingly, between July 1961 and March 1962, JFK and Labor Secretary Arthur Goldberg met on four occasions with David McDonald, head of the Steelworkers Union, whose contract was coming up for negotiation, and with Roger Blough, chairman of United States Steel, the third largest corporation in the country. The president and Goldberg urged the union to accept a noninflationary settlement, so that the steel companies would be able to avoid raising their prices. Labor cooperated; management did not.

On March 31, the Steelworkers ratified a two-year contract that included a wage freeze. Since there was to be no wage increase, prices could remain stable. The president telephoned union headquarters and steel industry executives to congratulate both groups on their "industrial statesmanship" and to extend "the thanks of the American people." On April 10, scarcely a week after the settlement had been reached, Blough called at the White House to announce his company was raising its prices by six dollars per ton. Both Kennedy and Goldberg felt betrayed. "My father always told me," JFK remarked to several aides, "that all businessmen were sons-of-bitches, but I never believed it till now." The secretary of labor said his own credibility had been ruined and announced he was resigning. Kennedy agreed the increase in steel prices was "a hell of a note" but asked Goldberg: "What if we roll them back?" The labor secretary decided he wouldn't resign after all.

At a press conference the next day, Kennedy unleashed his wrath. "The American people will find it hard, as I do, to accept a situation in which a tiny handful of steel executives, whose pursuit of power and profit exceeds their sense of public responsibility, can show such utter contempt for the interests of 185 million Americans." Ted Sorsensen, who was in the audience, heard reporters gasp at JFK's harsh statement. But the presidential offensive went far beyond words.

Shortly before Blough dropped his bombshell, newspapers had quoted Edmund Martin, head of Bethlehem Steel, as saying, "There shouldn't be any price rise." Bethlehem, the nation's second largest steel company, then promptly followed the lead of U.S. Steel and increased its prices. Since that seemed just a little too coincidental, the administration suspected the steel industry was involved in the practice of artificial price-fixing. In order to get the exact wording of Martin's statement, Bobby asked the FBI to check with journalists who had been present at the time. When it was revealed that the agents had gone to the home of one of the reporters at 3 A.M., the action was widely criticized, and Bobby was certain Hoover had ordered it to again embarrass the Kennedys.

But despite the outcry over the predawn visit, the administration kept up the pressure. The Justice Department announced it would convene a grand jury to see if antitrust laws had been violated. The Department would also consider the question of whether U.S. Steel should be broken up, on the grounds it had a monopolistic power to set prices for the entire industry. The White House released facts and figures proving the company did not need a price increase. Senator Albert Gore declared he would propose legislation to control steel prices; Estes Kefauver said his Senate Antitrust and Monopoly Committee would investigate; the House Antitrust Committee decided it would also look into the situation. A $5.5 million Pentagon order for armor plate, used in the making of Polaris submarines, was placed with one of the steel companies that had not raised its prices.

By noon on Friday, April 13, Bethlehem rescinded its increase, and that afternoon, U.S. Steel followed suit. Seventy-two hours had passed since Roger Blough paid his call at the White House.

The administration had won the battle, but the war continued. "We are aware of the disadvantages of victory," one presidential spokesman wryly commented. Signs of the "disadvantages" were everywhere. "After this display of naked power," said the *Christian Science Monitor*, "how free will the American economy be?" The *Wall Street Journal* was almost hysterical. "The Government set the price. And it did this by the pressure of fear—by naked power, by threats, by agents of the state security police." At a press conference on May 9, JFK commented that he was reading the newspapers more, but "enjoying it less."

On May 29, the stock market, which had been sliding for months, went into the largest one-day decline since the crash of 1929, and continued to go down for a month. A joke made the rounds that Kennedy had assured an executive the economic outlook was good and said, "If I weren't President, I'd be buying stock myself." To this, the businessman replied, "If you weren't President, so would I." The subject inevitably came up at a press conference, when a reporter commented big business was using the market slump as a means of forcing Kennedy to be more sympathetic. "Their attitude is," the reporter said, " 'Now we have you where we want you.' " JFK smilingly responded: "I can't believe I am where business, big business, wants me!"

The president knew that the same could also be said for many white Southerners.

When John F. Kennedy accepted his party's nomination at the 1960 Democratic National Convention, he pledged that the New Frontier would demand "an end to racial discrimination in all parts of our community life." During the second televised debate with Richard Nixon, JFK vowed that, if elected, he would end segregation in federal housing programs with "one stroke of the pen." He had even won over Eleanor Roosevelt by proclaiming he intended not only to push for civil rights legislation, but to take executive action "on a bold and large scale."

Following through on his campaign promises proved more difficult after election day. The Eighty-seventh Congress, which convened in January 1961, held a bare Democratic majority, but a coalition of Republicans and Southern Democrats blocked almost every measure in the sweeping legislative program the new president sent to Capitol Hill. Questioned at a press conference about why his list of proposals did not include a civil rights bill, JFK responded, "When I believe we can usefully move ahead in the field of legislation, when I feel that there is a necessity for Congressional action, with a chance of getting that Congressional action, then I will recommend it." Kennedy was concerned about winning passage of any number of social programs, especially Medicare, a plan of federal health insurance for the elderly. He told Martin Luther King not to expect major antidiscriminatory measures to be submitted in the near future. "If we get into a long fight in

Congress, it will bottleneck everything else and still get no bill," he explained to King.

The one piece of civil rights legislation Kennedy was able to promote was a constitutional amendment banning poll taxes, which were used in the South as a way to prevent low-income blacks from voting in national elections. After Congress passed the amendment in August 1962, it was submitted to the states for ratification. Too late for JFK to relish the victory, the ban finally became the Twenty-fourth Amendment to the Constitution in January 1964. It was Kennedy's only legislative achievement for civil rights during his first two years in office. The president was a political realist; he knew it was hopeless to push for more.

Instead, his administration took a long-range view and worked to increase voter registration throughout the Deep South, where in most sections fewer than 15 percent of eligible blacks had been permitted to register. With a goal of adding a million blacks to the voting ranks, it was hoped more moderate Southern Democrats would eventually be elected. Martin Luther King approved of the strategy; the right of suffrage, he said, was a central issue. "It will give us the concrete tool with which we ourselves can correct injustice."

In other areas, also not subject to congressional approval, small gains were made. At JFK's first Cabinet meeting, he had instructed its members to make certain segregation was not practiced within their departments, and followed up at another meeting later in the year by asking for a breakdown of the number of blacks on each staff. Administration officials were told to refuse speaking engagements before nonintegrated audiences, and were asked to resign memberships in all-white private clubs. Blacks were appointed to a number of important sub-Cabinet government posts. Kennedy established the Committee on Equal Employment Opportunities, with Lyndon Johnson as chairman, and charged it with instigating equitable hiring practices in both the government and the companies with which the government did business. Black employment at one such firm, the Lockheed Corporation, increased by 26 percent. Even the Washington Redskins, who played in a federally financed stadium, were persuaded to integrate their team.

But the progress was incremental. In the area of civil rights, Kennedy had gone at a pace faster than any other president had dared attempt, but it was not fast enough. For blacks, racial discrimination was a fact of the American way of life, and they were growing impatient. JFK had made them a promise, and that promise was still unfulfilled. The Freedom Rides in the spring of 1961 were just a hint of things to come. And eventually the president, in spite of his preoccupation with foreign affairs, would confront the domestic issue of civil rights with a passion he had once reserved for the Cold War.

On the day after John Kennedy took office, a man named James Meredith, inspired by the inaugural address and what he envisioned as a "new age" in the United States, applied for admission to the University of Mississippi. Meredith was black, and Ole Miss, as it was called throughout the South, was white—all white. Nevertheless, Meredith, who had attended the black Jackson State College, wanted "something more"—not just a better education, which he could have gotten at any number of northern schools—but "something more" for his people. Meredith believed he had a responsibility "to break White Supremacy in Mississippi," and thought Ole Miss was the place to start. But the university had no interest in playing an historic role; his application for admission was rejected.

With the support of Medgar Evers, local director of the National Association for the Advancement of Colored People, Meredith filed suit, stating he had been turned down because of his race. The case went all the way to the Supreme Court, which ordered his admission by upholding a circuit court decision that Meredith had indeed been refused enrollment "solely because he was a Negro." When Mississippi governor Ross Barnett responded by announcing, "We will not surrender to the evil and illegal forces of tyranny," the battle lines were drawn.

On September 20, 1962, accompanied by two hundred federal marshals, Meredith arrived at the Ole Miss campus in Oxford. The governor was there to greet him with a long proclamation reiterating his position that the young man would be refused admittance. After reading it aloud, Barnett handed the document to Meredith and said, "Take it and abide by it."

The attorney general of the United States and the governor of the state of Mississippi spent a great deal of the latter half of that month on the phone with each other. Between September 15 and September 25, the two spoke twenty times. On Sunday, September 23, there was another attempt to enroll Meredith, who this time was surrounded by more marshals and a growing white mob. As Barnett again blocked his entrance, the crowd shouted, "Go home, nigger." In a conversation with Bobby Kennedy that night, the governor said of Meredith: "It's best for him not to go to Ole

Miss." Bobby replied: "But he likes Ole Miss." On September 25, Barnett told the attorney general that Meredith was "backed by the NAACP which is a communist front," and that he would rather spend the rest of his life "in a penitentiary" than allow the university's admittance of "that boy." Bobby responded he intended "to enforce the laws of the United States." Under court order, the governor had until October 2 to get Meredith enrolled, and the order, Bobby said, was "going to be upheld."

It was obvious the situation was moving toward a showdown. Three days later, Bobby met with General Maxwell Taylor, chairman of the joint chiefs, to discuss the logistics of sending troops to the Ole Miss campus. While truckloads of angry whites descended on Oxford from all over the state, maps of Mississippi were being unrolled in the Pentagon.

On Saturday, September 29, the president entered the drama, placing the first of seven calls to Barnett. "I don't know Mr. Meredith, and I didn't put him in there," he informed the governor. "But under the Constitution I have to carry out the law. I want your help in doing it." Instead Barnett promptly made matters worse. During the Ole Miss football game that afternoon, he gave an emotional "I Love Mississippi" speech, arousing the spectators to such an extent that one student said the scene reminded him of a Nazi rally. After learning that conditions on campus were explosive and that local law-enforcement officers could not be counted on to keep control, JFK federalized the Mississippi National Guard and ordered U.S. Army troops to a base in Memphis, from which they could, if needed, quickly be flown to Oxford. He also requested air time to speak to the nation on television Sunday evening.

The next morning Barnett called the attorney general with a new proposal. He would agree to Meredith's registration if he could be photographed capitulating at gunpoint. Bobby replied that would be a "foolish and dangerous show." The governor then suggested Meredith be brought to Ole Miss that afternoon. It had been announced he would enroll on Monday, and those who intended to make trouble wouldn't be expecting him to show up a day early. Since it was a Sunday, state police would be able to keep the few outsiders off-campus; there was no need for the Army or the National Guard to be called in.

Although Bobby agreed to the governor's request, he felt uneasy and asked Deputy Attorney General Nicholas Katzenbach to fly to Oxford, to "be in charge of things." As Katzenbach, along with an assistant attorney general, Edwin Guthman, and two other Justice Department lawyers, prepared to depart, Bobby gave his deputy a typical Kennedy farewell: "If things get rough, don't worry about yourself. The President needs a moral issue." His flippancy masked a deep concern. Bobby feared he might be sending Katzenbach into a war zone.

Late Sunday afternoon, while James Meredith was surreptitiously taken to a dormitory, Katzenbach and his group entered the Ole Miss administration building, which was surrounded by five hundred federal marshals. Far from being deserted, as Barnett had promised, the campus was crowded with twenty-five hundred racists, some armed with shotguns and rifles. The mob ringed the building, chanting "2-4-1-3, we hate Ken-ned-dy" and "kill the nigger-loving bastards." Despite Katzenbach's protests, the state police had been withdrawn, and his small band felt very vulnerable. After dark, the mood grew uglier, and the crowd began to throw bricks and bottles. Then, using a stolen fire engine and a bulldozer, they attempted to batter their way inside. When it seemed the mob would succeed in storming the building, Katzenbach ordered the marshals to use tear gas.

In the meantime, JFK had given his television address based on Barnett's statement that Meredith was safely on campus, sneaked in, the governor told Mississippians, without his knowledge. Kennedy, unaware that the situation had become violent, said that Meredith's enrollment had "been accomplished, thus far without the use of National Guard or other troops." When the president went off the air and learned events in Oxford had taken an alarming turn, he immediately called Barnett. The governor had issued another proclamation declaring his state would "never surrender"— defiant words, he assured JFK, he was speaking "just to Mississippi." Kennedy insisted the state police be sent back to the campus, and slammed down the phone in the midst of Barnett's protest. Finally, fifty local law-enforcement officers showed up.

Throughout the night, the president and the attorney general sat in the Cabinet Room of the White House, waiting to learn if the United States was about to become embroiled in its second Civil War. "I haven't had such an interesting time since the Bay of Pigs," JFK commented. Connected to an open phone line in the Ole Miss administrative building, Bobby relayed the news. "This place is sort of like the Alamo," Edwin Guthman told him. Vehicles and campus buildings were burning, shots were being fired, two bystanders were dead. Hearing that appalling report, Kennedy ordered in the National Guard and the U.S. Army. Near dawn, peace was finally restored. Two hundred people had been arrested, two hundred marshals injured, a French journalist and a towns-person fatally wounded. But at eight o'clock that morning, when James Meredith registered as a student at the University of Missis-sippi, the civil rights movement took another step forward on its long path.

It had been a very tense two weeks in Washington, D.C. and Oxford, Mississippi. But they were nothing compared to two weeks in the following month—when America and Russia finally met at the brink.

I SEE
A STORM COMING

Since the Bay of Pigs, the two superpowers had been moving inexorably toward another confrontation. Kennedy realized his limited show of strength in Berlin had not been enough; sometime, somewhere, JFK was going to have to prove he was tough enough to risk the ultimate showdown. Khrushchev saw America as a paper tiger, unwilling to bare its nuclear teeth. Because Fidel Castro was convinced the United States intended to attack his small island, the Russian leader concluded it was the obvious place to display communist power.

Although the Kennedy administration was not contemplating an invasion of Cuba, Castro was right to fear American intentions. After a decade of covert action against leftist governments, the CIA was confident of its mandate to get rid of the only communist leader in the Western Hemisphere—using whatever dirty tricks were necessary.

In addition to the time he devoted to civil rights, Bobby had persevered in what he described as "chasing bad men." Members of the Organized Crime Section were regarded as the most elite group at Justice. The attorney general had even managed to somewhat deflect the FBI from its avid pursuit of subversives in order to turn the Bureau's expertise against the underworld. High on Bobby's list of "bad men" were two mobsters he remembered from their appearances before the McClellan Committee: Johnny Roselli and Sam Giancana.

The CIA, which hoped to conceal its dealings with the syndicate, was alarmed by the attorney general's determination to make war on organized crime. If the Justice Department prosecuted Giancana, the whole messy story of the Agency's involvement with the underworld might come out. The Chicago crime boss was a notorious loudmouth and, once on the witness stand, would undoubtedly reveal his connection with the most secretive organization in government.

In May 1962, CIA general counsel Lawrence Houston was sent to Bobby's office to tell him about the assassination scheme devised in the fall of 1960 between the Agency and the mob. Inspired by Operation Mongoose, Technical Services had already brewed up a new batch of poisons to pass on to Roselli. But CIA officials led Houston to believe the plan had been canceled, and that was the information he gave the attorney general. Houston later described Bobby's reaction: "If you have seen Mr. Kennedy's eyes get steely and his jaw set and his voice get low and precise, you get a definite feeling of unhappiness." Since his days with McClellan, Bobby had despised the underworld and was incensed, he told Houston, that the Agency had tried "to do business" with "gangsters."

Bobby had even greater reason to be upset than the CIA lawyer realized. The Kennedy administration had become involved with the very people he hated above all others, and in a plot to murder a foreign head of state. That organized crime was aware of the nasty scheme, and in a position to blackmail the government, was bad enough. But the president's affair with Judith Campbell compounded the dilemma. JFK had been seeing a woman who simultaneously had a relationship with one of the most infamous mobsters in the country—the very man the CIA had approached to assassinate Castro.

The previous February, Bobby had received a memorandum from J. Edgar Hoover. It stated that in the course of an ongoing FBI investigation of Johnny Roselli and Sam Giancana, agents had discovered the two men had a mutual friend: Judith Campbell. A check of the young woman's phone records revealed she had placed calls to the private White House number of the president's secretary, Evelyn Lincoln. "The relationship between Campbell and Mrs. Lincoln, or the purpose of these calls, is not known," the memo concluded. Judith Campbell, however, had been under surveillance since November 1961, and Hoover was well aware her "relationship" was not with Mrs. Lincoln. Having warned the attorney general that he knew all about JFK's imprudent activities, Hoover was surprised to learn calls between Campbell and the White House continued.

The FBI director had been in his job for thirty-eight years, and he intended to keep it. He would turn seventy on January 1, 1965; because there was no affection between him and the Kennedys, Hoover knew he would probably not be reappointed if the president was elected to a second term. The director maintained files on the private lives of many important people, and wasn't above using that information to get what he wanted. The attempt to put pressure on JFK through his brother obviously hadn't worked. Hoover concluded that Bobby—whom the president described as "a puritan" with "strict personal ethics"—didn't know about JFK's affair with Campbell and therefore had missed the whole point of the memo. If that were the case, the director thought, he would have to go right to the top. On March 22, J. Edgar Hoover had a private luncheon with John Kennedy. Official White House logs show the last of what had been a total of seventy calls between Campbell and JFK was placed that afternoon.

Although the president had at last come to his senses and severed the reckless connection to Campbell, the CIA continued its involvement with her underworld friends, despite Bobby's determination to bring Sam Giancana to trial. The head of the Chicago syndicate thought that his Agency contacts and potential for blackmailing the president would protect him from federal prosecution. But even with the risks it posed to his brother's administration, Bobby ordered intensified FBI surveillance on the syndicate boss. "They can't do this to me," Giancana protested to a lawyer. "I'm working for the government." The pressure continued. "Bobby pushed to get Giancana at any cost," said William Hundley, head of the Organized Crime Section. On the afternoon of November 22, 1963, the attorney general was scheduled to continue a discussion begun that morning with Hundley and other staff members, reviewing the Justice Department's case against Giancana. The meeting was canceled, and never rescheduled.

Having made a decision to continue his pursuit of the underworld regardless of the possible consequences to the Kennedy presidency, Bobby still had the assassination plot to consider. Historical opinion is divided as to whether he was upset at the CIA's association with organized crime, or because it had put itself in the murder business.

Lawrence Houston was under the impression the attorney general objected only to the involvement of "gangsters." But Bobby himself told two aides he had learned of a scheme to assassinate Castro and had "turned it off." Richard Bissell later said he "assumed" the project had presidential approval. Richard Helms, Bissell's replacement, thought the plan was ongoing because of "the intensity of the pressure" being brought by the Kennedys to do something about Castro. Operation Mongoose made it clear they wanted to get rid of the Cuban leader, but the problem lay in the CIA's interpretation of exactly what that meant.

Neither JFK nor Bobby ever ordered the Agency to kill Castro, and Helms said nobody wanted to embarrass the president by discussing it in front of him. The original plot had begun in the previous administration, and the CIA had not inquired if the scheme should be continued. Following a policy of "plausible denial"—originated by Eisenhower to protect himself and other senior government officials—the Agency consulted neither the new president nor John McCone, the man he had appointed to succeed Allen Dulles. William Harvey, a high-ranking Agency official in charge of "Executive Actions," had dispatched still another supply of poison pills to Roselli. Yet Harvey was, "for a variety of reasons," given Helms's approval not to tell McCone. The CIA director was a convert to Catholicism and deeply religious; both Helms and Harvey assumed he would veto the plan. Yet because there were few people more devout than Bobby Kennedy, it is odd the Agency would assume his endorsement of a murder plot.

Although the president was much less religious than his brother, he was on record as being against assassination. In May 1961, Kennedy sent the CIA a memo, never later withdrawn or amended, stating the United States could not condone such an action against any foreign leader. The following November, the same month in which he approved Operation Mongoose, JFK told Tad Szulc, Latin American correspondent for the *New York Times*, that he was "under terrific pressure" to approve Castro's murder—a statement which contradicts Helms's assertion that the plot was not discussed in Kennedy's presence. Both he and Bobby, JFK said, felt strongly that the United States "for moral reasons" should never resort to assassination. Richard Goodwin, a White House Latin American specialist and the originator of Operation Mongoose, sat in on the president's conversation with Szulc. He later asked Kennedy about "the crazy idea" of killing the Cuban premier. "If we get into that kind of thing," JFK replied, "we'll all be targets."

And if the Kennedys had been determined to kill Castro, they had the perfect opportunity to do so in the fall of 1962. It was then that both the president and the attorney general rejected a proposal to bomb and invade Cuba—a course of action urged by influential Democrats and Republicans alike, a plan that would almost certainly have resulted in Castro's death.

Tuesday, October 16, was three weeks before congressional election day, and President Kennedy was under considerable political pressure. In a campaign speech two years earlier, he had stated, "The transformation of Cuba into a communist base of operations a few miles from our coast—by jet plane, missile, or submarine—is an incredibly dangerous development to have been permitted by our Republican policymakers." Now the shoe was on the other foot. The Republican campaign committee had announced Cuba would be "the dominant issue of the 1962 campaign." Some senators were calling for an immediate invasion to oust Fidel Castro and his government.

Since late July, naval ships and planes, supplemented by twice monthly U-2 flights, had been photographing an unusual number of Russian ships in Cuban waters. The Soviets, it appeared, were unloading tanks, guns, planes, and personnel on the island. After observing the increased activity for three weeks, the CIA reported to the president that "something new and different" was taking place; five thousand Russian military specialists were in Cuba, and some sort of construction was under way. When Kennedy requested the U-2 flights be stepped up to once a week, photographs revealed the presence of defensive weapons: antiaircraft surface-to-air missiles (SAMs) with a twenty-five-mile range, and torpedo boats equipped with short-range, ship-to-ship rockets. The Agency concluded that the Soviet Union, in response to American campaign rhetoric urging an invasion, had decided to protect its only ally in the Western Hemisphere from external attack.

Soviet ambassador Anatoly Dobrynin, in a meeting with Bobby Kennedy on September 4, said Khrushchev had given him a message for the president. No offensive surface-to-surface missiles were being placed in Cuba; all military activity there was purely defensive and of no significance. Bobby responded that the buildup was being carefully watched, and that the placement of offensive weapons on the island would have "the gravest consequences." That afternoon, JFK issued a statement which echoed Bobby's warning. Should evidence reveal a "significant offensive capability" on the island of Cuba,

Kennedy said, "the gravest issues would arise." Two days later, Dobrynin requested Ted Sorensen to relay another message from Khrushchev to the president: "Nothing will be undertaken before the American Congressional elections that could complicate the international situation or aggravate the tension in the relations between our two countries."

Kennedy was not convinced, and on September 7 asked Congress for the authority to activate 150,000 reservists. The action was necessary, he explained, so that the United States could react promptly and effectively "to challenges which may be presented in any part of the free world." The Russians responded belligerently on September 11. "Our nuclear weapons are so powerful in their explosive force and the Soviet Union has so powerful rockets to carry these nuclear warheads" that placing missiles in Cuba was unnecessary. The statement concluded, "If the aggressors unleash war, our armed forces must be ready to strike a crushing retaliatory blow at the aggressor." At his press conference two days later, Kennedy reiterated that should Cuba at any time become an offensive military base for the Soviets, America would do "whatever must be done to protect its own security."

In spite of the increasingly volatile Cold War dialogue, few believed Russia would go beyond the installation of defensive weapons. Such a move would give the United States an excuse to invade Cuba—the very thing Russia said it was trying to prevent. All of the president's intelligence advisors agreed on that point, with the exception of John McCone. The CIA director was afraid the SAMs might be intended as protection for surface-to-surface missile sites, but since he was alone in that opinion, the newly married McCone decided to go ahead with a honeymoon on the Riviera. Even there, McCone continued to worry, and on September 7, 10, 13, and 16, sent off what would become known as the "honeymoon telegrams" to his deputy, Marshall Carter. These were distributed only within the Agency, and the president was not informed of McCone's concern. On September 20, the director telegraphed Carter with another thought: if the Soviets did successfully install offensive weapons in Cuba, he said, they would greatly improve their bargaining position with the United States—in Berlin or wherever else they might decide to use it.

Four U-2 flights over the eastern part of the island during the last week of September and the first week of October showed no evidence of anything other than the defensive sites. Photo surveillance of western Cuba was not currently under way; SAMs were believed to be operational in that area, and no one wanted to risk another Francis Gary Powers incident. When McCone returned from France and learned there had been no flights over the west end of the island in a month, he urged it be photographed immediately. But there were delays. Over the protests of his deputy, the Agency director accepted a suggestion by Robert McNamara that the missions be flown by pilots of the Strategic Air Command. If anyone was shot down and taken prisoner, the defense secretary wanted him to be a member of the Air Force and not, as with Powers, a CIA pilot. Cloudy conditions over Cuba resulted in another postponement; aerial photographs could not be taken from a U-2 when the sky was overcast. Finally, on October 14, the clouds cleared.

At 8:30 the next night, the Agency notified National Security Adviser McGeorge Bundy that the photos had been developed and analyzed. The unthinkable had happened. Near San Cristobal, construction was beginning on a base for medium-range ballistic missiles. With an eleven-hundred-mile range, MRBMs, armed with nuclear warheads, could within little more than a week be aimed straight at Washington, D.C.

The president had just returned from three days of campaigning for Democratic candidates in six different states, where he hoped his appearances would help elect congressional members more sympathetic to the Kennedy legislative program. Instead, many audiences had seemed to care more about JFK's lack of action against Fidel Castro. A Cincinnati demonstrator held up a sign which read, WHERE ARE THOSE FIGHTING IRISH? Another said, OK, WE LICKED MISSISSIPPI. NOW HOW ABOUT CUBA? JFK arrived back from his exhausting trip at 2 A.M. on October 15, and spent part of the day in conference with the prime minister of newly independent Algeria. That evening, he had dinner with his visiting parents, and a session with the incapacitated Joe Kennedy was always a strain. Bundy decided to let the president get a good night's sleep and to wait until early the next day to give him the results of the latest U-2 reconnaissance.

For Kennedy, Tuesday, October 16, 1962, seemed at first like any other morning in the White House. He read the newspapers, ate breakfast, and looked forward to a visit from astronaut Wally Schirra, who had a few days earlier completed America's third successful orbital flight. But with the appearance of Bundy at 8:45, the peaceful routine of the morning was shattered, and the thirteen-day Cuban missile crisis began.

Under pressure from his own military leaders, Khrushchev had made a dangerous decision. The "missile gap," which candidate Kennedy had used to such advantage, did not, in fact, exist. In spite of the Russian saber-rattling statement on September 11, the United States had great nuclear supremacy. Intercontinental ballistic missiles were expensive to build, and the Soviet Union had pressing economic problems. It would be less costly to install medium and intermediate-range missiles in Cuba than to increase production of ICBMs. The American president had not followed through at the Bay of Pigs, had sat still for Khrushchev's bullying in Vienna, had allowed the Berlin Wall to be built. Now the Russian leader was gambling Kennedy would let the missiles stay in Cuba.

Aboard *Air Force One* on the way back from the summit conference in June 1961, Evelyn Lincoln had been straightening JFK's papers. She came across a note which Kennedy had written to himself, paraphrasing words Abraham Lincoln had written on the eve of his own presidency: "I know there is a God—and I see a storm coming." Sixteen months later, the storm had arrived. The shocked and angered president called a meeting on October 16 of what would soon be known as "Excom": the Executive Committee of the National Security Council. The NSC had been established in 1947 to counsel the president on defense and foreign policy. But in this crisis, Kennedy wanted to pick his own advisors, some who were NSC members and some who were not. It was a group of fifteen men, from the departments of State and Defense, along with the attorney general, the director of the CIA, the secretary of the Treasury, the national security adviser, and the presidential counsel, Ted Sorensen. Sitting in on some Excom meetings would also be the vice-president, Kenny O'Donnell, Adlai Stevenson, and former secretary of state Dean Acheson.

That morning, they listened and watched in dismay as the results of the latest U-2 surveillance were displayed. The missiles were there, ninety miles from the Florida coast; they were offensive weapons; they would soon be operational. Now the committee would have to decide what to do about them. It was important their meetings be kept secret, Kennedy cautioned, in order to avoid alerting the Soviets or frightening the American public. He requested Excom make a study, and to recommend one or several courses of action. They had a little time to consider the alternatives; intelligence experts estimated the launch sites wouldn't be completed for ten days. The group's immediate reaction was that there would probably be only one feasible solution: an air strike. Listening to a discussion of a surprise attack, Bobby passed a note to his brother. He now understood, it read, how the Japanese commander felt "when he was planning Pearl Harbor."

JFK left the meeting to go about his business as usual; the White House press corps would quickly notice if the presidential routine changed. That afternoon he spoke at a State Department conference for editorial writers and commentators, where one participant asked Kennedy about the repeated criticisms of his lack of action against Castro. Since he could reveal nothing of the current situation, JFK left the unsuspecting audience laughing when he concluded with a poem:

> *Bullfight critics ranked in rows*
> *Crowd the enormous Plaza full.*
> *But only one is there who knows*
> *And he's the man who fights the bull.*

Excom met for the second day, the group puzzling over Khrushchev's motivation for his provocative plan. There were several theories. Perhaps he was testing the country's resolve. One member quoted a Russian adage: "If you strike steel, pull back. If you strike mush, keep going." Maybe Khrushchev expected Kennedy to turn to "mush" rather than risk nuclear war. If the president backed down, the Soviet Union might assume it could force the United States out of Berlin. America had missiles in Turkey, pointed at Moscow; this could be a ploy to have them removed. Republican cries for an invasion had no doubt alarmed Castro; possibly he had requested military assistance. A few of those present knew about Operation Mongoose; it was conceivable Cuban intelligence sources had also learned of the plan to overthrow their government. Only one thing was clear. The Soviet undertaking, it was estimated, would cost one billion dollars, and the economically troubled nation would never have invested such a sum unless the missiles were being installed for an alarming purpose. They would have to go.

Robert McNamara alone seemed to disagree with that premise. ICBMs in Russia were already trained on the United States, he said, and "A missile is a missile. It makes no great difference whether you are killed by a missile fired from the Soviet Union or from Cuba." But, it was pointed out, whether or not the Cuban missiles changed the actual balance of power, the credibility of the United States was at stake. As a result of State Department prodding, Latin American nations had earlier in the year voted to exclude Castro's government from the Organization of American States. Adlai Stevenson commented that the OAS countries were directly involved and threatened, and would "not consider this a remote quarrel between the United States and Russia." As for the missiles, Stevenson disagreed with the defense secretary. "We just had to get them out of there."

But there was no time for the diplomatic approach Stevenson would have preferred. U-2 photographs taken Wednesday, October 17, showed work was proceeding on at least sixteen and possibly as many as thirty-two MRBM sites. Experts now predicted they would be operational within a week. Worse yet, excavation was under way for three intermediate-range missile sites. At the present rate of construction, the IRBMs would be ready by early December; with a twenty-two-hundred-mile range, they could hit almost any target within the continental United States. Now convinced that some action was required, McNamara proposed a U.S. naval blockade against Soviet ships then en route to Cuba and presumed to be carrying nuclear warheads. It would be a limited response, which could, if necessary, later be escalated, and it gave Khrushchev a while to reconsider his dangerous course.

Air strike advocates disagreed with the suggestion. A blockade would not remove the missiles that were already on the island. The Pentagon, however, could not guarantee the success of a limited bombing attack: a "surgical" air strike against only the missile sites. That action would leave Soviet planes and other weapons untouched. There was also the possibility that not all the sites would be destroyed, perhaps leading to an instant nuclear retaliation against the United States. The joint chiefs instead recommended a massive bombing to eliminate all the missiles, planes, weapons, and—not incidentally—Fidel Castro.

Arguments against an attack from the air were that even a limited strike would kill Russian personnel. As many as twenty-five thousand Cubans, it was estimated, might also die. Latin Americans were certain to be appalled by the killing of innocent civilians, and Europeans, long accustomed to living in the shadow of Soviet missiles, would find the U.S. reaction excessive. Perhaps, instead, an invasion was called for. The debate dragged on, and time was running out. Photographs taken on Thursday, October 18, showed the Russians were moving ahead more quickly. Now it was thought they would have the first MRBM site completed within eighteen hours. Its missiles were aimed at specific cities within the United States. If they were fired, as many as 80 million Americans would be dead within minutes. Hearing that horrifying statistic, the attorney general asked with grim humor, "Can they hit Oxford, Mississippi?"

JFK kept to his normal schedule, burdened with the knowledge he would soon have to make a choice that could ultimately result in the destruction of two nations. During a campaign appearance in Connecticut, he was jeered by Yale students holding signs that read: MORE COURAGE, LESS PROFILE. The group wasn't booing a Harvard man; ironically, they were protesting Kennedy's failure to get rid of Castro.

On Thursday, the president invited Dean Acheson to the White House. The former secretary of state had attended the previous day's meeting of Excom, at which he had endorsed an air strike. The attorney general sharply disagreed. Repeating his Pearl Harbor analogy, Bobby said a sneak attack "would blacken the United States in the pages of history." Acheson had no patience for that argument; Bobby was being "emotional." JFK had twice warned the Russians, on September 4 and 13, what would happen if they made moves in Cuba that endangered American security. Therefore, Acheson said, there was no question of a "surprise" attack. Now, in the Oval Office, Kennedy also brought up Pearl Harbor. Acheson was scornful. It was a silly comparison, he told JFK, and "it is unworthy of you to talk that way." The president got up from his chair and stared out the window. Finally, after a long silence, he said, "Well, I guess this is the week I earn my salary."

That afternoon, Kennedy kept a previously scheduled appointment with Soviet foreign minister Andrei Gromyko, who was en route to Moscow after attending a meeting at the UN. Kennedy had considered confronting him with the U-2 photographs. But since the American response was still undecided, the president chose to remain silent about the missiles' presence and listened instead to what Gromyko had to say. When the subject of Cuba came up, the foreign minister said Russia's sole objective was to aid in its agriculture and land development, to "give bread to Cuba in order to prevent hunger in that country." The few defensive Soviet armaments were to guard against American aggression, and did not constitute a threat to the United States. Kennedy sat impassively through Gromyko's remarks. "I was dying to confront him with our evidence," he later told Kenny O'Donnell. "It was incredible to sit there and watch the lies coming out of his mouth."

While JFK conferred with the Soviet foreign minister, Excom was in session at a State Department conference room. The president had called a late-night meeting to hear the committee's recommendations, and its members were trying to arrive at a consensus. Acheson was not present to make his formidable arguments for an air strike, and now most of the others seemed to favor a blockade.

It provided flexibility; if the Soviet vessels refused to stop, military action could then, as a last resort, be taken. Khrushchev had stated on September 11 that an American move against Cuba would lead to nuclear war; there was also concern that in the event of an air strike or invasion, Castro would execute the Bay of Pigs prisoners. But most of all, there was the moral question, which Bobby had raised again and again over the past three days. With a majority having agreed on a blockade, the group left to meet with the president. Ten of them rode in the attorney general's limousine, to avoid a conspicuous number of official vehicles parked outside the White House. "It will be some story if this car is in an accident," one of its passengers commented.

In the Cabinet Room, the options were reviewed again. The joint chiefs were still pushing for a military solution. General Curtis LeMay, Air Force chief of staff, predicted the Russians would "do nothing" in the event Cuba was bombed. "Can you imagine LeMay saying a thing like that?" JFK asked O'Donnell after the meeting. The generals, he said, had an advantage. "If we listen to them, and do what they want us to do, none of us will be alive later to tell them that they were wrong." Having heard the alternatives and the reasons why most Excom members favored a blockade, Kennedy agreed it was probably the best approach, although, he added, "Whatever you fellows are recommending today you will be sorry about a week from now." A wrong decision could mean the end of civilization. "You're in a pretty bad fix, Mr. President," remarked General David Shoup, commandant of the Marine Corps. "You're in it with me," Kennedy replied. Everyone laughed, and the meeting adjourned.

On Friday, October 19, JFK left for a weekend on the campaign trail. It would be his last trip before the election, he told his aides. "This blows it. We've lost anyway"—the Republicans, he said, had been right about Cuba. Before departing, the president spoke with Bobby and Ted Sorensen. He wanted a final consensus from Excom, and he was relying on them "to pull the group together quickly." When a decision had been reached, Bobby was to phone him and Kennedy would fly back to Washington. But at their meeting that day, the committee seemed further apart than ever, with many of its members having second thoughts. After spending the night mulling over the Agency's grisly estimate that Soviet missiles were aimed at millions of Americans, most now felt a blockade was an inadequate response. Sorensen protested it wasn't fair to JFK to reverse their recommendation of the night before. But Dean Acheson pushed for military action, saying "the sooner we get to a showdown, the better." McCone, Bundy, and Treasury Secretary Dillon all agreed with General Maxwell Taylor's call for an air strike.

Then Bobby spoke up. They were fighting, he said, for something more than survival; a sneak attack would betray America's heritage and ideals. Neither the Soviet Union nor Cuba had broken any international law. It would be very difficult for the president to order a bombing, "with all the implications this would have for us in whatever world there would be afterward." Many in the room were deeply moved by Bobby's comments. A State Department representative said the attorney general's "good sense and his moral character were perhaps decisive." Certainly his remarks had convinced Dillon. "As he spoke, I felt that I was at a real turning point in history." What changed his mind, the Treasury secretary said, was Bobby's argument "that we ought to be true to ourselves as Americans," a consideration that had not occurred to him until the attorney general raised it "so eloquently." But other air-strike advocates would not back down, and the next morning Bobby called his brother. Excom couldn't make the decision, he said. It was up to the president.

JFK was in Chicago, where an anti-Castro group was gathered in front of his hotel with now familiar signs: LESS PROFILE, MORE COURAGE. On Saturday morning, October 20, Press Secretary Pierre Salinger announced Kennedy had developed a cold and would cancel the rest of his trip to return to the White House. Journalists who regularly covered the president watched as he boarded his plane. Yes, they agreed, JFK must really be ill; he was wearing a hat. But once back in the nation's capital, the cover story began to fall apart. The vice-president, who had been campaigning in Hawaii, also had a "cold" and was flying to Washington. While Salinger fended off calls from reporters, Kennedy spent the afternoon in a meeting with Excom.

Again JFK heard all the options. Adlai Stevenson thought the president could perhaps bargain with Khrushchev and Castro. He asked if Kennedy would consider giving up the American naval base at Guantánamo, near Santiago. A 1903 treaty with Cuba had guaranteed the United States could hold the base in perpetuity, but for three years Castro had been demanding American withdrawal. Stevenson suggested Kennedy could also offer to pull U.S. Jupiter missiles out of Turkey, where they posed a threat to the Soviet Union no less great than the Cuban missiles did to the United States. The president rejected both proposals. Guantánamo would not be surrendered under pressure; instead, it would be reinforced. Nor would America remove the admittedly outdated Jupiters. Because they were land-based, their usefulness had been superceded by maneuverable Polaris submarines, and Kennedy had already ordered that they be dismantled. Under the circumstances, however, European allies might interpret removal of the missiles as an indication that America was prepared to risk their security in order to protect its own. For the time being, the Jupiters would have to stay.

Although General Taylor reiterated the case for an air strike, there was still the problem that it would not necessarily destroy all the sites. Critics of a blockade had pointed out it wouldn't get rid of the missiles. But that could also be the case with bombs, and at least a naval embargo posed less risk of nuclear retaliation. The president made his decision; he would "fight the bull" with a blockade.

Only the details of the crisis could now be kept secret. By Sunday, October 21, messages had been sent to America's allies and embassies informing them of the situation. A special briefing was held for members of the OAS, who gave the president their unanimous approval for his proposed actions. Congressional leaders, most of them campaigning in their home states, were asked to fly back to Washington. Hale Boggs of Louisiana, the House majority whip, was fishing in the Gulf of Mexico; the request for his return was dropped in a bottle tossed out of an Air Force plane.

Newspapers were filled with speculation about an impending crisis. By Monday, October 22, when it was announced the president would address the nation that night, most of the country realized something ominous was going on in Washington.

Thirty minutes before Kennedy's address, a copy of the speech was delivered to Khrushchev in Moscow, along with a personal letter from JFK. The president wrote of his concern that the Russian government "would not correctly understand the will and determination of the United States." He had not assumed, Kennedy continued, that Khrushchev or "any other sane man would, in this nuclear age, deliberately plunge the world into war which it is crystal clear no country could win and which could only result in catastrophic consequences to the whole world, including the aggressor."

At 7 P.M. the president went on the air. "Good evening, my fellow citizens. This government, as promised, has maintained the closest surveillance of the Soviet military buildup on the island of

Cuba." The Berlin speech in July 1961 had been chilling; this one was much worse. Kennedy explained that the Russians had, for the first time, placed offensive weapons outside their own country, and now there were missiles ninety miles off the American coastline. He outlined the U.S. government's planned response. "It shall be the policy of this nation," JFK continued, "to regard any nuclear missile launched from Cuba against any nation in the Western Hemisphere as an attack by the Soviet Union on the United States, requiring a full retaliatory response upon the Soviet Union." To millions of people listening all across the world, it was the most terrifying sentence they would ever hear.

An overnight Gallup poll showed one in five Americans thought the Cuban missile crisis would result in World War III. The percentage was somewhat higher in the cities of Washington and New York, presumed to be the most likely targets of a Russian nuclear strike. On Tuesday, October 23, reconnaissance pilots for the first time flew just above tree-top level over Cuba. Their photographs showed that two MRBM sites now appeared to be operational. In the nation's capital, evacuation plans were readied for the president and members of a skeleton government, who would have only an eighteen-minute warning before the attack. Kennedy asked Jackie to take the children and move closer to their assigned underground shelter outside Washington; she refused to leave him alone in the White House. Robert Kennedy said he would not evacuate. If it came to that, he told Edwin Guthman, there would be at least "sixty million Americans killed and as many Russians or more. I'll be at Hickory Hill."

Massive military preparations had been made. Polaris submarines, armed with nuclear missiles, began to move toward the Soviet Union. Bombers of the Strategic Air Command, loaded with atomic weapons, circled the globe. Almost 180 American ships were in the Caribbean, with 22 surrounding Cuba. One hundred thousand combat troops, the largest U.S. force since D-Day, were in Georgia and Florida, ready to launch an invasion.

All day on October 23, surveillance planes reported that at least twenty-five Soviet ships, accompanied by six submarines, were holding on course for Cuba. That night, Khrushchev sent Kennedy a message which warned that the blockade would not be observed. America's actions, he said, were "the folly of degenerate imperialism," and the president was pushing their two nations "to the abyss of a world missile-nuclear war."

At an Excom meeting on Wednesday the 24th, the group was informed that several Russian vessels, escorted by a submarine, were approaching the point of no return five hundred miles outside Cuba. Everyone now assumed the worst. Navy ships and planes from the carrier *Essex*, posted near the blockade line, would have to fire on the Soviet ships if they refused to stop. The Russians would respond by launching the operable missiles in Cuba, or with ICBMs from the Soviet Union. Although outwardly calm, JFK was doodling on a pad: *serious . . . serious . . . submarines . . . submarines. . . .* He and the attorney general stared at each other across the table. Bobby felt almost as if only the two of them were there, and thought, inexplicably, of Joe Jr.'s death, of Jack's near-fatal illnesses. Minutes dragged by, the fate of the world hanging in the balance. "We were on the edge of a precipice," Bobby later described the scene, "with no way off."

Then a messenger came into the room. "Mr. President, we have a preliminary report which indicates that some of the Russian ships are stopping." Several were circling at reduced speeds; others were dead in the water. Most of the ones that continued on course toward Cuba were tankers. "We're eyeball to eyeball," Secretary of State Dean Rusk said quietly, "and I think the other fellow just blinked."

But both Kennedy and Khrushchev were aware that the reason for the showdown was ongoing; the missiles were still in Cuba. The two were in touch several times a day, since there was always the possibility of that factor JFK most feared: "a miscalculation." The communication system between Russia and the United States, which played, as Pierre Salinger described it, "a fateful role," was a comparatively antiquated tool in a potential nuclear confrontation. Kennedy's messages were sent to the American embassy in Moscow, but the process of coding, transmitting, decoding, and translating took four hours. If the diplomatic channels were bypassed, and proposals or responses given directly to the press, the time was cut down to an hour. But that meant no private communication between the two leaders was possible, and the crisis was far from over.

On Thursday, October 25, the first tanker and an East German passenger ship reached the blockade; the president instructed they be allowed through. At a meeting of the UN Security Council that evening, there was a sharp exchange between Adlai Stevenson and the Soviet ambassador to the United Nations, V. A. Zorin. The Russian charged the CIA had manufactured evidence to prove there were offensive weapons in Cuba. Stevenson spoke: "Do you, Ambassador Zorin, deny that the USSR has placed and is placing medium and intermediate range missiles and sites in Cuba? Yes or no? Don't wait for the translation. Yes or no?" When Zorin answered he was not in an American courtroom, Stevenson pointed out that the Russian ambassador was in the court of world opinion. "I am prepared to wait for my answer until hell freezes over. . . . And I am also prepared to present the evidence in this room—now!" With that, the U-2 photographs were brought into the room. After his presentation, which showed the Cuban countryside being transformed into a nuclear installation, Stevenson concluded: "Our job here is not to score debating points. Our job, Mr. Zorin, is to save the peace. And we are ready to try, if you are."

To prove the blockade was still very much in effect, the first Soviet ship, a freighter, was stopped on Friday, the 26th, and boarded by armed parties from two American destroyers. After being searched, it was found to be carrying only trucks and truck parts and was passed through the blockade. One of the destroyers which had intercepted the freighter was the *Joseph P. Kennedy, Jr.* Its involvement in the action was coincidental, but JFK ruefully told Salinger the press would never believe it hadn't been used in the encounter "just to give the family publicity."

Aerial photographs taken that day showed that all the MRBMs would be operational within a few days, the IRBMs within a month. Some Excom members began pushing again for an air strike or invasion. But a secret communication from Khrushchev to Kennedy on Friday night raised everyone's hopes that the Soviet Union might be willing to meet America's conditions. "If you have not lost your self-control," Khrushchev wrote, "we and you ought not to pull on the ends of the rope in which you have tied the knot of war." The Russian premier insisted he wanted to avoid "the catastrophe" of a nuclear conflict, and said "let us not only relax the forces pulling on the ends of the rope, let us take measures to untie that knot." Despite their ideological differences, Khrushchev said he wanted the United States and the Soviet Union "to compete peacefully, not by military means." The missiles would be withdrawn, under inspection by the UN, if America agreed not to invade Cuba.

An optimistic Excom met on Saturday morning, the 27th, to draft a reply. But during the meeting came a second, much more militant announcement from Khrushchev—and this one had been made publicly over Radio Moscow. There was no mention of the previous night's message; now the Soviet Union was demanding the removal of the Jupiter missiles in Turkey. Excom also heard a worrisome report from the FBI. In New York, Russian personnel were destroying documents in the time-honored tradition of diplomats whose country was about to go to war. Then ominous news. U-2 flights had been increased to one every two hours; now a pilot had been shot down and killed over Cuba. The joint chiefs said a decision could no longer be postponed. There must be an immediate air strike followed by an invasion.

"The noose was tightening on all of us, on Americans, on mankind," Bobby thought, and it couldn't be allowed to happen. He had a suggestion: ignore that day's demands by Khrushchev, respond instead to the conciliatory message of the night before. The president liked the idea, and within an hour had sent a reply. It made no mention of the Jupiters, but accepted the Soviet leader's offer to remove the Cuban missiles under the supervision of inspectors chosen by the United Nations. In return, Kennedy said, America would halt the blockade and give assurances it would not invade Cuba. At 9 A.M. on Sunday, October 28, Khrushchev accepted the president's terms. It was over.

The missiles were crated and returned to Russia, their sites dismantled and plowed under. Operation Mongoose was terminated. On November 6, in spite of Kennedy's fears of a Republican sweep in the congressional elections, the Democrats gained four seats in the Senate and lost only two in the House. On November 19, Khrushchev announced his country would concentrate on domestic economic problems instead of pursuing an international offensive. There was no more pressure in Berlin, and the Russian leader said he would welcome suggestions from the West in finding a solution to the dilemma of that divided city. Having looked into the abyss, Khrushchev now believed that "in the next war, the survivors will envy the dead." Never again, he stated, should the world come to the edge—as it had at the height of the missile crisis, when "the smell of burning hung in the air."

Heeding his own fearful words, Khrushchev agreed to begin off-the-record preliminary test ban negotiations in December. On Christmas Eve, the Bay of Pigs prisoners were released in return for $53 million of privately donated baby food and medical supplies. In April 1963, the Jupiter missiles were removed from Turkey. Four months later, Kennedy announced "a shaft of light" had cut into the darkness with what he regarded as the finest achievement of his presidency: Russia's signing of the nuclear test ban treaty. At about the same time, a "hot line" teletype link was also set up between Moscow and Washington, so there could be instant communication between the leaders of the two superpowers. In the autumn of 1963, the United States sold surplus wheat and flour to the Soviet Union, which helped take some of the pressure off the ailing Russian economy. That same fall, JFK began to quietly explore ways to open channels of communication with Castro.

Shortly after the end of the Cuban missile crisis, British prime minister Harold Macmillan said he thought the future would prove that it was then that the tide of the Cold War began to turn. And— at least for a little while—it did.

21

WINDS
OF CHANGE

The president's State of the Union message in January 1963 was filled with hope. "We are not lulled by the momentary calm of the sea or the somewhat clearer skies above," he said. "We know the turbulence that lies below, and the storms that are beyond the horizon this year. But now the winds of change appear to be blowing more strongly than ever." With the conclusion of the missile crisis, the problem of Cuba, which dominated so much of Kennedy's first two years in office, had begun to fade. After almost two decades of distrust, there was renewed optimism that the United States and the Soviet Union might begin to move at last toward détente. Nevertheless, there were difficult months ahead. "Beyond the horizon" lay Vietnam, and in the South, "winds of change" were reaching hurricane force.

The previous November, JFK had, with the long-promised "stroke of a pen," signed an executive order to eliminate discrimination in federally financed housing. It called for "appropriate agencies to use their good offices to promote and encourage the abandonment of discriminatory practices that may now exist." After waiting two years for Kennedy to take action on segregated housing, civil rights leaders were disappointed with the halfhearted tone of the order. "If tokenism were our goal," Martin Luther King said, "the administration moved us adroitly towards it."

Three months later, the president sent a message to Congress recommending passage of legislation to ensure black voting rights, to give financial assistance to schools that were voluntarily integrating, and to expand and strengthen the Commission on Civil Rights. He detailed the high costs of segregation: it increased delinquency, crime, disorder, welfare; it hampered economic growth; it diminished America's moral position as a world leader. But, JFK said, "above all, it is wrong." He promised "the full force of federal executive authority is being exerted in the battle against racial discrimination."

Kennedy's message only added to the frustration of civil rights activists, who thought the proposed measures overlooked the most important issues. Black unemployment was two and a half times greater than that of whites. In defiance of the 1954 Supreme Court decision, more than two thousand Southern school districts were still not integrated. Even the national government was cooperating in the preservation of segregationist traditions. No federal grant to any of the Southern states carried a stipulation that the funds be used in nondiscriminatory ways. The Federal Aviation Agency had recently given Jackson, Mississippi, $2 million to build an airport; the new facility would have, in keeping with local practices, "for whites only" rest rooms and restaurants. To black leaders, it seemed the president's latest proposal was typical of all his statements on civil rights: eloquent words and empty phrases.

But JFK, who characterized himself as an "idealist without illusions," felt he was moving as quickly as he dared. The November election had not been a Republican sweep, but neither had it been a mandate for the Democratic administration. There was no compelling reason to align himself with the activists; it would only harm him politically and doom all the other pending Kennedy legislation: Medicare, federal aid to education, a tax cut. Intellectually, the president knew segregation was detestable, but emotionally he had yet to be aroused. Then came Birmingham.

Martin Luther King called it "the most thoroughly segregated big city in the U.S."—and that made it, King knew, the ideal place to spotlight the cause of civil rights. Along with the racist mayor, Arthur Hanes, police commissioner Bull Connor had just been voted out of office, and a more moderate city government would soon be in charge. Bobby Kennedy urged King to postpone any action in Birmingham until the new administration had taken over, but the black leader had planned his timing very carefully. Connor had vowed "blood would run in the streets" before Birmingham agreed to desegregate. King responded by saying his group of nonviolent protestors would force racists like the police commissioner to "commit his brutality openly—in the light of day—with the rest of the world looking on."

During a demonstration on Good Friday, April 12, the participants remained true to the principle of passive resistance and, unprotesting, were arrested. King was placed in solitary confinement, in what he later described as a dark dungeon, without a mattress, pillow, or blanket. His lawyers were not allowed to see him. Then conditions suddenly improved; the Kennedys were now involved. When Mrs. King had not heard from her husband by Easter Sunday, she asked Bobby to have the FBI check the Birmingham jail. The next morning, the president himself phoned to reassure her that King was all right. Outgoing mayor Hanes was infuriated by the Kennedys' intervention and called King a "nigger who has got the blessing of the Attorney General and the White House."

When the protests resumed after King's release, Connor played into the black leader's hands by ordering his men to "Let 'em have it." The police responded by unleashing their dogs, then using electric cattle prods and high-pressure fire hoses on the marchers. Anyone who fell was savagely beaten with billy clubs. Across the nation, millions of Americans saw the spectacle on televised newscasts. The president, too, was watching, and the sight of a woman being attacked by a police dog made him "sick." Kennedy told black leaders he would no longer ask, as he had so often over the last two years, for their patience. After seeing the news, JFK said he could well understand why they were "tired of being asked to be patient." Something had to be done.

But what? The president's problem was that he could not legally take action against Birmingham officials. The national government was responsible for safeguarding interstate travelers, so the Justice Department had been able to respond to the plight of the Freedom Riders. Ross Barnett had defied an order of the Supreme Court, which allowed Kennedy to send U.S. troops to Oxford. But no federal law had been broken in the current situation.

The only solution, JFK said, was to get "both sides together to settle in a peaceful fashion the very real abuses too long inflicted on the Negro citizens of that community." He decided to send Burke Marshall, the assistant attorney general for civil rights, to negotiate with Birmingham's civic leaders. With the city on the verge of chaos, business had dropped by ten percent since the beginning of the demonstrations. Even the most ardent of the segregationist merchants accepted the inevitable, and on May 10 Marshall got their agreement to King's demands for increased black employment and integrated lunch counters, rest rooms, fitting rooms, and water fountains at major local stores. The demonstrations were suspended; Bull Connor's month-long reign of terror came to an end.

Then George Wallace spoke up. He would not, the Alabama governor announced, "compromise on the issues of segregation." His defiant stand inspired a new round of violence in Birmingham: the home of King's brother and the protestors' headquarters were bombed. In response, blacks rioted for the first time in the history of the South. Windows were broken, shops burned; even some members of Connor's detested police force were attacked. The mayor blamed the situation on Bobby. "I hope that every drop of blood that's spilled he tastes in his throat," Hanes said, "and I hope he chokes to death."

But despite the violence, Burke Marshall's negotiated agreement held up; Martin Luther King had achieved what he'd wanted in Birmingham. The president was quick to realize what King had known all along. "The civil rights movement should thank God for Bull Connor," Kennedy said. "He's helped it as much as Abraham Lincoln."

But now another problem was brewing in Alabama, the last holdout in the nation to continue a policy of segregation in its state universities. On May 21, a federal district court ruled that black students must be admitted to the summer session of the University of Alabama at Tuscaloosa. There was every reason to think it would be another Oxford. George Wallace had hailed his state as "the Cradle of the Confederacy" and the "very heart of the great Anglo-Saxon Southland." He would draw a line in the dust, the governor promised, "and toss the gauntlet before the feet of tyranny. And I say, segregation now! Segregation tomorrow! Segregation forever!" As the summer term approached, Bobby hoped to head off a confrontation, and Wallace reluctantly agreed to a meeting.

Accompanied by Burke Marshall and Edwin Guthman, Bobby went to Montgomery. State troopers, wearing steel helmets painted with the confederate flag, surrounded the Capitol building. A middle-aged white woman stood protectively on the spot where

Jefferson Davis had been sworn in as president of the Confederacy, just to make sure Bobby didn't step on it. Inside, Wallace opened the meeting by asking that the conversation be taped; Bobby realized the governor planned to later impress his constituents with the way he had talked back to the attorney general of the United States. Wallace said he would "never submit" to integration of an Alabama school system, and that the state would not "be ready for it in my lifetime." There was a great deal of discussion about federal troops; the governor seemed to relish the prospect of an encounter at bayonet point.

The young blacks were to enroll on June 11, and Bobby, now back in Washington, again sent Nicholas Katzenbach to handle the situation. Martin Luther King thought Wallace was "perhaps the most dangerous racist" in America, but Bobby didn't want to give the Alabama governor that much importance. "Dismiss George Wallace as a sort of second-rate figure," he advised his deputy, "wasting your time, wasting the students' time, causing a great fuss down there." When the two men confronted one another at the doorway of the registration building, Katzenbach was irritated to notice the governor carefully stood in semicircles painted to indicate his best position for the TV cameras. Katzenbach read the president's proclamation that the students must be admitted, and stood with a long-suffering expression in the near one-hundred-degree heat as the governor read a proclamation of his own, denouncing and forbidding "this illegal and unwarranted action by the central government." JFK, watching the ritual on television, immediately federalized the Alabama National Guard. But by the time they arrived at the campus, Wallace had decided he didn't want to "toss the gauntlet" after all. Although there wasn't a single bayonet in sight, the governor said he could not "fight bayonets with my bare hands." He stepped aside, the students were registered—and the University of Alabama was finally integrated.

Nineteen sixty-three marked the one hundredth anniversary of the Emancipation Proclamation. And that night, just hours after George Wallace's performance, John F. Kennedy went on the air to give the speech black Americans had waited a century to hear.

He began by referring to the afternoon's events in Tuscaloosa: because of "a series of threats and defiant statements," the National Guard had been called out to ensure the enrollment of two qualified students. He asked all Americans, no matter where they lived, to examine their consciences about what had been happening throughout the South. "We are confronted," he said, "primarily with a moral issue. It is as old as the Scriptures and is as clear as the American Constitution. . . ."

If an American, because his skin is dark, cannot eat lunch in a restaurant open to the public, if he cannot send his children to the best public school available, if he cannot vote for the public officials who represent him, if, in short, he cannot enjoy the full and free life which all of us want, then who among us would be content to have the color of his skin changed and stand in his place? Who among us would then be content with the counsels of patience and delay?

One hundred years of delay have passed since President Lincoln freed the slaves, yet their heirs, their grandsons, are not fully free. They are not yet freed from the bonds of injustice. They are not yet freed from social and economic oppression. And this nation, for all its hopes and all its boasts, will not be fully free until all its citizens are free.

We preach freedom around the world, and we mean it, and we cherish our freedom here at home, but are we to say to the world, and, much more importantly, to each other, that this is a land of the free except for the Negroes; that we have no second-class citizens except Negroes; that we have no class or caste system, no ghettos, no master race except with respect to Negroes?

The time had come, Kennedy said, for the nation to fulfill its promise. He would ask Congress to act, to make a commitment "to the proposition that race has no place in American life or law."

It was a moving speech, unlike any other by a U.S. president, partially extemporaneous, given in spite of the fact that all of JFK's advisers said he shouldn't get involved. But he was deeply concerned. Throughout the South that spring, thousands of demonstrators had been brutally beaten and then arrested for "disturbing the peace." As the number of protests grew, so did the violence. Then, only hours after Kennedy concluded his speech, Medgar Evers, who had helped to bring about James Meredith's admission to Ole Miss, was shot to death in front of his home in Jackson, Mississippi—the response of a white racist to the eloquent presidential plea for human decency.

As he had known it would, the address had harmful political consequences for Kennedy. Nationwide, his popularity was dropping in the Gallup polls: from a record high of 83 percent, it went down: to 66, then 61, then 53. Almost half of the country said JFK was moving "too fast" on civil rights, and more and more Americans were taking that view. Kennedy was already hated throughout the South, and now there was also a "white backlash" in the North. Democrats in New York and Chicago warned the president he might well lose the 1964 election because of his stand on integration.

Risking his popularity, his other legislative proposals, and perhaps even his political future, Kennedy nevertheless sent his civil rights program to Congress. The bill provided for an end to discrimination in public facilities and employment practices, and would give the attorney general authority to implement the Supreme Court's school desegregation ruling, in order to quicken the pace of "deliberate speed" the court had specified. JFK's accompanying message asked congressional members to put aside political pressure and to look into their hearts, "not in search of charity, for the Negro neither wants nor needs condescension—but for the one plain, proud, and priceless quality that unites us all as Americans: a sense of justice." He asked Congress to stay in session until it had passed the Civil Rights Act of 1963.

Near the end of June, the president met with a group of twenty-nine black leaders to discuss ways to guarantee passage of the bill. There was talk of a late summer march on Capitol Hill to demonstrate public pressure for the legislation. Kennedy was lukewarm to that idea. "We want success in Congress, not just a big show at the Capitol," he commented. "Some of these people are looking for an excuse to be against us." The only effect of a march, JFK thought, would be to "create an atmosphere of intimidation," and that would give "some members of Congress an out."

But Martin Luther King thought the march would serve a purpose. Even if it seemed ill-timed, he said, "I have never engaged in any direct action movement which did not," adding, "Some people thought Birmingham was ill-timed." The president responded, smiling: "Including the Attorney General." He went on more seriously. The latest poll showed his public approval had dropped again, to 47 percent. "We may all go down the drain," JFK stated, as a result of the civil rights proposal. After considering Kennedy's remarks, the black leaders decided the march should proceed from the Washington Monument to the Lincoln Memorial, rather than to the Capitol building.

JFK publicly backed the demonstration, but privately he was worried. Its planners were predicting one hundred thousand people would participate. If there were considerably fewer, the president told Arthur Schlesinger, some congressional members would regard the call for legislation as "greatly exaggerated." Then, too, the march could get out of hand. The American Nazi Party and the Ku Klux Klan were planning counterdemonstrations. A few congressmen were asking that the Capitol be protected, a Virginia senator feared thousands of blacks would "swarm" over its committee rooms and offices, a senator from Georgia complained about legislating on "the basis of threat and intimidations from mobs." Mississippi senator James Eastland said the whole thing was a communist plot. Many people who lived in Washington feared there would be a massive riot and decided to stay indoors on the day of the march. Clearly, violence would be a disaster—for the cause of civil rights and for the administration.

Everyone's worries were in vain. On August 28, a quarter of a million people gathered peacefully in front of the Lincoln Memorial, to hear a memorable speech by Martin Luther King. He began with a prepared text, but overwhelmed by the emotional day, King soon abandoned it and spoke from the heart:

In spite of difficulties and frustrations, he said, "I still have a dream. It is a dream deeply rooted in the American dream. I have a dream that one day this nation will rise up and live out the true meaning of its creed, 'We hold these truths to be self-evident, that all men are created equal.' I have a dream that one day on the red hills of Georgia, the sons of former slaves and the sons of former slave owners will be able to sit down together at the table of brotherhood. . . . I have a dream that my four little children will one day live in a nation where they will not be judged by the color of their skin, but by the content of their character. I have a dream. . . ."

King concluded that one day "all of God's children, black men and white men, Jews and Gentiles, Protestants and Catholics, will be able to join hands and sing in the words of the old Negro spiritual, 'Free at last! Free at last! Thank God Almighty, we are free at last!' "

Less than three weeks later, fifteen sticks of dynamite exploded in a Birmingham church. Four small black girls were killed.

In October, under pressure from J. Edgar Hoover, the attorney general authorized a wire tap on King's telephone. FBI assistant director William Sullivan later said, "Bobby Kennedy resisted, resisted, and resisted tapping King," but the bureau had "twisted the arm of the Attorney General" until he agreed. Hoover despised King as much as he did the Kennedys, and he hoped to discredit all three by hinting the black leader had ties to communism. Bobby was certain that the tap would prove King's innocence, and he was afraid of what the director might do if he didn't go along with it. Several Southern congressmen were already willing to believe the movement was backed by communists; if Hoover succeeded in smearing Martin Luther King, the proposed legislation would be doomed.

In the end, it didn't make any difference. Congress adjourned in December without having even voted on the Civil Rights Act of 1963. Its passage would come in the next year, and under another president.

THE NUMBER
ONE PRIORITY

His new resolve to fight discrimination in America had not ended JFK's fascination with foreign affairs. But having once stood at the brink, his perspective on the world had changed. With a lethal arsenal his to command, the president had come to realize, "It is much easier to make the speeches than it is finally to make the judgments." After the Bay of Pigs, Kennedy had stated, "our restraint is not inexhaustible." After the missile crisis, he said, "I hope our restraint—or sense of responsibility—will not ever come to an end."

On June 10, Kennedy delivered the commencement address at American University. Journalists, as well as Soviet officials in Moscow and Washington, were told in advance that the speech would be an important one. The president's theme, which he called "the most important topic on earth," was peace. "Not merely peace for Americans, but peace for all men and women; not merely peace in our time, but peace for all time." War, he said, had a new face, and total war made "no sense in an age when the deadly poison produced by a nuclear exchange would be carried by wind and water and soil and seed to the far corners of the globe and to generations yet unborn." Kennedy deplored the stockpiling of weapons, which "can only destroy and never create," which cost billions of dollars that could be "better devoted to combating ignorance, poverty, and disease."

Since the end of World War II, public exchanges between the leaders of the superpowers had usually been filled with accusations, threats, and boasts of military superiority. The president was determined to make a fresh start, to emphasize positive U.S.-Soviet relations, to change the way Americans viewed the Cold War. He called for a new attitude toward peace, which many thought could never be achieved. "But that is a dangerous, defeatist belief. It leads to the conclusion that war is inevitable, that mankind is doomed, that we are gripped by forces we cannot control. We need not accept that view. Our problems are man-made; therefore, they can be solved by man."

Kennedy also asked Americans to reexamine their attitudes toward the Soviet Union. "Let us not be blind to our differences, but let us also direct attention to our common interests and to the means by which those differences can be resolved. And if we cannot end now our differences, at least we can help make the world safe for diversity. For, in the final analysis, our most basic common link is that we all inhabit this small planet. We all breathe the same air. We all cherish our children's future. And we are all mortal."

Khrushchev thought it was the best speech made by any president since Franklin Roosevelt. Its full text was reprinted in the Soviet press. In England, the *Manchester Guardian* called it "one of the great state papers of American history." But in the United States, newspapers gave it little attention, and Republicans thought the speech was a "dreadful mistake" which would "accomplish nothing."

It was a month of extraordinary presidential speeches. On June 22, JFK left for a ten-day European visit. Germany was the first stop. When the threat of nuclear war hung over the world only months before, no one had felt more vulnerable than the citizens of that country. Now Kennedy was seeking universal peace, and the Germans hailed him as a conquering hero.

But in West Berlin on the morning of June 26, Kennedy got emotionally carried away by his first sight of the Wall. No matter how many photographs he had studied, he was unprepared for its grim reality, or for the contrast between the communist and democratic sections of the city. Shocked and angered, JFK forgot the spirit of the American University address. It was estimated that more than 60 percent of the two-and-a-third-million population had turned out to see him, and in a square outside the city hall, people were packed as far as he could see in every direction. Now, as the crowd chanted his name, Kennedy gave them what they wanted to hear—in the most truculent speech of his presidency:

"Two thousand years ago, the proudest boast was '*Civis Romanus sum.*' Today in the world of freedom, the proudest boast is '*Ich bin ein Berliner.*' " A pause, as his remark was translated. "I appreciate my interpreter translating my German," JFK said, laughing. Then he turned serious.

"There are many people in the world who really don't understand, or say they don't, what is the great issue between the free world and the communist world. Let—them—come—to—Berlin!

"There are some who say that communism is the wave of the future. Let—them—come—to—Berlin!

"And there are some who say in Europe and elsewhere we can work with the communists. Let—them—come—to—Berlin!"

With the repetition of the phrase, the crowd had begun to roar. "Ken-ah-dee! Ken-ah-dee!"

"All free men, wherever they may live, are citizens of Berlin, and therefore, as a free man, I take pride in the words, '*Ich bin ein Berliner.*' "

"Ken-ah-dee! Ken-ah-dee! Ken-ah-dee!" The crowd was almost hysterical. JFK, at first exhilarated by the reaction, soon was disturbed. If he had told his listeners to march on the Wall and tear it down, the president later said, they would have done so. Even more worrisome was the fact he had risked undoing the success of his "peace" speech of two weeks earlier. That afternoon, in an address at the Free University in Berlin, his remarks were more tempered. "I do believe in the necessity of the great powers working together to preserve the human race."

From Germany, Kennedy flew to Ireland, for a visit his aides had done their best to discourage. McGeorge Bundy said the sentimental journey offered no political advantages; Kenny O'Donnell thought it would be criticized as nothing more than a "pleasure trip." Finally JFK put his foot down with his appointments secretary. A pleasure trip was exactly what he wanted, he said, and added, "Let me remind you of something. I am the President of the United States, not you. When I say I want to go to Ireland, it means that I'm going to Ireland." In spite of his parents' determination to downplay their heritage, Kennedy had always been fascinated with the land from which all eight of his great-grandparents had emigrated. He loved Irish literature and was intrigued with the history of Ireland's struggle to win its freedom from the British. He often even traveled with a record album of his favorite Irish songs. Now, during the flight from Berlin to Dublin, JFK reminisced about Pamela Churchill's condescending reaction to their New Ross visit in 1947. "I felt like kicking her out of the car," he told Kenny.

The crowd that awaited the president was completely different from the one he had left in Berlin. The Irish too had gone mad, but with pride instead of frustration. Children sat on their fathers' shoulders to see him; women held their rosaries up as if to be blessed; nuns danced in the streets. Everyone's eyes seemed to be filled with tears of joy. The Secret Service wanted Kennedy to stay in his car; he refused, waded out among the people, and was almost crushed.

The next day, accompanied by his sisters Eunice and Jean, JFK went once again to New Ross in County Wexford. In his speech at New Ross, Kennedy pointed out the spot from which his great-grandfather had sailed for America. If he had not left, JFK added, to the delight of his audience, "I would be working today over there at the Albatross Company"—a local fertilizer plant.

That afternoon, the president and his sisters paid a call at the family farm, where they were greeted by their cousin Jimmy Kennedy and his sister, Mary Ryan. Jimmy commented on JFK's last visit. "Sure you were only a tall slight lad when you were here before." Having prepared a great spread for her neighbors and for anyone who could claim a connection with the Kennedys, Mrs. Ryan served tea, fresh salmon from a nearby river, and scones she had baked herself. JFK raised his cup in a toast: "We will drink a cup of tea to all the Kennedys who have gone away and to all those who have remained at home."

Mrs. Ryan later described "Cousin Jack" as "an ordinary member of the family," and said "the sisters were lovely too. Not a bit of false pride in them, for all their money." The president stayed as long as he could, although, Mrs. Ryan commented, "the government men with him kept telling him he had to go, that he must be on schedule. As he was leaving we gave him the presents. There was a large white wool blanket made from sheep right here. A bit of china for his wife. A blackthorn walking stick for himself. A handkerchief for Caroline. A hand-carved wooden boat for the little boy." When he said good-bye, Eunice and Jean were astonished to see their usually undemonstrative brother give Mrs. Ryan a hug and a kiss.

From New Ross, JFK went to the town of Wexford, where he told the crowd: "There is an impression in Washington that there are no Kennedys left in Ireland, that they are all in Washington, so I wonder if there are any Kennedys in the audience." He asked for a show of hands. "Well, I'm glad to see a few cousins who didn't catch the boat." In Cork, he was greeted by a sign which read, "Don't worry, Jack. The Iron Curtain will rust in peace." There the president met four Fitzgerald cousins, who said they were tired of hearing about the Kennedys of New Ross. After all, they pointed out, his mother's family had also originally come from County Wexford. That fact was less well-known, JFK explained, because Honey Fitz, the consummate politician, had told different constituents he was from Galway or Limerick or Donegal—whatever each person wanted to hear.

In Galway, Kennedy visited the Collegiate Church of St. Nicholas, where legend had it that Christopher Columbus had attended Mass before departing Europe on his voyage of discovery to the New World. Now, almost five centuries later, the bells of that same church rang out "The Star-Spangled Banner." In Limerick the next day, JFK's audience knew his itinerary called for a visit to England after leaving Ireland. The crowd roared when he said, "From here I go to . . . another country." He went on: "This is not the land of my birth, but it is the land for which I hold the greatest affection." And he made them a promise: "I will certainly come back in the springtime." The visit to Ireland, Kennedy later said, had been "the three happiest days" of his life.

The president returned to find there was little good news in Washington. He was becoming increasingly disturbed by events in that part of the world which had so long held his interest: Southeast Asia. Rejecting the Eisenhower "domino theory" that all of Indochina would be lost if the communists gained a foothold in Laos, JFK had allowed the United States for the first time to participate in creating a government that included communist representation. Thus Laos, the area of original concern, was for the time being stabilized under a coalitionist regime. But in the partitioned country of Vietnam, conditions were deteriorating.

The military struggle there was not being waged on a conventional battlefield; there was no front, and no national boundary had been violated. It was instead fought within South Vietnam itself, in what JFK called a "subterranean" war. The army of President Ngo Dinh Diem, assisted by American aid and advisers, was pitted against leftist guerrilla troops, called the Vietcong. Although some had infiltrated from the North, most of the guerrillas were South Vietnamese, who were winning the battle for control of their country.

Government forces outnumbered the Vietcong eight to one, yet to defeat guerrilla action would require a ratio of fifteen to one. The leftists' strategy was to strike, destroy, and vanish—while Diem's army was pinned down guarding vital installations that were the target of Vietcong saboteurs. Although much of the Vietcong equipment was American, captured from South Vietnamese-government soldiers, North Vietnam had also increased its support of the guerrillas. Intent on unifying the nation under communism, the North sent arms and ammunition down the Ho Chi Minh trail, a roadway hacked through the jungle.

As the situation worsened, the U.S. Joint Chiefs of Staff proposed bombing the supply lines from the North and deploying American combat troops to the South. Initially President Kennedy also favored increased involvement by the United States, although with the less conventional response: that of "counterinsurgency," a flexible, mobile military action which would emulate the style of the leftist guerrillas. If the South Vietnamese army was trained in that technique, JFK hoped it could hold the Vietcong at bay, while a program to liberalize the national government would win back the loyalty of the people.

But the Joint Chiefs had little enthusiasm for counterinsurgency, and Kennedy began to have serious doubts about continuing America's military commitment. In May 1963, the president approved a plan he had requested from the Pentagon, establishing a timetable to phase out all U.S. advisers in Vietnam by the end of 1965. An earlier withdrawal, JFK told Kenny O'Donnell, would lead to "another Joe McCarthy red scare." Even then, after his presumed reelection, Kennedy thought the plan would result in his becoming the most unpopular president in history, damned as a communist appeaser. "But I don't care," he said.

Kennedy had come to realize Vietnam was less a war zone than the scene of a political struggle. Since the very nature of the guerrillas' tactics was to fight only in a time and place of their choosing, the Vietcong could never be defeated as long as they had widespread support throughout the countryside. And because of the repressive policies of the South Vietnamese government, that support was expanding.

Throughout his years as president, Diem had grown increasingly aloof and dictatorial. He had outlawed elections in rural villages, a process with which even the French colonial rulers had never interfered. He then appointed his own officials to supervise the villages; but because they preferred to live in neighboring cities, Diem completely lost touch with the people in outlying areas. As the government in Saigon became more remote, the Vietcong were able to broaden their control in rural regions.

There was also growing unrest in urban areas. Buddhists, who made up a large proportion of the country's population, had suffered increasing discrimination under the Catholic president and his brother, Ngo Dinh Nhu, head of the secret police. On May 8, 1963, a group of Buddhist priests paraded in Hue, to protest Diem's ban on displaying ceremonial flags—an order which a U.S. embassy official compared to "a presidential proclamation in the United States outlawing carol singing at Christmas." Government security troops opened fire on the crowd, and it was reported that nine people had been killed.

One month later came an antigovernment demonstration that shocked the world. On a busy Saigon street, about 350 Buddhist nuns and monks gathered in a circle around an elderly priest, Quang Duc, who was seated on a cushion. After two monks poured gasoline over him, the priest lit a match. For almost ten minutes, while an Associated Press reporter photographed the scene, Quang Duc sat calmly as he burned to death. Over the next few months, six more self-immolations followed. Diem's sister-in-law, the beautiful, vitriolic Madame Nhu, claimed she "gaily clapped her hands" at news of each Buddhist "barbecue."

The United States vigorously protested government actions against the Buddhists, and Diem gave his assurances they would be stopped. But in August, pagodas throughout the country were raided by the secret police; holy relics were destroyed, and fourteen hundred monks and nuns arrested. Madame Nhu called it one of the happiest days of her life, while her husband bragged he had "taught the Buddhists and the Americans a lesson." College, high school, and grade school students, outraged by the anti-Buddhist campaign, went on strike to show their opposition to the government. It responded by closing the schools and jailing even the youngest of the students.

Long dissatisfied with Diem's conduct of the war and alienated by the increasing power of the secret police, Army generals were alarmed by rumors that Nhu intended to have them arrested and to declare martial law. When Diem gave his brother even more authority, a high-ranking member of the government told American officials that unless Nhu was removed, all of South Vietnam would be lost to the Vietcong in six months. The United States notified Diem it could no longer tolerate Nhu's growing domination. If American support was to continue, the Vietnamese president had to get rid of his brother. But there was little hope that this would happen. Frederick Nolting, outgoing U.S. ambassador in Saigon, said it would be like trying to separate Siamese twins.

In an interview on September 2, CBS newsman Walter Cronkite asked President Kennedy about the situation in Vietnam. "Unless a greater effort is made to win popular support," JFK replied, the war could probably not be won. "In the final analysis, it is their war. They are the ones who have to win it or lose it. We can help them, we can give them equipment, we can send our men out there as advisers, but they have to win it." In the last two months, he continued, "The government has gotten out of touch with the people." Cronkite asked if the Diem government had time to regain support. "With changes in policy and perhaps in personnel, I think it can," Kennedy answered. "If it doesn't make those changes, I would think that the chances of winning it would not be very good."

Vietnamese generals had already informed U.S. officials they were contemplating a takeover of the government. In late September, JFK sent Robert McNamara and General Maxwell Taylor on a fact-finding mission to Saigon. When the two returned early the next month, they recommended withdrawing one thousand advisers and cutting back on economic aid. That action, McNamara said, would either "push us toward a reconciliation with Diem or a coup to overthrow Diem." As rumors grew of an impending plot to overthrow the government, one Saigon official commented that a successor to the South Vietnamese president must first of all "be an only child."

Although the administration was unwilling to openly intervene in order to keep Diem and his brutal brother in power, there was concern in Washington and Saigon as to the possible fate of the man who had so long shared America's anticommunist goals. Kennedy sent an old friend, Massachusetts congressman Torbert Macdonald, to talk to Diem. Macdonald reported back he had told the Vietnamese president to seek sanctuary in the U.S. embassy.

"They're going to kill you," he warned. On November 1, Henry Cabot Lodge, newly appointed American ambassador to South Vietnam, also expressed concern to Diem about his personal safety.

The following day, word reached the White House that Diem and Nhu had been assassinated during a coup. Kennedy was horrified. He "leaped to his feet and rushed from the room with a look of shock and dismay," Maxwell Taylor later recalled. The president blamed the CIA, which had been in close touch with the dissident generals. "I've got to do something about those bastards," Kennedy said angrily to his friend George Smathers. "They should be stripped of their exorbitant power."

South Vietnam became more politically unstable over the next few weeks. On November 21, Henry Cabot Lodge flew from Saigon to Honolulu, en route to a meeting in Washington that JFK had scheduled for the following Sunday. That same day, Kennedy was preparing to leave for a brief political tour of Texas. But the situation in Southeast Asia was very much on his mind. "The first thing I do when I'm re-elected, I'm going to get the Americans out of Vietnam," he told a Hyannis Port neighbor, Larry Newman. It was, the president said, his "number one priority."

23

THE PAY IS GOOD AND I CAN WALK TO WORK

Although the president claimed things always looked better when he was away from Washington, he had come to love life in the White House. His mornings began at 7:30 in the living quarters on the second floor. While eating breakfast, JFK pored over several of the thirteen papers to which he subscribed; no day could get under way until, reading almost three thousand words a minute, he had gone through the *New York Times*, the *Wall Street Journal*, the *Washington Post*, the *Baltimore Sun*, the *St. Louis Post-Dispatch*. His aides came to dread the ringing of the telephone before they left for work. It was usually the president asking if they had seen some item or other, and what they intended to do about it.

About eight o'clock, Caroline and John would noisily arrive to wish their father a good morning. Kennedy took a hot bath before dressing, and sometimes John, along with several toy ducks, would get in with the president. Since every moment of the day was precious, JFK worked even in the tub, and as a result aides often received slightly moist memos in his scribbled handwriting. While the children watched cartoons on TV, their father got dressed, first putting on a leather brace to support his lower spine. By 9 A.M. the president—accompanied by Caroline, John, and two Secret Service men—was ready to go to his office on the ground floor of the West Wing.

The Oval Office had a nautical theme, reflecting JFK's lifelong love of the sea. On its walls hung naval paintings, as well as several ship models, among them a replica of PT 109 and a nineteenth-century American whaler that was a gift from Nikita Khrushchev. On Kennedy's desk was a small plaque which read, "Oh, God, thy sea is so great and my boat is so small," and the coconut shell into which he had carved his message while waiting to be rescued in the Solomon Islands.

The desk itself was made of timbers from a British warship, which Queen Victoria had presented to President Rutherford B. Hayes. Jackie found it being used as a sawhorse in the White House basement, and had the desk refinished to the delight of both her husband and son. On one side it had a hinged panel which opened like a door, and after Caroline had gone off to her nursery school upstairs, John sometimes remained behind, hidden inside what he called "my house." Unsuspecting visitors were startled to hear a scratching noise coming from the desk, and the president saying, "Is the Bunny Rabbit in there?" Then John would open the panel and emerge, screaming with laughter.

Opposite the desk were sofas and JFK's rocking chair, which he had used for years because it provided a comfortable sitting position for his back. Although most doctors agreed the rocker had no real medical value, the president insisted it helped and the chair became a symbol of the Kennedy White House. Behind the desk was a door, through which only Bobby and Lyndon Johnson were allowed to enter, and which opened into the Rose Garden. Since he used the garden to entertain guests, JFK took a personal interest in its layout and even designed the steps which led to it from his office. Kennedy waited impatiently for the garden to show its first signs of spring. Pierre Salinger once found him staring gloomily out the window of the Oval Office. There was no world crisis; the president simply wanted to know, "Isn't that damned lawn ever going to grow?"

A Secret Service man was always stationed in the garden when the president was at work, and in extreme weather Kennedy worried about whoever was on duty. One winter night JFK asked the agent to come inside and get warm. The man refused, saying he had to stay on patrol outside. A few minutes later Kennedy returned with his own coat and insisted the agent wear it. Soon he was back again, this time with hot chocolate. Coatless himself, the president sat down on the icy steps and the two drank the hot chocolate together.

JFK was consistently thoughtful of others, in spite of his crowded agenda; on an average day, he received as many as seventy scheduled visitors, a number that did not include the droppers-by.

There were also briefings, meetings, press conferences, speeches, reports, congressional bills, and a stack of correspondence to cope with. Kennedy signed about two hundred letters daily, and tried to see at least one out of every hundred of the seventeen thousand letters he received weekly from ordinary American citizens. And always there was a constant reminder of his most awesome responsibilities: twenty-four hours a day, only a few feet away, sat "The Bagman": an Army officer with a double-locked slender black briefcase. The case contained a code with which the president could order a nuclear attack.

The pressure was so great that Kennedy tried to take a two-hour break in the middle of the day. Almost every afternoon, he and Dave Powers swam for fifteen minutes in the heated White House pool, where JFK could relax, gossip, talk sports, reminisce about past political campaigns. Dave said he had to learn to do the breaststroke because it was the only way he could swim and talk at the same time. Afterwards, Kennedy did a series of exercises which had been designed to strengthen his back. When he had no business luncheon, the president ate alone with Jackie. During that private time, the doors were closed, the phones turned off, and the staff stayed away. After a brief nap, Kennedy returned to his office for a routinely hectic afternoon and evening.

At 7:30, Caroline and John would drop by in their pajamas and bathrobes to say good night. Aides who had been unable to see JFK earlier took advantage of the evening hours to present their problems, and the children would come in to greet their father's visitors: Caroline with a curtsy, John with a handshake which Ted Sorensen described as worthy of Honey Fitz himself. Then they would wait patiently in Evelyn Lincoln's adjoining office, where a dish of candy and toys were kept. When Kennedy finished work, he called Caroline and John in and the three played on the floor. The children pounded on their father, jumped up and down, were all over him—and for those moments, JFK stopped being president of the United States.

No matter what event was scheduled for later in the evening, JFK first took another swim and did more exercises to relieve the stiffness in his back. The Kennedys liked to entertain close friends with small dinner parties, followed by a movie in the White House projection room. The president loved movies; *Casablanca* was his favorite, and he had seen it several times. But Kennedy also had a low boring point, and if a film didn't hold his interest, he would go back upstairs to read in preparation for the next day.

JFK had the busiest job in the world, a fact he dismissed with a typical self-deprecating quip: "The pay is good and I can walk to work." Yet because of the intensity of life in the White House, the president felt it was important for him and his family to get away at least once a week. During the summer and fall, weekends were usually spent at Hyannis Port; in the winter and spring, they often went to Palm Beach. Neither place any longer gave the family much privacy, and since JFK's election Hyannis Port had become overrun with tourists. The Kennedys rented a Virginia farm, Glen Ora, in the hope of finding some escape. But the house was close to a road which was soon lined with photographers using telescopic lenses. Finally they decided to build their own home on Rattlesnake Mountain, a few miles from Glen Ora. While it was under construction, the Kennedys occasionally went to the official presidential retreat at Camp David in Maryland, where neither the press nor the public were allowed inside without invitation.

Trying to maintain any sort of private life was a constant battle. There had never been a family like them in the White House, and curiosity about the Kennedys was insatiable. No matter what one thought about JFK's politics, most people had to admit the Kennedys had class. The United States no longer had to feel culturally inferior to England or France. Now it had a royal family, one which had brought elegance and style to the White House. Even British prime minister Harold Macmillan admitted, "They certainly have acquired something we have lost, a casual sort of grandeur about their evenings, pretty women, music and beautiful clothes and champagne and all that."

Those who had never tasted *Gigot d'Agneau aux flageolets* or *Mousse aux Concombres* were nevertheless pleased such courses were served at Jacqueline's dinner parties. To many, Shakespeare might be a bore; still it was somehow a source of pride to know his plays were being performed in the East Ballroom. Perhaps they didn't quite get the joke, yet everyone knew JFK had said something marvelously clever when, at a dinner honoring Nobel Prize winners, he quipped that the group was the most extraordinary collection of talent and knowledge ever gathered at the White House, "with the possible exception of when Thomas Jefferson dined alone." People who had never heard of Pablo Casals were delighted that the cellist, ending a self-imposed exile because the United States recognized the fascist regime in his native Spain, agreed to play for the Kennedys simply because he admired the president. Some weren't even sure where Pakistan was, but they were charmed when Jacqueline gave the head of its government a state dinner at Mount Vernon, the first ever held outside the White House. On that occasion, guests arrived for an evening at George Washington's historic home after sailing down the Potomac aboard two presidential yachts, the *Honey Fitz* and the *Patrick J.* When the Kennedys formally entertained, the whole nation vicariously enjoyed their celebration of American excellence and style.

The public's obsession with the Kennedys also extended to their daughter, who would soon turn six, and their son, who was almost three. A respected journalist phoned Pierre Salinger at 3 A.M. to verify a rumor that one of Caroline's hamsters had drowned. The usually sedate *New York Times* headlined the fact that PRESIDENT'S SON GETS A HAIRCUT AND A PART. People were captivated to hear that John called his father "Foo-Foo Head," and that he and Caroline had taken off their clothes to play in a fountain on the White House lawn.

Everyone was also charmed by a number of stories which demonstrated the children's disregard for presidential protocol. One morning John decided to take part in a breakfast conference between JFK and several staff members. Nothing could persuade the little boy to leave, so Kennedy decided to ignore him and begin the meeting. "What have we got today?" he asked his aides. John was the first to reply: "*I've* got a glass of water." On another occasion, Ethiopian emperor Haile Selassie was in the Oval Office for an official visit. Having evaded his nurse, John walked in stark naked to greet the two heads of state.

Caroline, too, seemed to turn up in the most unlikely places throughout the White House. She once barged in on an important conference to tell the president, "Mommy wants you!" Another time she wandered into the press room, and in answer to a reporter's query said her father was "upstairs with his shoes and socks off, not doing anything." When a congressman told JFK his own daughter had said she wouldn't want to live in the White House, Kennedy replied, "That's not my trouble with Caroline. My problem is to keep her from holding press conferences."

The president and his children took the attention in stride. But Jackie made the transition less easily, and told a friend she felt as if she was living in a fish bowl with all the fish on the outside. Her face was plastered on magazines she wouldn't dream of reading. No matter where she was or what she was doing, the cameras found her: water-skiing, playing tennis, horseback riding;

in a boat, at a concert, on the beach; alone or with her family or friends; wearing a bathing suit, slacks, an elegant gown; talking, smiling, frowning—people just couldn't get enough of Jacqueline Kennedy.

She hated the loss of privacy, feared its effect on her marriage and her children, struggled to keep her sense of humor as she coped with the sudden elevation to being the most idolized woman in the world. Jackie asked to be addressed simply as "Mrs. Kennedy" because, she said, First Lady "sounds like a saddle horse." When asked what she intended to feed a new puppy, she smilingly replied, "Reporters." Salinger was bombarded with requests for interviews and photo sessions with John and Caroline, and their mother put up a fierce struggle to keep them out of the public eye. She wryly described herself as the greatest cross Salinger had to bear, and once sent him a note which began, "Don't worry—a nice calm memo." In spite of his many friendships among members of the press, even the president was reluctant to intervene. "My wife is a strong-minded woman," he explained. He agreed to a *Look* magazine request for a picture session with his son, but only at a time when Jackie would be away. Then JFK nervously asked the photographer to work quickly, because things would "get kind of sticky" if John's mother happened to catch them.

Jackie believed that "If you bungle raising your children, I don't think whatever else you do well matters very much." She made every effort to give Caroline and John a normal life. On Halloween, she wore a mask and took them trick-or-treating in Georgetown. Jackie liked to drive the family station wagon herself, taking the children to visit the Auchinclosses in Virginia or to the Maryland countryside to look at farm animals. But even a quiet expedition to buy her daughter a new dress didn't escape notice, and the next day a *Times* headline read: CAROLINE VISITS SHOP. Jackie worried constantly that the adulation would spoil her children, and reminded them again and again that their stay in the White House was only temporary.

Yet Jackie had done the impossible, turning a national monument into a home for her family. She had also made it a source of pride to all Americans. During the 1960 presidential campaign, the caption of a *New Yorker* cartoon had read: "Of course I'm voting for Nixon, but I can't help wishing I could see what Jackie would do with the White House." Eventually, almost one-third of the nation was able to see what Jackie had done when an hour-long taped TV special, *A Tour of the White House with Mrs. John F. Kennedy*, was broadcast simultaneously on CBS and NBC.

Ironically, the presidential mansion was the design of an Irish immigrant, James Hoban, who modeled it after a house in Dublin. Jackie had no quarrel with its classical facade. But the interior, she remarked before the inauguration, looked as if it had been "furnished by discount stores," a hodgepodge reflecting the varying tastes of previous residents. Jacqueline had resolved to transform the mansion. "Everything in the White House must have a reason for being there," she commented when explaining her plans. "It must be restored, and . . . that is a question of scholarship." The restoration became her own special project, and Jackie read every book she could find on the history of the White House.

In the beginning, she had surprisingly little support. The federal budget had no money for the undertaking, and the president was concerned about his wife getting involved in a fund-raising effort to redo her own home. But Jackie stuck to her guns. "Before everything slips away, before every link with the past is gone, I want to do this," she said, and announced she would appoint a committee of experts to advise on acquisitions. Realizing nothing would dissuade her, JFK asked Clark Clifford to draw up papers legalizing the committee. The lawyer confirmed Kennedy's fears. "The White House is a sacred cow to the American people," Clifford told him, "and woe to any President who touches it." But Jackie finally won both men over, although, she confided to a friend, a number of government officials had "warned, begged, and practically threatened" her not to go ahead.

All the dire predictions were wrong. "I approve of what you are doing to the White House," a woman wrote Jackie, "as much as I disapprove of your husband's policies." The restoration soon turned into what one writer described as "a national treasure hunt," as all across the country, people eagerly contributed money or antiques. Because of her triumph in Paris and the success of her restoration project, Jacqueline Kennedy often seemed to be on the front pages of newspapers as much as her husband.

Yet for all the changes she had brought to the White House, Jackie found the presidential mansion a difficult place in which to live. It was essentially, she said, an "office building," and once remarked that if people weren't happily married, "the White House would really finish it." But her husband's presidency had brought an unexpected bonus. After years of separation and strain, the

Kennedys had for the first time really gotten to know each other, and appeared to be deeply in love. Staff members were delighted to observe the president and his wife strolling hand in hand on the lawn, or through the corridors of the White House.

The couple drew even closer when, in August 1963, they suffered a tragic loss. Now that JFK was regularly at home, he and Jackie had looked forward to the arrival of another child. But Patrick Bouvier Kennedy was born with a respiratory problem and died after only thirty-nine hours. Just before the infant was buried, the president slipped into the casket a gold St. Christopher's medal, which he had worn since receiving it from Jacqueline on the day they were married. "He put up quite a fight," Kennedy said. "He was a beautiful baby." The death devastated JFK; no one had ever seen him so upset. He was the last to leave the funeral, weeping and clinging to the tiny casket. The president requested newspapers not publish photographs taken at that time. "I don't want to edit anybody," but "I'm asking it as a favor to me." It had been, he said, "a very personal moment." The pictures were never printed.

Five weeks after little Patrick's funeral, the Kennedys celebrated their tenth wedding anniversary at Hammersmith Farm, where it had all begun. Jackie's gift to her husband was a gold St. Christopher's medal.

Deeply depressed over the loss of the baby, Jackie left in October to accompany her sister Lee on a trip through the Aegean, aboard the yacht of wealthy Greek shipowner Aristotle Onassis. When Jackie's plans were made public, the press had a field day. The U.S. Maritime Association had sold Onassis fourteen surplus ships with the understanding they would remain under American registry. When he made a $20 million profit by transferring them to a foreign registry, the government sued for fraud, claiming Onassis was trying to avoid paying taxes to the United States. Including the wife of the American president among his guest list was viewed by some as a form of bribery, and newspapers made matters worse by running stories about the "luxury yacht," the "lavish shipboard dinners," the "crew of sixty, two coiffeurs, and a dance band." When she returned to Washington, Jackie was horrified by the reaction to her innocent vacation. But her husband, she told a friend, was being "really nice and understanding." There was a reason: Jackie's "guilt feelings," JFK confided to journalist Ben Bradlee, would work to his advantage.

The next presidential election was one year away, and Kennedy was determined to win by a big margin. There were so many things he wanted to accomplish, but little could be done unless he and Congress had a mandate from the American people. One state that loomed as a problem was Texas. There, the Democratic party was split into a conservative faction under Governor John Connally and a liberal coalition led by Senator Ralph Yarborough. Lyndon Johnson, once the most powerful political figure in the state, had failed in his attempts to unite the two groups. Those who backed Connally were put off by the vice-president's association with the New Frontier, while Yarborough followers distrusted LBJ's recent commitment to liberal causes.

Texas was too big, too important, to risk losing to the Republicans in 1964. Johnson thought Kennedy should pay a personal visit because presidential authority would be a powerful influence in healing the feud between the Democrats. JFK agreed, and decided it would be a good idea to have one of his greatest political assets accompany him. Campaign trips weren't exactly Jackie's style, but her Mediterranean cruise had embarrassed the Kennedy administration. "Maybe now you'll come with us to Texas," JFK said, smiling at his wife. "Sure I will, Jack," she replied.

24

I COULD
STAY HERE FOREVER

Texas was hardly Kennedy country. Its culture derived from
America's two most conservative regions, the South and West. The
Democratic ticket had barely carried the state in 1960, and its
citizens had come to like the administration's policies even less over
the three intervening years. Yet most Texans were patriotic and, no
matter how much they disapproved of his politics, were determined
to cordially welcome the president of the United States. That his
wife had chosen to accompany him guaranteed JFK an even warmer
reception.

The Kennedys' first stop, on November 21, was in San Antonio,
a city with a large Mexican-American population, and one of the
most liberal in the state. Even before *Air Force One* stopped taxiing
on the airport runway, the waiting crowd had begun to chant:
"Jackieee! Jackieee!" The presidential limousine made its way into
town under a blizzard of confetti. A school holiday had been
declared in honor of the visit, and it seemed most of the population
lined the route of the motorcade, many holding hand-lettered signs:
BIENVENIDO, MR. PRESIDENT and JACKIE, COME WATER-SKI IN
TEXAS! Kennedy was to dedicate a new Aerospace Medical Health
Center at a nearby air base, where nine thousand chairs had been
set up. Twenty thousand people turned out, including six high school
superintendents who tried to get into the press section by claiming
they were correspondents for their school papers.

From San Antonio, the presidential party flew on to the larger, more conservative city of Houston. Here some of the posters were less friendly: one said BAN THE BROTHERS; another read KENNEDY, KHRUSHCHEV, AND KING. But along the streets spectators stood ten and twelve deep, and the appearance of the limousine was greeted with cries of "Jackieee!" A *Time* magazine reporter interviewing the onlookers learned that most had come "for Jackie." JFK's aides agreed. When he asked Dave Powers to estimate the crowd, Dave mischievously replied, "You're doing just about average—but there's a hundred thousand extra here for Jackie." The manager of their hotel calmly greeted JFK, then completely lost his cool and babbled, "Good evening, Mrs. President" to Jackie.

Later that night, Kennedy spoke to the League of United Latin American Citizens, and concluded: "In order that my words will be even clearer to you, I'm going to ask my wife to say a few words also." Jackie made some brief remarks in Spanish, ending with *"Muchas gracias y viva las LULACs!"* The audience as one screamed *"Olé!"* The president himself was impressed; as they left the meeting, Dave Powers noted that Kennedy and his wife "exchanged eyes." Mrs. Lyndon Johnson, who was also watching the couple, thought JFK "looked beguiled."

The Kennedys spent the night in Fort Worth. On the morning of November 22, JFK was to address the local Chamber of Commerce, a mostly Republican group friendly to the conservative Governor Connally. Since working-class people had been excluded from the breakfast meeting, the president agreed to a request from Fort Worth Democrats that he make an earlier speech in the hotel parking lot. In spite of a drizzle, they began to gather before dawn: secretaries, clerks, waitresses, mechanics, housewives, railroad workers. By a little after eight o'clock, the crowd, now grown to five thousand, began to chant: "Come on Jackie, come on Jackie." Then there was a shout. "Here he is! Here's the President!" As Kennedy looked around, he noted wryly that outdoors in the rain stood his true constituents, more than twice the number of the privileged group which awaited him inside. JFK began to speak, referring at first to the weather: "There are no faint hearts in Fort Worth, and I appreciate your being here this morning." But his audience thought something was missing. "Where's Jackie?" one of the group called out. Everyone, including the president, laughed. "Mrs. Kennedy is organizing herself," he replied. "It takes her a little longer, but of course she looks better than we do when she does it."

After receiving thunderous applause in the parking lot, JFK went back to face what he was certain would be a less congenial group in the hotel. But even it was soon won over. The opening formalities had just begun when Raymond Buck, head of the Chamber of Commerce, announced, "And now, ladies and gentlemen, an event I know you have all been waiting for." Jackie entered the room, and pandemonium broke out. The entire audience of Fort Worth's elite began cheering, screaming, whistling; some even climbed on their seats to get a better look. Jackie was terrified, but she kept her eyes on her husband as she walked toward the table. JFK took her hand, and the crowd finally grew quiet.

Mr. Buck presented Jackie with a pair of ornate hand-tooled boots, and the president with a ten-gallon cowboy hat. Kennedy stood to accept it and looked almost sheepish when someone yelled, "Put it on, Jack!" Since absolutely nothing could have persuaded the president to do so, he smiled and said, "Come to Washington Monday and I'll put it on for you in the White House." Everyone laughed, and JFK began his address. "Two years ago I introduced myself in Paris by saying that I was the man who had accompanied Mrs. Kennedy to Paris. I am getting somewhat the same sensation as I travel around Texas." The president brought down the house when he added: "Nobody wonders what Lyndon and I wear."

After the breakfast, journalists sought out Dave Powers. They all agreed Jackie had been a sensation, and one reporter asked if she was going to make future campaign appearances. In their suite upstairs, her husband was wondering the same thing. When Kenny O'Donnell said there was a free hour before they had to leave for the airport, Jackie was grateful for the chance to relax. "Oh Jack, campaigning is so easy when you're President," she said. Kennedy was scheduled to make a West Coast trip in December, and he asked, "How about California in the next two weeks?" Jackie nodded. "I'll be there." Then she looked with surprise at JFK's appointments secretary. She had known him for ten years, but with her promise to go to California, Jackie for the first time saw the usually dour O'Donnell break into a huge grin.

The hour was up, and it was time to move on to the next stop: Dallas. As she prepared to leave her own hotel room, the wife of the vice-president noticed her hands were trembling. Just before the 1960 election, she and LBJ had been campaigning in Dallas, where they had been spat upon by an unruly crowd of right-wingers. The city had frightened her ever since; now she thought, "There might be something ugly today."

It was a worry shared by many. The president had been warned over and over again to stay away from Dallas. That oil-rich city aspired to culture and sophistication, but in the fall of 1963 a frontier philosophy still prevailed. In its downtown area, one out of five citizens carried guns. The state of Texas had more homicides than any other in the nation, and Dallas had the most murders in the state. Its leading newspaper, the *Morning News*, fanned the fires of hatred in editorials that claimed Washington, D.C., was inhabited by "subversives, perverts, and miscellaneous security risks."

The city was essentially ruled by the Dallas Citizens Council, a group of corporate heads who did little to mitigate the atmosphere of fanaticism. Indeed, young executives were required to attend right-wing seminars. Swastikas were painted on stores owned by Jews, radical-right literature was distributed in schools, the president's name was booed in classrooms. In October, Adlai Stevenson had been in Dallas to give an address on the United Nations. He was heckled throughout the speech, and police had to remove several members of the unruly audience. The UN ambassador finished by saying he believed "in the forgiveness of sin and the redemption of ignorance." But outside he encountered a spitting, screaming mob and was hit over the head with a protest sign. Although he was concerned about the president's visit only four weeks after his own, Stevenson was reassured by a letter from a group of prominent Dallas businessmen which apologized for the crowd's behavior and promised the incident would have an effect on the entire community.

Many feared that "effect" would be to arouse the citizenry even more. Representative Hale Boggs thought Kennedy would be going into "a hornet's nest"; Senator William Fulbright warned that "Dallas is a very dangerous place." Even Texans were frightened by the atmosphere in Dallas. An editor in Austin was sure the president would "not get through this without something happening to him." A woman in Dallas echoed that concern in a letter to Pierre Salinger. "Don't let the President come down here. I'm worried about him. I think something terrible will happen to him."

Some officials had the same nagging apprehension. Governor Connally thought the people of Dallas were "too emotional" and recommended Kennedy not visit there. Texas congressman Jim Wright was afraid of what might happen as a result of "the steady drum-beat of ultra right-wing propaganda with which the citizenry is constantly besieged."

By the morning of November 22, that propaganda was in full cry. Thousands of handbills had been distributed throughout the city. They showed front and profile photographs of JFK under the words WANTED FOR TREASON. Before leaving Fort Worth, the president scanned the *Morning News*. Inside was a full-page ad within a thick black border and the headline WELCOME MR. KENNEDY TO DALLAS. The ad accused the president of ignoring the Constitution, and asked twelve rhetorical questions. "WHY do you say we have built a 'wall of freedom' around Cuba when there is no freedom in Cuba today . . .? WHY have you approved the sale of wheat and corn to our enemies . . .? WHY have you ordered or permitted your brother Bobby, the Attorney General, to go soft on Communists . . .?" The ad concluded, "Mr. Kennedy, we DEMAND answers to these questions and we want them now." JFK handed the paper to Jackie and said, "We're heading into nut country today."

There was really no way around it; the president could not tour Texas and bypass one of its largest cities. He expected to encounter some ugly crowds, but nothing that the Secret Service couldn't handle. A man in JFK's position was aware there was always some danger. In his first year in office, he had received more than one thousand threatening letters and, like every occupant of the White House after Abraham Lincoln, knew he was vulnerable to a determined killer. But no American president had been assassinated since William McKinley in 1901, and JFK refused to worry about the possibility of it happening now; like Kenny O'Donnell, he believed politics and protection didn't mix. This was a political visit, and the Kennedys had to see and be seen by as many people as possible. They were in luck. The rain had stopped, and that meant the bubble-top on their limousine would not have to be used.

Everyone was in a good mood when *Air Force One* landed at Love Field in Dallas. As Kennedy and his wife waited for the doors to be opened, Dave Powers eyed them with approval. "You two look like Mr. and Mrs. America," he said. "Mr. President, remember when you're riding in the motorcade downtown to look and wave only at the people on the right side of the street. Jackie, be sure that you look only at the left side, and not to the right. If the both of you ever looked at the same voter at the same time, it would be too much for him!"

As soon as the Kennedys appeared in the plane's doorway, it seemed all the predictions of doom had been wrong. The greeting of the crowd was as warm and sunny as the day itself. The mayor's wife presented Jackie with a bouquet of red roses, and with the flowers cradled in her arm, she and JFK walked over to a wire fence behind which hundreds of people stood cheering. The president was on a tight schedule; after a meandering eleven-mile motorcade through downtown Dallas, he would speak to a group of civic leaders at the Trade Mart. Still, he and Jackie lingered at the fence, shaking as many hands as possible. Observing JFK, a Texas journalist wrote in his notebook, "Kennedy is showing he is not afraid." Nevertheless, the Dallas police were watchful. They had learned their lesson with the Stevenson incident, a local reporter commented. "After Kennedy leaves here they won't let anybody within ten feet of him."

It was 11:55, and time to go. In the lead car were Police Chief Jesse Curry, the county sheriff, and two Secret Service agents, followed by two policemen on motorcycles. Then came the presidential limousine: two agents in front, Governor and Mrs. Connally in the jump seats, the Kennedys in back with the roses lying between them. Four motorcycles followed the president's car and behind them, a convertible carrying Dave Powers, Kenny O'Donnell, and several more agents, including two each on the front and back bumpers. The Secret Service was unhappy about that positioning. Dallas was considered "hot"—dangerous—and Kennedy would have much more effective protection if agents were standing on the bumpers of his own limousine. But JFK was the boss, and he refused to ride through the streets of an American city surrounded by armed guards.

Several other cars followed that of the Secret Service. The Johnsons', with Senator Ralph Yarborough and more agents; then a pool of four journalists, one of whom was senior White House correspondent Merriman Smith of United Press International. His car's other occupants wryly reflected that if anything newsworthy took place, they wouldn't get a chance to report it, since the highly competitive Smith was sitting next to the dashboard radio phone. Half a mile behind Kennedy's limousine was the VIP bus carrying others in the presidential party, including JFK's physician, Dr. George Burkley. He was concerned; in case of an emergency, he would be much too far away. Still, Kennedy had never been healthier, and Burkley consoled himself that nothing would happen in the thirty or so minutes before the procession reached the Trade Mart. In fact, it seemed the only newsworthy event of the day would be the extent of the president's triumph in this most unlikely of settings.

As the motorcade proceeded through the city, Kennedy became increasingly delighted with the mood of the people. Although there were a few unfriendly signs, most of the extremists seemed to have stayed home, while the good citizens of Dallas had turned out to show JFK their city was not a frontier outpost of fascism. The crowds got larger as the procession moved into the downtown area, but Kennedy managed to spot a small hand-lettered poster: MR. PRESIDENT, PLEASE STOP AND SHAKE OUR HANDS. The limousine came to a halt. JFK stepped out and was nearly swamped by a bunch of excited children, one of whom was screaming, "It worked! It worked!" The motorcade resumed its course, then stopped again; this time Kennedy wanted to shake hands with a group of nuns.

At 12:21, the limousine turned onto the twelve-block-long Main Street, heart of the Dallas business district. Governor Connally stared with astonishment. The noise was deafening; in this bastion of conservatism, at least a quarter of a million people were cheering their hearts out for the liberal president. The sidewalks were thronged, the crowds spilling into the street until there was barely enough space for the cars to pass. Office workers hung out of windows, ignoring the noonday heat.

Higher up, on the top floors of the city's eight skyscrapers, it was cool. Here were the executive suites of the oil men: politically far to the right, millionaires, billionaires, some of whom annually paid only a few hundred dollars' income tax. Kennedy was offended by those tax loopholes, and by the extremist political views of the Dallas power structure. Although a Texas congressman warned JFK to be careful of what he said in that "tough town," a reporter who had gotten an advance copy of the Trade Mart speech said it would be a withering blast at the wealthy right-wingers. Now, in their lofty perches, that group heard the cheers grow fainter as the president they despised reached the end of Main Street.

The motorcade turned north, onto Houston Street, at 12:29. It had arrived at the outer edge of the downtown area, and the crowds were beginning to thin. Moving at eleven miles an hour, the presidential limousine drove for two blocks along the eastern side of a small park, Dealey Plaza, then to the intersection of Elm Street, which bounded the Plaza on the north. There were not many police stationed in the area; having anticipated fewer spectators in the stretch between Main, Houston, and Elm, Chief Curry had concentrated his men at Love Field and at the site where the president was scheduled to speak. After Kennedy's car made the short drive down Elm, it would reach a freeway leading to the Trade Mart.

The limousine made the 120-degree turn from Houston onto Elm. Now the motorcade was in front of the faded rust-brick facade of the Texas School Book Depository, a textbook warehouse. Its employees were on their lunch hour, and they too poured out onto the sidewalk or stood in the windows to get a look at the president of the United States. The Book Depository was only five minutes from the Trade Mart, and everyone began to relax.

Kennedy seemed pleased; he had been welcomed with obvious affection in what had been presumed to be hostile territory. Chief Curry was proudly thinking that he had never seen his city so hospitable. Just ahead, Jackie saw an underpass leading to the freeway. It would be nice to be in the shade for even a few seconds; the weather was unusually warm for November, and she was sweltering in a pink wool suit. A Secret Service man radioed another agent at the Trade Mart: the motorcade was almost there. Mrs. Connally looked back over her shoulder and said, "Mr. President, you can't say Dallas doesn't love you." Kennedy smiled, and turned to wave at a small boy whose father was holding him aloft.

It was 12:30.

In Hyannis Port, Joe Kennedy was sleeping. Rose had played nine holes of golf that morning, and she, too, decided to lie down to rest. At Hickory Hill, Bobby was just finishing lunch. He had spent all the previous day and that morning in meetings with members of his Organized Crime Section; now, he said, it was time to get back to the office. Across the Potomac, his younger brother sat half-listening to a debate on the need for federal library services. Freshmen senators were traditionally asked to preside when a quorum was not present, and today it was the junior senator from Massachusetts, Ted Kennedy. At the White House, his daughter and son were playing with their cousin John. As soon as they left, the little boy would be tucked in for his afternoon nap. Caroline was waiting to be picked up by the mother of one of her friends, excited because she was going to spend the night at a slumber party. For the last thirty minutes in Dallas, her mother had been listening to the now-familiar cries of "Jackieee! Jackieee!" Then there was a new sound; perhaps a motorcycle had backfired.

Something was horribly wrong. The president, no longer waving, was clutching his throat, slumping toward his wife. Jackie reached out for him. John Connally had recognized the sharp noise instantly and, filled with dread, turned toward Kennedy. Suddenly the governor felt a thudding pain in his back and fell over onto Mrs. Connally. From the front seat, the Secret Service agents looked around. It was the moment for which they had trained, but it couldn't be happening. They stared in disbelief, the limousine swerving, then almost coming to a halt. In the car behind, Dave Powers exclaimed, "Kenny, I think the President's been shot!" Another loud report, and there was no longer any doubt. Bone, blood, hair, brain fragments sprayed everyone in the limousine; a motorcycle patrolman was covered with red mist. Kennedy sprawled across the seat, his shattered head resting on the roses.

Six seconds had passed. Too late, the presidential limousine sprang forward. As it began to career down Elm Street, Jackie crawled out on the top of the trunk, perhaps looking for help. Clint Hill, one of the Secret Service agents in the car behind, reacted instantly. Jumping onto the trunk, he shoved Jackie back inside, using his body to shield the Kennedys and Connallys. Parkland Memorial Hospital was four miles away, and the trip was a nightmare. Sirens, radio, blood. The limousine racing along at eighty miles an hour, Mrs. Connally murmuring words to her husband that she didn't believe herself: "It's going to be all right." Jackie quietly sobbing, "He's dead. They've killed him. Oh Jack, oh Jack, I love you!" The press car, too, was rushing toward Parkland. At 12:34, Merriman Smith phoned the local bureau of UPI, and its teletypes instantly sent out the nation's first inkling that a tragedy had just occurred in Texas: THREE SHOTS WERE FIRED AT PRESIDENT KENNEDY'S MOTORCADE TODAY IN DOWNTOWN DALLAS.

When the limousine pulled up to the hospital entrance, the car carrying Dave and Kenny was right behind. Dave ran forward and looked down at his old friend. "Oh my God, Mr. President, what did they do?" He began to cry. Jackie held her husband protectively; people were swarming out of Parkland toward the car, and she didn't want strangers staring at him. Clint Hill said JFK must be gotten to a doctor immediately, but Jackie replied, "You know he's dead. Leave me alone." Realizing she couldn't bear for others to see her mutilated husband, Hill removed his jacket and handed it to Jackie to wrap around the president's head. With a few of the roses clinging to his chest, Kennedy was placed on a stretcher and carried into the hospital, his wife running alongside to keep the jacket in place.

Having seen JFK's limp form, Merriman Smith dashed to a phone. The horrified teletype operator became confused and slightly garbled Smith's words; yet the content was all too clear: FLASH FLASH KENNEDY SERIOUSLY WOUNDED PERHAPS SERIOUSLY PER-

HAPS FATALLY BY ASSASSIN'S BULLET. When Jack Bell of Associated Press called in his report, the distraught AP teletypist sent out an almost incomprehensible message. "Bloodstained" read as BLOOD STAINEZAAC RMBTHING, "he lay" as HE LAAAAAAAAAA, "Kenneth O'Donnell" as KENNETH O';$9,,3)). Other journalists crowded around Ralph Yarborough, who had been with the Johnsons only two cars behind the presidential limousine. Weeping, the senator said "a deed of horror" had taken place. Johnson himself was rushed to a remote booth in the hospital's emergency area, surrounded by Secret Service agents concerned that the shootings might be part of a plot to assassinate all of America's leaders. Anxiously awaiting some word on Kennedy's condition, the vice-president did not realize the ominous implication when The Bagman came into the booth.

Governor Connally was in Parkland's Trauma Room Two; although badly wounded, he would survive. But in Trauma One, the situation was hopeless. Unlike John Connally, John Kennedy had no pulse, no blood pressure. For a brief time, an electrocardiogram showed the uneven line of an irregular heartbeat; then the line went flat. Although the fourteen doctors crammed into the small room knew it was futile, they continued to work feverishly. Jackie waited in the hallway for ten minutes, watching the frenzied activity that she knew was a vain effort to keep her husband alive. Finally, over the protests of a nurse, she, too, entered the crowded Trauma One, explaining, "I want to be in there when he dies."

At one o'clock, a doctor drew up the sheet over Kennedy's face. Through radio, television, and word of mouth, more than 75 million Americans by then knew the president had been shot. Now came news that a priest had been summoned to Parkland Hospital. He was Father Oscar Huber, who had stood along the motorcade route with some young men from his parish, eagerly awaiting his first glimpse of the presidential limousine. When the limousine drove past, Kennedy turned to smile directly at him, and the boys had watched with amusement as their seventy-year-old priest jumped in the air and yelled, "Hurray!" One hour later, Father Huber drew down the sheet and looked again at the face of the president. Then the priest began to recite what for John F. Kennedy would be the fourth and final last rites of his church.

At 1:35 P.M. on November 22, 1963, hundreds of teletype machines finally clattered out the dreaded bulletin: FLASH PRESIDENT KENNEDY DEAD.

The announcement had been delayed in order to get LBJ out of Parkland and safely aboard *Air Force One*. Many now feared a conspiracy. With the first news of the shooting, almost everyone in Washington, D.C., had begun calling each other, and overloaded circuits caused a sudden massive breakdown of the telephone system. But some thought communications in the capital had been sabotaged, and remembered with growing unease that almost all the Cabinet members were in a plane far out over the Pacific, en route to Tokyo for trade agreement discussions. In those paranoid early afternoon hours, the government of the United States seemed vulnerable.

Once aboard the plane, Johnson turned on a television set to watch Walter Cronkite, who had gone on the air after the first bulletin. Although Dallas was the center of the day's horrible events, no one there was quite sure what was going on. But if either a domestic coup or a plot by a foreign power was under way, the New York networks would by now probably be aware of it. Since the newscast seemed to indicate that the assassination was an isolated incident, LBJ decided to hold the plane for Jacqueline Kennedy and the body of the thirty-fifth president. Soon hammering was heard from the rear section of *Air Force One* as seats were removed to make room for the casket.

But there was a delay at Parkland, where a brief ugly scene was taking place. Because a local judge said the assassination was "just another homicide case," the county medical examiner announced the body could not be removed until an autopsy had been performed. No one in the Kennedy group had even considered the possibility that Dallas bureaucracy would needlessly prolong Jackie's suffering. Torn with grief and anger, Kenny O'Donnell shoved the medical examiner aside and yelled, "Get the hell out of the way, we're leaving." Certain that local officials were in pursuit, the presidential party took off in a mad rush for the airport. At 2:15 John F. Kennedy boarded *Air Force One* for the last time.

O'Donnell urged that the plane take off immediately, before the medical examiner tried to stop its departure. But there was another delay; LBJ insisted on being sworn in before leaving Dallas. More minutes dragged by while an old friend of Johnson's, federal judge Sarah Hughes, made her way to the airport, and Nicholas Katzenbach called from Washington to dictate the precise wording of the presidential oath of office. Then, flanked by his wife and Jacqueline Kennedy, Lyndon Johnson raised his right hand: ". . . I will faithfully execute the office of President of the United States." *Air Force One* had landed at Love Field at 11:38 that morning; it was now 2:38.

During the sad flight, Jackie and her husband's aides sat in the rear compartment around the casket, holding an Irish wake. For the first time in her life, Jackie had a drink of scotch. She didn't like the taste, but it helped her, as it did the others, get through the interminable two-hour-and-twenty-minute trip. Then finally they were in Washington, and Bobby was running up the ramp to the plane's door, racing through its front compartment to get to the back. "Hi Jackie, I'm here," he said, putting his arm around her. Jackie thought as she so often had before: yes, he always was when she needed him.

All across the country flags were at half-mast and the nation was in mourning. Yet because events in Dallas had been so unexpected, there had been no live television coverage, and many found it difficult to grasp the fact that the assassination had actually happened. But the cameras were waiting in Washington, and for the first time horror became reality. President Kennedy had returned home, but this time no applause or shouts of excitement greeted him. The scene at the airport took place in utter silence, Bobby and Jackie holding hands in the doorway of *Air Force One* as they watched the casket being loaded into a waiting hearse. Jackie had refused to change her clothes, saying "Let them see what they've done." Now America recoiled in shock, shame, and grief; her suit and stockings were caked with the blood of her dead husband.

The weekend began, and the United States came to a standstill. Throughout Saturday, as the body of John Fitzgerald Kennedy lay in state in the East Room, tens of millions sat unmoving before their television sets. Film clips which showed the vigorously alive thirty-fifth president were almost too painful to watch. But struggling to comprehend the incomprehensible, people couldn't tear themselves away. All commercial programming had been canceled, yet on the average, Americans watched television for ten hours on that long, rainy day. They saw the lines of dignitaries come to pay their respects at the White House, and wreaths being laid in Dealey Plaza, many with cards attached: "Forgive us"; saw photos of Rose attending Mass in Hyannis Port, and weeping citizens in almost every city of the world. In Ireland, it was said, people had "cried the rain down," while in Russia, radio stations played nothing but dirges. Sometimes when describing these events, a commentator's voice would start to quaver; then the network would quickly switch to another scene, another reporter.

Saturday became Sunday. People arose to again switch on their sets, and thus became witnesses to the second incredible shock of the weekend and the first murder ever shown live on television.

On Friday afternoon in Dallas, a twenty-four-year-old employee of the Texas Book Depository, Lee Harvey Oswald, had been taken into police custody as the suspected assassin. Oswald had a peculiar background. He had been a radar operator in the Marines, stationed at a U-2 base near Tokyo. After leaving the service, Oswald defected to the Soviet Union, but thirty-two months later, traveling on a loan from the U.S. government, he had returned home to Texas with a Russian wife. Oswald then briefly lived in New Orleans. There he was in contact with both pro- and anti-Castro groups as well as an employee of the local underworld boss, before moving back to Dallas in October 1963. An avowed Marxist, Oswald let that city off the hook. In several Dallas schools, students had applauded when news of Kennedy's death was broadcast over the loudspeakers. Yet for all the concern about its virulent right-wing atmosphere, it seemed the president's assassin had come from the almost nonexistent other end of the Dallas political spectrum. Her husband, Jackie said, "didn't even have the satisfaction of being killed for civil rights"; instead, he had been shot by "some silly little communist."

Oswald denied he was the assassin, protesting he had been set up. But Dallas police announced the case against him was "cinched": Oswald had been in the Book Depository when the shots were fired, he had fled the scene, he had left behind a rifle with his fingerprints on it, he had allegedly killed a policeman who had stopped him for questioning. The evidence, police said, was airtight.

Lee Harvey Oswald would not have a chance to defend himself against the charge that he had committed the crime of the century. On Sunday morning, surrounded by detectives, reporters, and television cameras, he was being led through the basement of the city jail for transfer to the county prison. Suddenly Dallas strip-club owner Jack Ruby ran forward out of the crowd and, shoving a revolver into Oswald's ribs, fired one shot. Oswald died less than two hours later at Parkland Hospital, having never regained consciousness. Ruby's motivation, he claimed, was his great admiration for JFK.

While Oswald lay dying in Dallas, a majestic procession was under way in Washington. Led by six gray horses, a caisson bearing the body of John Kennedy moved slowly down Pennsylvania Avenue to the beat of muffled drums. Behind pranced a riderless horse, carrying empty boots reversed in the stirrups, an ancient symbol of a fallen leader. At the Capitol, the flag-draped coffin was carried up a long flight of stairs and into the domed rotunda, where there were brief eulogies and the presentation of a wreath from Lyndon Johnson. Then hand-in-hand the wife and daughter of the late president walked forward. Kneeling by the casket, Jackie gently kissed the flag while Caroline reached up to fumble underneath it, as if trying to touch her father. Even the rigid military discipline of the Joint Chiefs of Staff gave way, and, like everyone else watching the scene, they began to cry.

After the family and dignitaries left the rotunda, ordinary citizens had a chance to pay their last respects. The line outside the Capitol was three miles long. They knew there was nothing to see inside except the closed coffin with its military guard of honor. Yet they had to come, a quarter of a million Americans who stood patiently hour after hour throughout that long, cold day and night, waiting for their chance to say good-bye.

Finally it was Monday, and John Fitzgerald Kennedy could be laid to rest. The procession formed again, retracing the same route from the Capitol to the White House that the new young president had taken after his inauguration address scarcely a thousand days before. The caisson halted in front of the presidential mansion, and the mourners fell in behind. Jackie refused, she said, to go to her husband's funeral in a "fat black Cadillac." Others could do what they wished; she would walk from the White House to St. Matthew's Cathedral. Almost everyone joined her: family, friends, staff, government officials, servants, heads of state. There had been a series of anonymous assassination threats against several prominent participants, including Bobby, Lyndon Johnson, Supreme Court Chief Justice Earl Warren, Soviet first premier deputy Anastas Mikoyan. All refused to ride in limousines. Their attitude was much like that of Charles de Gaulle. When J. Edgar Hoover warned him that he might be in danger, the French president had a one-syllable reply: "*Pfft.*"

The procession was a sight no one would ever forget. At its head, between Bobby and Teddy, walked Jacqueline Kennedy. Her dignity made Americans, wracked with grief, again feel a sense of pride in their country, which three days before had brought them shame. "She gave an example to the whole world," de Gaulle said, "of how to behave."

It was John's third birthday, and during the Mass he started to fidget. "Where's my daddy?" he asked. Jackie, who had borne up through the nightmarish weekend, finally began to cry. Caroline reached over and took her mother's hand. "You'll be all right, Mummy," she murmured. "I'll take care of you."

The service was over. The flag-draped coffin was carried out and again strapped to the caisson. It was time for John F. Kennedy to begin his last journey. He was to be buried in Arlington Cemetery, a site JFK thought so beautiful he had once said, "I could stay here forever." Jackie and her children stood watching on the steps of the Cathedral, as the caisson moved slowly by. Then the nation's heart broke. Little John was saluting his father.

EPILOGUE

"So now he is a legend when he would have preferred to be a man."

One year after the assassination, Jacqueline Kennedy realized that myth-making had all but obscured her very human husband. Yet it was a legend she herself had begun, when she spoke of JFK in an interview during the bleak Thanksgiving weekend following his funeral.

"You must think of him," she told a journalist, "as this little boy, sick so much of the time, reading in bed, reading the Knights of the Round Table. . . ."

Something of the child was still there in the adult. In the White House, late at night, Kennedy had listened to records—and the lyric he loved most was from a Broadway musical about King Arthur:

Don't let it be forgot
That once there was a spot
For one brief shining moment
That was known as Camelot.

"There'll be great presidents again," Jackie said, "but there'll never be another Camelot." She had given the Kennedy administration its epitaph.

For more than a decade, America looked back to Camelot as a magical time—when its handsome leader had performed brave deeds, when its potential for greatness seemed without limit. And along the way, as Jackie had predicted, the man became a myth . . . lost as surely in the mists of legend as King Arthur had been lost fourteen centuries before.

By 1974, the country was reeling, torn apart by an unpopular war, by violent protests, by further assassinations, by political scandals. A nation founded in liberty had lost its way, and the search for an explanation began.

One result was the establishment of a Senate committee to study a quarter-century of questionable activities by the Central Intelligence Agency. The committee report, released in the spring of 1976, brought to light the CIA/Mafia scheme against Fidel Castro—and led to public disclosure of Kennedy's relationship with Judith Campbell.

Soon "Camelot" became a satirical description of a period in which the government was linked to the underworld and to plots against a foreign head of state, in which the president himself carried on an immoral private life while taking his country deeper into the morass of Vietnam. Romanticism about the Kennedy era gave way to disillusionment. It seemed that JFK had been all style and no substance, that his thousand days had represented neither the best nor the brightest.

As a mood of cynicism swept through America, the tarnished image of Camelot eclipsed its legacy of idealism and commitment—a legacy that reflected the awakened conscience of John F. Kennedy.

No one can ever know how different the United States might be today if Kennedy had lived to serve two full terms as president. The historic civil rights bill which was still pending in the autumn of 1963, and the attack on unemployment and poverty which he planned to launch in his second term, were but a part of JFK's concept for a better future.

He had proposed a broad legislative program: in addition to action on the poll tax, the space program, the test ban treaty, Food for Peace, the Alliance for Progress, and the Peace Corps, Kennedy requested funding for mass transit and urban renewal; an anticrime package; aid for education, medical care, mental health; an update of food and drug safety laws; expanded programs for school lunches and food distribution to the needy; a revision of welfare laws; the prevention of water pollution; the protection of wilderness areas from exploitation; agricultural controls; trade expansion; a tax cut and tax reform; an increase in the minimum wage and improvements in Social Security; a broadening of foreign aid.

To an obstreperous Congress, the list seemed endless, and almost all of JFK's proposals were bottled up on Capitol Hill at the time of his death. But in the emotional aftermath of the assassination, a flood of Kennedy legislation poured out of Washington under what President Johnson labeled his "Great Society." Ultimately, with the escalation of the Vietnam war, the massive number of social programs proved too expensive. It was not possible, as LBJ claimed in his 1966 budget proposal, for even the richest nation on earth to have both "guns and butter." The American economy was in a shambles, the communists were winning in Southeast Asia, yet Johnson refused either to raise taxes or to seek a negotiated settlement in Vietnam.

In March 1968, Bobby Kennedy, who thought the United States was "headed straight for disaster," reluctantly announced he would seek the Democratic presidential nomination against the incumbent. Two weeks later, Johnson withdrew from the campaign, and the stage seemed set for another Kennedy in the White House. But the United States was unraveling. In April one of the war's leading critics, Martin Luther King, was killed by a sniper. Nine weeks later, Bobby, too, was assassinated.

A nation that had united in grief over the death of its thirty-fifth president was now more divided than ever. As inflation sky-rocketed, so too did protests against the war, riots in black ghettos, crime, rebellion, alienation, drug use. America's middle class turned once more to the right, and in 1969, Richard Nixon was inaugurated president. But that administration was eventually torn apart by Watergate; faced with impeachment, Nixon resigned his office in 1974, and Vice-President Gerald Ford assumed leadership. By the following year, with South Vietnam on the verge of collapse, the last of the U.S. troops went home. Fifty-eight thousand of the more than two and a half million who served there had been killed in useless sacrifice: the communists had finally won all of Southeast Asia.

Vietnam symbolized far more than the nation's only defeat in war. America had also suffered wounds that would never heal— and the first had come a dozen years earlier, in Dallas . . .

On November 29, 1963, President Johnson appointed a seven-man commission, under the chairmanship of Supreme Court Chief Justice Earl Warren, to investigate the assassination. But people around the world were skeptical of its conclusion, ten months later, that Lee Harvey Oswald had acted alone. It seemed Kennedy's death would be robbed of all meaning unless he had been killed, not by the lone act of an irrational young man, but by a conspiracy of those who rejoiced at news of his death.

Although after a quarter of a century many still question the findings of the Warren Commission, nothing has ever come to light that could prove with certainty that anyone other than Oswald was involved. Perhaps in the end the truth behind the assassination of John F. Kennedy matters less than the fact that it happened at all . . . because in those six seconds in Dallas, America lost its innocence forever.

1917-1963

KEY TO
ABBREVIATIONS

Beschloss, *K and R*	*Kennedy and Roosevelt*
Bishop, *Life*	*A Day in the Life of President Kennedy*
Bishop, *The Day*	*The Day Kennedy Was Shot*
Boston Globe	*The Boston Globe.* "JFK, the man, the president"
Kennedy, *Profiles*	*Profiles in Courage*
Kennedy, *England*	*Why England Slept*
Manchester, *Death*	*The Death of a President*
Manchester, *Moment*	*One Brief Shining Moment*
Manchester, *Portrait*	*Portrait of a President*
NYT	*The New York Times*
Parmet, *Jack*	*Jack: The Struggles of John F. Kennedy*
Parmet, *JFK*	*JFK: The Presidency of John F. Kennedy*
Schlesinger, *Heritage*	*The Bitter Heritage*
Schlesinger, *Kennedy*	*Robert Kennedy and His Times*
Schlesinger, *Thousand*	*A Thousand Days*
White, *1960*	*The Making of the President 1960*
White, *1964*	*The Making of the President 1964*

NOTES

1   the Forest Service had sprayed green dye on the lawns: Collier and Horowitz, p. 258.

1   Army flamethrowers had to be used to melt the ice: ibid., p. 258.

1   At dawn the snow stopped, and by noon the sky was blue and cloudless Schlesinger, *Thousand*, p. 2.

1   Twenty thousand people . . . ringed the . . . Capitol building. A million more lined the streets: Reg Gadney, *Kennedy* (New York: Holt, Rinehart and Winston, 1983), p. 84.

1   eighty million people sat expectantly before their television sets: Faber, p. 152.

1   the youngest man ever elected to the presidency: Kennedy was forty-three years old. Theodore Roosevelt was forty-two when he succeeded President McKinley after the latter's assassination in 1901.

1   "Let's get this country moving again!": Sorensen, p. 178, says JFK used some variation of this phrase so often early in the campaign that his writers began including it in all his speeches.

2   a cold war in which it appeared communism would prevail: Moody, p. 159.

2   The day before, Kennedy had been briefed on the problems: Sidey, p. 38.

2   in the less than a minute it took to recite the oath: Faber, p. 149.

2   Kennedy had entered politics as a reluctant substitute: Whalen, p. 395.

2   Joe Kennedy wearing the same coat he had worn twenty years before: ibid., p. 465.

2   they squeezed each other's hands. No words were necessary: Rose Kennedy, p. 386.

2   the family Bible, in which the joys and sorrows of generations had been recorded: Goodwin, pp. 809–810.

2   At that same moment . . . bonfires were being lit: Collier and Horowitz, p. 259.

2   It was . . . the end of a journey which had begun more than a century before: ibid., p. 259.

5   The island had first been invaded by Britain in 1169: Woodham-Smith, p. 15.

5   the Irish rebelled again and again: Donald S. Connery, *The Irish* (New York: Simon and Schuster, 1968), p. 22.

5   Few of the landlords stayed behind: Whalen, p. 5.

5 the inexpensive and easily-cultivated potato: ibid., p. 6.

5 an acre and a half of land could raise enough: Woodham-Smith, p. 35.

5 Most of those . . . existed miserably in windowless mud huts: Whalen, p. 5.

5 there wasn't enough land to go around: Woodham-Smith, p. 32.

5 in a population of more than nine million, almost one-third . . . on the verge of starvation: ibid., pp. 31–32.

6 conditions . . . most deplorable in Europe: ibid., p. 19.

6 the sole concern was that Ireland might rise again in rebellion: Whalen, p. 5.

6 "not by love but by fear.": Woodham-Smith, p. 18.

6 that food, for which there was no substitute: ibid., p. 36.

6 The Irish had only two choices: Whalen, p. 6.

6 wagonloads of produce . . . sent from Ireland, while starving people watched: Woodham-Smith, p. 77.

6 Fires that had burned . . . for more than a century: ibid., p. 143.

6 England officially continued to look the other way: ibid., p. 146.

6 more than a million . . . died of hunger and disease: Connery, *The Irish*, p. 26.

6 where everyone was . . . prosperous: "the States.": Whalen, p. 7.

6 No one wanted the Irish in England, and fares to North America were kept as low as possible: Woodham-Smith, p. 210.

7 one out of three perished in the "coffin ships.": Whalen, p. 7.

7 the two had met . . . on board ship: Although other sources (Burns, Rose Kennedy, Whalen) state or imply that Patrick and Bridget met after their arrival in Boston, Davis, p. 10, says Joe Kennedy's sister asserts they met during the voyage.

7 ads were careful to specify "No Irish Need Apply.": Collier and Horowitz, p. 23.

7 whiskey barrels—steady employment, since the immigrants often turned to alcohol to forget: Whalen, pp. 9–10.

7 The slums were appalling: ibid., p. 10; Woodham-Smith, pp. 248–251.

7 Irish children . . . were "born to die," and over 60 percent . . . did not live to . . . five: Whalen, p. 13.

8 She took a job . . . which sold toiletries and household articles: Davis, p. 20.

8 P.J. helped out in the shop . . . dropped out to take a full-time job on the waterfront: Whalen, p. 13.

8 freedom . . . would have to be achieved within the . . . community: ibid., p. 14.

8 he preferred lemonade . . . and would rather listen: ibid., p. 14.

8 if a man needed a free drink, a small loan: ibid., p. 15.

8 he was able to expand: Parmet, *Jack*, p. 5.

8 By 1885, when Boston elected its first Irish mayor: Whalen, p. 17; Cameron, pp. 26–27. Davis, p. 30, says the year was 1884; Shannon, p. 182, says 1886; Collier and Horowitz, p. 27, say 1888. (Honey Fitz was the first mayor of Boston whose parents were born in Ireland: Burns, p. 12.)

8 their choice . . . resulted in a landslide victory: Whalen, p. 15. Although many sources (including Whalen) give the year as 1886, Rachlin, p. 14, gives the exact date as November 3, 1885.

9 P.J. continued his progression upward: Parmet, *Jack*, p. 5.

9 some in that community thought . . . Kennedy had aimed a little too high: Collier and Horowitz, p. 27.

9 Her husband's climb . . . continued upward: Whalen, p. 17.

9 to a position of genuine power behind the scenes: Parmet, *Jack*, p. 6.

9 his family was well-to-do: Whalen, p. 19.

9 Irish . . . who could afford to

have fruit in the house: McCarthy, p. 30.

9   Kennedy would spend his life trying to scale slippery new heights: Whalen, p. 17.

9   an elite . . . school which included five signers of the Declaration of Independence among its alumni: ibid., p. 22.

9   Joe did poorly in every subject except mathematics: ibid., p. 23.

9   His .667 batting average: ibid., p. 24.

9   It was a rare moment in an uneasy relationship: ibid., p. 24.

10   Honey Fitz was rumored to have a wandering eye for the ladies: Collier and Horowitz, pp. 248–249.

10   his stoic wife stayed home: Collier and Horowitz, p. 37.

10   Fitzgerald . . . achieved the office to which every Boston Irish politician aspired: ibid., p. 30.

10   Honey Fitz regarded his family as superior: Whalen, p. 28.

10   the local Catholic hierarchy thought all their young men should attend parochial schools: ibid., p. 24.

10   quick to accuse them of prejudice if he sensed a snub: Parmet, *Jack*, p. 6; Collier and Horowitz, p. 35.

10   he ridiculed their importance while yearning to be admitted: Parmet, *Jack*, p. 6.

10   He bought a sight-seeing bus for a few hundred dollars, and . . . ended up with a profit of five thousand dollars: Whalen, p. 30.

10   he dropped out of a banking course: McCarthy, p. 19.

11   the captain's own postgraduation business plans would depend on Joe being in the game: Whalen, p. 27.

11   an inevitable progression . . . the path smoothed by Protestantism, tradition, and family connections: ibid., p. 34.

11   Joe believed . . . *money*—was the only way to achieve true power: ibid., p. 34.

11   Kennedy, calling on the influence of his father and others, had himself appointed . . . at an annual salary of fifteen hundred dollars: ibid., p. 35. Goodwin, p. 239, says Joe got the job through Honey Fitz and gives the salary as twelve hundred dollars.

11   soon convinced it was a world he would be able to conquer: Goodwin, pp. 240–241.

11   Fascinated by the David-and-Goliath struggle, the press claimed that Joe was the youngest bank president: Rose Kennedy, p. 66. (See Davis, p. 37, re: the extravagance of the claim by journalists—and by Rose Kennedy herself.)

11   "I want to be a millionaire by the age of thirty-five.": Collier and Horowitz, p. 37.

12   Honey Fitz . . . now regarded the young man as a suitable son-in-law: Whalen, p. 39.

12   At fifteen . . . the youngest graduate . . . the prettiest senior: ibid., p. 40.

12   Because her shy mother shunned the spotlight, Rose had been . . . her father's official hostess: ibid., p. 40; Cameron, p. 41.

12   "two dinners and three dances a night . . .": Cameron, p. 49.

12   "my rambling Rose": Goodwin, p. 158.

12   "brimming with animation and charm . . .": Cameron, p. 52.

12   He sang it so often . . . people thought it was the national anthem: ibid., p. 50.

12   Only three things had ever clouded the adoring relationship: Goodwin, p. 144.

12   one out of every forty-two . . . was drawing a salary from the city: ibid., p. 119.

12   The mayor . . . created positions such as "City Dermatologist": Burner and West, p. 18.

12   and "Rubber Boot Repairman": Collier and Horowitz, p. 371.

12   "amazing exposure of payroll graft": Goodwin, p. 119.

13   "My biggest regret is not having gone to Wellesley.": ibid., p. 144.

13   To spare his favorite daughter the embarrassment . . . and to

avoid losing her: ibid., pp. 155, 217.

13 The mayor . . . was having an affair with . . . Toodles Ryan. . . . Honey Fitz withdrew: Parmet, *Jack*, p. 9.

13 the last modest home in which they would ever live: Cameron, p. 75.

13 none, to Joe, would ever rival the significance of his eldest son: Whalen, p. 227; Goodwin, pp. 275, 352; Parmet, *Jack*, p. 123; McTaggart, p. 13; Schlesinger, *Kennedy*, pp. 13, 58; Blair, p. 21. Virtually all Kennedy sources make this point.

14 his grandson would go to Harvard, serve as mayor . . . governor . . . "President of the United States": Goodwin, p. 262.

14 Joe . . . achieved his goal of becoming a millionaire: Collier and Horowitz, p. 43.

14 It was widely believed that the Kennedys . . . in the business of supplying liquor, went right on doing so: ibid., p. 44; Davis, pp. 48–49; Whalen, p. 58.

14 he made enormous profits using inside tips: Collier and Horowitz, p. 42; Whalen, p. 54.

14 a "private banker": Goodwin, p. 329.

14 "a gold mine": ibid., p. 340.

14 The women snubbed Rose, daughter of . . . mayor; their husbands blackballed Joe, son of an Irish barkeep: Whalen, p. 59.

15 "I was born here . . .". *Boston Globe*, p. 15.

15 If they weren't going to be allowed into Yankee society, the Kennedy family would become its own exclusive circle: Goodwin, p. 366; Cameron, p. 98.

15 Rose and the children boarded a private railroad car: Whalen, p. 74.

15 a friend asked Joe what he wanted . . . "Everything," he replied: Collier and Horowitz, p. 45.

16 Riverdale . . . with excellent schools nearby . . . wooded and rural: Cameron, p. 114.

16 Joe could commute to . . . the city: Parmet, *Jack*, p. 25.

16 For the next thirty-two months: Whalen, p. 99.

16 Kennedy was back and forth from one coast to the other: Collier and Horowitz, p. 49.

16 Hollywood's reigning queen, Gloria Swanson: Whalen, p. 93.

16 Kennedy lent the actress money: ibid., p. 94.

16 their affair soon became an open secret: Goodwin, pp. 393–397.

17 Rose was as skilled . . . in the home as her husband was in business: Collier and Horowitz, p. 49.

17 She oversaw a large staff: ibid., p. 49.

17 Rose was a compulsive note-writer: Cameron, pp. 99, 111–112.

17 She kept an index file: Rose Kennedy, pp. 83–84.

17 Jack's card was especially full: Blair, pp. 24–25; Parmet, *Jack*, pp. 16–17.

17 Perhaps because he was so often sick or convalescing, Jack became an avid reader: Rose Kennedy, p. 110.

17 An early favorite, which Rose thought very silly: ibid., p. 111.

17 *Billy Whiskers* . . . was allowed . . . only because his grandmother Fitzgerald had given it: ibid., p. 111.

17 lists Rose made up for each child: ibid., p. 110.

17 As they became older, the *New York Times* was added: Cameron, p. 114.

17 and at mealtimes they were usually questioned: Rose Kennedy, pp. 104–105.

17 appropriate dinner conversation was history or religion: ibid., p. 105.

18 "Mother, we know what happened to Jesus . . .": Cameron, p. 85.

18 Because of her own devout beliefs, Rose insisted that religion be an important part: Rose Kennedy, pp. 160–161.

18 Grace was recited before every

meal . . . rosary was a family event: Goodwin, p. 319.

18 Rose told all the children to wish for a happy death. Jack said he was instead going to wish for two dogs: ibid., p. 353.

18 Rose had clocks put in every room so that no child ever had an excuse: Cameron, p. 98.

18 Anyone who arrived after the meal had begun had to start with the course then being served: Rose Kennedy, p. 102.

18 Bobby took his mother's rule so seriously: ibid., p. 103.

18 he usually managed to cajole . . . the cook: ibid., p. 102.

18 a race . . . with the rest of the family trying to stall: ibid., pp. 129–130.

18 Rose kept a ruler in her desk: ibid., p. 132.

18 she sent the children off in different-colored bathing suits: Collier and Horowitz, p. 49.

18 the younger boy would often help himself to an outfit of his brother's: Rose Kennedy, pp. 119–120.

18 Joe Jr. had a bad temper and the two had to be pulled apart: ibid., p. 119.

18 Jack always lost: Whalen, p. 90.

19 Competing was a Kennedy compulsion, and winning was the only acceptable outcome: ibid., pp. 91, 361.

19 they were not to cry: Rose Kennedy, pp. 144–145.

19 Rivalry . . . most obviously so between the two oldest brothers: Whalen, p. 90.

19 bicycle race in which . . . Joe Jr. didn't get a scratch; Jack had . . . twenty-eight stitches: Parmet, *Jack*, p. 21.

19 a physical education teacher . . . to lead the group in calisthenics: Collier and Horowitz, p. 50; Cameron, p. 99.

19 In 1927 . . . the first of . . . several Kennedy sailboats: Damore, p. 25.

19 sailing races, which they . . . were always to win: Whalen, p. 91.

19 Contests were a part of life: Rose Kennedy, p. 143.

19 "Look at that fence . . .": Martin, p. 30.

19 There were "Twenty Questions" and charades, at which Jack . . . excelled: Rose Kennedy, p. 108; Cameron, p. 101.

19 "Five times three, add one . . .": Rose Kennedy, p. 108.

19 While math was an important . . . subject, money was not: ibid., p. 116; Whalen, p. 90.

19 The children were told their father was well-to-do, that money brought . . . responsibility: Rose Kennedy, p. 118.

19 at age five the children were given allowances of a dime: ibid., p. 97.

20 *A Plea for a raise*: Reproduced in Moody, p. 53, and Meyers, p. 6.

20 The increase was granted, and the saga ended with Chapter I: Rose Kennedy, p. 114.

20 "I don't know what's going to happen . . ."; "Well, kid, don't worry . . ."; Even Joe . . . had to laugh: Fay, pp. 10–11.

20 he never carried cash: Rose Kennedy, pp. 118–119.

20 They grew up a close-knit little band: ibid., pp. 122–123; Burns, p. 20; Goodwin, p. 366.

21 Irish history was never discussed: Davis, p. 54.

21 "I questioned his judgment . . .": Whalen, p. 96.

21 Five million dollars richer: ibid., p. 99.

21 Having received . . . tips from the young man who shined his shoes: ibid., p. 105.

21 Joe was richer than ever: Goodwin, p. 422.

21 ruthlessness and . . . cruelty . . . only the professional man: ibid., p. 350; Rose Kennedy, p. 138.

21 "If you make them independent . . .": Martin, p. 22.

21 "If that's the only way to hold them . . .": Schlesinger, *Kennedy*, p. 20.

21 the romance . . . had obviously cooled: Goodwin, p. 392.

22 In . . . six years . . . his wife made seventeen trips abroad: Collier and Horowitz, p. 58.

22 as Rose's limousine went down . . . Joe's limousine would be coming up: Martin, p. 30.

22 Joe Jr. . . . surrogate parent; despite Jack's occasional reluctance . . . Joe Jr.'s word was . . . final: Clinch, pp. 72, 77.

22 Bronxville . . . a point of departure for their boarding schools: Collier and Horowitz, p. 59.

22 Rose and Joe were forever united: Goodwin, pp. 320–321.

22 "the architect . . . of our lives.": Rose Kennedy, p. 57.

22 She relinquished her solitary position without regret: Whalen, p. 165.

22 Rose thought they should go to Catholic schools: Rose Kennedy, p. 162.

23 "pretty homesick, but it's O.K. now.": Burns, p. 24.

23 "I will be quite pius . . .": ibid., p. 24.

23 he had learned to play "baggamon": ibid., p. 24.

23 "If you study too much . . . you're liable to go crazy.": Burner and West, p. 33.

23 "did not know about the market slump . . .": Burns, p. 25.

23 Shriver commented on how "spunky" Jack was: Parmet, *Jack*, p. 27.

23 Joe put his foot down: Whalen, p. 167.

23 Jack was "quite different . . ."· Rose Kennedy, p. 175.

23 headmaster . . . would write . . . how two brothers could be so unalike· ibid., p. 182.

24 Joe Jr. was a conformist in a traditional school: ibid., pp. 169, 176–277.

24 "sarcastic and overbearing . . .": Goodwin, p. 354.

24 "Manly youth": Jack's letter is reproduced in Meyers, p. 12.

24 for Rose's benefit, an account of his religious activities: Cameron, p. 118.

24 "Received the prayer book . . .": ibid., p. 119.

24 "football pracite" and . . . "choclate pie with whipt cream.": Burns, pp. 24, 26.

24 "Jack studies at the last minute . . .": Rose Kennedy, p. 178.

24 Jack Kennedy was simply outclassed: Collier and Horowitz, p. 62; Blair, p. 31.

25 the senior who best combined scholarship and sportsmanship: Rose Kennedy, p. 170.

25 It was a decision which astonished even Rose: ibid., p. 170.

25 decided his eldest son was also going to be president: Krock, *Memoirs*, p. 329.

25 Rose declared he was a nuisance: Cameron, p. 119.

25 She was particularly annoyed that . . . oranges she had sent: Rose Kennedy, p. 177.

25 when as a junior Jack became . . . ill, the fact was not mentioned in the card file: Blair, p. 25.

25 Jack's . . . poor health . . . would prove to be a less easy diagnosis: Collier and Horowitz, p. 66.

26 Although Joe had emerged . . . richer than ever, the Depression frightened him: Beschloss, *K and R*, p. 65; Whalen, p. 112.

26 "Economic depression . . . cannot be cured . . .": Frederick Lewis Allen, *Since Yesterday*. (New York: Harper & Brothers, 1939), p. 38.

26 Joe Kennedy agreed with him: Beschloss, *K and R*, p. 69.

26 he contributed heavily . . . and worked to line up other influential backers: Whalen, p. 119.

26 secretary of the Treasury . . . would be . . . right: Rose Kennedy, p. 197.

26 In the world of Boston politics, those who backed a candidate: Davis, p. 63; Goodwin, p. 436.

26 he offered Kennedy the ambassadorship to Ireland: Collier and Horowitz, p. 75.

26 the position would emphasize a heritage Kennedy . . . trying to escape: ibid., p. 75.

26 the new president began to have second thoughts: ibid., p. 75.

27   financial community had been manipulating the market; The outcry . . . enabled FDR to fulfill another campaign promise: Allen, *Since Yesterday*, pp. 168–169.

27   to end the "callous and selfish wrongdoing": Beschloss, *K and R*, p. 84.

27   a man who had once manipulated . . . better than anyone: Whalen, p. 139; Beschloss, *K and R*, p. 87; Davis, p. 66.

27   "a thief to catch a thief.": Beschloss, *K and R*, p. 88.

27   "Boys, I've got nine kids . . .": Goodwin, p. 450.

27   "Definitely decided to stop fooling around . . .": Rose Kennedy, p. 180.

27   "to buck the system more effectively.": Goodwin, p. 486.

27   The more the school tried to enforce those standards: Parmet, *Jack*, p. 34.

28   The headmaster . . . had . . . two separate responsibilities: Meyers, p. 17.

28   "corrupting the morals and integrity of the other students"— a statement which made the group feel terribly important: Parmet, *Jack*, p. 35.

28   Roosevelt protested Kennedy's departure in vain: Cameron, p. 120.

28   "Don't let me lose confidence in you again . . .": Schlesinger, *Kennedy*, p. 16.

28   sixty-fourth in a class of one hundred twelve: Blair, p. 40.

28   Jack had rigged the election: Parmet, *Jack*, p. 40.

29   In the fall of 1935, Joe and Rose, accompanied by Jack and Kathleen: Rose Kennedy, p. 200.

29   he was losing one hundred thousand dollars a year. His salary . . . barely paid the telephone bills: Whalen, p. 174.

29   a kind of unofficial emissary . . . to report on economic conditions in Europe: Beschloss, *K and R*, p. 121.

29   called "Kick" because she reminded them of a high-spirited pony: Goodwin, p. 362.

29   Joe Jr. played the leading role in his father's grand plan: Whalen, p. 227.

29   Kick was . . . "especially special.": Peter Collier and David Horowitz, "The Kennedy Kick," *Vanity Fair*, July 1983, p. 50.

29   Joe Jr. had survived the school— as Joe knew he would—"untainted" by socialist thinking: Whalen, p. 172; Burns, p. 35.

30   "Now, Joe, what will you do about this . . .": Collier and Horowitz, p. 89.

30   The problem was . . . jaundice or hepatitis or . . . a "blood condition.": Rose Kennedy, p. 201; Parmet, *Jack*, p. 42.

30   Joe wanted all his sons to go to Harvard: Whalen, p. 183.

30   "If a mosquito bit Jack Kennedy . . .": Rose Kennedy, p. 202.

30   teased him about his ambitions by calling him "Prexy.": Collier and Horowitz, p. 89.

30   he was six feet tall and weighed only 149 pounds: Parmet, *Jack*, p. 43.

30   "Who the hell are you?": Martin, p. 31.

30   "You don't weigh enough and you're going to get hurt.": Goodwin, p. 505.

30   Jack suffered an injury to a spinal disk, aggravating his chronic back problems: Rose Kennedy, p. 215; Davis, p. 117.

30   he would periodically sneak out to practice his backstroke: Whalen, p. 226.

31   He had campaigned for . . . class president, but did not even make the runoff: Parmet, *Jack*, p. 43.

31   he could never measure up to his brother: Burns, p. 29.

31   "I want you to know I'm not bright like my brother.": Parmet, *Jack*, p. 44.

31   "Joe really had everything," but Jack was warmer, nicer, and "so much less self-centered.": Martin, p. 31.

31   Joe Jr.'s caustic sense of humor: Parmet, *Jack*, p. 44.

31   young Joe was so absorbed by the future that he "could never

fully enjoy the present.": Goodwin, p. 465.

31 Jack was free from the ambition which obsessed Joe Jr.: ibid., p. 478; Collier and Horowitz, p. 91; Parmet, *Jack*, p. 44.

31 "general feeling seems to be that there will not be another war." Another entry stated that ". . . France is much too well prepared . . .": Parmet, *Jack*, p. 51.

31 Italy lively and prosperous. "Fascism seems to treat them well": ibid., p. 53.

32 The people were haughty and insufferable: Blair, p. 65.

32 American handshakes were greeted with arrogant Nazi salutes of "Heil, Hitler.": Collier and Horowitz, p. 80.

32 regarded the Italian leader as a comic figure: ibid., p. 80.

32 they regretted having missed the mesmeric dictator: ibid., p. 80; Blair, pp. 64–65.

32 the tour of Germany had been an awful experience: Blair, p. 65.

32 He had written . . . he could get women as often as he wanted. Collier and Horowitz, p. 90.

32 "Looked pretty dull the first couple of days . . .": Parmet, *Jack*, p. 51.

32 in France . . . local custom required . . . a chaperone: ibid., p. 52.

32 "Very beautiful girls . . .": ibid., p. 52.

32 Jack was an abominable linguist: ibid., p. 31.

32 women . . . found him irresistible: Goodwin, p. 481; Blair, p. 401.

32 His younger brother's attraction for women was . . . another source of competition: Davis, p. 101.

32 "The girls really liked Jack . . .": Goodwin, pp. 481–482.

32 Jack decided to major in government. He did not plan to enter politics: Rose Kennedy, p. 216.

33 since his father . . . claimed that career for Joe Jr.: McCarthy, p. 59; Collier and Horowitz, p. 92.

33 Jack . . . might like to be a journalist: Rose Kennedy, p. 216.

33 Jack had told his father that the trip abroad had given him the incentive to study: Burns, p. 33.

33 he proceeded to get a D—in . . . "Continental Europe.": Parmet, *Jack*, p. 48.

33 As a freshman . . . C average, a lackluster performance he repeated: Burns, p. 31.

33 *I'm for Roosevelt* . . . ghostwritten by . . . Arthur Krock: Beschloss, *K and R*, p. 124; Parmet, *Jack*, p. 55.

33 implying . . . a more gratifying appointment in the future: Beschloss, *K and R*, p. 128.

33 "lousy shape."; "Why, there wasn't a guy in that room . . .": Whalen, p. 191.

33 he had also become less optimistic about the administration's economic policies: Burns, p. 18.

33 it was time to come through on his promise: Beschloss, *K and R*, p. 153; Whalen, p. 200.

33 The president was anxious to get Joe out of his hair: Cameron, p. 124.

33 Kennedy was too critical, too crass: ibid., pp. 200, 202; Burns, p. 33; Beschloss, *K and R*, p. 157.

34 "Kennedy is too dangerous to have around here.": Beschloss, *K and R*, p. 157.

34 "the greatest joke in the world.": ibid., p. 157.

34 the most glittering prize of the American diplomatic scene: Burns, p. 33.

34 only seven . . . "so as not to complicate the housing problem": Cameron, p. 126.

34 "the Father of His Country": Whalen, p. 211.

34 wrote . . . he was feeling much better: from Jack's letter reproduced in Meyers, p. 29.

34 Whether brought about by maturity: Whalen, pp. 226–227; Burns, p. 33.

34 liberation from . . . his older brother, Jack . . . made the dean's list: Parmet, *Jack*, p. 61.

34 Joe Jr. . . . wrote a friend that

Jack had come over "to begin his education.": Blair, p. 68.

34 a classroom could never rival . . . history in the making, and Jack was on the scene: Rose Kennedy, p. 240.

35 "so damned complicated that it is impossible to estimate the difficulties . . .": Collier and Horowitz, p. 99.

35 "crude, backward, hopelessly bureaucratic country.": Burns, p. 38.

35 his car . . . was pelted with bricks: Parmet, *Jack*, p. 65.

35 "The Poles will fight.": Burns, p. 38.

35 Joe believed another war would result in the destruction of European commercial centers . . . end of the capitalist system . . . triumph of communism: Whalen, p. 234; Beschloss, *K and R*, pp. 162–163; Goodwin, p. 551.

35 most frightening to Joe . . . if his country had to fight, so, too, would his sons: Whalen, p. 234.

35 "peace in our time"—a claim for which Joe Kennedy thought he himself should be given credit: Stevenson, p. 82.

36 paper was completed, with the help of five stenographers, just under the wire: Blair, p. 88.

36 pact . . . not the fault of England's rulers; instead . . . people . . . had been unwilling to pay the taxes: ibid., p. 89.

36 "Leaders are responsible . . ."; "English public opinion was not sufficiently aroused . . .": Whalen, p. 295.

36 the thesis was . . . a justification of his father's views: Burns, pp. 41–42.

36 Jack differed with Joe in regard to . . . Winston Churchill: Collier and Horowitz, p. 106.

36 "In light of the present-day war . . .": Parmet, *Jack*, p. 71.

36 "it seemed to represent a lot of work . . .": Blair, p. 88.

37 "I'll be interested to see what you think of it . . .": Whalen, p. 294.

37 summoned the faithful Arthur Krock: Parmet, *Jack*, p. 72; Krock, *Memoirs*, p. 343.

37 "You have gone too far . . ."; "thrown caution out of the window . . .": Blair, p. 91.

37 Jack listened to his father and amended the manuscript: ibid., pp. 91–94.

37 "You would be surprised . . .": Burns, p. 44.

37 Joe arranged . . . to send out 250 review copies: Parmet, *Jack*, pp. 73–74.

37 "painstaking scholarship."; "required reading . . ."; "sober, reliable . . .": all three reviewers' quotes are taken from the book jacket of *Why England Slept*.

37 *Washington Post* claimed the book was superficial: Parmet, *Jack*, p. 74.

37 A Harvard professor suggested . . . *Why Daddy Slept*: Collier and Horowitz, p. 106.

37 Harold Laski . . . deeply regretted its being published. He added . . . his doing so represented "much more real friendship . . .": Parmet, *Jack*, p. 75.

38 The book sold forty thousand copies in America and . . . in England: Burns, p. 44. Cameron, pp. 142–143, claims nearly a quarter of a million copies were sold in England.

38 *Why England Slept* was a bestseller and its author a celebrity: Parmet, *Jack*, pp. 76–77.

38 Jack . . . said it would never have had a chance "except for luck.": Martin, p. 35.

38 Harold Laski . . . pointed out that the only "luck" . . . was . . . Jack was the son of the American ambassador: Parmet, *Jack*, p. 75.

38 "The British have had it . . .": Collier and Horowitz, p. 106.

38 "What is our aim? I can answer in one word . . .": Davis, p. 82.

38 having endured fifty-seven straight nights of air raids: Whalen, pp. 321–322.

38 the embassy advised its personnel to find quarters outside the city: ibid., p. 322.

38 "Jittery Joe.": Collier and Horowitz, p. 107.

38 A British Foreign Office memo called him "undoubtedly a coward.": Davis, p. 83.

38 "a very foul specimen of double crosser and defeatist.": Collier and Horowitz, p. 104.

38 "His mind is as blank as uninked paper": ibid., p. 105.

39 "I cannot impress upon you strongly enough . . .": Whalen, p. 324.

39 nothing . . . but "blood, toil, tears, and sweat.": Whalen, p. 291.

39 an "errand boy," as Joe described himself: Collier and Horowitz, p. 106.

39 Henry Luce and many other . . . isolationists were urging him: Beschloss, *K and R*, p. 213.

39 he could put "25 million Catholic votes" behind FDR's . . . opponent: Stevenson, p. 149.

39 The president . . . asked Kennedy to come . . . "for consultation.": Collier and Horowitz, p. 107.

39 THE LIQUOR TRADE IN BOSTON IS NOW CHALLENGING: Stevenson, p. 149.

39 So Joe came home, ready for a showdown: Parmet, *Jack*, p. 81.

39 Rose . . . cautioned Joe: Cameron, p. 145; Davis, p. 85.

40 Joe's troubles . . . were the fault of the State Department; he himself was so involved; After the election . . . a thorough housecleaning: Whalen, p. 332.

40 The ambassador would have Roosevelt's blessing: ibid., pp. 332–333.

40 he would support Joe Jr. . . . for the governorship: Beschloss, *K and R*, p. 221.

40 The United States would stay out of war . . . Roosevelt shared this conviction: ibid., p. 219.

40 "I have a great stake in this country . . .": ibid., p. 220.

40 "Democracy is finished . . ."; It was a question of economics, and of "feeding people.": Whalen, p. 342.

40 a wonderful woman, "helpful and full of sympathy"; Mrs. Roosevelt, he added, "bothered us more . . .": ibid., p. 341.

40 Joe's reasons . . . and . . . Eleanor Roosevelt's kindness, were usually omitted: ibid., pp. 341–342.

41 In the eldest . . . Joe saw . . . his impossible goal: Clinch, p. 72.

41 Joe Jr. would achieve *everything*: Burner and West, p. 31.

41 "I find myself much more interested in what young Joe is going to do . . .": Goodwin, p. 617.

41 "To you mothers and fathers, I give you . . .": Burns, p. 46.

42 there was no point in . . . making plans: Parmet, *Jack*, p. 85.

42 Jack believed . . . the United States would soon be at war: Blair, p. 105.

42 few now paid much attention to Kennedy's familiar warnings: Whalen, p. 357.

42 Hoping that the warm California climate would improve his health, he had decided to audit courses: Blair, p. 103.

42 to pass the time until he was called into the service: Burns, p. 47.

42 the first peacetime draft; all men between . . . twenty-one and thirty-five; college students were exempt: Blair, p. 113.

43 the reason for his hospitalization was not disclosed: Davis, p. 121.

43 Joe had purchased property in Florida, a state which had no income tax: Parmet, *Jack*, p. 83.

43 That spring saw the most massive bombings yet inflicted on English cities: Leonard Mosley, *Battle of Britain* (Alexandria, VA: Time-Life Books, 1977), pp. 183–191.

43 it appeared the . . . invasion was about to begin: ibid., pp. 183, 191.

43 Japan . . . seemed intent on conquering all of Asia: Zich, pp. 21, 25.

43 "a most historic . . . pronouncement": Beschloss, *K and R*, p. 242.

43 "My ideas haven't changed . . .":
    Damore, p. 61.
43 "Wouldn't you know," he told
    everyone who cared to listen:
    Goodwin, p. 622.
43 the last time the Kennedys would
    all be together: Collier and Horo-
    witz, p. 113.
43 Visitors were taken aback . . .
    by the intensity with which Ken-
    nedy girls and boys alike played:
    McCarthy, pp. 109–110.
44 One visitor described the Ken-
    nedys . . . as existing outside the
    usual laws of nature. "There was
    no other group so handsome . . .":
    Collier and Horowitz, p. 113.
44 She was slow to learn to crawl,
    to walk, to talk: Whalen, p. 92.
44 "What can they do for her . . .":
    ibid., p. 92.
44 the Kennedys did their best not
    to let Rosemary know she was
    "different.": Rose Kennedy, pp.
    153–158.
44 as the children matured . . .
    Rosemary could not keep up:
    Collier and Horowitz, pp. 114–
    155.
44 A particular problem was her
    growing maturity: ibid., p. 115.
44 Rose feared Rosemary would be
    an easy victim: Cameron, pp.
    148–149.
44 Rosemary started to regress: ibid.,
    p. 149.
44 Her once docile personality
    changed, and she often threw
    tantrums . . . breaking objects
    and striking out: Rose Kennedy,
    p. 286.
45 finally . . . attacking her . . .
    grandfather: Collier and Horo-
    witz, p. 155.
45 lobotomy . . . was a new proce-
    dure for which there were high
    hopes: Goodwin, pp. 641–642.
45 At Joe's instigation and without
    even Rose's knowledge, the sur-
    gery was performed . . . with
    disastrous results: ibid., p. 642.
45 gone too was the ability to func-
    tion at more than a childlike
    level: Rose Kennedy, p. 286.
45 where, the Kennedys said, she
    had decided to devote her life

to . . . retarded children: Burns,
    p. 129.
45 It would be more than twenty
    years before even the sketchiest
    facts . . . were made public:
    Blair, pp. 22–23.
45 The Kennedy family had suffered
    a tragic loss—and the war hadn't
    even begun: Collier and Horo-
    witz, p. 114.
45 Joe Jr. had beaten him into the
    service, and . . . Jack was de-
    termined to follow: Whalen, p.
    360.
45 the Army . . . the Navy . . .
    turned him down because of his
    medical problems: Parmet, Jack,
    p. 86.
45 he followed a strict regimen of
    exercise and diet: Damore, p. 61.
45 his father pulled strings: Parmet,
    Jack, p. 86–87.
45 a period later omitted from his
    official naval biography: Blair,
    p. 132.
45 bulletins which summarized in-
    formation from foreign intelli-
    gence sources . . . then sent to
    the secretary of the Navy and
    other key naval personnel: ibid.,
    pp. 133–134.
45 By November relations . . . had
    become critical: ibid., p. 135.
45 The United States had broken
    Japan's diplomatic code, and
    messages . . . indicated the peace
    talks were a sham: ibid., p. 135;
    Zich, pp. 24, 51.
46 But where . . . ? Pearl Harbor
    . . . was the least likely: Blair,
    p. 135.
46 The Japanese . . . armada could
    not steam halfway across the
    Pacific without being detected:
    Zich, p. 27.
46 the ONI . . . had picked up no
    radio signals . . . since November
    16: ibid., p. 51.
46 The ONI decided . . . the carriers
    were in home waters: ibid., p. 52.
46 operating under radio silence . . .
    through the North Pacific, they
    were . . . 230 miles north of
    Oahu: ibid., p. 27.
46 Failure to anticipate the attack
    . . . had been one of the worst

intelligence blunders in history: Blair, p. 136.

46 The material to which Jack was privy was not highly classified: ibid., p. 153.

46 one of the ensigns . . . was having an affair with a woman suspected of being a Nazi spy: for the most complete background on Inga Arvad, and on her romance with Jack Kennedy, see ibid., pp. 144–164, 324, 547, 565–567.

46 The paper's theory . . . was that pretty finishing school graduates . . . were the most inexpensive source of labor: ibid., p. 138.

47 he had been approached by a beautiful student who asked him to find her a position in Washington: ibid., p. 146.

47 Like Joe Kennedy, Krock was always happy to oblige a pretty face: Wills, p. 21.

47 she seemed . . . the epitome of glamour: Parmet, *Jack*, p. 89.

47 won the title of "Miss Denmark": Davis, p. 92; McTaggart, p. 95. Inga's son, in an interview with the Blairs, says his mother won the title of "Miss Europe."

47 "the perfect example of Nordic beauty": Parmet, *Jack*, p. 89.

47 affronted, she said, because the Nazis had asked her to . . . spy: ibid., p. 89.

47 Kennedy was "playing around" with and "apparently spending the night" with Inga: ibid., p. 91.

47 On November 27, 1941, "Did You Happen to See . . ." was devoted to Jack: Blair, pp. 148–149.

48 Heads began to roll at ONI: ibid., p. 137.

48 Joe's influence saved his son again: Wills, p. 21.

48 Roosevelt himself had sent a memo . . . requesting that surveillance . . . be intensified: Parmet, *Jack*, p. 91.

48 Hoover now had . . . not for the last time—information that proved Jack's involvement with an inappropriate woman: ibid., p. 92; Powers, p. 360; Davis, pp. 93, 309, 353; Blair, p. 163.

48 no one was watching more closely than his father: Collier and Horowitz, p. 122.

48 Jack . . . announcing he wanted to marry Inga: Parmet, *Jack*, p. 90. See also Jack's letter to Lem Billings (Collier and Horowitz, p. 124) in which he refers to the possibility of the marriage.

48 There was more string-pulling: Parmet, *Jack*, p. 92.

48 "As you probably haven't heard . . .": Collier and Horowitz, p. 124.

49 In the early days . . . patrol torpedo boats were thought . . . glamorous: Blair, p. 175.

49 he had left . . . from the relative safety of one of its most heavily fortified islands: Zich, p. 95.

49 The general . . . sent their commander back . . . to lobby for a larger fleet: Blair, p. 175.

49 With so little good news . . . the Navy enthusiastically went along: ibid., p. 175.

49 PTs were small . . . PT torpedoes were often defective: ibid., p. 176.

49 The 1942 Naval Academy class . . . yielded exactly twenty men who chose . . . PT-boat service: ibid., p. 175.

49 Among the amateurs the Navy had better luck: ibid., p. 175.

49 For Jack Kennedy, they also seemed an answer to his problems: ibid., p. 177; Collier and Horowitz, p. 124.

49 In a letter to Lem, Jack mentioned . . . the fatality rate . . . "You have to be young, healthy . . .": Collier and Horowitz, p. 125.

50 Hidden from Navy brass was the fact . . . Jack had begun sleeping on a table: Goodwin, p. 646.

50 his own sleeve had only the single stripe of an ensign: Blair, p. 186.

50 the two brothers said good-bye for . . . the last time: ibid., p. 186.

50 The undersecretary of the Navy was a personal friend: Whalen, p. 367.

50 It was the first time . . . "Jack had won such an 'advantage' by

such a clear margin . . .": Rose Kennedy, p. 285.

50 tales of his brother's heroism would almost break Joe Jr.'s heart: Davis, p. 102.

51 After an eighteen-day sea voyage from San Francisco: Blair, pp. 190–191, 194.

51 a body of water which American Marines had dubbed "the Slot.": Steinberg, p. 33.

51 Their nocturnal forays, called "the Tokyo Express": ibid., p. 33.

52 Without U.S. supplies and troops, Australia could not have held . . . and the main line of defense would have moved back to the North American continent: ibid., p. 19.

52 On April 7, almost two hundred Japanese planes set out on the greatest air raid since Pearl Harbor: Donovan, p. 18.

52 "Condition Red": an air attack was imminent: ibid., p. 17.

52 A member of the crew threw him a rope, but the pilot . . . began to shoot: ibid., p. 21.

52 The LST responded with machine gun fire and the Japanese pilot sank from sight: Blair, p. 197.

52 KILL JAPS . . . KILL MORE JAPS: Donovan, p. 30.

52 The . . . raid had been followed by a . . . lull: Blair, p. 196.

52 The boat, eighty feet long and . . . made of plywood: Donovan, p. 31.

52 dirty and in need of paint after months of service . . . infested with cockroaches and rats: ibid., p. 54.

52 He was, for the first time, truly on his own: Blair, p. 128.

52 "If I were he, I would take as much time . . .": ibid., p. 210.

53 "As regards Bobby . . .": ibid., p. 210.

53 "P.S. Mother: Got to church Easter.": ibid., p. 211.

53 *The folks sent me a clipping . . .*: Donovan, p. 236.

53 The original crew had been transferred to another boat: Blair, p. 200.

53 The lull was over. The first major

allied offensive . . . began on June 30: Blair, pp. 211–212. The first American offensive, on Guadalcanal in August 1942, was conceived as a limited operation to check the Japanese advance eastward through the islands of the South Pacific. (Steinberg, p. 19).

53 a simultaneous attack . . . by General MacArthur and . . . Admiral Halsey: Steinberg, p. 75.

53 PT 109 was ordered into combat in mid-July . . . to the tiny island of Lumbari: Donovan, pp. 80, 90; Blair, p. 225.

53 Over the next two weeks, the boat went out on seven night patrols: Blair, p. 235, gives this as an estimated number. PT 109's logbook was lost in the sinking: Blair, pp. 228–229.

53 Japanese shipping was attempting to get through the Slot, and the mission of the PTs . . . was to intercept it: Donovan, p. 93.

53 The enemy had . . . a PT counterweapon: Blair, pp. 227–228.

53 "I hope it won't be taken as a sign of lack of confidence . . .": Goodwin, p. 651.

54 "If anything happens to me I have this knowledge . . .": Blair, p. 324.

54 PT 109 had . . . on three occasions, been attacked . . . two of the crew were wounded: ibid., p. 235.

54 shrapnel—fragments . . . Japan had imported: Donovan, p. 103.

54 on August 1 . . . a major Tokyo Express was expected: ibid., p. 114.

54 The message had no sooner arrived: ibid., p. 115.

54 eighteen Japanese dive bombers attacked . . . two PTs were destroyed: Blair, p. 237.

54 PT 109 . . . returned fire: Donovan, p. 117.

54 The air raid was a sign that the Express was in the area: Blair, p. 237.

54 fifteen PTs were sent out to meet it: ibid., p. 238.

54 Ross . . . on the night of July 20 . . . involved in a humiliating

mix-up: ibid., p. 231; Donovan, pp. 97–98.

54 Four Japanese ships went through . . . that night: Donovan, p. 136.

54 None . . . was destroyed. One suffered only slight damage: Blair, p. 265. Donovan, p. 136, says all four went through "without a scratch."

54 A naval historian later described the next few hours as the most confused and least effective action: Donovan, p. 136n.

54 the Japanese destroyers were probing . . . with searchlights and shooting . . . some PTs took evasive action: Blair, pp. 255, 262.

55 Some seem simply to have gotten lost: ibid., p. 252.

55 Of the ninty torpedoes . . . only thirty-two were fired . . . not a single one hit its target: ibid., pp. 243, 260, 265–266. Twenty-four of the thirty-two were fired as the Express was going to Kolombangara through a narrow body of water called Blackett Strait. PT 109 was rammed in this strait: ibid., p. 260.

55 Several . . . including 109, didn't fire any: ibid., pp. 249, 256–257; Donovan, p. 144.

55 Lookouts . . . saw the wake . . . assumed it was from another PT boat: ibid., p. 269.

55 Jack spun the wheel: Donovan, p. 144.

55 almost splitting it in half: Blair, p. 272.

55 Fearing the tanks would explode, Jack ordered the crew overboard. But after a few minutes . . . called out for everyone to climb back: ibid., p. 273.

55 Kennedy towed the older man to the boat: Donovan, p. 153.

55 "For a guy from Boston . . .": ibid., p. 154.

55 By sunup . . . the crew was terrified: ibid., p. 157; Blair, p. 277.

55 They were two miles east of Kolombangara: Donovan, pp. 160–161.

55 where ten thousand Japanese soldiers were based: Blair, p. 233.

55 Four miles in the opposite direction lay . . . Gizo . . . another enemy garrison: ibid., p. 276.

55 the wreckage was drifting southward, closer to . . . islands which might also be occupied: ibid., p. 277.

55 PT 109 appeared to be sinking: Donovan, p. 159.

55 Selecting the most remote . . . Jack, clenching the strap . . . towed the older man: ibid., pp. 162–163.

55 The trip took almost five hours: The soon-to-be-famous New Yorker/Reader's Digest article, reprinted in Meyers (pp. 40–44), says the trip took over five hours. Donovan, p. 165, says "fully four hours," while Blair, p. 281, says "about four hours."

55 About 6 P M, vomiting and exhausted, they crawled ashore: Blair, p. 281.

56 Within two hours, Jack swam out again . . . caught in a current and drifted . . . through the night: ibid., pp. 283–284.

56 The only source of food was coconuts, but these were unripened: ibid., p. 284.

56 the expedition took three hours, with Jack again towing McMahon: ibid., p. 287.

56 reluctant to explore . . . for fear of encountering the Japanese: ibid., p. 287; Donovan, p. 182.

56 the crew . . . licked at the foliage, but it was covered with bird droppings: Donovan, p. 173; Blair, p. 288.

56 Jack and Barney Ross set out to explore . . . Nauru: some sources, including Blair and Donovan, use the alternate spelling of "Naru" for this island. In his message carved on the coconut, Jack spelled it "Nauro": Donovan, p. 203. It was also known as Gross Island or Cross Island: Blair, p. 288.

56 because of the oppressive heat . . . the terrifying sounds of the jungle, the men were growing weak and despondent: Donovan, pp. 182–183.

56   the short swim . . . seemed effortless: ibid., p. 185.

56   they could see Rendova, thirty-
eight miles away: ibid., p. 185.

56   They came across a small canoe
. . . water . . . crackers and
candy: Blair, p. 289.

56   Jack tore a slat from the crate:
Donovan, p. 190.

56   he was amazed to find his men
. . . speaking pidgin English:
Blair, pp. 291–292.

57   Evans was a "coast watcher" . . .
on Kolombangara: ibid., p. 279.

57   He had . . . radioed news . . .
of the burning hulk . . . and been
asked to be on the lookout for
survivors: Donovan, p. 157.

57   NATIVE KNOWS POSIT: ibid., p.
203.

57   "No thanks . . . I've just had a
coconut.": Manchester, *Portrait*,
p. 162.

57   naval officials . . . realized the
story's potential. The survival . . .
of Joe Kennedy's son would
make very good reading . . .
back home: Blair, p. 296.

57   Typical of the coverage . . . was
one story that began: "The luck
of the Irish . . .": ibid., p. 299.

57   "To Ambassador Joe Kennedy
. . .": Collier and Horowitz, p.
131.

58   "By God, I'll show them.": ibid.,
p. 131.

58   The patrols . . . as long as fourteen hours . . . in rain and fog:
Blair, p. 387.

58   He would one day inherit . . .
almost two hundred thousand
acres: McCarthy, p. 85.

58   and eight great estates: Goodwin,
p. 546.

58   He was considered a possible
match for Princess Elizabeth:
Collier and Horowitz, p. 93.
("Princess Elizabeth" became
Queen Elizabeth II in 1953.)

58   The Duke . . . like most of
England's ruling class, disliked
Catholics and felt superior to the
Irish: ibid., p. 93; McTaggart, p.
47.

58   The antagonism was mutual: Rose
Kennedy, p. 291.

58   "You can't expect an American
girl to know how . . .": Peter
Collier and David Horowitz,
"The Kennedy Kick," *Vanity
Fair*, July 1983, p. 57.

58   what Rose called the heartbreaking and horrifying possibility that Kick might wed outside the Church: Goodwin, p.
677.

58   All through the winter, in a series
of letters and telegrams: Collier
and Horowitz, pp. 133–134.

59   "let all the rest of us go jump in
the lake," although he added . . .
"I'd be thrown right out in the
street.": Goodwin, p. 676.

59   Joe Jr. . . . kneel by his bed
every night to say his prayers
aloud: McTaggart, p. 158.

59   "I do know how you feel,
Mother . . . but I do think it
will be alright.": Goodwin, p.
678.

59   "In regard to Kick becoming a
Duchess . . . it would be rather
nice . . .": Collier and Horowitz,
p. 133.

59   Rose checked into a hospital:
Collier and Horowitz, p. 135, say
the reason was "minor surgery";
Goodwin, p. 680, says "a checkup" (although she claims Rose
entered the hospital after the
wedding). Rachlin, p. 90, says
Rose checked out only hours
after her daughter was married.
Most sources imply what Mc-
Taggart, pp. 162–163, states outright: "For two weeks prior . . .
the mother of the bride had been
sequestered away in a hospital
. . . to avoid being plagued by
reporters."

59   WITH YOUR FAITH IN GOD YOU
CAN'T MAKE A MISTAKE: Cameron,
p. 152.

59   Rose's only acknowledgment . . .
was to request . . . nuns to pray
"everything would turn out all
right.": ibid., p. 152.

59   "Once you've got your feet upon
the desk . . .": Parmet, *Jack*, p.
118.

59   He had returned . . . weighing
only 125 pounds: Burns, p. 53.

59 "In regard to the fascinating subject of my operation . . .": Sorensen, p. 40.

60 the Navy and Marine medal for "extremely heroic conduct . . .": Parmet, *Jack*, p. 121.

60 there had been a great deal of quiet criticism . . . even a rumor that MacArthur . . . said young Kennedy should be court-martialed: Blair, p. 376.

60 a long, laudatory piece . . . appeared in *The New Yorker*: as previously mentioned, this article (entitled "Survival") is reprinted in Meyers, pp. 40–44.

60 "Even I was wondering how it would all end.": Parmet, *Jack*, p. 119.

60 Joe . . . not satisfied . . . arranged to have the article reprinted in *Reader's Digest*: ibid., pp. 119 120.

60 Jack was a celebrity: Collier and Horowitz, p. 137.

60 his months in England had been filled with frustration: Blair, p. 387.

60 His own brother was . . . the pride of the Navy: ibid., pp. 387–388; Collier and Horowitz, p. 136; McTaggart, p. 169.

60 he had even disobeyed orders . . . the crew had complained of his recklessness: Collier and Horowitz, p. 134.

61 he was packed to go home: ibid., p. 136.

61 experienced pilots were needed for an extremely hazardous top-secret mission: ibid., p. 136.

61 intelligence sources had located their launch sites: Blair, p. 388.

61 losing in the process 154 planes and almost 800 men: ibid., p. 136.

61 a radio-controlled pilotless bomber, filled with twelve tons of explosives . . . Because its electronic equipment was incapable of controlling a takeoff, a pilot and copilot would be aboard: ibid., pp. 388–389.

61 they would bail out and . . . "mother planes" would assume control: ibid., p. 388.

61 after the war it would be revealed that the bunkers had been abandoned: Martin, p. 40.

61 the bomber, code-named Zootsuit Black: Collier and Horowitz, p. 136.

61 Joe . . . had been warned . . . the explosives' arming mechanism might malfunction: McTaggart, pp. 170–172.

61 "Nobody in my family needs insurance.": Collier and Horowitz, p. 137.

61 twenty-eight minutes into the mission, moments before its pilot and copilot were to bail out, Zootsuit Black had exploded: ibid., p. 137.

61 Elliott Roosevelt . . . had been momentarily blinded: Martin, pp. 39–40.

61 the largest nonatomic explosion of World War II: McTaggart, p. 173, says "ever engineered by man." Parmet, *Jack*, p. 2, says "what may have been the greatest nonnuclear explosion of all time."

61 Joe went to his room and locked the door: Whalen, p. 371.

61 His eldest son was dead. So, too, was a part of Joe Kennedy: ibid., p. 371; Krock, *Memoirs*, p. 348.

62 news of her brother's death brought Kick back to America: McTaggart, p. 175. (Several sources mistakenly say Kick was in Hyannis Port when the Kennedys heard the news of Joe Jr.'s death.)

62 Jack . . . was yellow from malaria . . . and frighteningly thin: ibid., p. 175.

62 Rose had not forgiven . . . the controversial marriage, and . . . was aloof: ibid., p. 177.

62 "Don't get worried about it . . .": Goodwin, p. 692.

62 "threw the letter on the table . . .": ibid., p. 692.

62 Nineteen years old and in uniform, he was still . . . an obedient little boy: Blair, pp. 392–393.

62 Kick . . . sneering at her younger brother to "get lost," took the scotch: McTaggart, p. 180; Collier and Horowitz, p. 142.

62 everyone was . . . clapping when . . . an upstairs window flew open. "Jack," his father's voice bellowed out, "don't you and your friends have any respect . . .": Blair, p. 393; McTaggart, p. 179.

62 Barney approached Joe to apologize, but the older man turned away: Blair, p. 393.

63 Billy Hartington had been shot through the heart by a German sniper: McTaggart, p. 184; Collier and Horowitz, p. 144.

63 Kick, who had spent only five weeks with her young husband, now prepared to return to England as a widow: McTaggart, p. 187.

63 the whole family . . . rallied around . . . A friend, bewildered by the charade, wondered how Kick could possibly keep up the pretense: ibid., p. 186.

63 that was the way they had all been raised: "Kennedys don't cry.": ibid., p. 186; Martin, p. 241.

67 "Red Fay isn't even a member of the family . . .": Fay, p. 150.

67 "You come down here with ten dollars' . . .": ibid., p. 151.

67 "It is the realization that the future . . .": Blair, p. 399.

68 Joe opened the cover, closed the cover: Krock, *Memoirs*, p. 349.

68 "I can feel Pappy's eyes . . .": Fay, p. 152.

68 "by reason of physical disability": Parmet, *Jack*, p. 128.

68 VISITED WITH HIS FATHER: Blair, p. 422.

68 his introspective nature: Clinch, pp. 115–119.

68 "an inner eye": Goodwin, p. 751. See also Martin, p. 75; Rose Kennedy, p. 326.

69 "There is a heritage of twenty-five years of distrust . . .": Blair, p. 428.

69 "Mustn't expect too much": Schlesinger, *Thousand*, p. 89.

69 He was one of the few journalists: Krock, *Memoirs*, p. 350.

69 "When the war is over . . .": Fay, p. 152.

69 "It was like being drafted . . .": Damore, p. 86.

69 "I got Jack into politics . . .": Whalen, p. 392.

69 The story became a legend: Burns, p. 57.

70 Later . . . both father and son tried to dismiss: Blair, p. 405.

70 controlled by an ambitious, domineering father: Whalen, p. 392.

70 "I guess Dad has decided . . .": Collier and Horowitz, p. 162.

70 "Jack went into politics because young Joe died . . .": McCarthy, p. 16.

70 "My brother Joe was the logical one . . .": Blair, p. 405.

70 "narrow-minded bigoted sons of bitches": Collier and Horowitz, p. 44.

70 who had accepted his wealth but not his religion: *Boston Globe*, p. 15.

70 Yet Boston newspapers had continued to follow Joe's career: Whalen, p. 393.

70 Boston's leading Irish-American family: ibid., p. 393; Burner and West, p. 47.

70 poorest in the state: Parmet, *Jack*, p. 142.

71 "Great Lovers in History . . .": Goodwin, p. 251.

71 hoping their detested rival would be victorious: Blair, p. 449.

71 "How can he lose? . . .": Clinch, p. 120.

71 business-as-usual in Boston politics could no longer be taken for granted: Blair, p. 477; Parmet, *Jack*, pp. 135–136.

72 Jack Kennedy's ability to be among those: Whalen, p. 395.

72 "altogether different from Jack . . .": McCarthy, pp. 16–17.

72 "withdrawn and quiet.": ibid., p. 17.

72 neither he nor Rose could picture their son: ibid., p. 17.

72 Jack just didn't have the traditional backslapping qualities: Whalen, p. 395.

72 "hard-boiled guys.": Meyers, p. 48.

72 "I never thought Jack had it in him": ibid., p. 48.

73 there were two Kennedy headquarters: Whalen, p. 397.

73 the real command post was at the Ritz: ibid., p. 397.

73 behind the scenes, Joseph P. Kennedy: Collier and Horowitz, p. 151.

73 Jack would run as: Blair, pp. 484–485.

73 through his pull in Washington, to get a destroyer named: Collier and Horowitz, p. 150.

73 "We're going to sell Jack . . .": Davis, p. 125; Clinch, pp. 98, 121.

73 "didn't know ten people in Boston": Blair, p. 451.

73 Honey Fitz had become a bit eccentric . . . Jack admitted: Collier and Horowitz, p. 152.

74 wisdom regarding Massachusetts politics: Rose Kennedy, pp. 307–308.

74 "Grampa, remember *I'm* the candidate.": Collier and Horowitz, p. 152. ("Grampa" is the spelling Rose uses when referring to Honey Fitz. Rose Kennedy, pp. 307–308.)

74 "Gramp, notwithstanding the impression . . .": Fay, p. 155.

74 Most of Kane's adult life: O'Donnell and Powers, p. 49.

74 "political engineer": Blair, p. 453.

74 "In politics, you have no friends . . .": ibid., p. 484.

74 Kane took one look . . . and yelled, "Get that son of a bitch . . .": ibid., p. 484.

74 "Who? *GRAMPA?*": ibid., p. 484.

74 "Either he goes or I do.": Collier and Horowitz, p. 152.

74 to meet almost everyone: Blair, p. 486.

74 the older ones wanted to mother him: Rose Kennedy, p. 319.

75 the Eleventh . . . three key areas: for a comprehensive description of the Eleventh Congressional District, see Blair, pp. 477–483.

75 trying to buy a congressional seat: O'Donnell and Powers, p. 66.

76 ill at ease and shy, but *aggressively* shy: O'Donnell and Powers, p. 53.

76 felt sorry for the son of a millionaire: Rose Kennedy, p. 311.

76 "I think I know how you feel . . .": ibid., p. 312.

76 "Then do you think . . ."; "I'm already with you.": O'Donnell and Powers, p. 55.

76 Voters were surprised and flattered: Whalen, p. 400.

76 "as if his life and Jack's . . .": Collier and Horowitz, p. 154.

76 Bobby . . . spaghetti and playing softball: Whalen, p. 401.

77 a greater understanding of politics: Cameron, p. 156; Rose Kennedy, pp. 314–315.

77 "It takes three things to win . . .": Whalen, p. 399.

77 "Regardless of how many young guys . . .": ibid., p. 398.

77 went to bed with their hands outside the covers: Damore, p. 90.

77 the area was saturated: Whalen, p. 399.

77 the wife of one of Jack's opponents: Blair, p. 540.

77 dishes, silverware . . . provided by Joe: Whalen, p. 399.

77 He had spent enough . . . to elect his own chauffeur: Burns, p. 65.

77 "the clincher.": Whalen, p. 401.

77 Seasoned observers . . . chortled: ibid., p. 401.

77 rented finery: Collier and Horowitz, p. 155.

77 just had their hair done: Rose Kennedy, p. 319.

77 his first and last public appearance: Whalen, p. 401.

78 "Daddy, do you really think . . ."; "You must remember . . .": Collier and Horowitz, p. 150.

78 "I'm shadowboxing in a match . . .": ibid., p. 146.

78 "I'm just filling Joe's shoes . . .": Damore, p. 91.

78 how effortlessly Joe Jr. could have met the people in the slums: Whalen, p. 395.

78 "do the job": Collier and Horowitz, p. 154.

78 "Sometimes we all have to do . . .": ibid., p. 154.

78 It was Jack: Whalen, pp. 395, 400; Blair, p. 486; Parmet, *Jack*,

pp. 154–155; O'Donnell and Powers, pp. 63–64.

79 "obligation as a rich man's son . . .": Goodwin, p. 719.

79 "light up the room": Damore, p. 87.

79 "Nobody asked me my address . . .": *Boston Globe*, p. 27.

79 "I seem to be the only person . . .": O'Donnell and Powers, p. 59.

79 ". . . hold it against me.": Martin, p. 45.

79 "Congratulations, John F. . . ."; "Governor? Someday that young man . . .": Rose Kennedy, p. 307.

80 "communism, fascism . . .": Parmet, *Jack*, p. 158.

80 the issue of Jack's wearing a hat: Blair, p. 530.

80 "Well, Mother . . ."; "Dear, it would have looked better . . .": Goodwin, p. 718.

81 became a sort of Washington branch office: Davis, p. 136.

81 paranoia had not yet reached its peak: Blair, p. 575.

82 a "Massachusetts Democrat": Clinch, p. 125.

82 The Wisconsin senator . . . visited . . . dated Patricia: Parmet, *Jack*, p. 172.

82 "into the elevator and asked me . . .": Burns, p. 71.

82 "god-awful.": Blair, p. 581.

83 Joe Kennedy had engineered the award: ibid., p. 585. Parmet, *Jack*, p. 164.

83 "for civic responsibility . . .": Blair, p. 586.

83 had "not had a constructive thought . . .": Burns, p. 75.

83 Friends urged Jack to retract: ibid., p. 76.

83 "Watch this young fellow . . .": Blair, p. 617.

84 KENNEDY COURTS CURLEY VENGEANCE: ibid., p. 629.

84 "a hell of a mistake . . .": Parmet, *Jack*, p. 184.

84 Jack was again on thin ice: Blair, p. 579.

84 to expose subversives . . . threatened economic and political order: Parmet, *Jack*, pp. 177–182.

84 "slave labor bill": ibid., p. 184.

85 Jack's first speech . . . "The grave error . . .": Blair, p. 621.

85 audience of little more than one hundred: *The* (McKeesport) *Daily News*, April 22, 1947, p. 1 (reprinted in *Boston Globe*, p. 28).

85 neither he nor Jack could recall: Blair, pp. 621–622.

86 "I would like to offer a toast . . .": Collier and Horowitz, p. 164.

86 a journey back in time: Burns, p. 3.

86 "surrounded by chickens . . ."; "She had not understood at all . . .": ibid., p. 4.

86 if they had a bathroom: Davis, p. 141.

86 gone "completely English": Collier and Horowitz, p. 164.

86 "It's rather nice not having to be a Kennedy . . .": ibid., p. 165.

87 the largest private residence . . . twenty-two thousand acres . . . one for every day of the year: McTaggart, p. 208.

87 wafers . . . left along the route to the dining hall, in order to find: ibid., p. 208.

87 It was Addison's disease: Blair, p. 646.

87 the adrenal glands, located near the kidneys: ibid., p. 642.

88 "That young American friend of yours . . .": ibid., p. 641.

88 On October 11, Jack sailed home on the *Queen Elizabeth*: Rachlin, p. 105; Parmet, *Jack*, p. 189.

88 once again the saga . . . was trotted out: Blair, p. 649.

88 "while studying labor conditions in Europe.": ibid., p. 649.

88 Jack . . . could not expect to live much past the age of forty: Parmet, *Jack*, p. 191.

88 "decrepit"; "a frail, sick, hollow man.": ibid., p. 165.

88 as long as they were attractive: ibid., p. 167.

88 "a smorgasbord": Burner and West, p. 51.

89 she would never see Kick again: McTaggart, p. 224.

89 she would leave him . . . publicly embarrass him: ibid., p. 224.

89 "especially special": Collier and Horowitz, "The Kennedy Kick," *Vanity Fair*, July 1983, p. 50.

89 "everything," Jack said, "moving in their direction.": Burns, p. 54.

89 he was living every day as if it was his last: Collier and Horowitz, p. 172.

89 "Well, I guess if you don't want to work for a living . . .": ibid., p. 172.

90 going through the motions: Parmet, *Jack*, p. 195.

90 the standard treatment . . . DOCA pellets implanted in the thigh: Blair, pp. 647–648.

90 safety deposit boxes all across the country: ibid., p. 648.

90 "almost magical.": ibid., p. 648.

91 "notable chiefly for its high absenteeism.": George V. Higgins, "Challenging the Kennedy 'Magic'," *NYT Magazine*, August 3, 1986, p. 21.

91 "hustle for three years": Burner and West, p. 52.

91 Jack Kennedy's . . . seat was safe as long as he wanted to stay in it: Whalen, p. 412.

91 "We're worms over in the House . . .": Burns, p. 93.

92 McCarthy . . . anticipating the 1952 election . . . looking for a campaign gimmick: Reeves, p. 200.

92 touched off years of communist witch hunting: Cook, p. 15.

92 "While I cannot take the time . . .": Reeves, p. 224.

92 McCarthy's startling charge: ibid., pp. 224–225.

92 "an old laundry list.": Cook, p. 16.

93 Within a week . . . a star of national headlines: Reeves, p. 233.

93 frequent host in Hyannis Port— where the Wisconsin senator even suffered a cracked rib: ibid., p. 203.

93 Joe contributed to McCarthy's cause: Parmet, *Jack*, p. 173.

93 as well as to the campaign fund of Republican Richard Nixon: ibid., p. 189.

93 In every race . . . the candidate who could sling the most red mud won: Reeves, p. 343.

93 "police action": Jones, p. 443.

94 "may have something." He also expressed his pleasure at Richard Nixon's victory: Parmet, *Jack*, p. 212.

94 "Tuesday to Thursday Club": Whalen, p. 416.

94 Having beaten four opponents . . . with five times . . . their votes, he had gone on to trounce the Republican . . . five to one: Rose Kennedy, p. 320.

94 Joe made sure his son's conferences were well covered: Parmet, *Jack*, pp. 217–218.

94 kept the two brothers from getting to know each other: Schlesinger, *Kennedy*, p. 96.

95 "a pain in the ass.": Collier and Horowitz, p. 181.

95 America . . . preached freedom and independence: Damore, pp. 104–105.

95 Communism would thrive . . . in an atmosphere of discontent: Schlesinger, *Kennedy*, p. 95.

95 "to die for.": ibid., p. 95.

95 Democracy must . . . be given that same aura . . . "We have only status quo . . .": ibid., p. 95.

95 Vietnam's Declaration of Independence, modeled on that of the United States, began "All men are created equal . . .": Schlesinger, *Heritage*, p. 4.

95 Ho . . . "an agent of world communism.": ibid., p. 4.

95 French were "an integral part of the world-wide resistance . . .": ibid., pp. 4–5.

95 "As it stands now . . ."; Seventy percent of the Vietnamese: Schlesinger, *Kennedy*, p. 96.

96 "quite unpopular"; "It doesn't seem to be a picture . . .": ibid., p. 96.

96 The Asian trip made a major impression: ibid., p. 97.

96 "Communism cannot be met . . ."; to build strong non-Communist sentiment; "too ready to buttress . . ."; "with the 'haves' . . .": ibid., pp. 96–97.

96 "We cannot reform the

world . . ."; "The things we cannot and must not do . . .": Damore, pp. 104–105.

96 to speak . . . in . . . 39 cities and 312 towns: O'Donnell and Powers, p. 81.

96 Jack told Dave Powers he would announce . . . as soon as the map was covered: ibid., p. 79.

96 compiled an index card file: ibid., pp. 79–80.

96 the nucleus of . . . the "Kennedy machine": Collier and Horowitz, p. 183.

97 "inferior peoples whose prolific issue . . .": Cameron, p. 25.

97 "ancestral portraits . . .": Rose Kennedy, p. 49.

97 "Do you think . . . Jews and Italians . . .": Collier and Horowitz, p. 30.

97 "As much right as your father or mine . . . It was only a difference . . .": Cameron, p. 33.

97 It had been Henry Cabot Lodge, Jr. who persuaded . . . Eisenhower: Brendon, pp. 211–212; Krock, *Memoirs*, p. 284.

98 "Tell Joe not to waste his money . . .": Whalen, p. 417.

98 "When you've beaten him . . .": ibid., p. 419.

98 "knock Lodge's block off.": Collier and Horowitz, p. 184.

98 Bobby asked . . . Kenneth O'Donnell: Schlesinger, *Kennedy*, p. 98.

98 Joe knew nothing "about politics . . .": ibid., p. 98.

98 "Don't drag me into it": O'Donnell and Powers, p. 83.

98 "absolute, catastrophic disaster": Schlesinger, *Kennedy*, p. 98.

98 "screw it up": ibid., p. 98.

99 "In return for one Irishman . . .": O'Donnell and Powers, p. 85.

99 "that Bobby had all this tremendous ability.": Schlesinger, *Kennedy*, p. 100.

99 "If you're not going to work . . .": ibid., p. 99.

99 a soon-to-be-famous image . . . Bobby Kennedy was "ruthless.": ibid., p. 99.

99 "I don't care if anybody around here likes me . . .": O'Donnell and Powers, p. 89.

99 "I know you're an important man . . ."; "Keep that fresh kid of yours . . .": Whalen, p. 421.

99 "I don't want my brother to get mixed up with politicians!": Collier and Horowitz, p. 185.

99 "My brother Jack couldn't be here . . .": Burns, p. 114.

100 Ethel . . . campaigned . . . up to the last possible moment: Collier and Horowitz, p. 187.

100 She "wowed them everywhere": McCarthy, p. 103.

100 In poor neighborhoods, simply dressed in a skirt and blouse: ibid., p. 103; Martin, p. 53; Cameron, pp. 163–164.

100 "Your son owes me one dollar and sixty-five cents.": Cameron, p. 166. Rose Kennedy, p. 311, gives a different version of this story.

100 one of his mother's ubiquitous notes: ibid., p. 164; see also Rose Kennedy, p. 359.

100 "Greetings. You have just made a political contribution.": Collier and Horowitz, p. 185.

101 the financially strapped *Boston Post* . . . received a half-million-dollar loan: Whalen, p. 430.

101 McCarthy . . . a three-thousand-dollar contribution: ibid., p. 427.

101 Despite his many avid admirers . . . the Wisconsin senator declined to campaign for . . . Lodge: Reeves, p. 442; Parmet, *Jack*, p. 249.

101 Joe also paid for almost a million copies: Whalen, p. 423.

101 "John Fulfills Dream of Brother Joe . . .": Collier and Horowitz, p. 188.

101 Inserted in each paper: Whalen, p. 423.

101 Having read an article about Jack in . . . *Time*: Goodwin, p. 766.

101 Hanani wrote that . . . Jack's election . . . a way of promoting "genuine friendship . . .": Damore, p. 126.

101 attributed to his ordeal in the Solomon Islands: Parmet, *Jack*, p. 239.

101 crutches . . . concealed in the car, gritting his teeth . . . closing

his eyes: O'Donnell and Powers, p. 79.

101 "extraordinarily likable.": Parmet, *Jack*, p. 253.

102 had found his opponents' faults and campaigned on them. But in Jack's case: ibid., p. 253.

102 Since there were few ideological differences . . . the campaign came down to one of personalities: Burns, p. 116.

102 Too late, he realized the entire state . . . was under siege: Whalen, p. 431.

102 the Kennedy family had shaken the hands of more than two million voters: ibid., pp. 431–432.

102 "Reception in honor of . . .": Burns, p. 113.

102 a veteran newspaper reporter . . . said "It was all they could do to keep those old gals . . . from curtsying.": Whalen, p. 432.

102 "What is there about Jack Kennedy . . .": ibid., p. 432.

102 he had shaken hands with more than 70,000; defeated his opponent by 70,737: Rose Kennedy, p. 326, O'Donnell and Powers, p. 89.

102 "It was those damned tea parties!": Whalen, p. 433.

102 Eisenhower . . . had taken the state by 208,800: Burns, p. 115.

102 "At last . . . the Fitzgeralds have evened the score . . .": Whalen, p. 434.

103 the new senator elect sang "Sweet Adeline.": Collier and Horowitz, p. 189.

104 "bumper crop . . .", "long convertible . . ."; "photographed with . . ."; "just about the most eligible bachelor . . .": Parmet, *Jack*, p. 258.

104 wearing a necktie . . . "Kennedy for President.": Whalen, p. 438.

104 It was time to put the playboy image behind him: Parmet, *Jack*, p. 258.

105 He had waged two campaigns the previous year: O'Donnell and Powers, p. 94.

105 the Bouviers through four generations in America: for a complete history of the American

Bouviers, see John H. Davis, *The Bouviers*. New York: Farrar, Straus & Giroux, 1969.

105 went into the mass production: Davis, p. 163.

105 By 1848, when Patrick Kennedy was bound for Boston: ibid., p. 163.

105 vast amounts of West Virginia coal land: ibid., p. 163; Birmingham, p. 20.

105 her father was estimated to be worth seven and a half million dollars, all made in the stock market: Birmingham, p. 7.

105 the same amount Joe Kennedy had amassed: Davis, p. 164.

105 by the 1930s, the Kennedy fortune far surpassed that of the Bouviers: ibid., p. 165.

105 The strain of their financial problems, along with Jack's fondness: ibid., pp. 176 177.

106 concealed the family's background: ibid., p. 170.

106 His mother-in-law was never allowed to meet guests: ibid., p. 171.

106 she was descended from "the Lees of Maryland," implying these nonexistent ancestors: Birmingham, pp. 9–10.

106 "leaned across the asparagus": Burns, p. 127.

106 "spasmodic courtship . . . He'd call me from some oyster bar up there . . .": ibid., p. 127.

107 When Jack telephoned her in London: Birmingham, p. 71.

107 she "has a tendency to think I'm not good enough . . .": Fay, p. 160.

107 The Kennedys were a step down socially: Davis, p. 212.

107 The marriage would bring Jacqueline immediate wealth: ibid., p. 213.

107 he was often mistaken for Clark Gable: Birmingham, p. 7.

107 "Kennedy" was a dirty word: ibid., p. 26.

107 "They talked about politics . . .": Parmet, *Jack*, p. 259.

108 the "rah rah girls": Davis, p. 160.

108 "a sorority hazing.": Collier and Horowitz, p. 193.

108 "The Debutante.": ibid., p. 193.
108 "Jacqueline" with . . . French pronunciation . . . "rhymes with queen": ibid., p. 193.
108 Ethel, who prided herself on being more Kennedy than the Kennedys: ibid., p. 193.
108 "With those feet of yours? . . .": ibid., p. 193.
108 "fell all over each other like gorillas.": ibid., p. 193.
108 she would enhance their social image as well as further Jack's political career: Davis, p. 213.
108 Jack Bouvier . . . was too drunk to show up: Birmingham, pp. 73–74. See Davis, pp. 214–222, for the reasons behind Bouvier's behavior.
108 which Joe made sure was well publicized: Davis, pp. 216–217.
108 the "Wedding of the Year": Birmingham, p. 72.
108 Before eight hundred notable guests . . . the father of the bride had been taken ill: NYT, September 12, 1953 (reprinted in Meyers, p. 68).
109 "too tanned and too handsome to be believed": Parmet, Jack, p. 261.
109 his face was scratched from . . . a rose bush: McCarthy, p. 114.
109 The newlyweds made a difficult adjustment: Burns, p. 131.
109 changes made him feel like "a transient.": Collier and Horowitz, p. 196.
109 As the wife of a well-known senator . . . Jackie soon realized the role: Parmet, Jack, pp. 296–298.
109 "I don't think there are any men . . ."; "Men are such a combination . . .": Collier and Horowitz, p. 197.
109 "so disciplined in so many ways . . .": ibid., p. 197.
110 Jackie was left alone at parties: ibid., p. 197.
110 "took a chair, turned it towards a corner . . .": Martin, p. 89.
110 "The trouble with you, Jackie . . ."; "The trouble with you, Jack . . .": ibid., p. 111.
110 "You're too old . . ."; "Well, you're too young . . .": ibid., p. 111.
110 she grimly responded, "I can't say I have any yet.": ibid., p. 89.
110 "wandering around looking like the survivor . . .": Collier and Horowitz, p. 197.
110 a registered pacifist and civil rights activist years before either cause was popular: Parmet, Jack, p. 264.
111 "an odd duck": ibid., p. 264.
111 "You've got to remember . . .": Collier and Horowitz, p. 198.
111 "to work on the legislative program . . .": Parmet, Jack, p. 265.
111 became an expert on . . . a region he had at first known little about: Burns, p. 123.
111 "The Suicide Senator": McCarthy, p. 130.
111 over and over again for twenty years . . . every senator and representative . . . voted against it: Sorensen, p. 58.
111 what was good for any area . . . would ultimately benefit the country as a whole: Parmet, Jack, p. 271.
111 the Chicago Merchandise Mart . . . greatest source of income: Whalen, pp. 379–380.
111 "ruining New England": Sorensen, p. 59.
112 "a turning point in the Seaway debate . . .": ibid., p. 59.
112 under the byline of Senator John F. Kennedy: Collier and Horowitz, pp. 198–199.
112 "Tuesday to Thursday Club": Whalen, p. 416.
112 "to enter the jungle . . .": Parmet, Jack, p. 285.
112 "no amount of American military assistance . . .": ibid., p. 284.
113 "deceived for political reasons . . .": ibid., p. 285.
113 "Keep your eye on young Democratic Senator . . .": ibid., p. 286.
113 "couldn't tie his own tie": Martin, p. 89.
113 "Make sure the socks Jack wears . . .": Rose Kennedy, p. 359.
113 Jack paid a high price: Parmet, Jack, p. 287.

113 he weighed only 140 pounds and was . . . using crutches: Meyers, p. 77.

113 he would rather die: McCarthy, p. 115.

113 It would be years before many liberal Democrats would forgive Jack: Burns, pp. 149–154.

114 At the start . . . he was probably no more anticommunist: Reeves, p. 200.

114 Truman's . . . had been "crawling with Communists.": ibid., p. 530.

115 By mid-1953, Joe McCarthy was at the height of his power: Burns, p. 136.

115 to criticize McCarthy might be construed as being "soft" on communism: Reeves, pp. 330–331.

115 To keep in the public eye, McCarthy had to make new . . . discoveries: Cook, p. 24.

115 communist infiltration of the United States Army: Schlesinger, Kennedy, p. 114.

115 But Eisenhower . . . refused to "get into the gutter with that guy.": Hughes, p. 92.

115 the Senate ordered a hearing to uncover the truth: Cook, p. 33.

115 heavy drinking: Reeves, p. 586.

115 His temper, his scowling face . . . to make him seem "the perfect stock villain.": ibid., p. 597; see also Schlesinger, Kennedy, p. 118.

115 Senator Karl Mundt . . . usually allowed McCarthy to speak: Cook, p. 9.

116 "Point of order, Mr. Chairman . . ."; His often irrelevant interruptions: Schlesinger, Kennedy, p. 118.

116 "Point of order . . ." became a national joke . . . fear had been replaced with laughter: Reeves, p. 597.

116 denounced the new committee as the "involuntary agent": Cook, p. 58.

116 Even his remaining admirers: ibid., p. 58.

116 a move . . . postponed until after Election Day: Reeves, pp. 651–652.

116 "the blackest act . . .": ibid., p. 662.

116 A woman . . . photographing the event for Life . . . led out amid cries of "Hang the Communist.": ibid., p. 662.

116 "Defeat the Republican congressional candidates . . .": ibid., p. 654.

116 Nixon . . . warning that Democrats tolerated internal subversion: ibid., p. 654.

117 twenty-two Republicans voting for . . . twenty-two against; McCarthy himself . . . voted "present"; forty-four Democrats . . . supported: ibid., p. 662.

117 might "have something": Parmet, Jack, p. 212.

117 Since then, he had neither given: Burns, pp. 141 143, 149.

117 There was the fact that his brother had worked for McCarthy's subcommittee: Whalen, p. 437.

117 appointment engineered by Joe: Schlesinger, Kennedy, p. 104.

117 "headed for disaster.": ibid., p. 109.

117 affable men who often behaved abominably and were surprised when someone took it personally: ibid., p. 110 (re McCarthy); Whalen, p. 328 (re Kennedy).

117 Roosevelt and . . . Eisenhower likened McCarthy to Hitler.: Reeves, p. 497 (re Roosevelt); Brendon, p. 275 (re Eisenhower).

117 When McCarthy eventually died of cirrhosis: Reeves, p. 672 (quoting Time).

117 "In case there is any question . . . I liked Joe McCarthy.": Whalen, p. 427.

118 he was warned his chances . . . were fifty-fifty: O'Donnell and Powers, p. 99.

118 a urinary tract infection developed and Jack slipped into a coma: Parmet, Jack, p. 309.

118 the only time . . . Joe had shown an emotion that equaled his response to the death of Joe Jr.: Krock, Memoirs, p. 349.

118 Jack "fought his way out of it": Whalen, p. 442.

118 A friend described his room as . . . one in a college dormitory: Collier and Horowitz, p. 204.

118 Jackie dropped in . . . to play checkers or Monopoly: Martin, p. 83.

118 too ill to confront the issue: Burns, p. 148.

118 young women . . . were "cousins.": Collier and Horowitz, p. 204.

118 he could certainly not have stood alone: Sorensen, p. 49; O'Donnell and Powers, p. 99.

119 "When I get downstairs I know exactly what's going to happen . . .": Parmet, *Jack*, p. 310.

119 Jack might never walk again: Collier and Horowitz, p. 205.

119 "It was a terrible time . . .": ibid., p. 205.

119 "I don't think I know anyone who has more courage . . .": Whalen, p. 442.

119 a silver plate . . . had . . . made his condition worse. Now . . . a bone graft: Parmet, *Jack*, p. 312.

119 Grace Kelly to wear a nurse's uniform . . . "I must be losing it.": Collier and Horowitz, p. 205.

119 "I know nothing can happen to him now . . .": O'Donnell and Powers, p. 102.

119 A hopeful bulletin . . . announced he planned to return . . . in March: Parmet, *Jack*, p. 312.

120 house was converted to . . . a hospital wing: Collier and Horowitz, p. 205.

120 a loose screw . . . resulted in a bad fall: Parmet, *Jack*, p. 313.

120 could sleep no more than an hour or two . . .; "That's where the book came from": Whalen, p. 442.

120 Jack had to work lying on a board: Krock, *Memoirs*, p. 354.

120 the final result would not be the effort of a single author: Parmet, *Jack*, pp. 324–327.

120 Sorensen . . . worked on the manuscript in Palm Beach: ibid., p. 327.

120 Schlesinger . . . Davids . . . several people: ibid., pp. 325–328.

120 Jackie had seldom left his bedside: Martin, p. 84.

120 She changed his dressings: Rose Kennedy, p. 353.

120 Jackie had suffered a miscarriage: Davis, p. 226.

120 He had used them . . . because he was afraid he couldn't kneel gracefully: Parmet, *Jack*, p. 319.

121 "conditions in Communist Poland.": ibid., p. 318.

121 Sorensen's "invaluable assistance" and of Jacqueline's "help during all the days . . .": *Profiles*, p. 17.

121 had written so thoughtfully . . . "about political integrity . . .": Parmet, *Jack*, p. 320.

121 "In the days ahead, only the very courageous . . .": *Profiles*, p. 39.

121 "A man does what he must . . ."; "supply courage itself. For this . . . each man must look into his own soul.": ibid., p. 266.

122 To many who were aware of Jack's schedule, it seemed unlikely: Parmet, *Jack*, p. 331.

122 Jack was irate. *Profiles in Courage* was a tribute to integrity, and now: Sorensen, pp. 68–69.

122 Sorensen made a sworn statement . . . ABC apologized: ibid., p. 69.

122 the retraction . . . had been written . . . by Ted Sorensen: ibid., p. 70.

122 "The concept of the book was Kennedy's . . .": Parmet, *Jack*, p. 324.

122 "too much profile . . .": Collier and Horowitz, p. 240.

123 "Leave it alone and don't get into the gutter . . .": O'Donnell and Powers, p. 105.

123 Adlai is "going to take a licking.": Whalen, p. 443.

124 not to "mention my name to anybody": O'Donnell and Powers, p. 106.

124 Joe Kennedy had given the *Boston Post* a half-million-dollar loan: Whalen, pp. 429–431. Privately, Jack told a journalist his father had virtually "bought" the paper.

124 in one front-page editorial after another: Sorensen, p. 78.

124 both Kennedy and Stevenson had socialist tendencies: O'Donnell and Powers, p. 108.

124 implied that Senator Kennedy was soft on communism: Parmet, *Jack*, p. 350.

124 "the gloves came off.": O'Donnell and Powers, p. 109.

124 "he hasn't got enough money to buy me.": Burns, p. 179.

124 "one thousand percent": ibid., p. 178.

125 "sudden entry into an intra-party dispute . . .": Parmet, *Jack*, p. 352.

125 Irish politician . . . Jack had always taken pains to avoid: O'Donnell and Powers, p. 112.

125 "They don't want you pushing one of your bright new faces . . .": ibid., p. 111.

125 timing could not have been less convenient: Parmet, *Jack*, pp. 353–354.

125 "a brawl of monumental proportions": O'Donnell and Powers, p. 116.

125 "a great victory in Massachusetts . . .": ibid., p. 116.

125 "Let's not try to kid anybody . . .": ibid., p. 116.

126 "All of us who were in contact with him . . .": Parmet, *Jack*, p. 357.

126 "Kennedy came before the convention tonight . . .": ibid., p. 367.

127 "I think he just wanted to put his foot in the water . . .": Schlesinger, *Kennedy*, p. 136

127 "an attitude of coolness . . .": Parmet, *Jack*, p. 370.

127 "terribly thin, terribly tired . . .": Martin, p. 95.

127 He had been persistently criticized . . . for being indecisive: Krock, *In the Nation*, p. 315.

128 "The choice will be yours . . . The profit . . .": Whitman and *NYT*, p. 154.

128 Jack nevertheless was going to "swim.": Schlesinger, *Kennedy*, p. 137.

128 Bobby . . . was asked for his autograph: O'Donnell and Powers, p. 121.

128 "Tell him I'm going for it.": ibid., p. 122.

128 "blue language.": ibid., p. 122.

128 Jack was "an idiot": ibid., p. 122.

128 he said "vigorously.": Rose Kennedy, p. 328.

128 "Whew! . . . Is he mad!": O'Donnell and Powers, p. 122.

128 "Let's go.": Sorensen, p. 90.

129 "Ladies and gentlemen of this convention . . .": Burns, p. 190.

129 "a moment of magic . . .": Martin, p. 104.

129 "the Indian who had a lot of arrows . . .": Parmet, *Jack*, p. 380.

129 "We did our best . . .": Whalen, p. 444.

129 "You wouldn't believe it . . .": O'Donnell and Powers, p. 126.

129 "Stevenson was just not a man of action . . .": Schlesinger, *Kennedy*, p. 141.

129 to a Kennedy . . . the worst thing one could say: Collier and Horowitz, p. 209.

129 "Don't feel sorry for young Jack Kennedy . . .": Parmet, *Jack*, p. 382.

130 "I have a feeling that he was the real hero . . .": ibid., p. 382.

130 "Joe was the star of our family . . .": Whalen, p. 444.

130 pick up "all of the marbles.": O'Donnell and Powers, p. 128.

131 "I see Dad's roughing it . . .": Collier and Horowitz, p. 209.

131 "God is still with you . . .": Whalen, p. 444.

131 Having received his father's blessing: Collier and Horowitz, p. 209.

131 "You knew that it you were in trouble . . .": Schlesinger, *Kennedy*, p. 138.

131 get "back to your wife . . .": Martin, p. 157.

131 Although Jackie had stayed by her husband's bedside: ibid., p. 157.

131 "a lousy husband" who had inherited not only his father's . . . "love for women": ibid., p. 82.

132 Next to her husband and her own father . . . "I love him more than anybody . . .": ibid., p. 85.

132 Joe Kennedy . . . offered her a

million-dollar bribe: Parmet, *JFK*, p. 110; Martin, p. 111.

132 He had turned forty . . . his well-known detachment: Parmet, *Jack*, p. 416.

133 Nineteen fifty-seven was . . . the most exciting time: O'Donnell and Powers, p. 129.

133 "Now I know his religion won't keep him out . . .": ibid., p. 129.

133 "Jack Kennedy has left panting politicians . . .": McCarthy, p. 126.

133 "confidently look forward to the day . . .": Sorensen, p. 35.

133 the presidential nomination would go to "Kennedy, period.": McCarthy, p. 126.

134 inundated with twenty-five hundred speaking invitations . . . accepted one hundred forty-four: ibid., p. 126.

134 "autographing pictures of himself.": Martin, p. 90.

134 a logical extension of his interest in Vietnam: Sorensen, p. 65.

134 "America's role in the continuing struggle . . .": Parmet, *Jack*, p. 401.

134 "the senator from Algeria.": ibid., p. 407.

134 Jack . . . could not logically condemn French colonialism . . . while ignoring Soviet treatment: ibid., p. 407.

134 Criticizing Russia was always a reasonably safe tactic: Halberstam, p. 95.

135 "Hunger has never been a weapon . . .": Parmet, *Jack*, p. 400.

135 New York gangsters were muscling in on unions: Guthman, p. 8.

135 The new organization had done little to curb wrongdoing . . . no effective laws to police union behavior: Schlesinger, *Kennedy*, p. 143.

136 knowing almost nothing about labor itself . . . still less about the Teamsters: ibid., p. 144.

136 Teamster management . . . involved in illegal financial dealings . . . violently enforce its policies: ibid., p. 148; Guthman, pp. 6–11.

136 Leading the opposition: Collier and Horowitz, pp. 219–220.

136 "some apprehensions about this . . .": Collier and Horowitz, p. 229.

136 "If the investigation flops . . .": O'Donnell and Powers, p. 132.

136 Beck was "a crook": Schlesinger, *Kennedy*, p. 149.

136 Its public hearings, which opened in February: Guthman, p. 34.

136 "the biggest, most spectacular congressional investigation . . .": Parmet, *Jack*, p. 423.

137 After a prolonged "vacation" out of the country: Collier and Horowitz, p. 220.

137 "the finest job I've ever seen done . . .": Schlesinger, *Kennedy*, p. 155.

137 Beck . . . sent to prison for larceny and income tax evasion: ibid., p. 155.

137 "If he's still at work . . .": Salinger, p. 19.

137 The Teamster leader regarded Bobby as a "spoiled jerk": Schlesinger, *Kennedy*, p. 160.

137 "far more sinister": ibid., p. 170.

137 underworld figures, all with some connection to Hoffa: Blakey and Billing, p. 193.

137 Sam Giancana, a friend of Frank Sinatra: Powers, p. 360.

137 and leader of organized crime in Chicago: Blakey and Billings, p. 54.

137 had used the local Brotherhood of Electrical Workers: Schlesinger, *Kennedy*, p. 172.

137 Red Dorfman . . . head of the mob-dominated . . . Union: Blakey and Billings, p. 284.

137 One person the police questioned . . . was Jack Rubenstein: ibid., p. 284; Schlesinger, *Kennedy*, p. 171.

137 "To the best of my recollection . . .": Schlesinger, *Kennedy*, p. 164.

138 Bobby was also exasperated with the FBI . . . and with the Justice Department: ibid., pp. 176, 190.

138 In spite of the hearings, Hoffa was elected president . . . Beck was given a fifty-thousand-dollar annual pension: Guthman, pp. 65–67.
The Teamsters' expulsion from the AFL-CIO ended in October 1987, when the union was reaffiliated with that organization.

138 Committee had changed nothing: he was still in charge . . . Bobby was still trying "to elect his brother . . .": Collier and Horowitz, p. 227.

138 Jimmy Hoffa was . . . evil: Schlesinger, *Kennedy*, pp. 169–170.

138 Hoffa supported Republican candidates: ibid., p. 177.

138 "close family life.": Collier and Horowitz, p. 222.

138 seldom called strikes . . . declared his belief in free enterprise: Schlesinger, *Kennedy*, pp. 146, 177.

138 condemned union leaders . . . to bring about social and economic changes: ibid., p. 177.

138 "We both recognize that in the writing in the clouds . . .": ibid., p. 177.

138 Hoffa claimed the Kennedys had set out to destroy his organization: O'Donnell and Powers, p. 133.

138 played on this fear . . . Reuther "the leader of Soviet America.": Schlesinger, *Kennedy*, p. 177.

138 "ignored continual demands . . .": ibid., p. 181.

139 the issue was more appropriate to bargaining table negotiation: O'Donnell and Powers, p. 134.

139 "fourteenth century attitude toward labor unions.": ibid., p. 134.

139 eight straight hours in one-hundred-degree heat . . . a break of two to five minutes: ibid., p. 134; Schlesinger, *Kennedy*, p. 183.

139 "sensational developments": O'Donnell and Powers, p. 135.

139 Brotz had died . . . the wrong column of figures: ibid., p. 135.

139 Republicans . . . began to stall . . . Goldwater no longer wanted to call Reuther: ibid., pp. 135–136.

139 what was essentially Bobby's show: Parmet, *Jack*, p. 420.

139 "build his United Auto Workers . . .": ibid., pp. 420–421.

139 Jack was furious . . . after five heated closed sessions: O'Donnell and Powers, p. 136.

140 "that all the dead people . . ."; "Oh, my God . . ."; ibid., p. 137.

140 "My brother's name was Joe . . .": Parmet, *Jack*, p. 422.

140 Kohler . . . found guilty of unfair labor practices . . . largest back payment sum in American history: Schlesinger, *Kennedy*, p. 188.

140 penetrating questioning of witnesses, had been the "star": O'Donnell and Powers, p. 137.

140 a "saint towards the UAW": Parmet, *Jack*, p. 423.

140 his own philosophical movement leftward: Burner and West, p. 77.

140 They were the people Jack Kennedy needed . . . the active intellectuals and professionals who . . . played a disproportionate role: ibid., pp. 79–80; Parmet, *Jack*, p. 440.

141 "All those men who had once been quite snotty . . .": Collier and Horowitz, p. 233.

141 the first member . . . to appoint a black: Sorensen, p. 49.

141 the money from his . . . award to the United Negro College Fund: Burns, p. 162.

141 Senator Eastland . . . would support Kennedy: Parmet, *Jack*, p. 409.

141 a motion . . . that gave the attorney general broad powers: ibid., p. 410; Burner and West, p. 60.

142 "to be on both sides at the same time" and wondered if . . . "more important to his career . . .": Parmet, *Jack*, pp. 411–412.

142 "received a terrific shock . . .": ibid., p. 412.

142 Arkansas National Guard to prevent enrollment of nine black students: Brendon, p. 344.

142 Faubus withdrew the Guardsmen, allowing a white mob to take control: ibid., p. 345.

142 That defiance . . . brought Southern fury to a level not seen since the days of Reconstruction: ibid., p. 346; Parmet, *Jack*, p. 413.

142 "to uphold law and order . . .": Parmet, *Jack*, p. 414.

142 "Thank you, Mr. Kennedy" said one caustic newspaper editorial: ibid., p. 414.

143 warnings of a "missile gap" began to be heard: ibid., p. 443.

143 a "wave of near hysteria.": Brendon, p. 348.

143 the nation was questioning: Burner and West, pp. 66–67, 69.

143 Jack was among the first to publicly fault the educational system: ibid., p. 66.

143 "lack of high quality education" . . . lead to "the undoing of our nation.": Parmet, *Jack*, p. 388.

143 "superiority in nuclear striking power" and . . . "a peril more deadly . . .": Collier and Horowitz, p. 232.

143 Lyndon Johnson . . . suggesting that Bobby Kennedy be put in charge: Schlesinger, *Kennedy*, p. 157.

143 "more dynamic leadership.": Brendon, p. 348.

144 "Jimmy Hoffa can rejoice . . .": Parmet, *Jack*, pp. 432–433.

144 His career . . . "really took off": Collier and Horowitz, p. 229n.

144 "The Rise of the Brothers Kennedy" which included sixteen photographs: Parmet, *Jack*, p. 438.

144 "trustworthy, loyal, brave . . .": ibid., p. 437.

144 Washington's "hottest tourist attraction.": ibid., p. 437.

144 some . . . regarded Jack as a celebrity rather than . . . worthy of consideration: ibid., p. 438.

144 "Month after month, from the glossy pages of *Life* . . .": ibid., p. 438.

144 "has three strikes against him: religion . . .": ibid., p. 440.

145 "they can't stop us for the presidency.": Whalen, p. 448.

145 to get the kind of record-breaking showing Jack needed to impress national Democratic leaders: O'Donnell and Powers, p. 139.

145 The candidate himself, sensitive to Adlai Stevenson's remark: ibid., p. 139.

145 "When Jackie was traveling with us . . .": ibid., p. 142.

145 "You really want *all* of the votes . . .": ibid., p. 143.

146 "I proudly call home": Damore, p. 161.

146 the first major Democrat to ever win . . . Cape Cod: ibid., p. 163.

146 "the Kennedy compound.": Rose Kennedy, p. 355.

146 would "keep the Kennedys together in the future.": Collier and Horowitz, p. 218.

146 "This is the most exclusive club in the world.": ibid., p. 218.

147 "nothing takes precedence over his oath . . .": Burns, pp. 243–244.

147 "If he is willing to answer questions on his views . . .": McCarthy, p. 141.

148 liberals were . . . less honest: Burner and West, p. 81.

148 she made no secret of her belief: Burns, p. 243; Burner and West, pp. 152–153.

148 "someone who understands what courage is . . ."; "oodles of money . . .": Whalen, p. 449; Parmet, *Jack*, p. 463.

148 challenged her to name "one such example . . .": Parmet, *Jack*, p. 463.

148 "commonly accepted as a fact.": ibid., p. 463.

148 "I am disappointed that you now seem to accept . . .": Burner and West, p. 80.

148 "I like Jack . . . But I don't like his daddy . . .": Whalen, p. 449.

148 "I'm not against the Pope . . .": Davis, p. 241.

148 "We send all our bills to Daddy . . .": Parmet, *Jack*, p. 439.

148 "I have just received the following wire . . .": ibid., p. 439.

149 "Let's not con ourselves . . .": Whalen, p. 450.

149 "average guy": McCarthy, p. 143.
149 "I have withdrawn completely from public life": Parmet, *Jack*, p. 437.
149 The plane . . . gave him a significant advantage: ibid., p. 512.
149 Mindful of the tapes: ibid., p. 523; Davis, pp. 234–235.
150 Joe's influential contacts in the press: Davis, p. 232.
150 Stories about the Kennedys appeared in *Life, Redbook*, etc.: ibid., p. 232.
150 "getting sick" of all those magazines . . . he replied, "These stories about me . . .": Martin, p. 107.
150 "did not intend to sacrifice . . .": Parmet, *Jack*, p. 441.
150 a "political banana peel.": Martin, p. 121.
151 "I have realized more and more . . .": ibid., p. 122.
151 he had kept the act from being a total disaster for labor: Parmet, *Jack*, p. 497.
151 The AFL-CIO called the new legislation worse than . . . Taft-Hartley: ibid., p. 497; Burns, p. 228.
151 "outstandingly provided" skill in the art of compromise: Burns, p. 228.
151 Jack Kennedy could fall into a well and come up dry: Martin, p. 121.
151 a "five-ring circus": Burns, p. 215.
151 Jacqueline hoped to provide . . . a restful setting: ibid., p. 216.
151 Caroline's first six words: ibid., p. 217.
152 he amazed fifteen advisors: White, *1960*, pp. 53–54.
152 His knowledge . . . was "remarkable.": ibid., p. 54.
152 He was aware of every delegate situation: Sorensen, p. 120; Burns, p. 234.
152 couldn't "match his knowledge . . .": Sorensen, p. 121.
152 An unofficial campaign headquarters, with only Steve Smith's name on the door: Parmet, *Jack*, p. 507.
152 divided the country into regions: ibid., p. 507.

152 more than forty thousand supporters: Collier and Horowitz, p. 236.
152 Four secretaries; Rows of filing cabinets; state maps: Burns, p. 233.
153 "still looks like a Harvard graduate student . . .": ibid., p. 259. Jack's office even received a suggestion that his current publicity photo . . . be scrapped: Parmet, *Jack*, p. 513.
153 "Do you think a 42-year-old . . ."; "I don't know about a 42-year-old . . .": ibid., pp. 438–439.
153 "There's no need to go outside of the family . . .": McCarthy, p. 143.
153 "He is," Joe agreed. "But I'm seventy-two . . .": Whalen, p. 450.
153 "Jack is the greatest attraction . . .": ibid., p. 446.
153 "And the others—the ones you *can* hire . . .": ibid., p. 446.
153 the "first and only choice": Sorensen, p. 117.
153 could be "trusted more implicitly . . .": Schlesinger, *Kennedy*, p. 201.
153 "All right, Jack, what has been done . . .": Fay, p. 6.
154 "Jack, how do you expect to run . . .": ibid., pp. 6–7.
154 "How would you like looking forward to that voice . . .": ibid., p. 7.
154 "we've been able to do a few things in your absence.": ibid., p. 7.
154 "compensate for a lot of other things.": Martin, p. 108.
154 "I am announcing today . . .": ibid., p. 123.
155 "If I were Protestant . . .": *Boston Globe*, p. 34.
155 more than twice the previous record: Sorensen, pp. 132–133.
155 would have the nomination wrapped up: White, *1960*, p. 85.
156 "My name is John Kennedy . . ."; "President of what?": O'Donnell and Powers, p. 153.
156 "the difference between the kinds of farms": Sorensen, p. 134.

156 It was a Kennedy blitz: *Life*, March 28, 1960, p. 28.

156 "They're all over the state . . .": O'Donnell and Powers, p. 157.

156 Sister Pat was a major attraction: O'Donnell and Powers, p. 158.

156 "Jackie's drawing more people . . .": ibid., p. 156.

156 "Just keep on with your shopping . . .": ibid., pp. 156–157.

156 "you could have heard a pin drop": ibid., p. 157.

156 "a corner grocer running against a chain store.": White, *1960*, p. 92.

156 more than any other candidate: Sorensen, p. 137.

156 He claimed a moral victory: O'Donnell and Powers, p. 160.

157 "Maybe . . . I can hitch a ride . . .": ibid., p. 160.

157 "Well, what are our problems?"; "There's only one problem . . .": ibid., p. 160.

157 "as if they were afraid . . .": ibid., p. 163.

157 "must have been a couple of visiting Catholics . . .": ibid., p. 163.

157 "We've never had a Catholic president . . .": White, *1960*, p. 105.

157 "We have enough trouble in West Virginia . . .": ibid., p. 108.

157 Coal mining had once been the leading industry: ibid., pp. 98–99.

157 "Is it true you're the son . . .": Collier and Horowitz, p. 237.

158 "My daddy and Jack Kennedy's daddy . . .": O'Donnell and Powers, p. 165.

158 Jackie visited miners' wives; a group of railroad workers: ibid., pp. 164–165.

158 "In the pitch dark . . .": Martin, p. 134.

158 Jack teasingly reminded him he wasn't old enough: Sorensen, p. 140.

158 "wasn't invited.": Rose Kennedy, pp. 368–369.

158 Against Bobby's advice . . . to meet the issue of his Catholicism head on: Martin, p. 134.

158 "And if he breaks his oath . . .": White, *1960*, pp. 107–108.

159 "A sin against God . . .": ibid., p. 108.

159 the finest TV broadcast: ibid., p. 107.

159 contributed more men and women: ibid., p. 100.

159 "Bobby must be tired": Martin, p. 136.

159 Jack would ask . . . if forty million Americans: O'Donnell and Powers, p. 166.

159 "That wasn't the country my brother died for . . .": ibid., pp. 166–167.

159 "Nobody asked me if I was a Catholic . . .": ibid., p. 166.

159 "To listen to their stuff . . .": White, *1960*, p. 106.

159 "Get your ass down here. You're winning by a landslide.": Martin, p. 137.

159 "This must be awful for poor Hubert . . .": O'Donnell and Powers, p. 171.

159 began to cry. Bobby cried with him: White, *1960*, p. 113.

160 "putting together the political bits and pieces.": O'Donnell and Powers, p. 172.

160 Those leaders had only one consideration: ibid., p. 172.

160 "twenty-five minutes on television.": Sorensen, p. 155.

161 not "to accept anyone as second best . . .": Whalen, p. 454.

161 "a man with the greatest possible maturity . . .": Sorensen, p. 152.

161 had promised . . . he would "remain neutral": Schlesinger, *Thousand*, p. 22.

161 While Jack had been winning primaries: Kearns, pp. 160–161.

161 "If I don't get it . . .": Schlesinger, *Kennedy*, p. 212.

161 Every vote for Stevenson, LBJ supporters reasoned: Schlesinger, *Thousand*, p. 35.

162 "with a touch of gray . . .": ibid., p. 27.

162 "I never thought Hitler was right.": Schlesinger, *Kennedy*, p. 214.

162 "I haven't had anything given to me . . .": Whalen, pp. 454–455.

162 "Jack was out kissing babies . . .": Martin, p. 146.

162 Jack had Addison's disease and was physically unfit to be president: Schlesinger, *Kennedy*, p. 214.

162 Johnson was even more vicious: ibid., p. 214; Collier and Horowitz, p. 241.

162 hinting that Jack's disease was terminal: Schlesinger, *Thousand*, p. 44; Collier and Horowitz, p. 241.

162 "You Johnson people are running a stinking damned campaign . . .": Collier and Horowitz, p. 241.

162 "young Jack": Sorensen, p. 156.

162 "a damned fool": Schlesinger, *Kennedy*, p. 214.

162 "But Daddy, how can Jack say no? . . .": Collier and Horowitz, p. 242.

162 Jack "will absolutely take this fellow apart.": Schlesinger, *Kennedy*, p. 215.

162 absenteeism of "some people.": Sorensen, p. 156.

162 "was talking about some other candidate": ibid., p. 156.

163 Bobby said they were "dead": Schlesinger, *Thousand*, p. 39.

163 It would be then . . . or never: Sorensen, p. 155.

163 "Does your wife know . . ."; "No, and don't tell her": O'Donnell and Powers, p. 183.

163 "Well, this is the day . . .": ibid., p. 183.

163 "Let's hope the breakfast tastes as good . . .": ibid., p. 184.

164 "Do not reject this man . . .": White, *1960*, p. 165.

164 That morning, Stevenson had phoned . . . Daley: ibid., p. 167.

164 "Don't worry, Dad": Collier and Horowitz, p. 242.

164 "Alabama casts twenty votes . . .": O'Donnell and Powers, p. 187.

164 "God Almighty! . . . I slave and knock my brains out . . .": ibid., p. 187.

164 "Do you mind, Bill?"; "Please don't worry . . ."; "Sit down . . .": ibid., p. 187.

165 Wyoming could nominate the next president; "Such support can never be forgotten . . .": Fay, p. 49.

165 "This may be it": O'Donnell and Powers, p. 188.

165 "Wyoming . . . casts all fifteen votes . . .": Martin, p. 152.

165 which little more than an hour before: White, *1960*, p. 171.

165 as the band began to play: Collier and Horowitz, p. 242.

165 "LBJ now means . . .": O'Donnell and Powers, p. 190.

166 Jack reluctantly made a decision . . . would see as betrayal: Schlesinger, *Thousand*, pp. 50–52, 57; Parmet, *JFK*, p. 27.

166 from Bobby on down: Schlesinger, *Kennedy*, pp. 218–220; Collier and Horowitz, pp. 243–244; Parmet, *JFK*, p. 27.

166 "a disaster": O'Donnell and Powers, p. 192.

166 "This is the worst mistake . . .": ibid., p. 192.

166 "Wait a minute . . . I'm forty-three years old . . .": ibid., pp. 192–193.

166 the ayes and nays were in equal proportion: Schlesinger, *Thousand*, p. 58.

166 "Yesterday was the best day of my life . . .": Schlesinger, *Kennedy*, p. 220.

167 Just forty-eight hours before . . . calling Joe a pro-Nazi: ibid., p. 221.

167 "Don't worry, Jack . . . Within two weeks . . .": ibid., p. 221.

167 "We stand today on the edge . . .": White, *1960*, p. 177.

167 "Now begins another long journey . . ."; The crowd cheered: ibid., p. 178.

168 "the personification of a kind of disciplined vigor . . .": Beschloss, *Mayday*, p. 181.

168 "a formidable candidate": Ibid., p. 181.

169 Central Intelligence Agency U-2: Ranelagh, p. 318.

169 "impossible" for Powers to be captured: Beschloss, *Mayday*, p. 34.

169 tried to give the impression: Brendon, p. 389.

169 the new "American Exhibition": Beschloss, *Mayday*, p. 261.

169 "proper cordiality.": ibid., p. 286.

169 had also been "torpedoed": ibid., p. 285.

169 postponed six to eight months: Brendon, p. 393.

169 Khrushchev was keeping an eye on: Beschloss, *Mayday*, p. 225.

169 Kennedy . . . was an unknown quantity: ibid., pp. 195, 225.

169 Stevenson . . . the most agreeable; Nixon . . . a disaster: ibid., p. 225.

169 more popular than ever: ibid., p. 303.

169 could easily have won a third term: Brendon, p. 396.

169 would have expressed "regret": Sorensen, p. 149.

169 YOU'RE UNFIT TO BE PRESIDENT: Beschloss, *Mayday*, p. 319.

169 "naive and inexperienced.": Sorensen, p. 185.

170 gathering state secrets: Beschloss, *Mayday*, p. 328.

170 ten years' "deprivation of liberty": ibid., p. 335. In February 1962, Powers was released from prison and returned to the United States in exchange for Soviet spy Rudolf Abel.

170 258 members of the police department: Szulc, p. 524.

170 get-together at the Plaza included James O'Connell . . . Robert Maheu . . . Johnny Roselli: ibid., p. 524; Wyden, pp. 41–42. Many sources, including Wyden, give the spelling of the latter's name as "Rosselli."

170 "a sensitive mission . . ."; "the liquidation of Fidel Castro.": Szulc, p. 523.

170 "in Latin America or around the world.": Sorensen, p. 170.

170 "solidarity with Cuba.": Szulc, p. 526.

170 "broad abeam.": ibid., p. 526.

171 "disgrace to civilization": Beschloss, *Mayday*, p. 338.

171 denouncing U.S. "aggression": Szulc, p. 527.

171 was booed; the Russian premier booed back: Beschloss, *Mayday*, p. 338.

171 tried to shout Macmillan down, called the UN a spitoon: Jones, p. 480.

171 pounded first his fist and then his shoe: Beschloss, *Mayday*, p. 339.

171 until it had chosen a new leader: White, *1960*, p. 295.

171 "the kind of man Mr. Khrushchev . . .": Beschloss, *Mayday*, p. 340.

171 Jack trailed Nixon . . . 53 to 47 percent: Collier and Horowitz, p. 244.

171 "I'm getting tired of these people . . .": O'Donnell and Powers, p. 206.

171 almost everyone on his staff advised against: ibid., p. 207.

171 "We can win or lose the election . . .": White, *1960*, p. 260.

172 "Do you realize that tonight . . .": O'Donnell and Powers, p. 208.

172 "where religious liberty is so indivisible . . .": Meyers, p. 97.

172 to convince Protestants: Sorensen, p. 191.

172 "side by side with Bowie and Crockett . . .": ibid., pp. 189–190.

172 "It was the best speech of his campaign . . .": ibid., p. 190.

172 Ten years before; now . . . 88 percent; four or five hours; forty million sets: White, *1960*, pp. 279–280.

172 Eisenhower had advised him not to accept: Sorensen, p. 196.

173 fuming about the lost time . . . caught a cold: White, *1960*, p. 273.

173 a long nap, piles of index cards: Sorensen, p. 198.

173 "This is a great country . . .": ibid., p. 198.

173 "moving again.": ibid., p. 199.

173 sounded weak. "I know Senator Kennedy feels as deeply . . .": ibid., p. 199.

173 boredom and amusement: O'Donnell and Powers, p. 213.

173 Nixon directed his responses at Jack: White, *1960*, pp. 287–288.

173 "the best qualities of Elvis Presley . . .": ibid., p. 331.

174 he should set the speech to music: Sorensen, p. 177.

174 "It was strictly involuntary . . .": *Boston Globe*, p. 22.

174 "If we'd really gone down . . .": Martin, p. 173.

174 "Where I grew up . . .": ibid., p. 179.

174 "We have not had much manure . . .": ibid., p. 179.

174 "So I ahsk what's wrong with the American fahmah . . .": ibid., pp. 179–180.

174 WHEN I GROW UP; IF I ONLY HAD A VOTE: ibid., p. 177.

174 The voting age be lowered to nine: Sorensen, p. 180.

174 Reporters entertained themselves counting empty shoes: Martin, p. 174.

174 "Women . . . literally leaped out of them": ibid., p. 174.

174 "Let me speak first . . .": Sorensen, p. 181.

174 "Here's your glass.": ibid., p. 181.

175 "I don't think you're going to get him,": ibid., p. 181.

175 "Get lost, Pals" Donrequint and Trctick, p. 67.

175 "between the comfortable and the concerned.": Sorensen, p. 184.

175 "I don't run for the office . . .": ibid., pp. 178–179.

175 "I want a world . . .": ibid., p. 183

175 The Soviets . . . "have made a spectacle . . .": Beschloss, Mayday, p. 339.

175 said he had access to more information: ibid., p. 339.

175 asked if there were no doubting Thomases in the Pentagon: ibid., p. 339.

175 "the party which gave us the Missile Gap.": ibid., p. 340.

175 an unwritten political law: White, 1960, p. 294.

176 49 percent for Kennedy: ibid., p. 295.

176 there was fear for his life: ibid., p. 322.

176 Three Southern governors: ibid., p. 322.

176 "Tell Jack that we'll ride it through . . .": Schlesinger, Thousand, p. 74.

176 "I made it clear . . . it was not a political call . . .": Wofford, p. 21.

176 "I've got a suitcase of votes . . .": White, 1960, p. 323.

176 "Imagine Martin Luther King having a bigot . . .": Schlesinger, Thousand, p. 74.

176 "Don't worry, son . . .": Whalen, p. 457.

176 "Jack and Bob will run the show . . .": ibid., p. 456.

177 "in his own way.": ibid., p. 457.

177 Joe . . . phoned him to end their . . . association: Krock, Memoirs, p. 366.

177 Joe refused to ever speak to him again: Collier and Horowitz, p. 247.

177 "Look, I can't control my father . . .": ibid., p. 247.

177 BE THANKFUL ONLY ONE CAN WIN: Whalen, p. 457.

177 "Where was I yesterday?": Martin, p. 172.

177 "Whatever you do, don't speak!": ibid., p. 172.

177 she had borrowed clothes from Jackie: ibid., p. 171.

177 "We went around by car . . .": ibid., p. 172.

177 "Thank God I get out of those dreadful chicken dinners . . .": ibid., p. 127.

177 too much status and not enough quo: ibid., p. 127.

177 "The American people just aren't ready . . .": ibid., p. 127.

178 "If he lost, I'd never forgive myself . . .": Sorensen, p. 207.

178 worse than Omaha Beach: ibid., p. 207.

178 felt the sides of the car bending: ibid., p. 207; Martin, p. 174.

178 Dave Powers estimated the crowd . . . to be one million: Meyers, p. 95.

178 "I assure you that my wife ": Martin, p. 202.

178 "I don't think Jack has changed . . .": ibid., pp. 199–200.

178 "Oh, I hope not . . .": ibid., p. 200.

178 "without the advantages of a powerful family.": ibid., p. 187.

178 loved everybody in "little Wyoming.": ibid., p. 187.

178 "Little Brother Is Watching You.": Schlesinger, Kennedy, p. 223.

178 "I don't give a damn . . .": ibid., p. 222.

178 "If you say anything more . . .":
Collier and Horowitz, p. 248n.

179 "Mr. Nixon may be very experienced . . .": Sorensen, p. 183.

179 "called him an ignoramus . . .":
ibid., pp. 207–208.

179 "the worst news . . ."; "It must
show that perhaps . . .": White,
1960, p. 298n.

179 "barefaced liar.": ibid., p. 326.

179 "Having seen him four times
close up . . .": ibid., p. 327.

179 "We do things for this guy . . .":
O'Donnell and Powers, p. 203.

179 "What do you suppose Nixon's
doing . . .": Sorensen, p. 179.

179 "five minutes allotted for the
candidate . . .": ibid., p. 179.

179 "I am going to last about five
more days . . .": ibid., p. 179.

179 A joke began making the rounds:
O'Donnell and Powers, p. 217.

180 "Dear Mr. President . . .": White,
1960, p. 299n.

180 no one should expect him "to
run a country . . .": Sorensen,
p. 194.

180 "I have a deep and abiding
faith . . .": O'Donnell and
Powers, pp. 217–218.

180 "If you give me a week . . .":
Brendon, p. 397.

180 That statement . . . caused some
embarrassment in the Nixon camp:
ibid., p. 398.

180 television viewers were inundated: White, 1960, p. 311.

180 "too close to call.": Sorensen, p.
209.

181 "You've seen those elephants . . .": O'Donnell and
Powers, p. 217.

181 Jack took his campaign home:
White, 1960, p. 338.

181 "We love you, Jack!": ibid., p.
339.

181 told the crowd he had promised
their mayor: ibid., p. 340.

181 "My God, isn't this unbelievable?": O'Donnell and Powers,
p. 221.

181 "Somebody asked her last
week . . .": Adler, p. 64.

181 Men and women alike were
screaming "I love you, Jack!":
White, 1960, p. 343.

182 "picking this country of ours
up . . .": Sorensen, p. 210.

182 "I come back to this old city . . .":
ibid., p. 210.

182 at midnight, the citizens of New
Hampshire: White, 1960, p. 3.

182 Jack . . . was tense and irritable:
Damore, p. 215.

182 a command post of thirty telephones and four wire-service
teletypes: White, 1960, p. 8.

182 news from ninety key districts:
Damore, p. 216.

182 Eunice . . . began to sing: Martin,
p. 206.

183 odds . . . at 100 to 1. Jack said
the computer was "nuts": Damore, p. 217.

183 By eight o'clock, the network
estimated . . . 51 percent: ibid.,
p. 218.

183 NBC . . . called the election a
"cliff-hanger.": Sorensen, p. 212.

183 "I see we won in Pennsylvania . . .": O'Donnell and
Powers, p. 223.

183 "Ohio did that to me.": Damore,
p. 219.

183 By 3 A.M. . . . the election hinged
on just four states: O'Donnell
and Powers, p. 224.

183 "where there are only fifty
voters . . .": ibid., p. 224.

183 "Is there any milk in the house?":
White, 1960, p. 24.

183 phone bill . . . came to ten
thousand dollars: ibid., p. 346.

183 "I'm worrying about Teddy . . .":
O'Donnell and Powers, p. 225.

184 one-tenth of one percent: White,
1960, p. 350.

184 By 7 A.M. Secret Service agents
had surrounded: ibid., p. 347.

184 "Good morning, Mr. President.":
Damore, p. 224.

184 the entire family burst into applause: ibid., pp. 226–227.

184 "So now my wife and I . . .":
ibid., p. 229.

184 Joe . . . had been standing alone:
Rose Kennedy, p. 377.

184 the president-elect of the United
States hugged the man: Damore,
p. 229.

187 "I thought this part of being
president . . .": Sidey, p. 12.

187 he had spent so much time: *Boston Globe*, p. 42.
187 "People, people, people . . .": Schlesinger, *Thousand*, p. 127.
188 his slender victory required: Powers, p. 357.
188 The announcement caused dismay: Collier and Horowitz, p. 253.
188 "I asked him how . . .": Parmet, *JFK*, p. 70.
188 "It was just as well . . .": O'Donnell and Powers, p. 229.
188 "I'm never there . . .": ibid., p. 233.
188 "both mother and son . . .": ibid., p. 233.
189 "twilight zone": Salinger, p. 51.
189 Clifford had asked for nothing: Sorensen, p. 229.
189 "I want the best men . . .": Opotowsky, p. 12.
189 might as well do it as a co-conspirator: Collier and Horowitz, p. 253n.
189 "There's nothing left at Harvard . . .": Opotowsky, p. 13.
189 "no raiding pact": ibid., p. 13.
190 wouldn't even consider the appointment: O'Donnell and Powers, p. 237.
190 On the afternoon: Opotowsky, p. 155.
190 "ten dullest jobs.": Parmet, *JFK*, p. 62.
190 "Harvard does not have . . .": Schlesinger, *Thousand*, p. 144.
190 pressure from liberals: O'Donnell and Powers, p. 236; Whitman and *NYT*, p. 219.
190 refusal to endorse: ibid., p. 317; Whitman and *NYT*, p. 220.
190 reluctantly accepted: Whitman and *NYT*, p. 221; Schlesinger, *Thousand*, p. 139.
190 geographical balance: Opotowsky, p. 25.
190 without regard to party affiliation: ibid., p. 22.
190 whom Richard Nixon might well have chosen: Schlesinger, *Thousand*, p. 135.
191 reassured Wall Street: Collier and Horowitz, p. 254; Parmet, *JFK*, p. 65; O'Donnell and Powers, p. 239.

191 "I can't.": Whalen, p. 467.
191 "anytime I want to.": ibid., p. 463.
191 "Jack doesn't belong anymore . . .": ibid., p. 462.
191 arrangements had been made: ibid., pp. 475–476; Collier and Horowitz, p. 255; Parmet, *JFK*, p. 75.
191 "Thank you very much . . .": Parmet, *JFK*, p. 64.
191 charges of nepotism: Whalen, p. 468.
191 "I changed my mind . . .": Opotowsky, p. 18.
191 "Well, I think I'll open . . .": Bradlee, p. 38.
192 "Damn it, Bobby . . .": Schlesinger, *Thousand*, p. 142.
192 "Don't smile too much . . .": Schlesinger, *Kennedy*, p. 243.
192 "If Robert Kennedy . . .": ibid., p. 243
192 could turn out to be an "unqualified disaster.": ibid., p. 244.
192 "a little legal experience . . .": Manchester, *Portrait*, p. 160.
192 "nine strangers and a brother.": Parmet, *JFK*, p. 62.
192 almost one hundred people: Sorensen, p. 237.
192 twenty-nine task forces: Schlesinger, *Thousand*, p. 160.
192 As a result, a Kennedy program: Sorensen, p. 239.
192 "to take the legislative initiative immediately.": ibid., p. 239.
192 anxious to be punctual: Parmet, *JFK*, pp. 73–74.
192 Jack had brought along a hat: ibid., p. 74.
193 "Good morning, Mr. President": ibid., p. 74.
193 "young whippersnapper": Schlesinger, *Thousand*, p. 126.
193 addressing his successor as "Senator.": Parmet, *JFK*, p. 74.
193 "tremendously impressed": Sorensen, p. 231.
193 "understanding of the world problems . . .": Schlesinger, *Thousand*, p. 126.
193 "I've shown my friend here . . .": Sidey, p. 38.
193 "This is one of the problems . . .": ibid., p. 38.

193 "would happen before we take over . . .": Sorensen, p. 640.

193 "things were really just as bad . . .": O'Donnell and Powers, p. 245.

193 "Are they expecting Castro . . .": ibid., p. 228.

193 "The Kennedys bought the Presidency and the Whitehouse.": Schlesinger, *Thousand*, p. 161.

193 "Grandpa," "Grandma," . . .: Sidey, p. 25.

193 "To Bobby . . .": Schlesinger, *Kennedy*, p. 243.

193 a spare tire: Sidey, p. 35.

194 "lost that lean, Lincolnesque look": Rose Kennedy, p. 391.

194 characteristically late: Sidey, p. 31.

194 "one of the most observed trips . . .": ibid., p. 31.

194 "I'm here to go over your grades.": Sorensen, p. 234.

194 "For of those to whom . . .": ibid., p. 234; Rose Kennedy, p. 388. For a more complete version of the Massachusetts legislature address, see Rose Kennedy, pp. 387–388.

194 Although Joe had no idea: Rose Kennedy, pp. 386–387.

194 Bonfires had been lit: Schlesinger, *Thousand*, p. 1.

194 instructed the driver: O'Donnell and Powers, p. 246.

194 "It's better than mine": ibid., p. 246.

195 "I suppose you'll be laughing it up . . .": ibid., p. 246.

195 "last carefree night on the town . . .": ibid., p. 246.

195 "study the secret": Sorensen, p. 240.

195 "had never used two or three words . . .": ibid., p. 240.

195 "*Let the word go forth* . . .": For complete text of the inaugural address, see ibid., pp. 245–248.

196 The duke and duchess of Devonshire: Goodwin, p. 812.

196 the little boy who always forgot: Rose Kennedy, p. 390.

196 his eyes glistened with tears.: ibid., p. 388; Whalen, p. 465.

196 "Oh, Jack, what a day": Schlesinger, *Thousand*, p. 5.

196 Jack stood up: Whalen, p. 466, says the president saluted both his parents; Goodwin, p. 816, says he tipped his hat only to his father.

197 "awfully quiet.": Sorensen, p. 249.

197 "Do you think it's adequate?": ibid., p. 249; Fay, p. 101.

198 "You never give us any hard news . . .": Salinger, p. 125.

198 "I speak today . . .": Parmet, *JFK*, p. 87.

198 "disturbing.": Rachlin, p. 181.

198 concerned about unemployment: ibid., p. 181.

198 "national household . . ." while abroad "weapons spread . . .": Parmet, *JFK*, p. 87.

198 "the world beyond the Cold War.": Rachlin, p. 181.

198 "wars of national liberation" made a deep impression: Collier and Horowitz, p. 265; Paper, p. 71; Parmet, *JFK*, p. 136. See also Schlesinger, *Thousand*, pp. 302–304.

198 "Asia, Latin America . . .": Sorensen, p. 530; Jones, p. 489.

198 proposed a Food for Peace program: Schlesinger, *Thousand*, p. 168.

199 "immense reservoir of dedicated . . .": ibid., p. 607.

199 "call forth your strengths . . .": Rachlin, p. 186.

199 "into a vast crucible . . .": Schlesinger, *Thousand*, p. 205; Sorensen, p. 534; Collier and Horowitz, p. 265.

199 To Americans, not even Nikita Khrushchev: Wofford, p. 344.

199 a fascinating revolutionary figure: Jones, p. 490.

199 "beginning of a new era": Szulc, p. 493.

199 almost a billion dollars' worth: *The Final Assassinations Report*, p. 118, gives the amount as $700 million; Szulc, p. 509, puts this figure at $850 million; Jones, p. 490, says "over $1 billion."

199 "We will take and take . . .": Jones, p. 490.

199 Its Technical Services staff: Wyden, p. 40; Schlesinger, *Kennedy*,

p. 502; Wofford, p. 302; Collier and Horowitz, p. 293; Davis, pp. 287–288.

200 The Agency secretly decided on . . . murder: Ranelagh, pp. 336–338, 344–345, 356; Szulc, p. 463; Schlesinger, *Kennedy*, pp. 473, 501–503, 506–508; Wyden, pp. 39–40; Wofford, p. 67; Collier and Horowitz, p. 294.

200 turned to the underworld: *The Final Assassinations Report*, pp. 131–136; Ranelagh, p. 356; Wyden, pp. 43–44; Wofford, pp. 392, 399; Schlesinger, *Kennedy*, pp. 173, 503–505; Parmet, *JFK*, p. 127; Szulc, p. 524; Collier and Horowitz, p. 293. (As previously noted, "Roselli" is spelled "Rosselli" in some sources.)

200 mob members such as Jack Ruby: Davis, p. 476; Hurt, pp. 175–180. See also Schlesinger, *Kennedy*, p. 504; Wofford, pp. 413–414.

200 developed poison pills: Schlesinger, *Kennedy*, p. 505; Wyden, pp. 109–110; Ranelagh, p. 357; Davis, p. 288; Szulc, p. 524.

200 began to have second thoughts: Schlesinger, *Kennedy*, p. 505.

201 list of ten most wanted criminals: Wyden, p. 44.

201 "several friends . . . was to be done away with . . .": ibid., p. 504; Ranelagh, p. 35.

201 President Kennedy himself was involved: Wyden, p. 44; Parmet, *JFK*, pp. 117–118; Collier and Horowitz, pp. 283, 292, 412–413; Schlesinger, *Kennedy*, pp. 515–516; Wofford, pp. 491–495; Hurt, p. 176.

201 records of phone calls: Schlesinger, *Kennedy*, p. 515; Parmet, *JFK*, p. 118; Wyden, p. 44.

201 Cuban exiles had been training: Wyden, p. 45.

201 U.S. HELPS TRAIN AN ANTI-CASTRO FORCE . . .: ibid., p. 46.

202 "He wanted the dignity of Harold Macmillan . . .": Collier and Horowitz, p. 265.

202 whatever was necessary: Wofford, p. 344.

202 "continued and accelerated.": Schlesinger, *Thousand*, p. 164.

202 "initial military success"; "ultimate success": Wyden, p. 90.

202 were given to understand: ibid., p. 92; Schlesinger, *Thousand*, p. 247; Parmet, *JFK*, p. 165; Sidey, p. 125.

202 "Don't forget we have a disposal problem.": Schlesinger, *Thousand*, p. 242.

203 "fix a malevolent image . . .": ibid., p. 240.

203 "I've reserved the right . . .": ibid., p. 256.

203 "To give this activity . . .": ibid., p. 251.

203 "It was a sort of orphan child . . .": Ranelagh, p. 360.

203 "only half sold": ibid., p. 360.

203 "You can't mañana this thing": Collier and Horowitz, p. 268.

203 later denied: Schlesinger, *Thousand*, p. 247; Ranelagh, p. 363.

203 one-fourth of the Cuban people: Schlesinger, *Thousand*, p. 247.

203 "melt away": ibid., p. 250.

203 wouldn't make the front page of the *New York Times*: Wyden, p. 151.

204 both Castro and the CIA would later agree: Ranelagh, p. 369.

204 the first shots: Wyden, p. 219.

204 the first frogmen: Schlesinger, *Thousand*, p. 274.

204 interpreted as seaweed: Wyden, p. 137.

205 would be asleep: ibid., p. 218.

205 without communications: ibid., p. 222.

205 "Castro's capability in certain specific respects . . .": Szulc, p. 555.

205 "Londonderry, Ireland.": Wyden, p. 242.

205 "Oh, hell . . .": Whalen, p. 474.

206 "I know that outfit . . .": Manchester, *Portrait*, p. 35.

206 "We will have to do something.": Schlesinger, *Thousand*, p. 276.

206 "I made a mistake . . .": ibid., p. 276.

206 "It was inconceivable . . .": Davis, pp. 296–297.

206 called Kennedy a traitor: ibid., p. 299.

206 "a Profile in Timidity and Indecision.": Parmet, *JFK*, p. 177.

206 "turned chicken.": Davis, p. 297.
206 "There is an old saying . . .": Sorensen, p. 308.
206 "an error doesn't become a mistake . . .": CBS Video, *John F. Kennedy*.
206 "decent interval": Parmet, *JFK*, p. 212.
206 "If this were the British government . . .": Wyden, p. 311.
206 "a bad idea" because he was "a Democrat, and brother.": Schlesinger, *Kennedy*, p. 478.
206 the president's unofficial watchdog: Schlesinger, *Thousand*, p. 428.
207 "Why couldn't this have happened to James Bond?": Sorensen, p. 388.
207 "How could I have been so far off base?": ibid., p. 309.
208 "channels of communication" and "lessen the chance . . .": ibid., p. 542.
208 "I have to show him . . .": O'Donnell and Powers, p. 286.
208 "The 'chickens are coming home to roost' . . .": Parmet, *JFK*, p. 179; Sidey, p. 154.
208 "would be a mistake . . .": Parmet, *JFK*, p. 178.
209 at the urging of the CIA: Halberstam, p. 148.
209 "the biggest funeral . . .": ibid., p. 133.
209 "is remote from the people . . .": ibid., p. 134.
209 "the Winston Churchill of Southeast Asia.": ibid., p. 135.
209 "He's the only boy we got out there": ibid., p. 135.
209 no matter what the Vietnamese people might want: Brendon, p. 291.
209 purchased in a toy store: Sorensen, p. 525.
210 "this tradition has been broken in extraordinary times . . .": Rachlin, p. 198.
210 "I believe that this nation . . .": ibid., pp. 198–199; Sorensen, p. 525.
210 "like a bulldog got a hold of them.": Wofford, p. 152.
210 disapproved of JFK's private life: Powers, p. 358.

210 He admittedly "hated" Bobby: ibid., p. 353; Schlesinger, *Kennedy*, p. 271n.
210 his youth: Powers, p. 354.
210 born the year after Hoover became head of the FBI: Navasky, p. 8.
210 his working in shirt sleeves: Schlesinger, *Kennedy*, p. 268.
210 bringing the family dog to the office: Powers, p. 355.
210 habit of throwing darts: Schlesinger, *Kennedy*, p. 268.
210 his refusal to kowtow: ibid., p. 268.
210 Hoover did not let the attorney general know: Wofford, p. 152.
210 agents stood watching: Schlesinger, *Kennedy*, p. 307; Powers, p. 368.
211 It was Mother's Day: Schlesinger, *Kennedy*, p. 307; Wofford, p. 152.
211 "The government is going to be . . . upset"; "somebody better get in the damn bus . . .": Schlesinger, *Kennedy*, p. 308.
211 agents watched and took notes: ibid., p. 309; Wofford, p. 154; Powers, p. 368.
211 "Get 'em, get 'em": Schlesinger, *Kennedy*, p. 309.
211 "Now, John, don't tell me that": ibid., p. 310.
212 "Oh, Dad, I don't have a cent . . .": Collier and Horowitz, pp. 275–276.
212 "a U.S. President is not under obligation . . .": Rose Kennedy, p. 400.
212 "*Jacqui. Jacqui* . . .": Martin, p. 306.
212 "Well, I'm dazzled.": ibid., p. 308.
212 "Your wife knows more French history . . .": O'Donnell and Powers, p. 289.
212 "*Elle est plus reine* . . .": Sidey, p. 183.
212 "probably because . . . I have such a charming wife.": O'Donnell and Powers, p. 289.
212 a French cartoonist: Martin, p. 308.
212 "I am the man who accompanied Jacqueline Kennedy . . .": Sidey, p. 188.

213 "at the summit . . .": Salinger, p. 175.

213 "miscalculation" seemed to annoy: Sorensen, p. 546; Schlesinger, *Thousand*, p. 361.

213 had misjudged the situation: Sorensen, p. 546.

213 "I hope you get to keep them.": Sidey, p. 196.

213 "area of accommodation.": ibid., p. 199.

214 "fall into our lap . . .": Halberstam, p. 90.

214 "Ideas cannot be stopped": Parmet, *JFK*, p. 191.

214 like "dealing with Dad . . .": Collier and Horowitz, p. 277.

214 "I'd rather shake hands with her.": Martin, p. 313.

214 like sitting next to Abbott and Costello: Schlesinger, *Thousand*, p. 367.

214 "Don't bore me with statistics": ibid., p. 367.

214 "Why don't you send me one?": ibid., p. 367.

214 "I'm afraid I asked Khrushchev for it . . .": ibid., p. 367.

214 "A thousand-mile journey . . .": ibid., p. 370.

215 would not be the one to break it: Sorensen, p. 544.

215 symbol of the struggle: Jones, p. 429.

215 two Germanys, two Berlins: ibid., p. 429.

215 a "bone in the throat.": ibid., p. 476.

215 situation was intolerable. Schlesinger, *Thousand*, p. 370.

215 "free city": Sorenson, p. 584.

216 "I'll step on your corns . . .": Martin, p. 312.

216 scraps of paper: Sorensen, p. 584.

216 "at any risk.": Sidey, p. 199.

216 "If that is true . . .": Sorensen, p. 586.

216 "a very sober two days."; "wholly different views . . .": Schlesinger, *Thousand*, p. 377.

216 "A peace treaty with Germany . . .": Parmet, *JFK*, p. 194.

216 "aggression" which would be "duly repulsed.": ibid., p. 194.

216 "apparently designed to heighten tension.": ibid., p. 195.

216 "holocaust or humiliation": Sorensen, p. 587.

216 "that son of a bitch . . .": Schlesinger, *Thousand*, p. 391.

217 "We cannot and will not . . .": ibid., p. 391.

217 "We seek peace . . .": Sorensen, p. 592.

217 speech was belligerent, and said Kennedy's moves were military hysteria: ibid., p. 592.

217 nearing flashpoint: ibid., p. 593.

217 "There wouldn't be any need of a wall . . .": O'Donnell and Powers, p. 303.

217 some sinister long-range Soviet plan: Schlesinger, *Thousand*, p. 395.

217 "brutal border closing": ibid., p. 395.

218 "most anxious moment": Sorensen, p. 594.

218 "inappropriate place from which to start World War III.": Davis, p. 359.

218 "Talking to Kennedy then . . .": Sidey, p. 240.

218 the odds were one in five: Salinger, p. 190.

218 "We have no other choice": Rachlin, p. 213.

218 "It's been a tough first year . . ."; "We're in better shape . . .": Sidey, p. 288.

218 "the worst one we've got": Parmet, *JFK*, p. 137.

218 "It's like taking a drink": Schlesinger, *Thousand*, p. 547.

219 to coordinate intelligence activities, propaganda, and guerrilla strikes: Blakey and Billings, p. 55.

219 Interpreting the scheme as one meant to revive their assassination attempts: Szulc, p. 573.

219 "Dad's gotten sick": Parmet, *JFK*, p. 125.

220 "The answer is . . .": Rachlin, p. 232.

220 "We have a long way to go . . .": Sorensen, p. 529.

220 "impossible.": Schlesinger, *Thousand*, p. 373.

221 with whom Kennedy was rumored to have had an affair: Collier and Horowitz, p. 413; Davis, pp. 610–611; Martin, p. 358; Parmet,

JFK, p. 304; Summers, p. 225 ff.
See also Gloria Steinem, *Marilyn*
(New York: Henry Holt and
Company, 1986), pp. 119–126;
C.D.B. Bryan, "Say Goodbye to
Camelot," *Rolling Stone*, December 5, 1985, p. 36.

221 "skin and beads": Schlesinger, *Kennedy*, p. 617.

221 "in such a sweet, wholesome way.": Summers, p. 284.

221 "As goes steel, so goes inflation": Sorensen, p. 443.

221 "industrial statesmanship" and to extend "the thanks . . .": ibid., p. 447.

221 "My father always told me . . .": Schlesinger, *Thousand*, p. 635.

221 The secretary of labor said his own credibility: Parmet, *JFK*, p. 238.

221 "a hell of a note": ibid., p. 238.

221 "The American people will find it hard . . .": Sidey, p. 298.

222 Sorensen . . . heard reporters gasp: Sorensen, p. 451.

222 "There shouldn't be any price rise.": Schlesinger, *Kennedy*, p. 420.

222 Bobby was certain Hoover had ordered it: ibid., p. 420.

222 "We are aware of the disadvantages . . .": Sidey, p. 306.

222 "After this display . . ."; "The Government set the price . . .": Schlesinger, *Kennedy*, p. 423.

223 "enjoying it less.": Salinger, p. 73; Parmet, *JFK*, p. 239.

223 "If I weren't President . . .": Sorensen, p. 462.

223 "Their attitude is . . ."; "I can't believe . . .": ibid., p. 465.

223 "an end to racial discrimination . . .": Wofford, p. 58.

223 "one stroke of the pen.": ibid., p. 63.

223 "on a bold and large scale.": ibid., p. 63.

223 "When I believe we can . . .": Sorensen, p. 476.

223 "If we get into a long fight . . .": Wofford, p. 140.

224 fewer than 15 percent: Schlesinger, *Thousand*, p. 935.

224 "It will give us the concrete tool . . .": ibid., p. 935.

224 increased by 26 percent: Wofford, p. 144.

224 Even the Washington Redskins: Sorensen, p. 478.

224 progress was incremental . . . Kennedy had gone at a pace: Burner and West, p. 169.

225 with a passion he had once reserved: ibid., p. 170.

225 "new age": Schlesinger, *Thousand*, p. 940.

225 "something more"—not just . . .: Sidey, p. 317.

225 "to break White Supremacy . . .": Schlesinger, *Kennedy*, p. 330.

225 "solely because he was a Negro.": Schlesinger, *Thousand*, p. 941.

225 "We will not surrender . . .": ibid., p. 941.

225 "Take it and abide by it.": ibid., p. 941.

225 the two spoke twenty times: Schlesinger, *Kennedy*, p. 331.

225 "Go home, nigger.": Schlesinger, *Thousand*, p. 942.

225 "It's best for him . . .": ibid., p. 942.

226 "But he likes Ole Miss.": ibid., p. 942.

226 "backed by the NAACP . . .": Navasky, p. 215.

226 "in a penitentiary . . .": ibid., p. 215.

226 "going to be upheld.": ibid., p. 215.

226 While truckloads . . . maps of Mississippi were being unrolled: Schlesinger, *Kennedy*, pp. 332–333.

226 "I don't know Mr. Meredith . . .": Schlesinger, *Thousand*, p. 944.

226 "I love Mississippi" speech . . . that one student said . . . a Nazi rally: Navasky, p. 263.

226 capitulating at gunpoint: ibid., p. 263; Guthman, p. 200.

226 "a foolish and dangerous show.": Schlesinger, *Thousand*, p. 946.

226 "be in charge of things.": Schlesinger, *Kennedy*, p. 335.

227 "If things get rough . . .": ibid., p. 335.

227 "2-4-1-3 . . .": Schlesinger, *Thousand*, p. 947.

227 sneaked in . . . without his knowledge: Sorensen, p. 485.

227 "never surrender": ibid., p. 486.
227 "just to Mississippi.": Burner and West, p. 171.
227 "I haven't had such an interesting time . . .": ibid., p. 171.
227 "This place is sort of like the Alamo": Schlesinger, *Thousand*, p. 947.
229 superpowers . . . moving inexorably toward another confrontation: Szulc, p. 562.
229 paper tiger . . . nuclear teeth: Hilsman, p. 48.
229 the Kennedy administration was not contemplating an invasion: Szulc, pp. 572–573.
229 After a decade of covert action: James Reston, "File and Forget": *The New York Times*, July 22, 1987, p. A27.
229 "chasing bad men.": Collier and Horowitz, p. 269.
229 elite group at Justice: ibid., p. 269.
229 to turn the Bureau's expertise against the underworld: Schlesinger, *Kennedy*, p. 281.
229 two mobsters he remembered: Collier and Horowitz, p. 269.
230 alarmed by the attorney general's determination: Schlesinger, *Kennedy*, p. 514; Blakey and Billings, p. 59.
230 a new batch of poisons to pass on to Roselli: Schlesinger, *Kennedy*, p. 515; Ranelagh, p. 383.
230 led Houston to believe the plan had been canceled, and that was the information: Schlesinger, *Kennedy*, p. 514.
230 "If you have seen Mr. Kennedy's eyes . . .": Blakey and Billings, p. 59.
230 "to do business" with "gangsters.": Schlesinger, *Kennedy*, p. 515.
230 in a plot to murder a foreign head of state: Wofford, p. 404.
230 in the course of an ongoing FBI investigation: Davis, p. 332.
230 "The relationship between Campbell and Mrs. Lincoln . . .": Blakey and Billings, p. 380.
231 The director maintained files on the private lives: Powers, pp. 266, 359.

231 wasn't above using that information: ibid., p. 266.
231 "a puritan": Bradlee, p. 142.
231 official White House logs show: Wofford, p. 401.
231 The head of the Chicago crime syndicate: Collier and Horowitz, pp. 226–227.
231 Bobby ordered intensified FBI surveillance: Wofford, p. 405.
231 "They can't do this to me" . . . "I'm working . . .": Schlesinger, *Kennedy*, p. 516.
231 "Bobby pushed to get Giancana . . .": ibid., p. 516.
231 On the afternoon of November 22, 1963: Blakey and Billings, p. 199.
232 under the impression the attorney general objected . . . involvement of "gangsters.": Davis, p. 334.
232 "turned it off.": Schlesinger, *Kennedy*, p. 515.
232 "assumed" the project had presidential approval: ibid., p. 509.
232 "intensity of the pressure": Ranelagh, p. 385.
232 Neither JFK nor Bobby ever ordered: Blakey and Billings, p. 393.
232 nobody wanted to embarrass the president: Schlesinger, *Kennedy*, p. 510.
232 the CIA had not inquired: ibid., p. 510.
232 "plausible denial"—originated by Eisenhower: Ranelagh, p. 341; Szulc, p. 523.
232 "for a variety of reasons": Schlesinger, *Kennedy*, p. 510.
232 sent the CIA a memo, never later withdrawn or amended: ibid., p. 518.
232 "under terrific pressure": ibid., p. 513; Szulc, p. 558.
232 "for moral reasons": ibid., p. 513; ibid., p. 558.
232 originator of Operation Mongoose: Blakey and Billings, p. 55.
232 "the crazy idea": Schlesinger, *Kennedy*, p. 513.
232 "If we get into that kind of thing . . .": ibid., p. 513.
233 had the perfect opportunity to do so: ibid., p. 519. Other sources disagree with Schlesinger, et al.,

and believe one or both Kennedys played an active role in the plot to assassinate the Cuban leader. Ranelagh, p. 385, says "both the President and the attorney general had a good idea that plans were being made to kill Castro" and that "in all probability, President Kennedy was behind these moves." Parmet, *JFK*, p. 221, says "It is impossible to absolve the Kennedys of responsibility for the attempts on Castro's life." The author of this book agrees with the opinion of Fidel Castro himself, quoted in Szulc, p. 560: "It is hard for me to believe that Kennedy would have given a direct order of that nature."

233 "The transformation of Cuba into a communist base . . .": Abel, p. 12.

233 "the dominant issue of the 1962 campaign.": Sorensen, p. 670.

233 "something new and different": Schlesinger, *Thousand*, p. 797.

233 Khrushchev had given him a message: ibid., p. 798.

233 "the gravest consequences.": Robert Kennedy, p. 26.

233 "significant offensive capability": Schlesinger, *Thousand*, p. 798.

234 "Nothing will be undertaken . . .": Sorensen, p. 667.

234 "to challenges which may be presented . . .": Rachlin, p. 244.

234 "Our nuclear weapons are so powerful . . .": Schlesinger, *Thousand*, p. 799.

234 "If the aggressors unleash war . . .": ibid., p. 799.

234 "whatever must be done . . .": Rachlin, p. 244.

234 with the exception of John McCone: Sorensen, p. 670.

234 "honeymoon telegrams": Abel, p. 23.

234 These were distributed only within the Agency: ibid., p. 23.

234 the president was not informed of McCone's concern: Sorensen, p. 670.

234 they would greatly improve their bargaining position: Abel, p. 24.

235 no one wanted to risk another Francis Gary Powers incident: ibid., p. 25.

235 Over the protests of his deputy: ibid., p. 27.

235 WHERE ARE THOSE FIGHTING IRISH? Another said, OK, WE LICKED MISSISSIPPI: Sidey, p. 358.

235 to let the president get a good night's sleep: Sorensen, p. 673.

236 The "missile gap" . . . did not . . . exist: Collier and Horowitz, p. 265; Abel, p. 36.

236 "I know there is a God . . .": Evelyn Lincoln, pp. 175, 274; Wofford, p. 50.

237 only one feasible solution: Robert Kennedy, p. 31.

237 "when he was planning Pearl Harbor.": ibid., p. 31.

237 *Bullfight critics ranked in rows . . .*: Parmet, *JFK*, p. 286. O'Donnell and Powers, p. 316, and Abel, p. 54, both give slightly different translations of this poem by a Spanish bullfighter.

237 "If you strike steel . . .": Sorensen, p. 677.

237 "A missile is a missile . . .": Abel, p. 51.

238 "not consider this a remote quarrel . . .": ibid., p. 60.

238 "We just had to get them out of there.": ibid., p. 60.

238 "Can they hit Oxford, Mississippi?": Schlesinger, *Kennedy*, p. 529.

239 MORE COURAGE, LESS PROFILE. The group wasn't booing a Harvard man: Abel, p. 56.

239 "would blacken the United States . . .": Sorensen, p. 684.

239 "emotional.": Schlesinger, *Kennedy*, p. 530.

239 "it is unworthy of you . . .": ibid., p. 531.

239 "Well, I guess this is the week . . .": Wicker, p. 59.

239 "give bread to Cuba . . .": Robert Kennedy, p. 41.

239 "I was dying to confront him . . .": O'Donnell and Powers, p. 319.

240 "It will be some story . . .": Sorensen, p. 691.

240 "do nothing" in the event Cuba was bombed: O'Donnell and Powers, p. 318.

240 "Can you imagine LeMay . . .": ibid., p. 318.

240 "Whatever you fellows are recommending . . .": Schlesinger, *Thousand*, p. 805.

240 "You're in a pretty bad fix . . ."; "You're in it with me": Robert Kennedy, p. 37.

240 "This blows it . . .": Sidey, p. 335.

240 "to pull the group together . . .": Sorensen, p. 692.

241 "the sooner we get to a showdown . . .": Schlesinger, *Kennedy*, p. 531.

241 "with all the implications this would have . . .": ibid., p. 532.

241 "good sense and his moral character . . .": ibid., p. 532.

241 "As he spoke, I felt that I was at . . .": ibid., p. 532.

241 "that we ought to be true . . .": Abel, p. 80.

242 Many critics of JFK's actions during the missile crisis deplored his unwillingness to withdraw the obsolete Jupiter missiles from Turkey, apparently choosing to risk nuclear confrontation rather than seek a negotiated settlement. However, on Saturday, October 27, Bobby met with Soviet ambassador Anatoly Dobrynin to "personally convey the president's great concern." (News of this meeting was first made known in Bobby's memoir of the crisis, *Thirteen Days*, p. 106.) When Dobrynin raised the subject of the Turkish missiles, Bobby responded that within a few months the matter would "be resolved satisfactorily," although the deal would be off should Russia make it public (Schlesinger, *Kennedy*, p. 545). Both Kennedys believed it was vital that the discussion with Dobrynin remain secret, in order to avoid an inevitable uproar from the Congress, the Pentagon, and the countries of NATO, who would view the president's proposal as another example of "caving in" to the Soviets. In March 1987, Dean Rusk for the first time revealed that on the same day as Bobby's meeting with Dobrynin, JFK requested Rusk contact U Thant, Secretary General of the United Nations. According to Rusk, Kennedy suggested that if necessary, U Thant use his position at the UN to propose the simultaneous removal of the missiles in Cuba and Turkey. This was another sign, McGeorge Bundy said upon hearing of Rusk's surprising disclosure, that JFK had been prepared "to go the extra mile to avoid a conflict, and to absorb whatever political costs that may have entailed" (J. Anthony Lukas, "Class Reunion," *New York Times Magazine*, 8/30/87, pp. 58–61).

242 bottle tossed out of: Salinger, p. 260.

242 "would not correctly understand . . .": O'Donnell and Powers, p. 330.

242 "Good evening, my fellow citizens . . .": Sorensen, p. 703.

243 "It shall be the policy of this nation . . .": ibid., p. 700.

243 she refused to leave him alone: O'Donnell and Powers, p. 325.

243 at least "sixty million Americans killed . . .": Guthman, p. 126.

243 "the folly of degenerate imperialism": Jones, p. 499.

244 doodling on a pad: *serious . . . serious*: Sorensen, p. 705.

244 as if only the two of them were there, and thought, inexplicably, of Joe Jr.'s death: Robert Kennedy, p. 70.

244 "We were on the edge of a precipice . . .": ibid., p. 70.

244 "Mr. President, we have a preliminary report . . .": O'Donnell and Powers, p. 332.

244 "We're eyeball to eyeball . . .": ibid., p. 332.

244 "a fateful role": Salinger, p. 269.

245 "Do you, Ambassador Zorin . . .": Whitman and *NYT*, p. 248.

245 "I am prepared to wait . . .": ibid., p. 248.
245 "Our job here is not to score . . .": Schlesinger, *Thousand*, p. 824.
245 "just to give the family publicity.": Salinger, p. 271.
245 "If you have not lost your self-control . . .": Robert Kennedy, p. 89.
245 "the catastrophe": ibid., p. 90.
245 "let us not only relax . . .": ibid., p. 90.
245 "to compete peacefully . . .": ibid., p. 87.
246 Russian personnel were destroying documents: Parmet, *JFK*, p. 295.
246 "The noose was tightening . . .": Robert Kennedy, p. 97.
246 sites dismantled and plowed under: Sorensen, p. 720.
246 Operation Mongoose was terminated: Szulc, p. 588.
246 the Democrats gained four seats: Sidey, p. 362.
246 Khrushchev announced his country: O'Donnell and Powers, p. 343.
246 Russian leader said he would welcome suggestions: Sorensen, p. 725.
246 "in the next war, the survivors will envy the dead.": Manchester, *Death*, p. 653.
246 "the smell of burning . . .": Hilsman, p. 157.
246 off-the-record preliminary test ban negotiations: Sorensen, p. 728.
246 "a shaft of light": Schlesinger, *Thousand*, p. 910.
246 what he regarded as the finest achievement of his presidency: Sorensen, p. 740.
247 ways to open channels of communication with Castro: Szulc, pp. 558–559, 588–589; Schlesinger, *Kennedy*, pp. 577–579; Blakey and Billings, p. 144.
247 it was then that the tide of the Cold War began to turn: Sorensen, p. 719.
248 "We are not lulled by the momentary calm . . .": Sidey, p. 8.
248 long-promised "stroke of a pen": Sorensen, p. 481.

248 "appropriate agencies to use . . .": Parmet, *JFK*, p. 263.
248 "If tokenism were our goal . . .": Martin, p. 372.
249 He detailed the high cost of segregation: Schlesinger, *Thousand*, p. 951.
249 "above all, it is wrong.": ibid., p. 951.
249 "the full force of federal executive authority . . .": Parmet, *JFK*, p. 264.
249 Black unemployment was two and a half times greater: Schlesinger, *Kennedy*, p. 957.
249 more than two thousand Southern school districts: ibid., p. 956.
249 No federal grant; The Federal Aviation Agency: Schlesinger, *Kennedy*, p. 951.
249 an "idealist without illusions": Schlesinger, *Boston Globe*, p. 3.
249 Then came Birmingham: Parmet, *JFK*, p. 264.
249 "the most thoroughly segregated big city . . .": Sorensen, p. 489.
249 the ideal place: Parmet, *JFK*, p. 264.
249 Bobby Kennedy urged King: Schlesinger, *Kennedy*, p. 341.
250 "blood would run in the streets": Oates, p. 212.
250 "commit his brutality openly . . .": ibid., p. 212.
250 a dark dungeon: Bennett, p. 137.
250 without a mattress, pillow, or blanket: Oates, p. 221.
250 conditions suddenly improved: ibid., p. 221.
250 "nigger who has got the blessing . . .": Martin, p. 453.
250 Connor played into the black leader's hands: Bennett, p. 151.
250 "Let 'em have it.": Oates, p. 234.
250 unleashing their dogs: ibid., p. 234.
250 beaten with billy clubs: Bennett, p. 152; Oates, p. 235.
250 made him "sick.": Schlesinger, *Thousand*, p. 959.
250 "tired of being asked to be patient.": ibid., p. 959.
250 Something had to be done. But what?: Parmet, *JFK*, p. 265.
251 on the verge of chaos: Bennett, p. 153.

251 business had dropped by ten percent: Parmet, *JFK*, p. 266.

251 even the most ardent of the
segregationist merchants: Oates,
p. 239.

251 increased black employment and
integrated lunch counters, etc.:
ibid., p. 240.

251 at major local stores: Parmet,
JFK, p. 265.

251 reign of terror: Navasky, p. 235.

251 "compromise on the issues of segregation: Schlesinger, *Thousand*,
p. 959.

251 for the first time in the history
of the South: Schlesinger, *Kennedy*, p. 343.

251 "I hope that every drop of
blood . . .": ibid., pp. 343–344.

251 "The civil rights movement should
thank God . . .": Sorensen, p.
489.

251 the last holdout in the nation:
ibid., p. 492.

251 "Cradle of the Confederacy" and
the "very heart . . .": Schlesinger,
Kennedy, p. 351.

251 "and toss the gauntlet . . .":
ibid., p. 351.

251 State troopers wearing steel helmets: ibid., p. 352.

251 A middle-aged white woman:
Guthman, p. 208.

252 the governor planned to later impress his constituents: Schlesinger, *Kennedy*, p. 352.

252 "never submit"; not "be ready
for it in my lifetime.": ibid., p.
352.

252 seemed to relish the prospect:
Guthman, p. 209.

252 "perhaps the most dangerous
racist": Schlesinger, *Kennedy*, p.
351.

252 "Dismiss George Wallace . . .":
ibid., p. 355.

252 Katzenbach was irritated to notice: ibid., p. 355.

252 long-suffering expression: ibid.,
p. 355.

252 near one-hundred-degree heat:
Guthman, p. 215.

252 denouncing and forbidding "this
illegal and unwarranted action . . .": ibid., p. 217.

252 although there wasn't a bayonet

252 in sight . . . could not "fight
bayonets with my bare hands.":
Schlesinger, *Kennedy*, p. 356.

252 He stepped aside: ibid., p. 356.

253 "We are confronted . . .": Quotations from the president's civil
rights address are taken from the
complete text in Meyers, pp. 197–
198.

253 unlike any other by a U.S. president: Parmet, *JFK*, p. 267.

253 partially extemporaneous: Sorensen, p. 495.

253 JFK's advisers said he shouldn't
get involved: Schlesinger, *Kennedy*, p. 357.

253 white racist: Burner and West,
p. 173.

254 83 percent: Sidey, p. 156.

254 66, then 61, then 53: Parmet,
JFK, p. 272.

254 moving "too fast": ibid., p. 272.

254 now there was also a "white backlash": Schlesinger, *Thousand*, p.
967.

254 might well lose the 1964 election:
ibid., p. 968.

254 "not in search of charity . . .":
Rachlin, p. 266.

254 "We want success in Congress . . .": Schlesinger, *Thousand*, p. 969.

254 "create an atmosphere of intimidation": ibid., p. 969.

254 "I have never engaged . . .":
ibid., p. 970.

254 "Including the Attorney General.": ibid., p. 970.

254 47 percent. "We may all go down
the drain": ibid., p. 971.

255 planners were predicting one
hundred thousand people: ibid.,
p. 972.

255 "greatly exaggerated.": Schlesinger, *Kennedy*, p. 365.

255 blacks would "swarm": Parmet,
JFK, p. 273.

255 "the basis of threat and intimidation . . .": ibid., p. 273.

255 He began with a prepared text:
Oates, p. 260.

255 "I still have a dream . . .": For
the full text of Martin Luther
King's "I have a dream . . ."
speech, see ibid., pp. 259–262.

256 "Bobby Kennedy resisted . . .";

"twisted the arm . . .": Schlesinger, *Kennedy*, p. 375.

256 Hoover despised King: ibid., p. 378; Powers, pp. 353, 373.

256 hoped to discredit: Navasky, p. 170; Schlesinger, *Kennedy*, p. 366.

256 certain that the tap would prove King's innocence: Schlesinger, *Kennedy*, p. 375.

256 if Hoover succeeded in smearing . . . King: ibid., pp. 370, 372; Powers, p. 372.

257 "It is much easier to make the speeches . . .": Meyers, p. 174.

257 "our restraint is not inexhaustible"; "I hope our restraint . . .": Sorensen, p. 727.

257 Journalists, as well as Soviet officials: ibid., p. 731.

257 "Not merely peace for Americans . . .": Quotations from the president's address at American University are taken from the complete text in Meyers, pp. 193–195.

258 Khrushchev thought it was the best speech: Schlesinger, *Thousand*, p. 904.

258 Its full text was reprinted: Sorensen, p. 733.

258 "one of the great state papers . . .": ibid., p. 733.

258 newspapers gave it little attention; "dreadful mistake"; "accomplish nothing.": ibid., p. 733.

258 a month of extraordinary presidential speeches: Schlesinger, *Thousand*, p. 965.

258 hailed him as a conquering hero: Parmet, *JFK*, p. 322.

258 emotionally carried away: O'Donnell and Powers, p. 360.

258 No matter how many photographs he had studied: Richard H. Rovere, in Meyers, p. 200.

258 he was unprepared: Schlesinger, *Thousand*, p. 884.

258 Shocked and angered: ibid., p. 884.

258 more than sixty percent: Richard H. Rovere, in Meyers, p. 199.

259 packed as far as he could see: O'Donnell and Powers, p. 360.

259 gave them what they wanted to hear: Parmet, *JFK*, p. 322.

259 most truculent speech of his presidency: Collier and Horowitz, p. 306.

259 "Two thousand years ago . . .": Sorensen, p. 601.

259 "I appreciate my interpreter translating my German": CBS Video, *John F. Kennedy.*

259 "There are many people . . .": Schlesinger, *Thousand*, pp. 884–885.

259 The crowd was almost hysterical: Manchester, *Moment*, p. 210.

259 march on the Wall and tear it down: Schlesinger, *Thousand*, p. 885.

259 he had risked undoing: Collier and Horowitz, p. 306; O'Donnell and Powers, p. 360.

259 "I do believe in the necessity . . .": O'Donnell and Powers, p. 361.

259 no political advantages; a "pleasure trip": ibid., p. 358.

259 "Let me remind you of something . . .": ibid., p. 359.

259 He loved Irish literature . . . history: Hennessy, pp. xi, 31, 36–38.

260 traveled with a record album: Martin, p. 433.

260 "I felt like kicking her out of the car": O'Donnell and Powers, p. 362.

260 Children sat on their fathers' shoulders: Martin, p. 433.

260 Everyone's eyes seemed to be filled with tears: O'Donnell and Powers, p. 362.

260 The Secret Service wanted: Martin, p. 434.

260 "I would be working today . . .": O'Donnell and Powers, p. 363.

260 "Sure you were only a tall slight lad . . .": Hennessy, p. 61.

260 tea, fresh salmon: Davis, p. 385.

260 "We will drink a cup of tea . . .": Hennessy, pp. 61–62.

260 "Cousin Jack" . . . ; "the government men . . .": Meyers, p. 205.

260 astonished to see: O'Donnell and Powers, p. 364.

261 "There is an impression in Washington . . .": Rachlin, p. 267.

261 "Don't worry, Jack . . .": O'Donnell and Powers, p. 365.

261 met four Fitzgerald cousins: Hennessy, p. 68.

261 legend had it that Christopher Columbus: ibid., pp. 90, 95.

261 rang out "The Star-Spangled Banner.": ibid., p. 95.

261 "From here I go . . .": O'Donnell and Powers, p. 370.

261 "This is not the land . . ."; "I will certainly come back . . .": ibid., p. 370.

261 "the three happiest days": Martin, p. 435.

261 increasingly disturbed: Sorensen, p. 658.

261 Rejecting the Eisenhower "domino theory": Paper, pp. 63, 129.

261 JFK had allowed the United States for the first time to participate in creating a government which included communist representation: ibid., p. 367.

261 "subterranean" war: Hilsman, p. 413.

262 most of the guerrillas were South Vietnamese: ibid., p. 428; Schlesinger, *Thousand*, p. 539.

262 eight to one; fifteen to one: Hilsman, p. 429.

262 guarding vital installations: ibid., p. 429.

262 much of the Vietcong equipment: ibid., p. 428; Schlesinger, *Thousand*, p. 539.

262 flexible, mobile military action: Schlesinger, *Thousand*, p. 541.

262 emulate the style of the leftist guerrillas: Hilsman, p. 425.

262 In May 1961, the president approved a plan: Schlesinger, *Kennedy*, pp. 742–743.

262 "another Joe McCarthy red scare.": O'Donnell and Powers, p. 16.

262 "But I don't care": ibid., p. 16.

262 Vietnam was less a war zone than the scene of a political struggle: ibid., p. 15; Schlesinger, *Thousand*, p. 988.

263 had outlawed elections in rural villages: Schlesinger, *Thousand*, p. 418.

263 "a presidential proclamation . . .": Rust, p. 94.

263 Government security troops: ibid., p. 95.

263 nine people had been killed: Hilsman, p. 468.

263 about 350 Buddhist nuns and monks: ibid., p. 473.

263 two monks poured gasoline: Rust, p. 98.

263 For almost ten minutes: Hilsman, p. 474.

263 the beautiful, vitriolic Madame Nhu: ibid., p. 418; Sorensen, p. 659.

263 "gaily clapped her hands": Schlesinger, *Thousand*, p. 987.

263 Buddhist "barbecue.": Hilsman, p. 474.

263 Diem gave his assurances: Schlesinger, *Thousand*, p. 989.

263 fourteen hundred monks and nuns arrested: Rust, p. 107.

263 one of the happiest days: Schlesinger, *Thousand*, p. 990.

263 "taught the Buddhists and the Americans . . .": Hilsman, p. 485.

263 Long dissatisfied with Diem's conduct of the war: Rust, p. 2; Schlesinger, *Thousand*, p. 540.

264 South Vietnam would be lost: Hilsman, p. 485.

264 like trying to separate Siamese twins: Schlesinger, *Thousand*, p. 989.

264 "Unless a greater effort is made . . .": Hilsman, p. 497.

264 "push us toward a reconciliation . . .": Collier and Horowitz, p. 308.

264 "be an only child.": Schlesinger, *Thousand*, p. 996.

264 Although the administration was unwilling to openly intervene: ibid., p. 997.

264 Kennedy sent an old friend: Parmet, *JFK*, p. 335.

264 "They're going to kill you": ibid., p. 335.

264 expressed concern to Diem: ibid., p. 334.

265 Kennedy was horrified: Martin, p. 440. Observers felt JFK's reaction was moral rather than political: Rust, p. 175.

265 He "leaped to his feet . . .": Parmet, *JFK*, p. 334.

265 which had been in close touch with the dissident generals: Ranelagh, p. 435.

265 "I've got to do something about those bastards . . .": Parmet, *JFK*, pp. 334–335.

265 "The first thing I do . . ."; "number one priority.": Martin, p. 442. The question of what Kennedy would have done about Vietnam is unanswerable. His own plan for phasing out American military personnel there by the end of 1965 was almost immediately "erased" by President Lyndon Johnson, the *New York Times* noted on January 11, 1964 (Schlesinger, *Kennedy*, pp. 742–743). Among others, Ranelagh, p. 420; Jones, p. 508; Davis, p. 376; and Parmet, *JFK*, p. 336, believe Kennedy too would have continued U.S. involvement after the expansion of North Vietnamese support to the Vietcong in 1965. Halberstam, pp. 299–301, and Schlesinger, *Kennedy*, p. 758, describe JFK's mixed legacy: himself with grave doubts about the wisdom of America's commitment, but belatedly or failing altogether to pass those doubts on to the public and to his own advisers, many of whom stayed on in the Johnson administration to play important roles in escalating the war. Rust, p. 181; Paper, p. 380, and others believe the president had become sufficiently aware of the danger and would not have ordered combat troops to Vietnam. This author agrees with the statement of newspaper columnist Mary McGrory (quoted in Martin, p. 440), who said of Kennedy: "He would not stand for long the sight of pine coffins coming back from a futile battle."

266 things always looked better: Schlesinger, *Thousand*, p. 1019.

266 he had come to love life in the White House: ibid., p. 671.

266 His mornings began at 7:30: Sorensen, p. 371.

266 the thirteen papers to which he subscribed: Salinger, p. 117.

266 reading almost three thousand words a minute: Bergquist and Tretick, p. 15. Fay, p. 194, says Kennedy read between twenty-two and twenty-four hundred words a minute. In Martin, p. 87, a friend is quoted as saying JFK "must have read . . . eighteen hundred words a minute." Sidey, p. 65, says twelve hundred to two thousand.

266 if they had seen some item or other: O'Donnell and Powers, p. 256; Salinger, p. 89.

266 John, along with several toy ducks: Martin, p. 242.

266 often received slightly moist memos: Salinger, p. 89.

266 leather brace to support his lower spine: Parmet, *JFK*, p. 119.

267 "Oh, God, thy sea is so great . . .": Manchester, *Death*, p. 7.

267 being used as a sawhorse: Salinger, pp. 75–76.

267 what he called "my house.": Bergquist and Tretick, p. 125.

267 "Is the Bunny Rabbit in there?": ibid., p. 126.

267 screaming with laughter: O'Donnell and Powers, p. 251.

267 JFK's rocking chair: Parmet, *JFK*, p. 119.

267 only Bobby and Lyndon Johnson were allowed to enter: O'Donnell and Powers, p. 254.

267 designed the steps: Evelyn Lincoln, p. 298.

267 "Isn't that damned lawn ever going to grow?": Salinger, p. 75.

267 had to stay on patrol outside: Martin, p. 233.

267 as many as seventy scheduled visitors: ibid., p. 237.

268 about two hundred letters daily: Manchester, *Portrait*, p. 52.

268 at least one out of every hundred: ibid., pp. 52–53.

268 "The Bagman": Manchester, *Death*, p. 62.

268 double-locked slender black briefcase: Manchester, *Portrait*, p. 56.

268 had to learn to do the breaststroke: Bishop, *Life*, p. 54.

268 During that private time: Martin, p. 248.

268 Caroline with a curtsy, John with a handshake: Sorensen, pp. 375, 380.

268 The children pounded on their father: Martin, pp. 237–238.

268 *Casablanca* was his favorite: Manchester, *Portrait*, p. 26.

268 low boring point: Salinger, p. 91. Occasionally JFK would ask to see the last reel of a film before making his early exit: Manchester, *Portrait*, p. 27.

269 "The pay is good . . .": Martin, p. 236.

269 felt it was important . . . to get away: Sorensen, p. 376.

269 Hyannis Port . . . overrun with tourists: Damore, p. 243.

269 road . . . lined with photographers using telescopic lenses: Salinger, p. 85.

269 There had never been a family like them: Sidey, p. 94.

269 "They certainly have acquired something . . .": Davis, p. 392.

269 *Gigot d'Agneau aux flageolets* or *Mousse aux Concombres*: from the White House dinner menu, November 7, 1961. Reprinted in Anne H. Lincoln, p. 11.

269 "with the possible exception of when Thomas Jefferson dined alone.": Schlesinger, *Thousand*, p. 733.

269 ending a self-imposed exile: Sidey, p. 277.

269 because he admired the president: Faber, p. 308.

270 the first ever held outside the White House: Davis, p. 392.

270 aboard two presidential yachts: ibid., p. 392.

270 the whole nation vicariously enjoyed: Anne H. Lincoln, p. 16.

270 to verify a rumor . . . Caroline's hamster had drowned: Salinger, p. 315.

270 PRESIDENT'S SON GETS A HAIRCUT: Faber, p. 195.

270 "Foo-Foo Head": Fay, p. 239.

270 "What have we got today?" he asked. "*I've* got a glass of water.": Sorensen, p. 380.

270 John walked in stark naked: Bergquist and Tretick, p. 6.

270 "Mommy wants you!": Evelyn Lincoln, p. 247.

270 "Upstairs with his shoes and socks off . . .": Salinger, p. 313.

270 "That's not my trouble with Caroline . . .": Bergquist and Tretick, p. 81.

270 on magazines she wouldn't dream of reading: Faber, p. 195.

270 No matter where she was: Bishop, *Life*, p. 85.

271 First Lady "sounds like a saddle horse.": Martin, p. 247.

271 "Reporters.": ibid., p. 257.

271 the greatest cross Salinger had to bear: ibid., p. 257.

271 "Don't worry—a nice calm memo.": Salinger, p. 311.

271 "My wife is a strong-minded woman": Martin, p. 257.

271 "get kind of sticky": Bergquist and Tretick, p. 124.

271 "If you bungle raising your children . . .": Sorensen, p. 382.

271 On Halloween, she wore a mask: Schlesinger, *Thousand*, p. 669.

271 Jackie liked to drive: ibid., p. 669; Bishop, *Life*, p. 71.

271 CAROLINE VISITS SHOP: Faber, p. 195.

271 "Of course I'm voting for Nixon . . .": Manchester, *Portrait*, p. 84.

271 almost one-third of the nation: Wolff, p. 9. Rachlin, p. 229, says over forty-five million watched the telecast; Davis, p. 395, says there were fifty-six million viewers.

272 simultaneously on CBS and NBC: Rachlin, p. 229. Salinger, p. 166, says ABC also broadcast the program.

272 "furnished by discount stores": Martin, p. 221.

272 "Everything in the White House . . .": Schlesinger, *Thousand*, p. 670.

272 "Before everything slips away . . .": Sidney, p. 283.

272 "The White House is a sacred cow . . .": Davis, p. 393.

272 "warned, begged, and practically threatened": Salinger, p. 305.

272 "I approve of what you are doing . . .": Sidey, p. 280.

272 "a national treasure hunt": Martin, p. 253.

272 "office building": Martin, p. 249.

272 if people weren't happily mar-

ried, "the White House would really finish it." ibid., p. 239.

272 After years of separation: Sorensen, p. 382; Schlesinger, *Thousand*, p. 671; Sidey, p. 96; Fay, p. 181.

273 had looked forward to the arrival of another child: Sorensen, p. 367; Salinger, p. 101.

273 slipped into the casket a gold . . . medal: O'Donnell and Powers, p. 378.

273 "He put up quite a fight," Kennedy said. "He was . . .": ibid., p. 377.

273 no one had ever seen him so upset: Collier and Horowitz, p. 310.

273 the last to leave the funeral: ibid., p. 310.

273 "I don't want to edit anybody . . .": Martin, p. 466.

273 Jackie's gift to her husband: Davis, p. 414.

273 under American registry. When he made a $20 million profit: Martin, p. 468.

273 a form of bribery: Parmet, *JFK*, p. 338.

273 "luxury yacht," the "lavish shipboard dinners," etc.: Bradlee, p. 219.

273 "really nice and understanding.": ibid., p. 219.

273 "guilt feelings" . . . would work to his advantage: ibid., p. 219.

274 The Democratic party was split: Schlesinger, *Thousand*, p. 1019; Parmet, *JFK*, p. 337.

274 presidential authority would be a powerful influence: ibid., p. 1019; ibid., p. 337.

274 "Maybe now you'll come with us . . ."; "Sure I will, Jack.": Bradlee, p. 220.

275 Even before *Air Force One* stopped taxiing . . . "Jackieee! Jackieee!": Manchester, *Death*, p. 71.

275 BIENVENIDO, MR. PRESIDENT; JACKIE, COME WATER-SKI: ibid., p. 75.

275 six high school superintendents: ibid., p. 75.

276 BAN THE BROTHERS; KENNEDY,

KHRUSHCHEV, AND KING: ibid., p. 79.

276 "for Jackie.": ibid., p. 80.

276 "you're doing just about average . . .": White, *1964*, p. 5.

276 "Good evening, Mrs. President": O'Donnell and Powers, p. 22.

276 "In order that my words . . .": Manchester, *Death*, p. 84.

276 "*Muchas gracias* . . .": ibid., p. 84.

276 "exchanged eyes.": O'Donnell and Powers, p. 22.

276 JFK "looked beguiled.": Manchester, *Death*, p. 84.

276 "Come on Jackie . . .": Bishop, *The Day*, p. 55.

276 "Here he is! . . .": ibid., p. 60.

276 "There are no faint hearts . . .": ibid., p. 61.

276 "Where's Jackie?": ibid., p. 61.

276 "Mrs. Kennedy is organizing herself . . .": O'Donnell and Powers, p. 23.

277 "And now, ladies and gentlemen . . .": Bishop, *The Day*, p. 77.

277 "Put it on, Jack!": ibid., p. 78.

277 "Come to Washington Monday . . .": Wicker, p. 46.

277 "Two years ago I introduced myself . . .": Manchester, *Death*, pp. 117–118.

277 "Oh Jack, campaigning is so easy . . .": ibid., p. 120.

277 "How about California . . ."; "I'll be there.": O'Donnell and Powers, p. 24.

278 "There might be something ugly today.": Bishop, *The Day*, p. 47.

278 aspired to culture and sophistication: Manchester, *Death*, p. 43.

278 one out of five citizens carried guns: Bishop, *The Day*, p. 52.

278 The state of Texas had more homicides: Manchester, *Death*, p. 43.

278 Its leading newspaper . . . fanned the fires of hatred: Schlesinger, *Thousand*, p. 1021.

278 "subversives, perverts . . .": Manchester, *Death*, p. 49.

278 Dallas Citizens Council: ibid., p. 47; Schlesinger, *Thousand*, pp. 1021–1022.

278 young executives were required; swastikas were painted, etc.: Manchester, *Death*, p. 44.

278 "in the forgiveness of sin . . .": Schlesinger, *Thousand*, p. 1020.

278 effect on the entire community: ibid., p. 1021.

278 "a hornet's nest": Manchester, *Death*, p. 14.

278 "Dallas is a very dangerous place.": ibid., p. 39.

278 "not get through this without something happening . . .": ibid., p. 39.

278 "Don't let the President . . .": Salinger, p. 1.

278 "too emotional": Manchester, *Death*, p. 39.

278 "the steady drum-beat of ultra right-wing propaganda . . .": Schlesinger, *Thousand*, p. 1025.

279 WANTED FOR TREASON: Bishop, *The Day*, p. 26.

279 WELCOME MR. KENNEDY TO DALLAS: Manchester, *Death*, p. 109.

279 "WHY do you say . . .": Bishop, *The Day*, pp. 24–25.

279 "Mr. Kennedy, we DEMAND answers . . .": Manchester, *Death*, p. 109.

279 "We're heading into nut country today.": ibid., p. 121.

279 "You two look like Mr. and Mrs. America . . .": O'Donnell and Powers, p. 26.

280 "Kennedy is showing he is not afraid.": Manchester, *Death*, p. 131.

280 "After Kennedy leaves here . . .": ibid., p. 130.

280 Dallas was considered "hot": Bishop, *The Day*, p. 134.

280 the highly competitive Smith: Manchester, *Death*, p. 134.

280 He was concerned: ibid., pp. 131–132.

281 "It worked!": Bishop, *The Day*, p. 150.

281 Connally stared with astonishment: ibid., p. 135.

281 at least a quarter of a million people: Blakey and Billings, p. 13.

281 some of whom annually paid only a few hundred dollars' . . . tax: Bradlee, p. 118.

281 be careful of what he said in that "tough town": Manchester, *Death*, p. 127.

281 a withering blast at the wealthy right-wingers: Manchester, *Death*, p. 127.

282 had never seen his city so hospitable: Bishop, *The Day*, p. 168.

282 Jackie saw an underpass: Manchester, *Death*, p. 154.

282 "Mr. President, you can't say Dallas doesn't love you.": Moody, p. 198.

282 to wave at a small boy: Manchester, *Death*, p. 155.

282 Joe Kennedy was sleeping. Rose had played nine holes of golf: Rose Kennedy, p. 442.

282 perhaps a motorcycle had backfired: Manchester, *Death*, p. 155.

282 Connally had recognized the sharp noise: ibid., p. 155.

282 thudding pain in his back: ibid., p. 157.

283 swerving, then almost coming to a halt: Bishop, *The Day*, p. 174.

283 "Kenny, I think the President's been shot!": O'Donnell and Powers, p. 27.

283 his shattered head resting on the roses: Bishop, *The Day*, p. 179.

283 the presidential limousine sprang forward: Manchester, *Death*, p. 161.

283 perhaps looking for help: O'Donnell and Powers, p. 29.

283 "It's going to be all right.": Manchester, *Death*, p. 163.

283 "He's dead. They've killed him . . .": ibid., p. 163.

283 THREE SHOTS WERE FIRED: United Press International, p. 22.

283 "Oh my God, Mr. President . . .": O'Donnell and Powers, p. 29.

283 "You know he's dead . . .": Manchester, *Death*, p. 171.

283 roses clinging to his chest: Bishop, *The Day*, p. 198.

283 FLASH FLASH: United Press International, p. 22.

284 "Bloodstained" read as BLOOD STAINEZAAC RMBTHING: Manchester, *Death*, p. 169.

284 "a deed of horror": ibid., p. 172.
284 "I want to be in there . . .": ibid., p. 186.
284 "Hurray!": ibid., p. 136.
284 FLASH PRESIDENT KENNEDY DEAD: ibid., p. 221.
285 "just another homicide case": O'Donnell and Powers, p. 34.
285 "Get the hell out of the way . . .": ibid., p. 34.
286 For the first time . . . Jackie had a drink of scotch: Manchester, *Death*, p. 349.
286 "Hi Jackie, I'm here": ibid., p. 387.
286 yes, he always was: ibid., p. 387.
286 no applause or shouts of excitement: White, *1964*, p. 10.
286 "Let them see what they've done.": Manchester, *Death*, p. 348.
286 Tens of millions: United Press International, p. 43.
286 All commercial programming had been canceled: White, *1964*, p. 12.
286 watched television for ten hours: Manchester, *Death*, p. 497.
286 lines of dignitaries . . . wreaths being laid: United Press International, p. 43.
286 "Forgive us": ibid., p. 60.
286 "cried the rain down": Joseph Roddy, "They Cried the Rain Down That Night," *JFK Memorial Book* (Cowles Magazines and Broadcasting, Inc., 1964), unpaginated.
286 Russia . . . nothing but dirges: Manchester, *Death*, p. 498.
286 voice would start to quaver: ibid., p. 466.
287 both pro- and anti-Castro groups: *The Final Assassinations Report*, p. 61.
287 an employee of the local underworld boss: ibid., p. 177.
287 students had applauded: Manchester, *Death*, p. 250; Schlesinger, *Thousand*, p. 1027n.
287 "didn't even have the satisfaction . . ."; "some silly little communist.": Manchester, *Death*, p. 407.
287 protesting he had been set up: Blakey and Billings, p. 20.

287 case against him was "cinched": United Press International, p. 62.
287 Ruby's motivation: Blakey and Billings, p. 280.
288 gently kissed the flag while Caroline reached up: Manchester, *Death*, p. 542; *Life*, December 6, 1963, p. 38.
288 they began to cry: Manchester, *Death*, p. 542.
288 line . . . was three miles long: ibid., p. 563.
288 They knew there was nothing to see: United Press International, p. 94.
288 a quarter of a million Americans: White, *1964*, 16.
288 retracing the same route: Manchester, *Death*, p. 578.
288 "fat black Cadillac.": ibid., p. 485.
288 "Pfft.": ibid., p. 575.
288 "She gave an example to the whole world . . .": Rose Kennedy, p. 447.
289 "Where's my Daddy?": Manchester, *Death*, p. 584.
289 "You'll be all right . . ."; "I'll take care of you.": ibid., p. 589.
289 "I could stay here forever.": Dora Jane Hamblin, "Mrs. Kennedy's Decisions Shaped All the Solemn Pageantry," *Life*, December 6, 1963, p. 49.
291 "So now he is a legend . . .": Jacqueline Kennedy in *JFK Memorial Book* (unpaginated).
291 "You must think of him as this little boy . . .": Theodore H. White, "For President Kennedy, an Epilogue," *Life*, December 6, 1963, p. 159.
291 the lyric he loved most was from a Broadway musical about King Arthur: *Don't let it be forgot . . .*: ibid, p. 159.
291 "There'll be great presidents again . . .": ibid., p. 159.
291 She had given the Kennedy administration its epitaph: Theodore H. White, *In Search of History* (New York: Warner, 1978), p. 524. Pages 518–525 contain a fascinating description of exactly how the Camelot legend came to be.

291 a magical time—when its handsome leader had performed brave deeds: ibid., pp. 524–525.

292 as King Arthur had been lost more than fourteen centuries before: Norma Lorre Goodrich, *King Arthur* (New York: Watts, 1986), p. 361, estimates the fatal wounding of Arthur to have taken place between the years 515–542.

292 a Senate committee to study questionable activities of the Central Intelligence Agency: Ranelagh, p. 594.

292 The committee report, released in the spring of 1976, brought to light the CIA/Mafia scheme: *The Final Assassinations Report*, pp. xxxi–xxxii.

292 led to public disclosure of Kennedy's relationship with Judith Campbell: The Senate committee, headed by Democrat Frank Church, tried to tiptoe around this point; its November 1975 *Interim Report* referred to Campbell only as a "close friend of President Kennedy": Davis, p. 614*n*. Four days before the report was released, Republican committee members leaked Campbell's identity to the press (ibid., pp. 614–615; Collier and Horowitz, pp. 412–413).

292 Soon "Camelot" became a satirical description: Arthur Schlesinger, Jr., *Boston Globe*, p. 3.

292 JFK had been all style and no substance, that his thousand days had represented neither the best nor the brightest: ibid., p. 3.

292 the attack on unemployment and poverty which he planned to launch: Schlesinger, *Thousand*, pp. 1006–1007; Richard Wilson, "What Happened to the Kennedy Program," *JFK Memorial Book* (unpaginated).

292 He had proposed a broad legislative program: ibid; See also Sorensen, pp. 759–760.

293 in the emotional aftermath . . . a flood of Kennedy legislation poured out: Richard Wilson, *JFK Memorial Book*.

293 what President Johnson labeled

his "Great Society.". Kearns, pp. 210–211.

293 It was not possible, as LBJ claimed in his 1966 budget proposal . . . to have both "guns and butter.": David Osborne, "Winning Battles, Losing the War," *Mother Jones*, June 1986, p. 20.

293 The American economy was in a shambles . . . yet Johnson refused . . . to raise taxes: ibid., p. 20; Kearns, p 296.

293 "headed straight for disaster": Wofford, p. 422.

293 reluctantly announced he would seek . . . the nomination: His decision to risk splitting the Democratic party was one of the most difficult Bobby ever had to make. See Schlesinger, *Kennedy*, pp. 858–895.

293 Fifty-eight thousand of the more than two and a half million who served there: had been killed: Rust, p. 181.

293 its conclusion . . . that Lee Harvey Oswald had acted alone: In the summer of 1975, five days before he was scheduled to testify before the Senate committee investigating the CIA, Sam Giancana was shot to death in his Chicago home. Less than two weeks later, Jimmy Hoffa disappeared from the parking lot of a Detroit restaurant; his body has never been found. Johnny Roselli made two appearances before the committee, during which he speculated that Santos Trafficante—the third member of the Mafia triumvirate recruited by the CIA to kill Fidel Castro—had been responsible for President Kennedy's death. Four months after his testimony, Roselli's decomposed body was found stuffed in an oil barrel floating off Miami Beach (Blakey and Billings, pp. 204, 388–391).

Spurred by the Senate committee report, and by a Gallup Poll which found that eighty percent of the American people believed JFK's death had been the result of a conspiracy, a House committee was established in the fall of 1976 to investigate the assassination. Its report, published three years later, stated that "available evidence does not preclude" the possibility that members of organized crime and/or anti-Castro Cuban groups may have been responsible for the murder of John F. Kennedy (*The Final Assassinations Report*, pp. xxxv, 153, 177).

Four out of five Americans remain convinced Oswald did not act alone. Some critics believe the House committee managed to "avoid opening some of the most tantalizing doors" that have been locked for a quarter-century, and that the truth behind the Kennedy assassination is buried deep within the vaults of U.S. intelligence agencies—most particularly, those of the CIA (Hurt, pp. 34, 439).

Photo insert following page 116:

infamous "NINA" ads: Collier and Horowitz, p. 23.
Rose moved back in with her parents: Goodwin, p. 307.
"give her a black eye": Rose Kennedy, p. 76.
"pugnacious personality": Burns, p. 28.
Joe encouraged his children . . . to make history themselves: Whalen, p. 439.
allergic reaction to the little dachshund: Collier and Horowitz, p. 80.
the royalties from his 1940 bestseller: McTaggart, p. 84; Whalen, p. 296.
"There's more of us . . .": Schlesinger, Kennedy, p. 684.
Red Fay and Barney Ross were making bets: Fay, p. 141.

"We enjoyed it more . . .": McCarthy, p. 141.
charmed—and bribed—a clerk: Manchester, *Moment*, pp. 37–38.
"It all depends on the weather . . ."; Sorensen, p. 368.
"queen of the circus"; "the man on the flying trapeze": Birmingham, p. 81.
Kennedy passed through a kind of political sound barrier: Meyers, p. 81.
McClellan would be his second choice: Parmet, *Jack*, p. 436.
Jackie suggested "Acapulco."; offered to stuff a pillow in her dress: Bergquist and Tretick, pp. 170, 172.
"You won't believe it . . ."; "Oh my God! . . .: Schlesinger, *Kennedy*, p. 218.

Photo insert following page 212:

Caroline's vocabulary had expanded: Lowe, p. 81.
"like young Lincoln.": Rose Kennedy, p. 374.
"did not look well.": Gadney, p. 42.
might get "clobbered.": Damore, p. 217.
the "longest night in history.": Lowe, p. 123.
"That goddamned Arthur Krock.": Tom Wicker, quoted in Meyers, p. 177.
"I assume it passed unanimously.": Adler, p. 81.
"Well, Dad, it looks as though . . .": Martin, p. 385.

Teddy . . . had considered changing his name: *Boston Globe*, p. 41.
"You're doing pretty well . . .": Manchester, *Moment*, p. 232.
Photographers claimed wars . . . were less terrifying: Bergquist and Tretick, p. 105.
"Lancer" and "Lace": Manchester, *Death*, p. 61.
"Five more minutes . . .": ibid., p. 153.
The photographer carefully angled his camera: ibid., pp. 324–325.
"In the light of history . . .": O'Donnell and Powers, p. 36.

BIBLIOGRAPHY

Abel, Elie. *The Missile Crisis*. Philadelphia: Lippincott, 1966.

Adler, Bill, ed. *The Kennedy Wit*. New York: Citadel, 1964.

Bennett, Lerone, Jr. *What Manner of Man*. 6th rev. ed. Chicago: Johnson, 1986.

Bergquist, Laura, and Stanley Tretick. *A Very Special President*. New York: McGraw-Hill, 1965.

Beschloss, Michael R. *Kennedy and Roosevelt*. New York: Norton, 1980.

——. *Mayday*. New York: Harper & Row, 1986.

Birmingham, Stephen. *Jacqueline Bouvier Kennedy Onassis*. New York: Grosset & Dunlap, 1978.

Bishop, Jim. *A Day in the Life of President Kennedy*. New York: Random House, 1964.

——. *The Day Kennedy Was Shot*. New York: Funk & Wagnalls, 1968.

Blair, Joan and Clay, Jr. *The Search for J.F.K.* New York: Berkley, 1976 (Book Club ed.).

Blakey, G. Robert, and Richard N. Billings, *The Plot to Kill the President*. New York: Times Books, 1981.

The Boston Globe special section (in conjunction with the dedication of The John F. Kennedy Library). "JFK, the man, the president." October 20, 1979.

Bradlee, Benjamin C. *Conversations with Kennedy*. New York: Norton, 1975.

Brendon, Piers. *Ike: His Life and Times*. New York: Harper & Row, 1986.

Burner, David, and Thomas R. West. *The Torch Is Passed*. New York: Atheneum, 1984.

Burns, James MacGregor. *John Kennedy*. New York: Harcourt, Brace, 1959.

Cameron, Gail. *Rose*. New York: G. P. Putnam's Sons, 1971.

Clinch, Nancy Gager. *The Kennedy Neurosis*. New York: Grosset & Dunlap, 1973.

Collier, Peter, and David Horowitz. *The Kennedys*. New York: Summit, 1984.

Cook, Fred J. *The Army-McCarthy Hearings*. New York: Watts, 1971.

Damore, Leo. *The Cape Cod Years of John Fitzgerald Kennedy*. Englewood Cliffs, NJ: Prentice-Hall, 1967.

Davis, John H. *The Kennedys*. New York: McGraw-Hill, 1984.

Donovan, Robert J. *PT 109*. New York: McGraw-Hill, 1961.

Exner, Judith, with Ovid Demaris. *My Story*. New York: Grove, 1977.

Faber, Harold, ed. *The Kennedy Years.* New York: Viking, 1964.

Fay, Paul B., Jr. *The Pleasure of His Company.* New York: Harper & Row, 1966.

The Final Assassinations Report. Report of the Select Committee on Assassinations, U.S. House of Representatives. New York: Bantam, 1979.

Goodwin, Doris Kearns. *The Fitzgeralds and the Kennedys.* New York: Simon and Schuster, 1987.

Guthman, Edwin. *We Band of Brothers.* New York: Harper & Row, 1971.

Halberstam, David. *The Best and the Brightest.* New York: Random House, 1972.

Hennessy, Maurice N. *I'll Come Back in the Springtime.* New York: Ives Washburn, 1966.

Hilsman, Roger. *To Move a Nation.* Garden City, NY: Doubleday, 1967.

Hughes, Emmet John. *The Ordeal of Power.* New York: Atheneum, 1963.

Hurt, Henry. *Reasonable Doubt.* New York: Holt, Rinehart, and Winston, 1985.

Jones, Howard. *The Course of American Diplomacy.* New York: Watts, 1985.

Kearns, Doris. *Lyndon Johnson and the American Dream.* New York: Harper & Row, 1976.

Kennedy, John F. *Profiles in Courage.* Memorial ed. New York: Harper & Row, 1964.

———. *Why England Slept.* New York: Wilfred Funk, 1961 ed.

Kennedy, Robert F. *Thirteen Days.* New York: W. W. Norton, 1969.

Kennedy, Rose Fitzgerald. *Times to Remember.* Garden City, NY: Doubleday, 1974 (Book Club ed.).

Krock, Arthur. *In the Nation: 1932–1966.* New York: McGraw-Hill, 1966.

———. *Memoirs: Sixty Years on the Firing Line.* New York: Funk and Wagnalls, 1968.

Lincoln, Anne H. *The Kennedy White House Parties.* New York: Viking, 1967.

Lincoln, Evelyn. *My Twelve Years with John F. Kennedy.* New York: David McKay, 1965.

Lowe, Jacques. *Kennedy: A Time Remembered.* New York: Quartet Books, 1983.

Manchester, William. *The Death of a President.* New York: Harper & Row, 1967.

———. *One Brief Shining Moment.* Boston: Little, Brown, 1983.

———. *Portrait of a President.* Rev. ed. Boston: Little, Brown, 1967 (Book Club ed.).

Martin, Ralph G. *A Hero for Our Time.* New York: Macmillan, 1983 (Book Club ed.).

McCarthy, Joe. *The Remarkable Kennedys.* New York: Popular Library, 1960.

McTaggart, Lynne. *Kathleen Kennedy: Her Life and Times.* Garden City, NY: Dial, 1983.

Meyers, Joan, ed. *John Fitzgerald Kennedy . . . As We Remember Him.* New York: Atheneum, 1965.

Moody, Sidney C., Jr., ed. *Triumph and Tragedy.* New York: The Associated Press, 1968.

Navasky, Victor S. *Kennedy Justice.* New York: Atheneum, 1971 (Book Club ed.).

Oates, Stephen B. *Let the Trumpets Sound: The Life of Martin Luther King, Jr.* New York: Plume/New American Library, 1983.

O'Donnell, Kenneth P., and David F. Powers, with Joe McCarthy. *"Johnny, We Hardly Knew Ye."* Boston: Little, Brown, 1970.

O'Neill, Tip, with William Novak. *Man of the House.* New York: Random House, 1987.

Opotowsky, Stan. *The Kennedy Government.* New York: E. P. Dutton, 1961.

Paper, Lewis J. *The Promise and the Performance.* New York: Crown, 1975.

Parmet, Herbert S. *Jack: The Struggles of John F. Kennedy.* New York: Dial, 1980.

———. *JFK: The Presidency of John F. Kennedy.* New York: Dial, 1983.

Powers, Richard Gid. *Secrecy and Power: The Life of J. Edgar Hoover.* New York: Free Press/Macmillan, 1987.

Rachlin, Harvey. *The Kennedys.* New York: Pharos/World Almanac, 1986.

Ranelagh, John. *The Agency.* New York: Simon and Schuster, 1986.

Reeves, Thomas C. *The Life and Times of Joe McCarthy*. New York: Stein and Day, 1982.
Rust, William J. *Kennedy in Vietnam*. New York: Scribner, 1985.
Salinger, Pierre. *With Kennedy*. Garden City, NY: Doubleday, 1966.
Schlesinger, Arthur M., Jr. *The Bitter Heritage*. Boston: Houghton Mifflin, 1967.
————. *Robert Kennedy and His Times*. Boston: Houghton Mifflin, 1978 (Book Club ed.).
————. *A Thousand Days*. Boston: Houghton Mifflin, 1965.
Shannon, William V. *The American Irish*. New York: Macmillan, 1963.
Sidey, Hugh. *John F. Kennedy, President*. New York: Atheneum, 1963.
Sorensen, Theodore C. *Kennedy*. New York: Harper & Row, 1965.
Steinberg, Rafael. *Island Fighting*. Alexandria, VA: Time-Life, 1978.
Stevenson, William. *A Man Called Intrepid*. New York: Harcourt, Brace Jovanovich, 1976.
Stoughton, Cecil, Chester V. Clifton, and Hugh Sidey. *The Memories*. New York: W. W. Norton, 1973.
Summers, Anthony. *Goddess: The Secret Lives of Marilyn Monroe*. New York: Macmillan, 1985 (Book Club ed.).
Szulc, Tad. *Fidel*. New York: Morrow, 1986.
United Press International. *Four Days*. New York: American Heritage, 1964.
Whalen, Richard J. *The Founding Father*. New York: New American Library, 1964 (Book Club ed.).
White, Theodore H. *The Making of the President 1960*. New York: Atheneum, 1961.
————. *The Making of the President 1964*. New York: Atheneum, 1965.
Whitman, Alden, and *The New York Times*. *Portrait: Adlai E. Stevenson*. New York: Harper & Row, 1965.
Wicker, Tom. *Kennedy Without Tears*. New York: Morrow, 1964.
Wills, Garry. *The Kennedy Imprisonment*. Boston: Atlantic–Little, Brown, 1982.
Wofford, Harris. *Of Kennedys and Kings*. New York: Farrar, Straus, Giroux, 1980.
Wolff, Perry. *A Tour of the White House with Mrs. John F. Kennedy*. Garden City, NY: Doubleday, 1962.
Woodham-Smith, Cecil. *The Great Hunger*. New York: Harper & Row, 1962.
Wyden, Peter. *Bay of Pigs*. New York: Simon and Schuster, 1979.
Zich, Arthur. *The Rising Sun*. Alexandria, VA: Time-Life, 1977.

Videos

CBS Video. *John F. Kennedy*. CBS Inc., 1981.
Maljack Productions Inc. *The Kennedys*. MPI Home Video, 1985.
David John Mendelsohn Productions. *Thank You, Mr. President*. Worldvision Home Video Inc., 1983.

INDEX

Houston, Lawrence, 230, 232
Houston, Texas: 1960 Ministerial
    Association speech, 171–172; 1963
    Kennedy trip to, 276
Huber, Father Oscar, 284
Hughes, Sarah, 285
Humphrey, Hubert, 128; 1960
    presidential campaign of, 155–159
Hundley, William, 231
Hyannis Port homes, 15, 22, 43–44, 57,
    60, 62, 86, 107, 121, 146, 152, 163,
    178, 182–184, 211–212, 218, 269,
    286

Illinois, 152, 160–161, 164, 177, 183,
    184. See also Chicago
I'm for Roosevelt (Joseph P. Kennedy),
    33
Inauguration, JFK's, 194–196
India, 95
Indiana, 161; 1960 presidential
    primary, 160
Inflation, 221, 293
Intercontinental ballistic missiles
    (ICBMs), 236, 237; Soviet, in Cuba,
    237, 238; Soviet development of, 143
International Brotherhood of Team-
    sters, 135, 144, 151; McClellan
    Committee investigation of, 135–140
Iowa, 152, 164, 174
Ireland, 58, 86; and JFK's death, 286;
    1963 Kennedy trip to, 259–261;
    Potato Famine, 5, 6, 106
Irish-Catholicism: in Boston politics,
    8–10, 11, 12–15, 26, 71, 73, 84, 97,
    123; history in America, 6–10; as
    issue in JFK's political career, 123,
    129, 133, 147–149, 157, 158–159,
    171–172, 179–180; prejudice against,
    9, 10, 11, 14–15, 21, 58, 97, 107–108,
    157
Iron Curtain, 134, 261
Italy, 31, 32, 131
Ives, Irving, 138, 144, 150

Jackson State College, 225
Japan, 71, 101; World War II, 43, 45–
    46, 49, 51–57, 60
Jefferson, Thomas, 194, 269
Johnson, Lady Bird, 276, 277–278, 280,
    284, 285
Johnson, Lyndon B., 143, 277, 280;
    Bobby Kennedy's dislike for, 166–
    167; on civil rights, 166, 224; and
    Cuban missile crisis, 236, 241;
    debates JFK, 162; and JFK's

Johnson, Lyndon B. (continued)
    assassination and funeral, 284, 285,
    288, 293–294; 1960 presidential
    hopes, 161–162, 164; as 1960 vice-
    presidential candidate, 165–166,
    176, 183; 1961 Saigon visit, 209;
    as president, 293–294; as Senate
    majority leader, 161, 166; sworn in
    as president, 285; as vice-president,
    209, 241, 267, 274
Joint Chiefs of Staff, 175, 202, 262, 288
Joseph P. Kennedy, Jr. (destroyer), 73,
    245
Justice Department, 98, 138, 222, 230,
    231, 251; Organized Crime Section,
    229, 231, 282

Kane, Joe, 74; as JFK's campaign
    advisor, 74–75, 77, 79, 80
Kansas, 152, 196
Katzenbach, Nicholas, 226–227, 252,
    285
Kefauver, Estes, 128–129, 222
Kelly, Grace, 119
Ken-Air Corporation, 149
Kennedy, Bridget Murphy, 7, 8
Kennedy, Caroline Bouvier, 132, 133,
    151–152, 182, 184, 282; and JFK's
    death, 288, 289; life in the White
    House, 266, 267, 268, 270, 271;
    public interest in, 150, 270
Kennedy, Edward (Teddy), 21, 70, 76,
    86, 100, 131, 133, 146, 282, 288;
    birth of, 21; role in JFK's political
    rise, 145, 152, 156, 158, 164–165,
    176, 177, 178, 183–184; as Senator,
    191, 219
Kennedy, Ethel Shakel, 94–95, 100,
    108, 110, 146, 158, 177
Kennedy, Jacqueline Bouvier, 105, 182,
    184, 219; birth of Caroline, 132;
    birth of John, Jr., 188–189; as
    campaign asset, 145, 156, 158, 177–
    178, 274, 276, 277, 279; childhood
    of, 105–106; cold Kennedy recep-
    tion of, 107–108; courtship and
    marriage to JFK, 106–109; and
    Cuban missile crisis, 243; and death
    of Patrick, 273; dinner parties of, 269–
    270; early married life to JFK, 109–
    110, 118–122, 130–133; education of,
    106; fondness for Joe Kennedy, 132;
    glamour of, 177, 212–213; Irish
    background of, 106–108; and JFK's
    assassination, 282–287; and JFK's
    extramarital affairs, 109–110, 131;

Kennedy, Rose Fitzgerald, 2, 10, 12, 39, 45, 50, 97, 165, 177, 193–194, 282; childhood of, 12; courage of, 119; courtship and marriage to Joe Sr., 12–13; early married years, 13–15; education of, 12–13; grandchildren of, 146; Jackie likened to, 109; and JFK's death, 286; at JFK's inauguration, 196; and Kathleen's controversial romances, 59, 62, 87, 88; marital problems of, 16, 21–22; as a mother, 13–21, 22; 1961 trip to France, 212; relationship with her father, 12–13; religious beliefs of, 17–18, 58–59, 87; role in JFK's political rise, 76–77, 80, 100, 102–103, 113, 156, 158, 163, 178, 196

Kennedy, Rosemary, 14; mental retardation of, 44–45

"Kennedy machine," 96–102

Kentucky, 193

Khrushchev, Nikita, 168, 175, 176, 193, 198, 207, 229, 258; and Berlin crisis, 215–218; and Cuban missile crisis, 233, 234, 236, 237, 238, 240, 242–247; and Jackie Kennedy, 214; and 1960 presidential election, 169, 170–171, 176, 179; at 1961 Vienna summit, 213–216; on space race, 220. *See also* Soviet Union

King, Coretta Scott, 176, 250

King, Martin Luther, Jr., 176, 223, 248, 252, 253; assassination of, 293; 1961 Montgomery Freedom Ride, 211; 1963 Birmingham demonstrations, 249–251, 255; 1963 Lincoln Memorial speech, 254–255; on voting rights, 224

King, Martin Luther, Sr., 176

"Kitchen Debate," 168, 172

Kohler strike, 138–140

Kolombangara Island, 54, 55, 57

Korean War, 93, 115

Krock, Arthur, 33, 37, 46–47, 68, 98, 106, 118, 150, 177

Ku Klux Klan, 210–211, 255

Labor issues, 84–85, 190; European, 86; JFK's prolabor stance, 85–86, 138–140, 143–144, 150–151; the Landrum-Griffin Act, 150–151, 166; McClellan Committee investigation and proposed legislation, 139–140, 143–144, 150–151; steel price controversy (1962), 221–222; Taft-Hartley Law, 85

Ladies' Home Journal, 150

Landrum, Philip, 150

Landrum-Griffin Act. 150–151, 166

Laos, 208–209, 213–214, 218, 261. *See also* Southeast Asia

Laski, Harold, 25, 30, 37–38

Latin America, 73, 170–171, 198–199, 237; Alliance for Progress, 199, 219; Bay of Pigs operation, 201–208, 213; Cuban missile crisis, 233–247. *See also specific countries*

Lawford, Patricia Kennedy, 15, 76, 82, 100, 126, 146, 156, 177, 178, 181

Lawford, Peter, 126, 146, 156

Lawrence, David, 160

League of United Latin American Citizens (LULAC), 276

Lee, James, 106

LeMay, General Curtis, 240

Lenin Peace Medal, 213

Lewis, Joe, 83

Life magazine, 107, 116, 144, 150

Lincoln, Abraham, 195, 236, 279

Lincoln, Evelyn, 230, 236, 268

Lincoln Memorial speech of Martin Luther King (1963), 255

Lismore Castle, Ireland, 86–87

Little Rock Central High School desegregation issue (Arkansas), 142

Lockheed Corporation, 224

Lodge, Henry Cabot, Jr., 97–98, 101–103, 105; as ambassador to South Vietnam, 264, 265; as 1960 vice-presidential candidate, 167, 180

Lodge, Henry Cabot, Sr., 97

London School of Economics, 25, 29–30

Look magazine, 144, 147, 150, 271

Los Angeles Democratic convention (1960), 161–167

Louisiana, 152

Luce, Henry, 37, 39, 150

Lumbari Island, 53, 54

Lynch, John "Pat," 125

MacArthur, General Douglas, 49, 53, 60, 208–209

Macdonald, Torbet, 264

Macmillan, Harold, 171, 202, 247, 269

Maheu, Robert, 170, 200

Maine, 175, 181

Mao Tse-tung, 92, 201

Maritime Commission, 93

Marshall, Burke, 250–251

Marshall, George, 85

Marshall Plan, 85, 215